AF291173

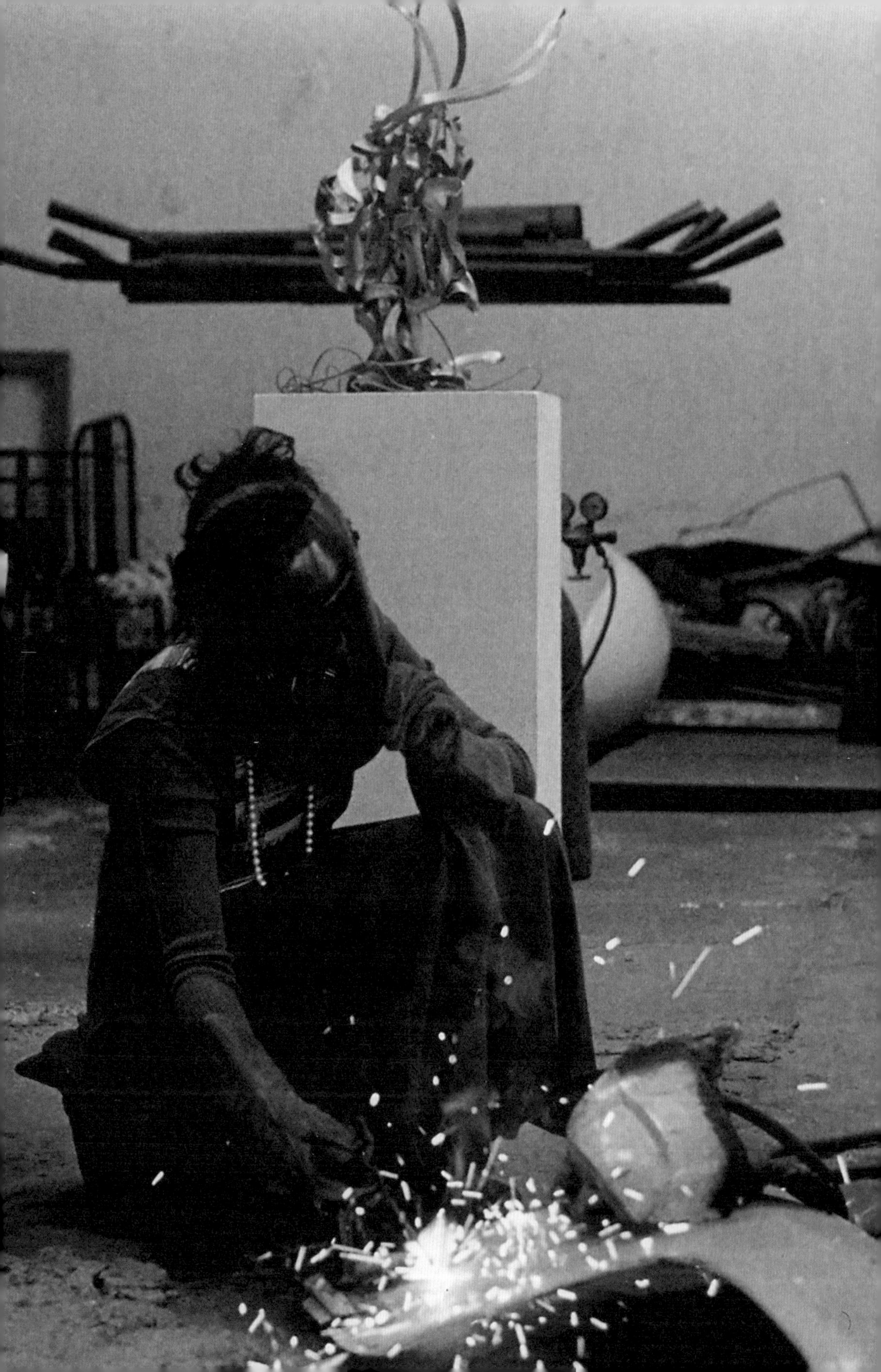

Feliza Bursztyn

This book was published
on the occasion of the exhibition
Feliza Bursztyn: Welding Madness
Muzeum Susch
18 December 2021 – 26 June 2022

Curated by
Marta Dziewańska, Abigail Winograd

PUBLICATION

Editors
Marta Dziewańska
Abigail Winograd

Managing Editor Muzeum Susch
Agnieszka Sosnowska

MUZEUM SUSH / ART STATIONS
FOUNDATION CH

*Founder and Chairwoman of Foundation
Board*
Grażyna Kulczyk

Curator of Muzeum Susch
Pierre-Henri Foulon

Curator of Publicaziuns Susch
Agnieszka Sosnowska

Curator of Acziun Susch
Joanna Leśnierowska

Advisor
Maciej Chorążak

Registrar
Sabina Schumpf

Producer
Aleksandra Wojtaszek

Technician
Jan Steffen

Finance and Administration Secretary
Cornelia Koch

Assistant & Receptionist
Brigitte Janikowski
Manuela Bonifazi

Invigilator
Carlos Goncalves

ART STATIONS FOUNDATION CH BOARD

*Founder and Chairwoman of the Foundation
Board*
Grażyna Kulczyk

Board Members
Carolina Müller-Möhl, *Founder and President
Müller-Möhl Group & Müller-Möhl Foundation*
Andrzej Przywara, *Co-Founder and Director
Foksal Gallery Foundation, Warsaw*
Dr. Andreas Ritter, *Attorney*

The publisher gratefully acknowledges the
generous support of the Institute for Studies
on Latin American Art (ISLAA)

INSTITUTE FOR
STUDIES ON
LATIN AMERICAN ART

Acknowledgements
Muzeum Susch and curators would like
to thank the following individuals without
whom the exhibition and the accompanying
publication would not have been possible:
Pablo and Camilo Leyva, Catalina Casas,
Paula Bossa, and Ana Maria Reyes of
Galeria Casas Riegner, Ariel Aisiks and the
Institute for Studies on Latin American Art,
Estrellita Brodsky, Lilly Scarpetta, Director
María Wills Londoño and Chief Curator
Laura Paola Zarta from the Museo del Banco
de la República, Director María Mercedes
González and Chief Curator Emiliano Valdés
from the Museo de Arte Moderno Medellín,
Director Julia Restrepo Tirado and the
Museo Nacional de Colombia, Museo la
Tertulia, Tate Modern, Sylvia Súarez, Gina
McDaniel Tarver, Cecilia Fajardo-Hill, Julia
Buenaventura, Lynn Zelevansky, Daniel
Muzyczuk, Lucas Ospina, José Roca,
and Ana María Romano G.

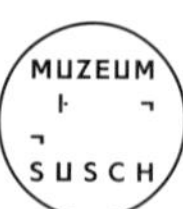

Feliza Bursztyn
Welding Madness

edited by
Marta Dziewańska
Abigail Winograd

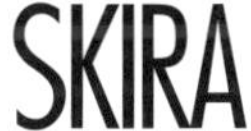

Cover
Feliza Bursztyn in her studio in Bogotá,
c. 1961
Courtesy of the Archive of Pablo Leyva.
Photo: Hernan Díaz

Page 2
Feliza Bursztyn welding in her studio in
Bogotá, 1981
Courtesy of the Archive of Pablo Leyva.
Photo: Rafael Moure

Design
Luigi Fiore

Editorial Coordination
Emma Cavazzini

Copy Editing
Carlotta Santuccio

Layout
Sara Marcon

Iconographical Research
Paola Lamanna

First published in Italy in 2022 by
Skira editore S.p.A.
Palazzo Casati Stampa
via Torino 61
20123 Milano, Italy
www.skira.net

Printed and bound in Italy. First edition

ISBN: 978-3-033-09114-6
(Muzeum Susch)
ISBN: 978-88-572-4722-9
(Skira editore)

Distributed in USA, Canada, Central & South
America by ARTBOOK | D.A.P.,
75 Broad Street, Suite 630,
New York, NY 10004, USA.
Distributed elsewhere in the world by
Thames and Hudson Ltd., 181 A High
Holborn, London WC1V 7QX, United
Kingdom.

Contents

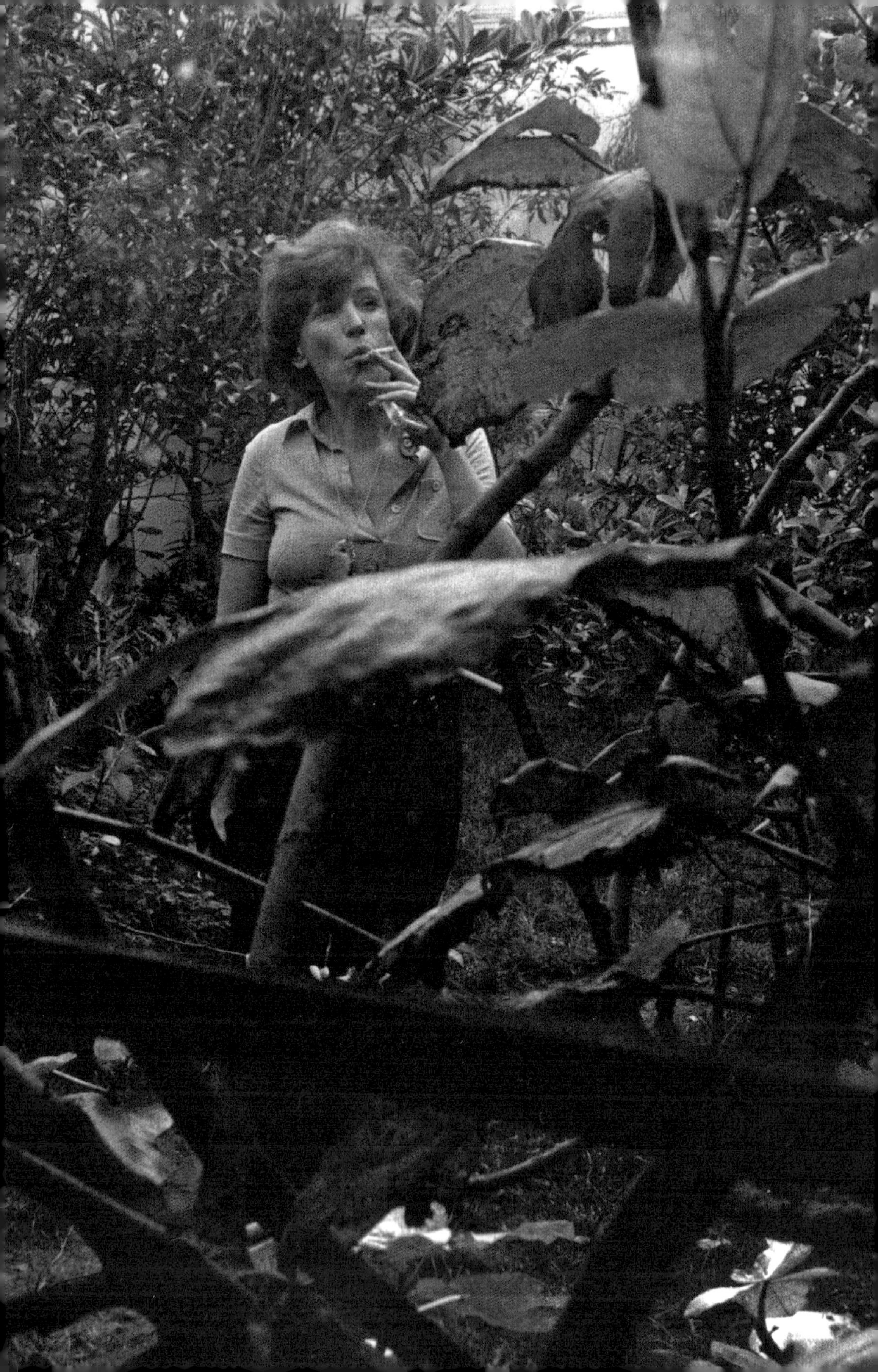

Preface

Feliza Bursztyn: Welding Madness. **A Retrospective**

Feliza Bursztyn's highly experimental oeuvre situates her as an outstanding female pioneer in the international avant-garde movements of the 1960s and 1970s. The Colombian sculptor of Jewish-Polish descent lived through some of the most challenging historical events of the twentieth century on both sides of the Atlantic.

Since her family emigrated from Poland in 1933 – the year of the artist's birth – Feliza Bursztyn grew up in Colombia's conservative and patriarchal society and subsequently became an ardent advocate of women's emancipation and liberal social politics. In reaction to the rapid modernization of Colombian society and its deep-reaching consequences, Burstyn began to create metal sculptures out of industrial detritus with ghostlike yet comical humanoid traits. The artist's objects and installations can be considered as sites of aesthetic resistance that reveal the troublesome face of modernity.

Since the late 1960s Bursztyn has given her sculptures an increasingly feminist agenda. Reflecting on her ground-breaking series *Las camas* (The Beds) and *Las histéricas* (The Hysterical Ones), the artist stated: "In a sexist country, pretend to be the mad one!". Bursztyn harshly criticized the living conditions of women in Colombia and confronted the social conventions of her country. Her progressive political views and lifestyle resulted in persecution by the state security forces, and in 1981 she was in exile in Paris, where she died prematurely at the age of forty-nine. The exhibition *Feliza Bursztyn: Welding Madness* showcases the artist's tragically cut-short yet exceptional career path.

1. The artist in her studio garden, c. 1975
Courtesy of the Archive of Pablo Leyva. Photo: Gorka Dorronsoro

I am proud and honoured to host the first international museum retrospective of this seminal artist. This career-spanning exhibition positions Bursztyn as one of Latin America's most outstanding sculptors of the twentieth century whose life and work resonate today with widely established artists of her generation like Gego and Mira Schendel, with whom Bursztyn shared the biographical trajectory of Jewish immigration to Latin America. The artist's feminist engagement, which manifested in a profound and original way in her work, opens another central narrative in the matrilinear research and exhibition focus of Muzeum Susch.

I would like to thank the exhibition curators, Marta Dziewańska and Abigail Winograd, for their intense academic research and curatorial investigation into the oeuvre of this hitherto underrecognized artist.

I would like to express my special gratitude to Pablo and Camilo Leyva for their unwavering support of this project.

I would like to extend my special thanks to all private and institutional lenders: Museo de Arte Moderno de Bogotá (MAMBO); Museo Nacional de Colombia; Museo La Tertulia; Collection of El Banco de la República; Tate, London; Instituto de Visión; Patrimonio Fílmico Colombiano; Private Collection, Bogotá; Private Collection, New York; Private Collection, courtesy Casas Riegner, Bogotá.

I would like to thank Estrellita Brodsky, Lilly Scarpetta, and the Institute for Studies on Latin American Art (ISLAA) for their generous support to the exhibition and the accompanying publication.

I am grateful to all the authors of this publication for their invaluable contributions, which recontextualize Feliza Bursztyn's complex oeuvre placing her in a broader art historical narrative: Julia Buenaventura, Cecilia Fajardo-Hill, Camilo Leyva, Daniel Muzyczuk, Lucas Ospina, Sylvia Suárez, Gina Tarver, and Lynn Zelevansky.

I further cordially acknowledge Catalina Casas, Ana María Durán, and Paula Bossa from Casas Riegner, Bogotá, for their continuous assistance throughout the project.

I would like to thank the following exhibition partners for their trusting collaboration: the Colombian institutions Museo del Banco de la República, here Director María Wills Londoño and Chief Curator Laura Paola Zarta Gutiérrez, and the Museo de Arte Moderno de Medellín, Director María Mercedes González and Chief Curator Emiliano Valdés.

Finally, I would like thank the team of Muzeum Susch for their commitment in the realization of this complex exhibition project throughout its extended preparation period.

Grażyna Kulczyk
Founder and Chairwoman of the Board
of Art Stations Foundation CH

Feliza Bursztyn: Life in Images

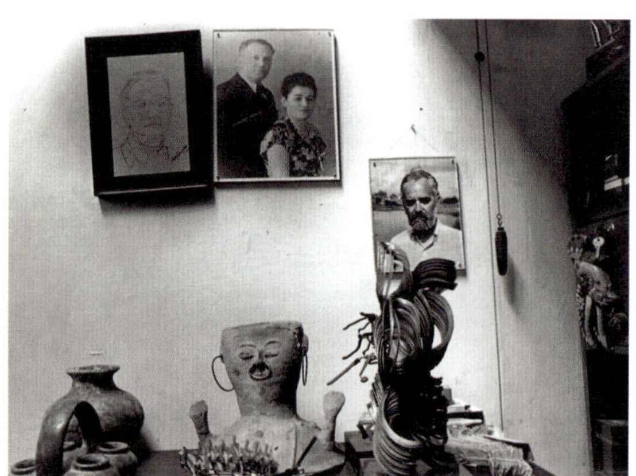

Feliza Bursztyn was born on 9 September 1933 to Polish Jewish immigrants, Yaakov and Chaja Bursztyn. In Bogotá, her father became a successful businessman. When his daughter returned to Colombia from Paris in 1961 to become an artist, he gave her a vacant garage next to one of his factories. It became her studio and her home. This picture from the artist's studio, taken in the 1960s, features a photograph of her parents flanked by Bursztyn's drawing of her father on the left and a photo of Hernando Valencia Goelkel on the right. The table displays pieces from Bursztyn's collection of pre-hispanic pottery and several examples of her own work.

Interior of Feliza Bursztyn's studio in Bogotá, c. 1975
Courtesy of the Archive of Pablo Leyva. Photo: Pablo Leyva

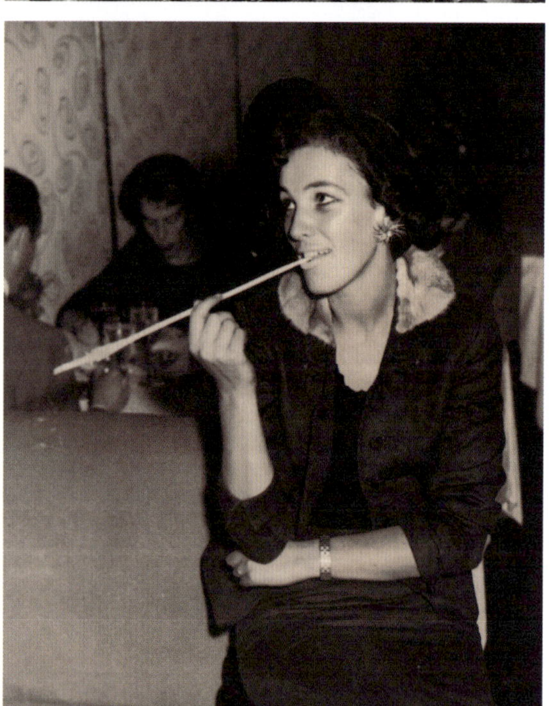

Bursztyn left Bogotá in 1947 to finish high school in New York. After graduation, she studied at the Arts Students League for two years. In 1952, she married Larry Laurence Fleischer and had three daughters. The couple returned to Bogotá in 1956 and divorced shortly thereafter, in 1957. Following her divorce, Bursztyn departed for Paris to study with Ossip Zadkine at the Académie de la Grande Chaumière.

Portrait of the artist out for the night, c. 1958
Courtesy of the Archive of Pablo Leyva

Inspired by her training in Europe and by her peers, more specifically the Nouveaux Réalistes, Bursztyn began her *Chatarras* (Junk Sculptures) series. Bronze, the material she was trained to work in Paris, was scarce in Colombia so she turned to junkyard detritus – discarded fragments of machines, cables, bolts, and other metal bits. She welded them together into rough, abstract compositions significantly challenging prevalent ideals of beauty and nobility and was the first Colombian artist to use "non-art" materials.

Sculptures from the *Chatarras* series in the artist's studio in Bogotá, c. 1964
Courtesy of the Archive of Pablo Leyva. Photo: Federico Hecht

In 1965, Bursztyn won first prize at the XVII Salón de Artistas Nacionales in the National Museum with her work *Mirando al norte* (Looking North). Marta Traba, founding director of the Museo de Arte Moderno de Bogotá, critic, and close friend of the artist, was part of the jury and defended Bursztyn when the press expressed outrage over her victory.

Mirando al norte in the artist's studio in Bogotá, c. 1965
Courtesy of the Archive of Pablo Leyva

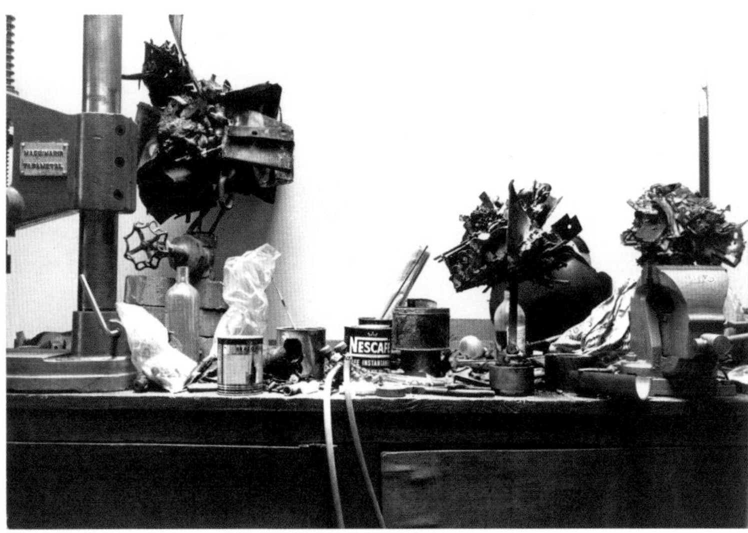

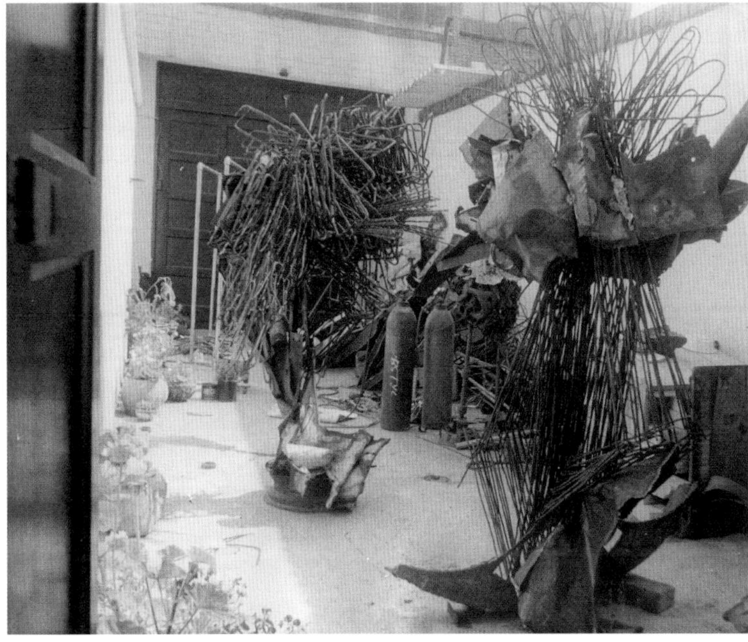

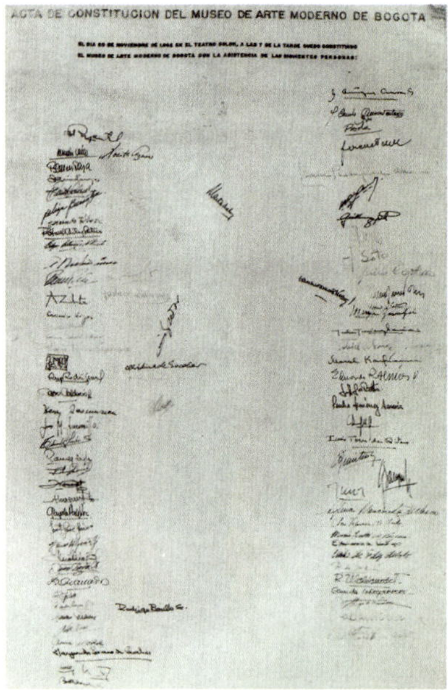

MAMBO founding document with signatures, 1962
"Acta de constitución del Museo de Arte Moderno de Bogotá", published in *El Museo de Arte Moderno de Bogotá: Recuento de un esfuerzo conjunto* (Bogotá: Litotechninon, [198?])

Bursztyn was a central figure in the post-war artistic developments in Bogotá. She was present at the founding of the Museo de Arte Moderno de Bogotá on 20 November 1962 and was among the assembled members of the artistic community who signed MAMBO's articles of association as a witness. One of the driving forces behind the museum's founding was Traba, the Argentine critic and writer, who was a crucial figure in the development of modern art in Colombia. Traba was also a close friend and fervent supporter of Bursztyn's work.

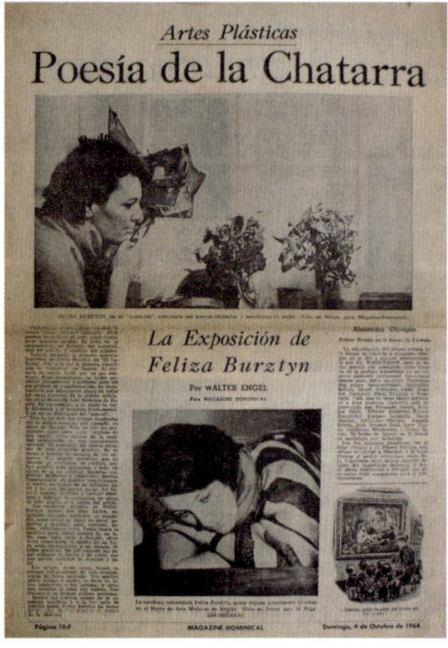

When Bursztyn presented the first of her eleven *Chatarras* (Junk Sculptures) in 1961, Walter Engel, one of Colombia's leading art critics, summarily dismissed the work as lacking spiritual truth and plastic value. By 1964, however, on the occasion of her second solo show at MAMBO, where she showed fuller, flower-like compositions made of coffee cans, Engel changed his position and celebrated her ability to transform scrap into poetry.

Walter Engel, "Poesía de la Chatarra: La Exposición de Feliza Burztyn", *El Espectador: Magazine Dominical* (Bogotá), 4 October 1964
◀

Bursztyn frequently collaborated with artists working in multiple disciplines and her studio became an important gathering site for the artistic community in Bogotá and beyond. The theatre director Santiago García, who trained with Bertolt Brecht, was a frequent visitor and important formative figure. Over the course of her career, Bursztyn grew more and more interested in the performing arts and her installations became increasingly theatrical. Patricia Ariza and García were the founders of Teatro La Candelaria in Bogotá, one of the most influential theatre troupes to emerge in post-war Latin America. Ariza still runs the theatre today.

Santiago García, Patricia Ariza, and Feliza Bursztyn in the artist's studio in Bogotá, c. 1963
Courtesy of the Archive of Pablo Leyva. Photo: Roberto Álvarez
▶

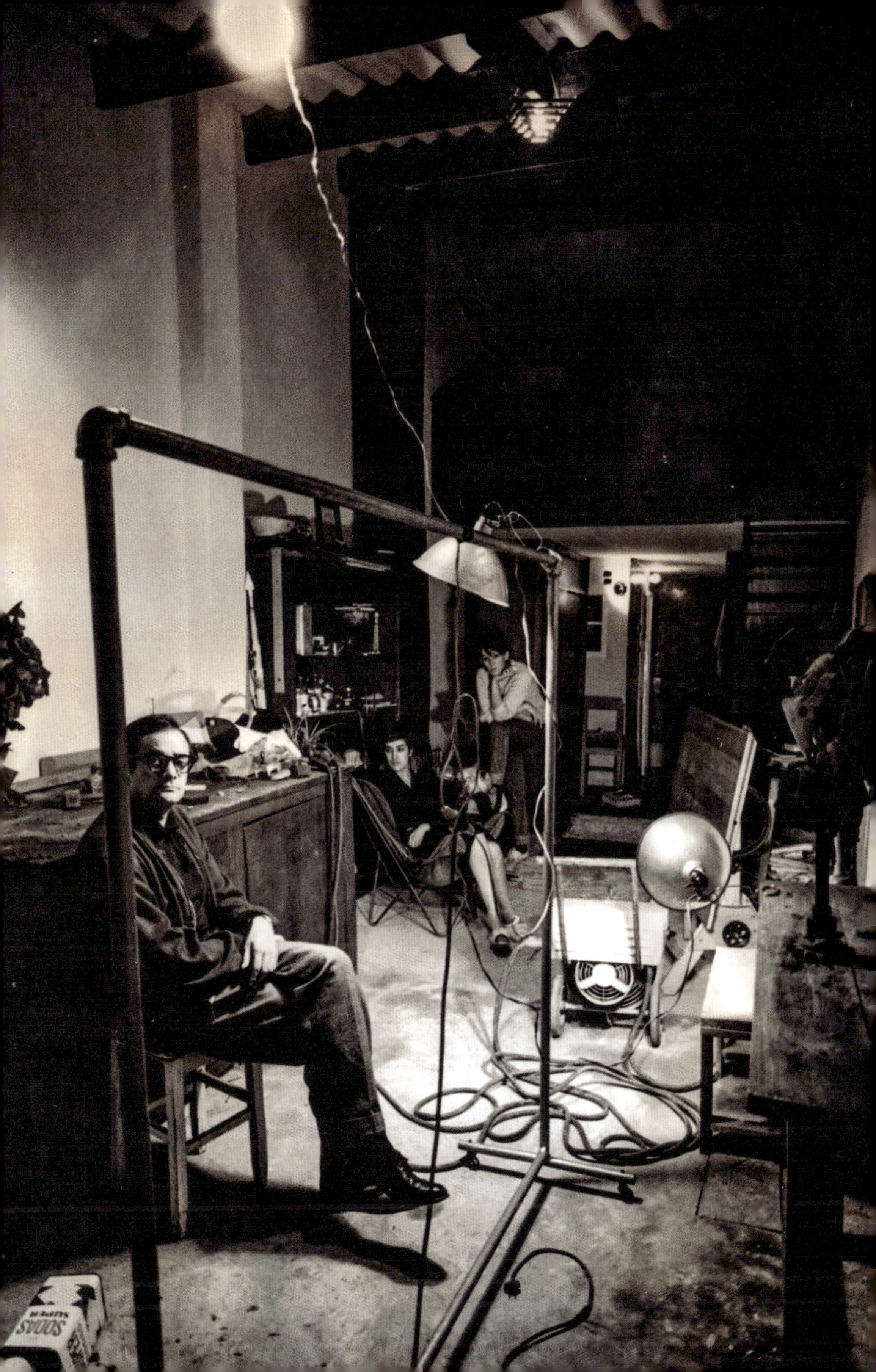
SODAS SUPER

In 1968, Feliza Bursztyn unveiled a new body of work, made of
stainless steel scrap and with a kinetic component, which she
titled *Las histéricas* (The Hysterical Ones). Her new materials,
even if different from the scraps previously used, also
demonstrated connections to industry. Combining them with a
small electrical motors, left visible, she set her work in motion
and activated various aspects of the exhibition space.

Feliza Bursztyn welding in her studio in Bogotá, c. 1971
Courtesy of the Archive of Pablo Leyva. Photo: Pablo Leyva

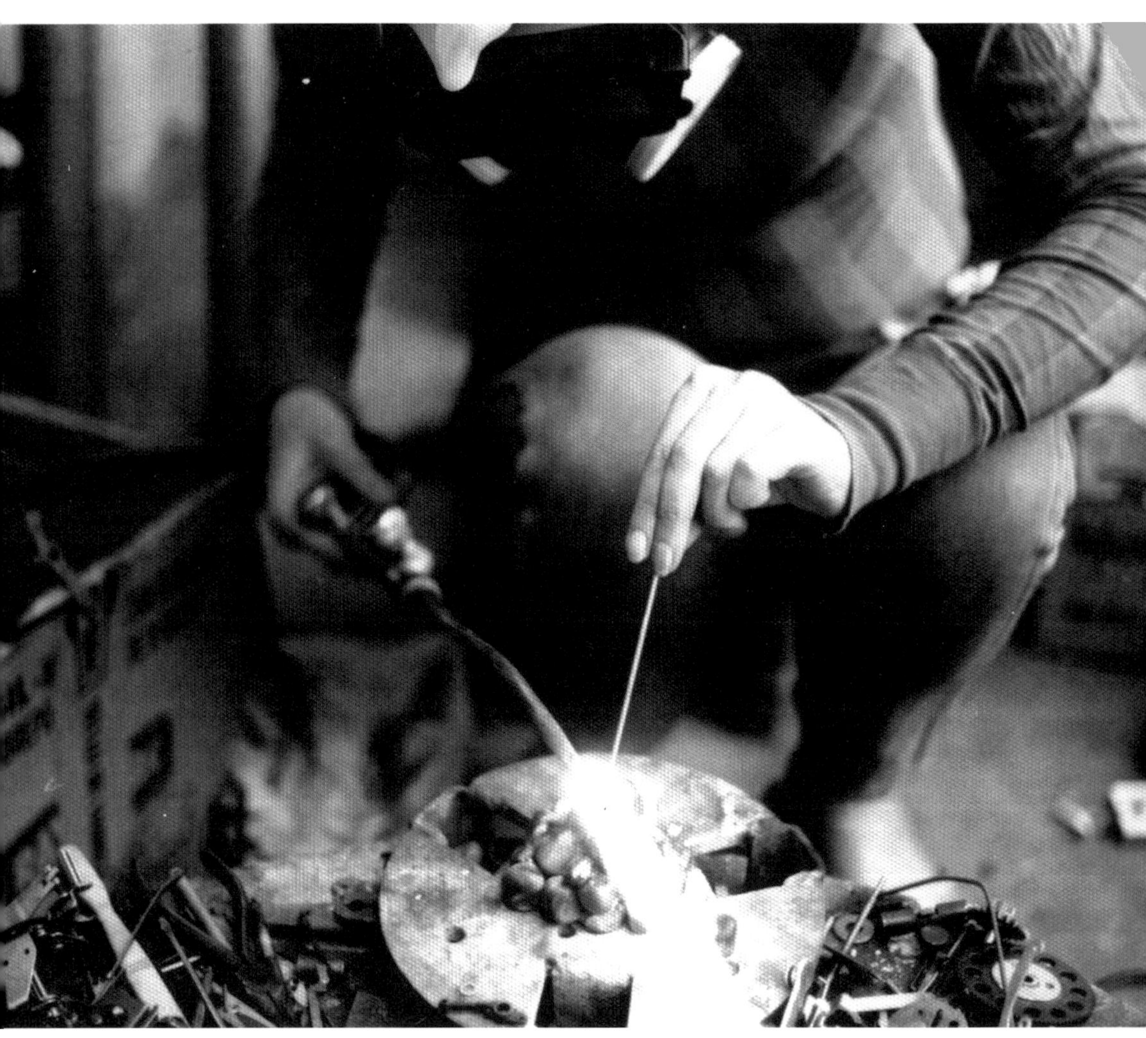

Feliza Bursztyn's *Las histéricas* (The Hysterical Ones) were occasionally presented in immersive environments that included not only a loud mechanical sound but were also accompanied by a short film titled *Hoy Feliza* (Today Feliza, 1968), created by her friend, experimental filmmaker Luis Ernesto Arocha. This incorporation of movement, sound, and other immersive effects contributed forcefully to questioning and undermining the conventional definitions of sculpture in Colombia.

Exhibition booklet for *Histéricas*, Museo de Arte Moderno de Bogotá, February–March 1968

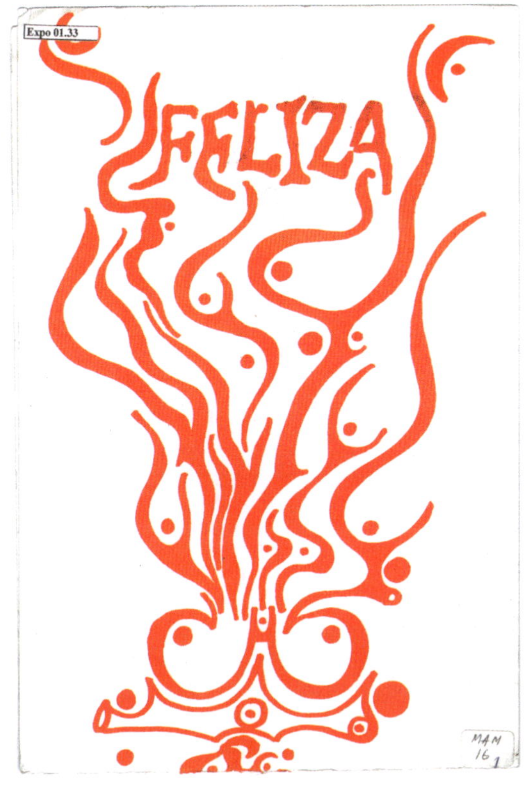

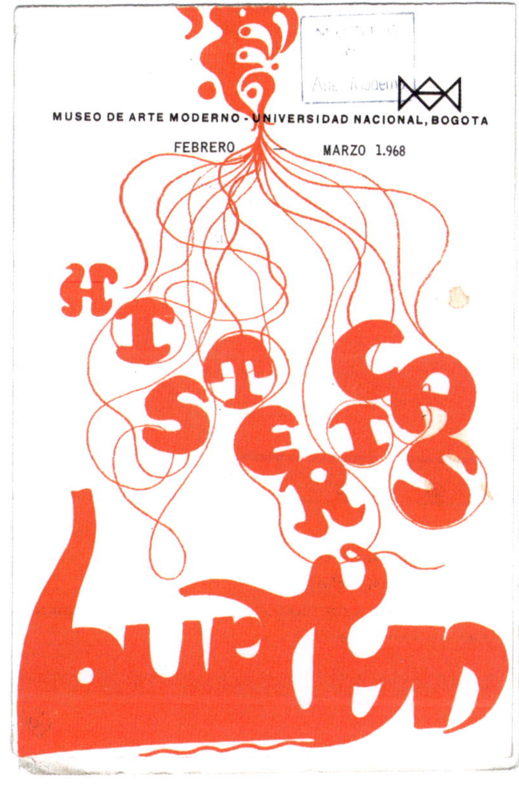

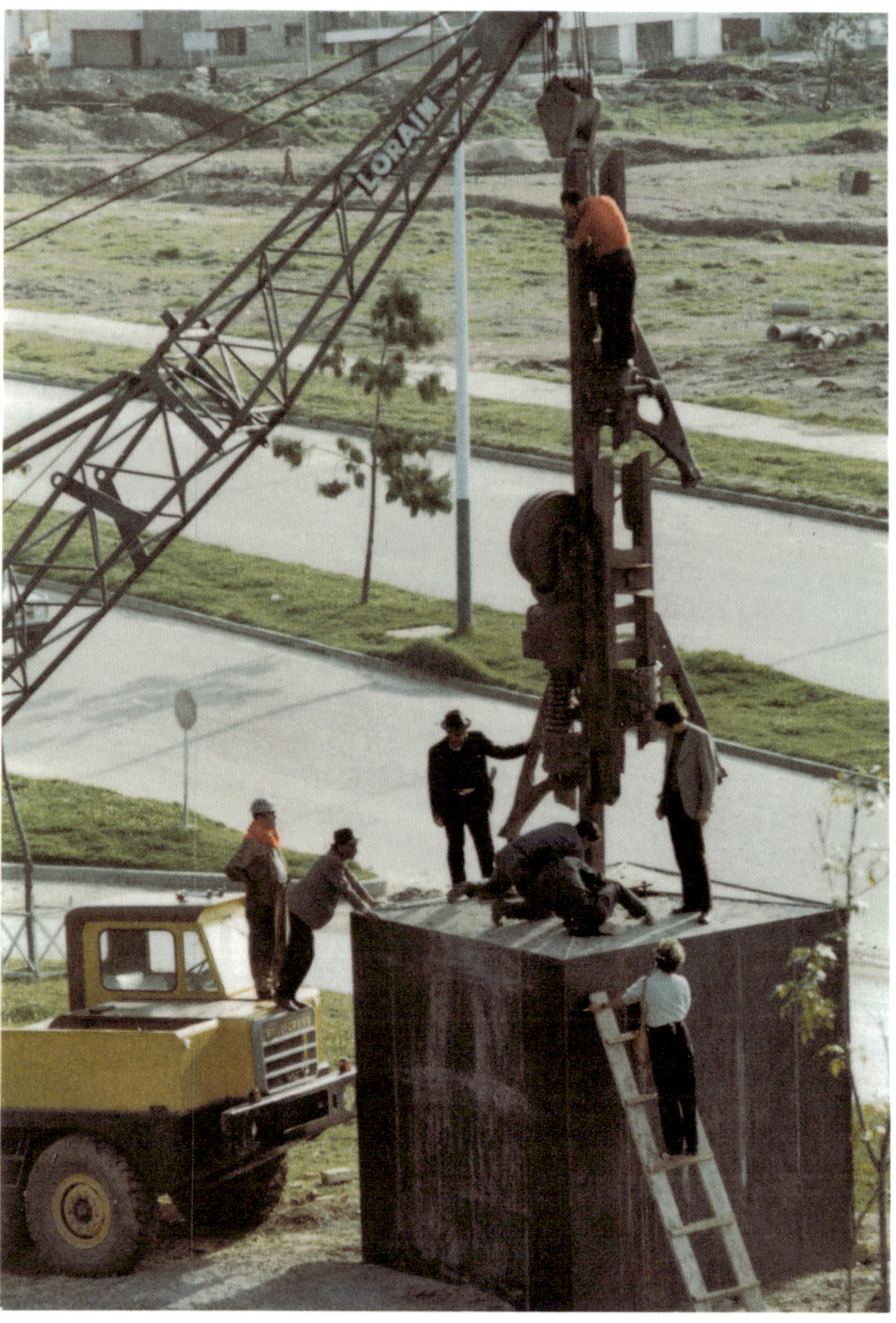LORAIN

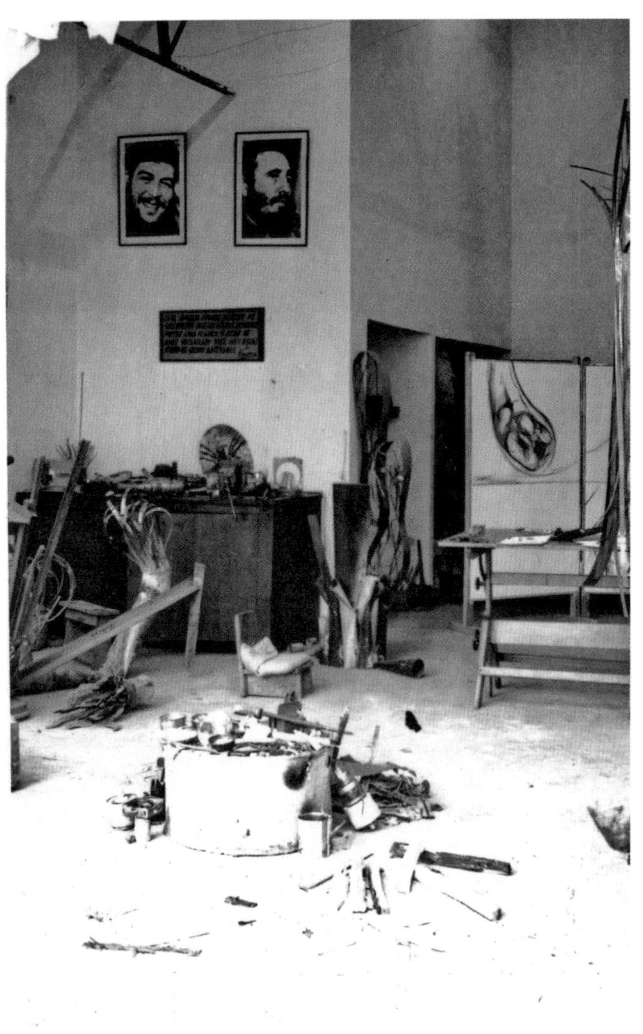

Over time, Bursztyn translated her *Chatarras* (Junk Sculptures) into larger scale objects and created several public sculptures on commission. The first public sculpture to be erected, in 1971, was *Homenaje a Gandhi* (Homage to Gandhi). Composed of a bulldozer chassis, the statue still towers over the traffic on Carrera 7a at the intersection with Calle 100 in Bogotá.

Feliza Bursztyn installing *Homenaje a Gandhi*, 1971
Courtesy of the Archive of Pablo Leyva. Photo: Pablo Leyva
◀

An ardent supporter of the Cuban Revolution, Bursztyn was sceptical of the pervasive enthusiasm among political and cultural elites for developmentalism which, in her view, exacerbated extant social and economic divisions. Her vocal enthusiasm for left wing causes and relationship with political activists caused the authorities in Colombia to view Bursztyn with suspicion.

The artist's studio in Bogotá, 1974
Courtesy of the Archive of Pablo Leyva. Photo: Pablo Leyva
▲

Bursztyn also maintained close friendships with artists and poets, among them Alejandro Obregón, who was one of the most important modern painters in post-war Colombia. She referred to him as the "*madre*" (mother) of modern painting. Juan Gustavo Cobo Borda was one of the editors of *Revista Eco*. He authored several articles about and dedicated poems to the artist. In fact, writing poems dedicated to Bursztyn was a practice common among poets in Colombia at the time.

The artist was also close to Nobel Prize-winning author Gabriel García Márquez, whom she met in the 1950s. It was Bursztyn who introduced Gabo, as he was affectionately known, to Jorge Gaitán Durán, her then lover and publisher of the magazine *Mito*, which first published García Márquez's fiction. Gaitán Durán died in 1962 when the plane he was on crashed on the island of Guadeloupe en route from Paris to Bogotá.

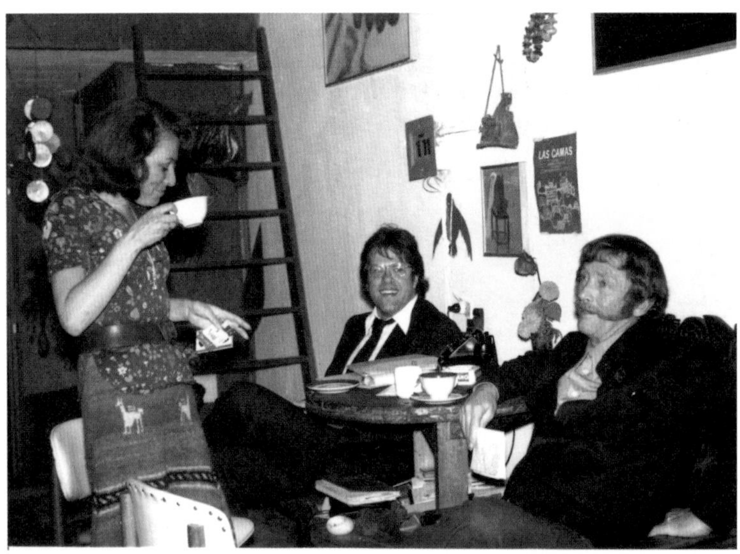

Alejandro Obregón, Juan Gustavo Cobo Borda,
and Feliza Bursztyn in the artist's home in Bogotá, 1974
Courtesy of the Archive of Pablo Leyva. Photo: Pablo Leyva

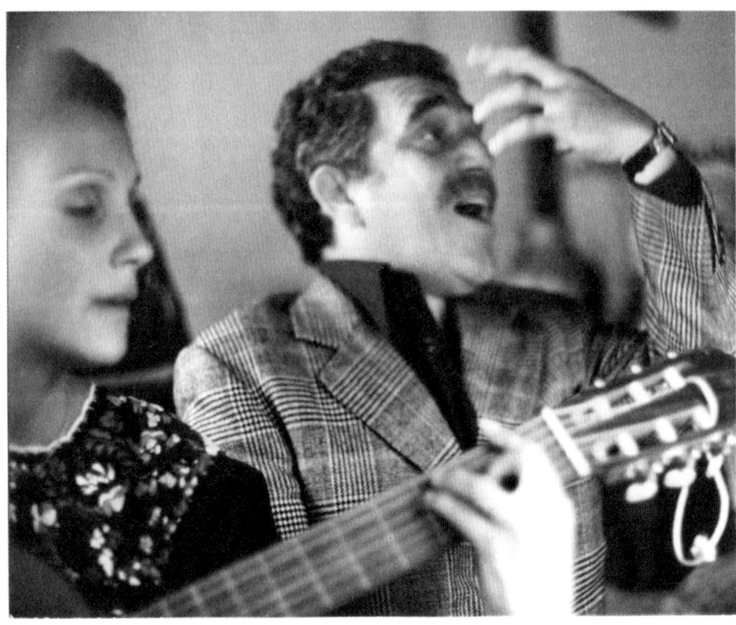

Gabriel García Márquez singing in the artist's studio
in Bogotá, after 1971
Courtesy of the Archive of Pablo Leyva. Photo: Pablo Leyva

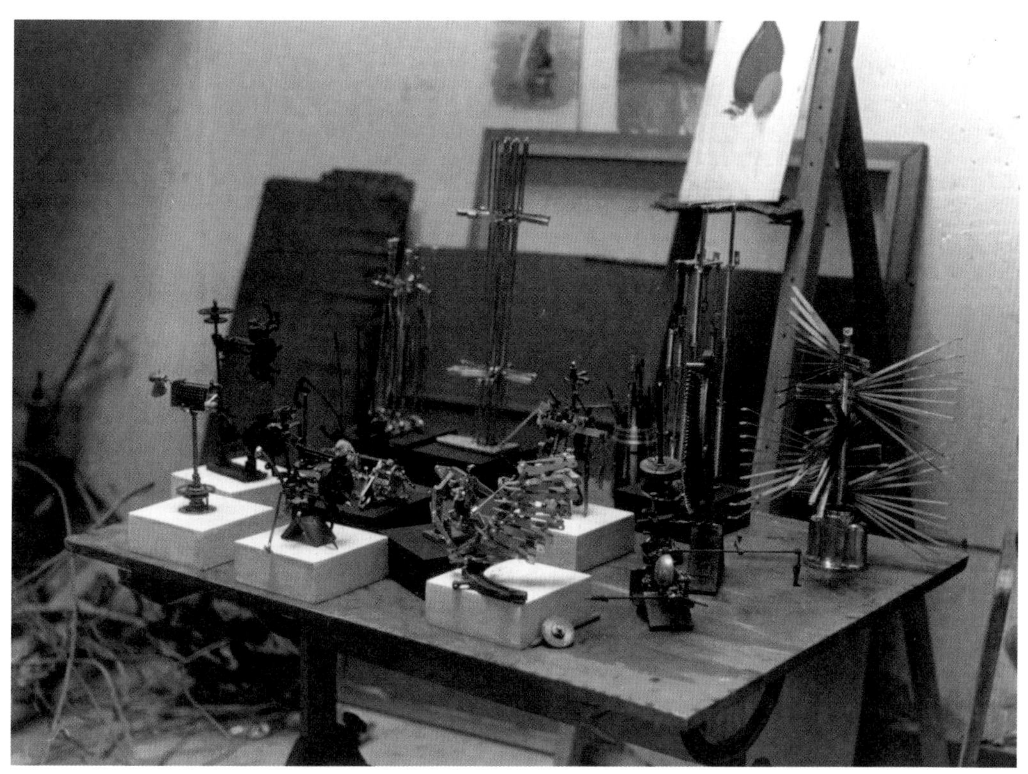

Throughout the 1960s, the scale of Bursztyn's work increased exponentially. With the *Minimáquinas* (Minimachines), she reversed course and began producing smaller-scale works while recovering in the hospital following a car accident. They are intricate structures, made from disassembled typewriters and other small manual machines. To compound the preciousness lent to them by their detail and, often, delicacy, Bursztyn chrome-plated some of them in gold and silver. The artist intended these intimately sized constructions to be manipulated by the audience, thereby creating yet another connection between spectator and artwork. They demonstrated Bursztyn's commitment to public engagement in the form of "open proposals", enabling a critique of the hegemonic models of politics and culture of her time.

Table in the artist's studio with multiple sculptures from the *Minimáquinas* series, c. 1973
Courtesy of the Archive of Pablo Leyva. Photo: Pablo Leyva

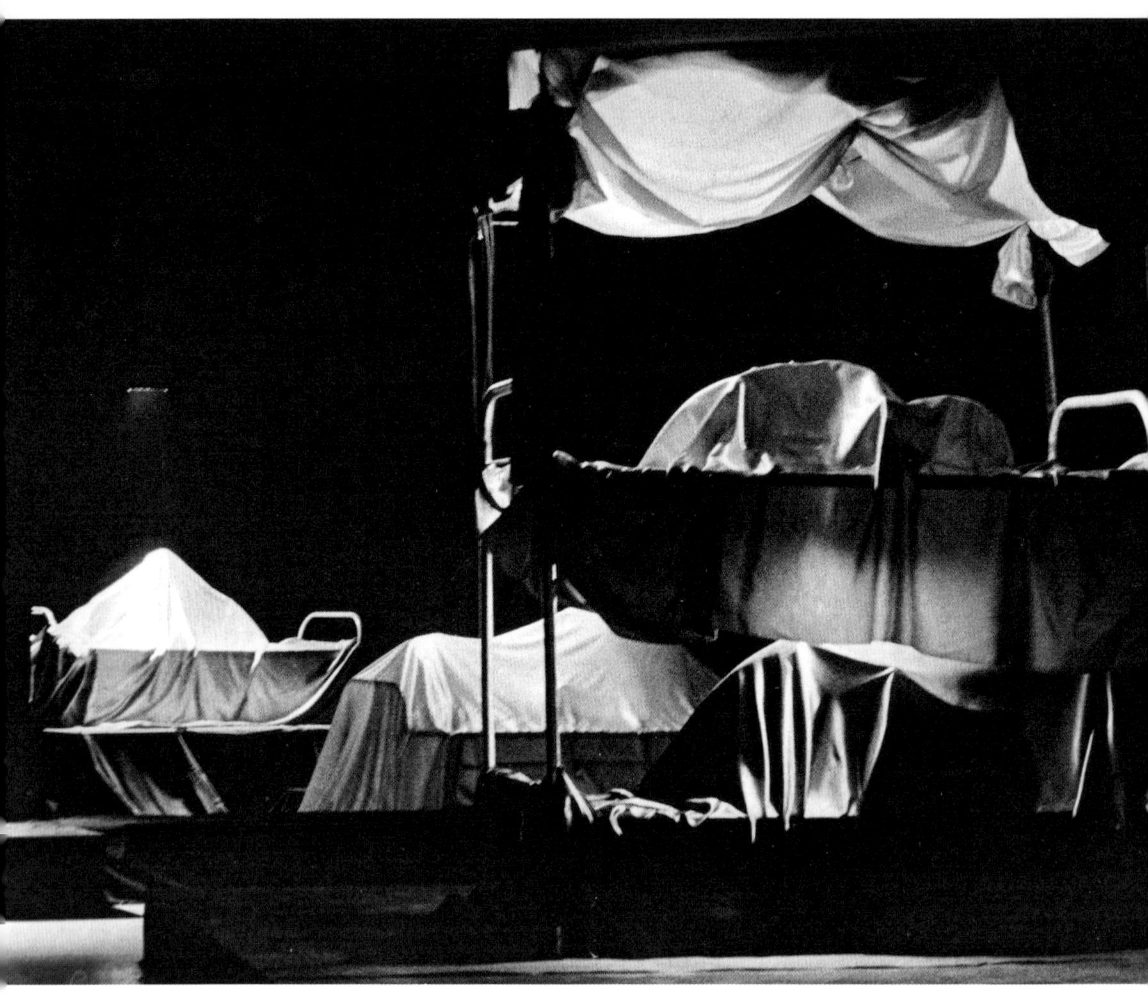

In 1972, Bursztyn began her series *Las camas* (The Beds). The
sculptures consisted of metal bed frames fitted with motors and
draped in satin fabric. Bursztyn debuted the first *Cama (Construcción
en movimiento)* (Bed: Construction in Motion) at the third Bienal de
Artes Coltejer in Medellín and was awarded first prize for the work at the
first Salón Nacional de Artistas de la Universidad Jorge Tadeo Lozano
that same year. The exhibition *Las camas* took place in 1974 at the
Museo de Arte Moderno de Bogotá. Bursztyn installed thirteen
individual works in a room-sized installation. The suggestive vibration
lent the installation a blatantly erotic charge.

Las camas installed by Feliza Bursztyn in her exhibition at the
Museo de Arte Moderno de Bogotá in 1974
Courtesy of the Archive of Pablo Leyva. Photo: Pablo Leyva

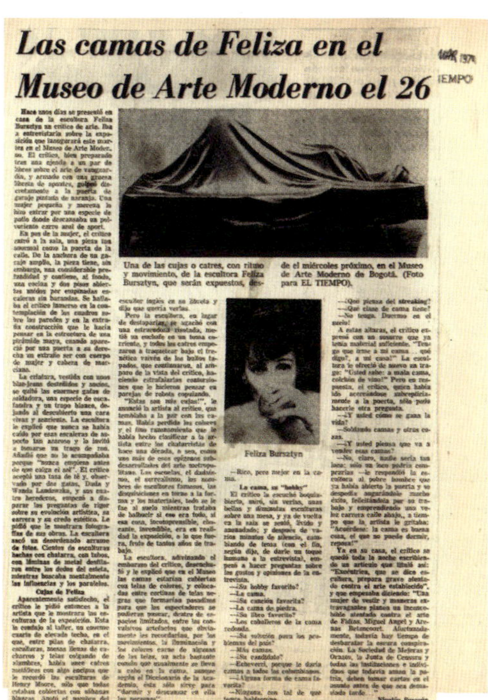

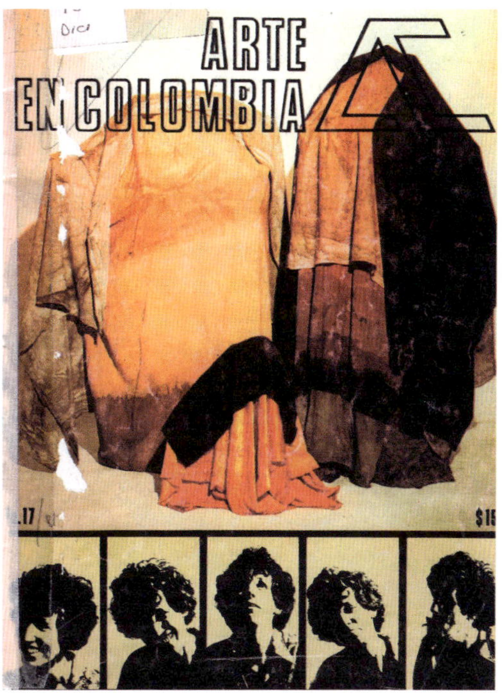

Bursztyn loved giving interviews. The article devoted to the *Camas* exhibition at MAMBO was written by Nicolas Suescún, a renowned poet and friend. Over the years Suescún reviewed many of Bursztyn's shows, always with an ironic, comic tone. Here, he asked Bursztyn about her hobby and her favourite book and song: the questions were meant to be a parody of those frequently asked in women's magazines. Bursztyn's answers all included the word "bed". So, when asked to suggest a solution for the country's problems, she replied: "more beds".

"Las camas de Feliza en el Museo de Arte Moderno el 26", *El Tiempo* (Bogotá), March 1974

La baila mecánica (The Mechanical Ballet) premiered on 5 April 1979 at the Galeria Garcés Velásquez in Bogotá. It represented the pinnacle of Bursztyn's experiments with material, light, sound, and movement. The theatricality of this work was also reflected in the exhibition brochure that mimicked a program for a ballet or theatre play. "El VII Salón Atenas" is one of the last articles that Traba wrote about the Colombian art scene. After being forced to resign from all her official posts and to refrain from political commentary (for openly criticising the military seizure of the campus of the National University of Colombia where MAMBO was located), she permanently left the country in 1969.

Marta Traba, "El VII Salón Atenas: 'Ya que estamos'", *Arte en Colombia* (Bogotá), no. 17 (December 1981)

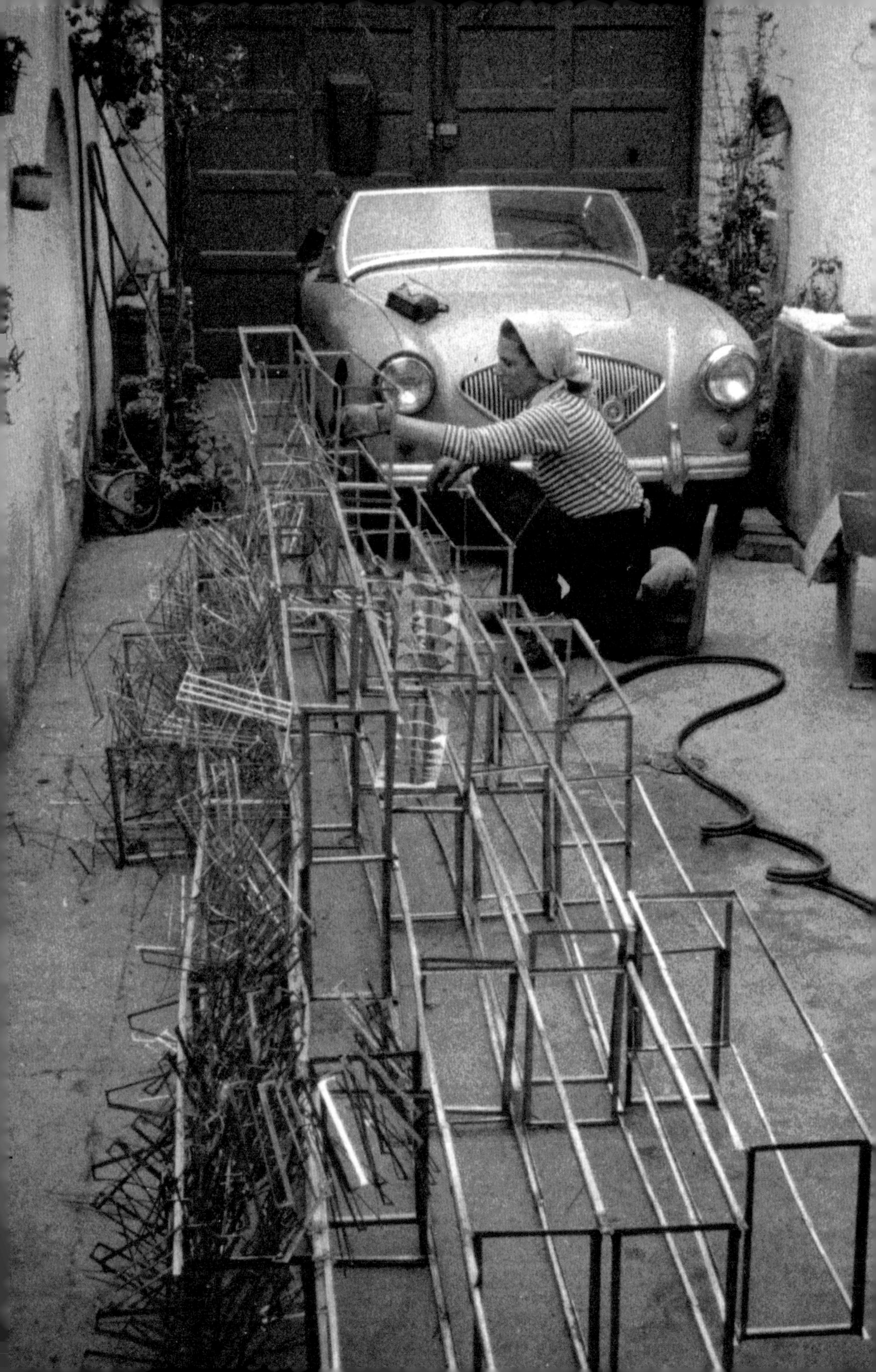

Over the course of her career, Bursztyn received several commissions
for private installations. One such composition, *Homenaje a Da Vinci*
(Homage to Da Vinci, 1973), was made for Rita de Agudelo. De Agudelo
was the director of Galería San Diego, one of the most important
galleries in Bogotá and the site of several exhibitions by the artist. The
work was composed of the remnants from the production of pressed
aluminium kitchen utensils.

Feliza Bursztyn working on *Homenaje a Da Vinci*, a commission for
Rita de Agudelo in the yard of her studio in Bogotá, c. 1973
Courtesy of the Archive of Pablo Leyva. Photo: Pablo Leyva
◄

In 1979, Bursztyn was interviewed by Maritza Uribe de Urdinola, the
founder of the Museo de Arte Moderno La Tertulia in Cali. Bursztyn
reflected on her life, family, and work. She also uttered the phrase that
encapsulated the strategy that had defined her work for decades: "En un
país de machistas, ¡hágase la loca!". In a patriarchal society, women have
no choice but to feign madness.

Maritza Uribe de Urdinola, "En un país de machistas, ¡hágase la loca!",
El Tiempo: Revista Carrusel (Bogotá), 30 November 1979
▼

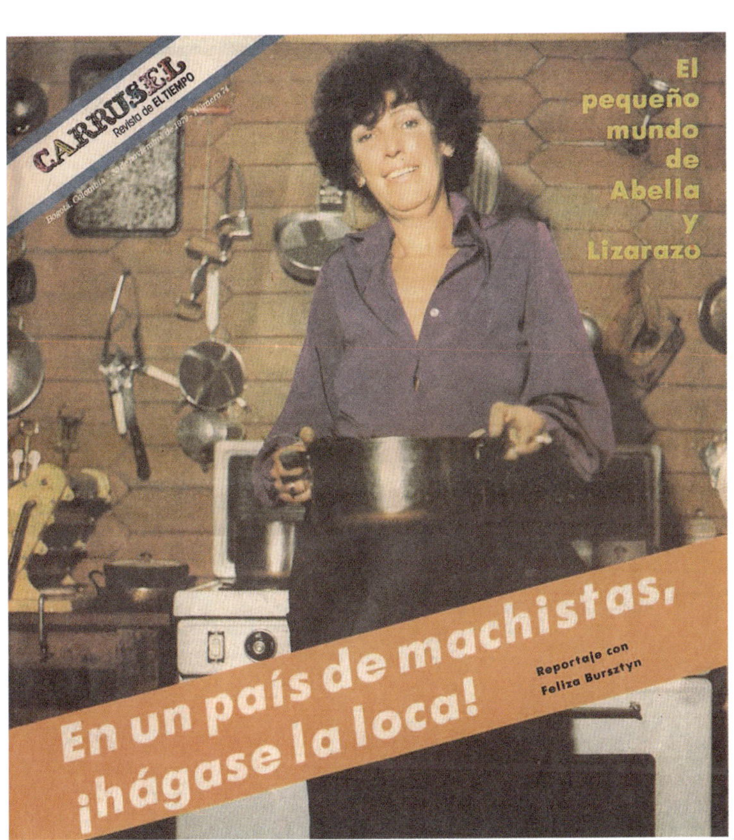

Bursztyn frequently installed her works in the garden of her home
and studio. The articles written about Bursztyn often emphasized how
the sculptures in her garden seemed to imitate the natural environment
despite being made of industrial debris. Also visible in the photo is one
of the artist's early works from the *Color* (Colour Series) series,
composed of car parts. There is a biographical element inscribed in this
series of works: in 1968 Bursztyn was involved in a terrible car accident
while travelling with her friend, fellow artist Beatriz Daza. Daza was killed
and Bursztyn severely injured. She would suffer pain for the rest of her
life and undergo multiple surgeries in the years following the crash. In
1981, García Márquez wrote: "Feliza has never done something more
subversive than turning car accidents into artworks".

Feliza Bursztyn in her studio in Bogotá, c. 1979
Courtesy of the Archive of Pablo Leyva. Photo: Rafael Moure

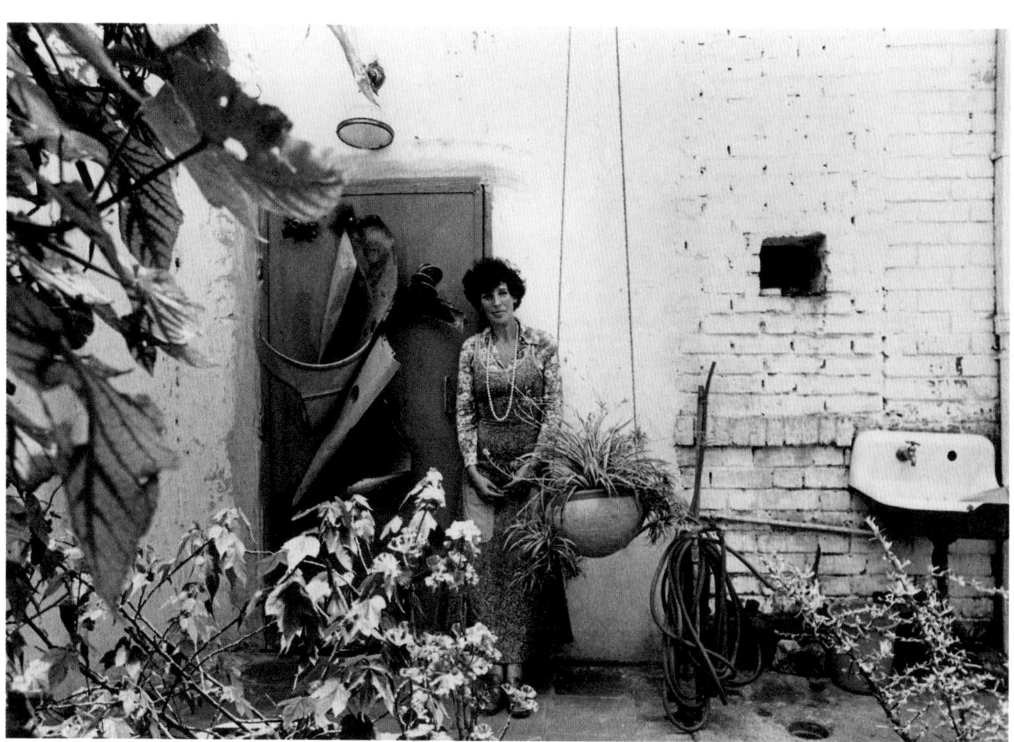

Bursztyn's decision to be a sculptor was a scandal in a country that
considered art, in general, and sculpture, in particular, to be male pursuits.
The artist consistently challenged these perceptions by sharing pictures of
herself emphatically dressed in feminine attire. Here, she welds one of her
Color (Colour Series) pieces in a silk kimono and pearls.

The artist welding in her studio in Bogotá, c. 1980
Courtesy of the Archive of Pablo Leyva. Photo: Pablo Leyva

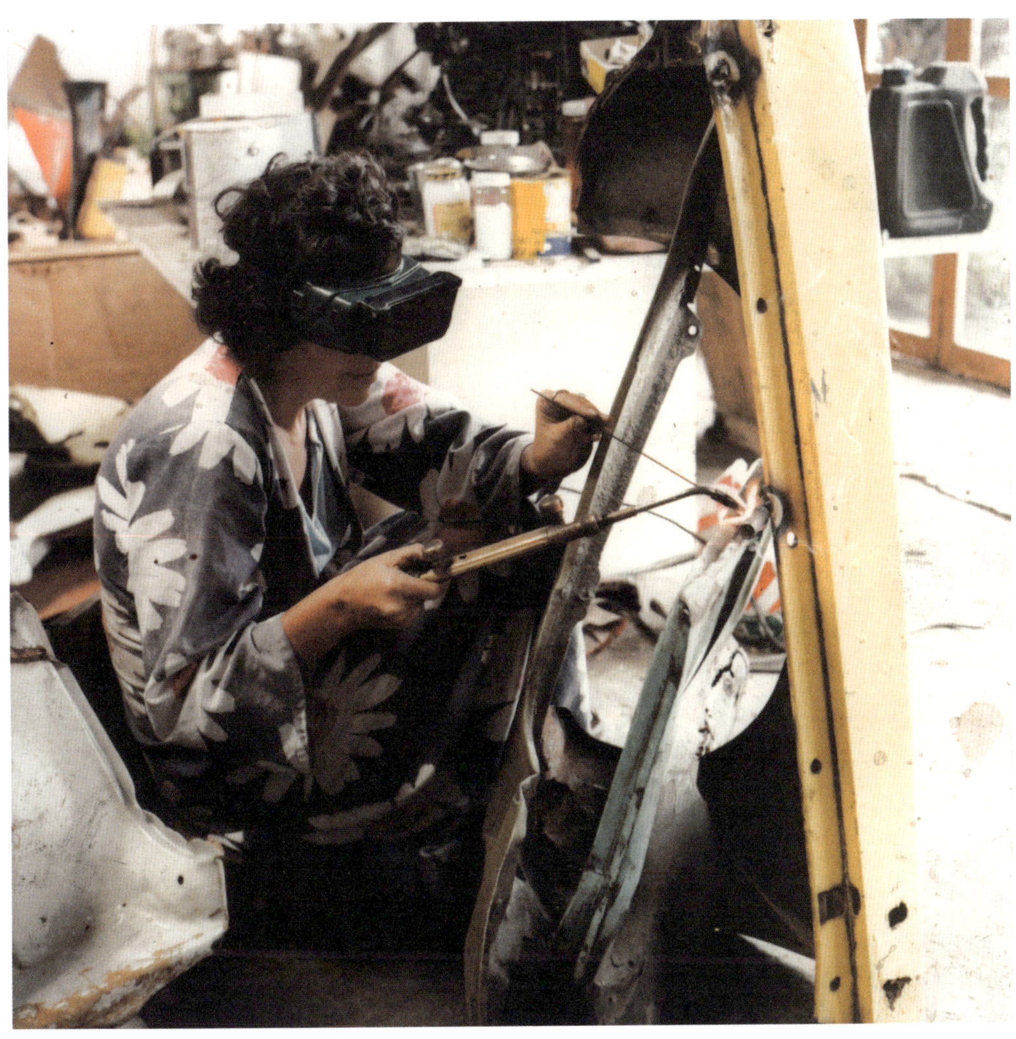

Bursztyn regularly exhibited her work in Cuba. Her embrace of the Cuban Revolution drew the suspicion of the authorities in conservative, US-allied Colombia. Her last exhibition, *Dos Escultores Colombianos: Feliza Negret* (Two Colombian Sculptors: Feliza Negret), took place in Havana on 13 July 1981. Shortly after she returned, she was arrested in her home in the early morning of 24 July and detained for forty-eight hours. No specific reason was given for her arrest but it was authorized under the McCarthyist umbrella of the "Estatuto de seguridad" (Security Statute). The Security Statute was passed by President Julio César Turbay Ayala (1978–82) in 1978 purportedly in response to an increase of violent attacks by guerrilla groups.

Invitation to the exhibition *Dos Escultores Colombianos: Feliza Negret* at the Galería Latinoamericana, Casa de las Américas, Havana, 13 July 1981
Courtesy of the Archive of Pablo Leyva

On 5 August 1981 Pablo Leyva, Bursztyn's second husband, drove to the Mexican Embassy while she lay on the floor in the car's backseat. Fearing for her safety following her detention, the couple had contacted García Márquez who arranged for Bursztyn to take refuge in the Mexican Embassy. She was granted asylum and on 8 August boarded a plane for Mexico City, where she stayed at Garcia Marquez's house. It was there that she produced her last sculptures which are now lost.

"Autorizan salida del país a Feliza Bursztyn", *El Espectador* (Bogotá), August 1981

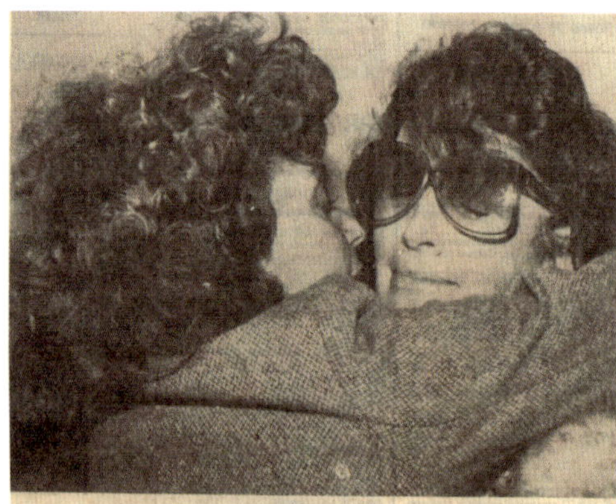

Viajó Feliza

La escultora colombiana Feliza Bursztyn viajó a México en calidad de asilada política y en el aeropuerto Eldorado fue despedida por familiares, amigos y artistas, entre ellos la comediante y actriz Fanny Mickey, con quien se abraza efusivamente. Feliza se asiló tras ser investigada por supuestos actos de subversión. (Foto Mauricio Angel, EL TIEMPO).

Bursztyn's absence was keenly felt by the artistic community of Bogotá. In a show of support, a group of artists and other intellectuals penned an open letter protesting her kidnapping by military forces and asking the government to stop such detentions and tortures.

Comunicado, 1981
Courtesy of the Archive of Pablo Leyva

Bursztyn's death was widely reported in the Colombian press. García Márquez wrote two obituaries and pictures of Feliza's coffin returning to Colombia, her funeral, and the graveside service all appeared in the newspaper. The feeling of grief occasioned by the loss of the artist was pervasive.

Caricatura "Locombia" by Dick Salazar, *El Espectador* (Bogotá), 13 January 1982

following pages
After several months in Mexico City, Bursztyn and Leyva decided to opt for exile in Paris. Bursztyn hoped to create a new life for herself in a city she knew and loved. In addition, she had been granted a stipend by the French government to pursue her work. On the evening of 8 January 1982, at dinner, Bursztyn suffered a heart attack and died in the restaurant. She was surrounded by her friends García Márquez, his wife Mercedes Barcha, Enrique Santos Calderón, María Teresa Rubino, and Leyva. She was forty-nine years old. The photo captures the artist's studio as she left it on her departure in 1981.

Feliza Bursztyn's studio after she left Bogotá for her exile in Paris, 1981
Courtesy of the Archive of Pablo Leyva. Photo: Pablo Leyva

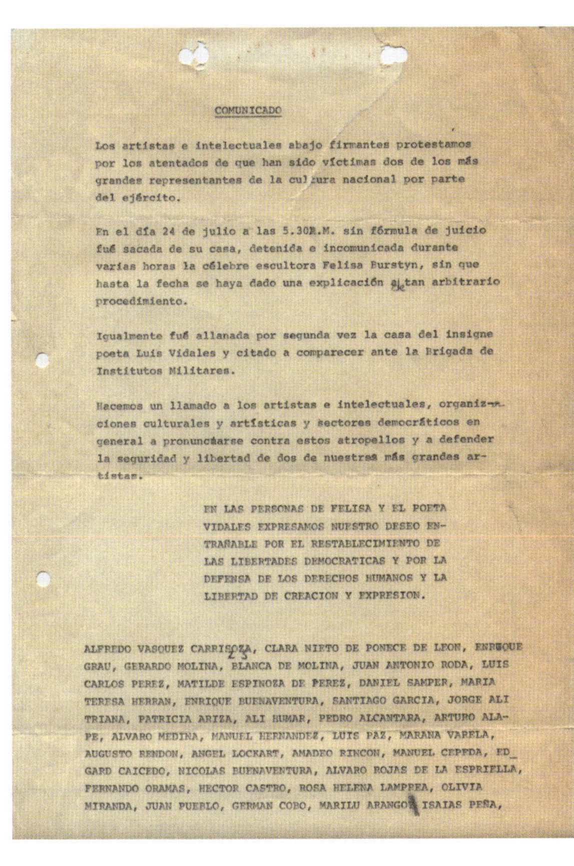

COMUNICADO

Los artistas e intelectuales abajo firmantes protestamos por los atentados de que han sido víctimas dos de los más grandes representantes de la cultura nacional por parte del ejército.

En el día 24 de julio a las 5.30P.M. sin fórmula de juicio fué sacada de su casa, detenida e incomunicada durante varias horas la célebre escultora Felisa Burstyn, sin que hasta la fecha se haya dado una explicación a tan arbitrario procedimiento.

Igualmente fué allanada por segunda vez la casa del insigne poeta Luis Vidales y citado a comparecer ante la Brigada de Institutos Militares.

Hacemos un llamado a los artistas e intelectuales, organiza-ciones culturales y artísticas y sectores democráticos en general a pronunciarse contra estos atropellos y a defender la seguridad y libertad de dos de nuestras más grandes artistas.

EN LAS PERSONAS DE FELISA Y EL POETA VIDALES EXPRESAMOS NUESTRO DESEO EN-TRAÑABLE POR EL RESTABLECIMIENTO DE LAS LIBERTADES DEMOCRATICAS Y POR LA DEFENSA DE LOS DERECHOS HUMANOS Y LA LIBERTAD DE CREACION Y EXPRESION.

ALFREDO VASQUEZ CARRIZOZA, CLARA NIETO DE PONECE DE LEON, ENRIQUE GRAU, GERARDO MOLINA, BLANCA DE MOLINA, JUAN ANTONIO RODA, LUIS CARLOS PEREZ, MATILDE ESPINOZA DE PEREZ, DANIEL SAMPER, MARIA TERESA HERRAN, ENRIQUE BUENAVENTURA, SANTIAGO GARCIA, JORGE ALI TRIANA, PATRICIA ARIZA, ALI HUMAR, PEDRO ALCANTARA, ARTURO ALA-PE, ALVARO MEDINA, MANUEL HERNANDEZ, LUIS PAZ, MARANA VARELA, AUGUSTO RENDON, ANGEL LOCKART, AMADEO RINCON, MANUEL CEPEDA, ED_GARD CAICEDO, NICOLAS BUENAVENTURA, ALVARO ROJAS DE LA ESPRIELLA, FERNANDO ORAMAS, HECTOR CASTRO, ROSA HELENA LAMPREA, OLIVIA MIRANDA, JUAN PUEBLO, GERMAN COBO, MARILU ARANGO, ISAIAS PEÑA,

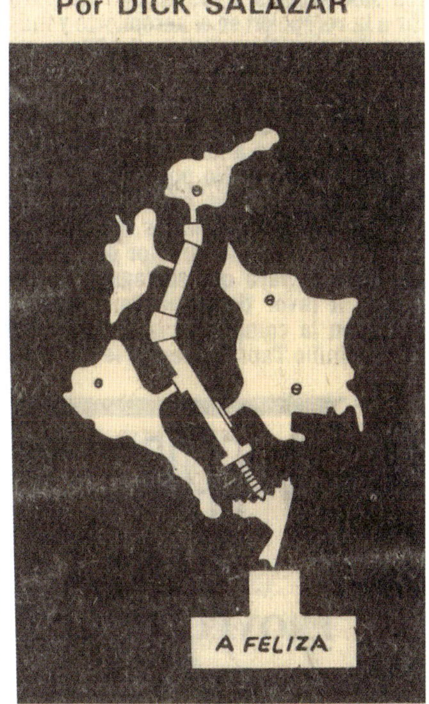

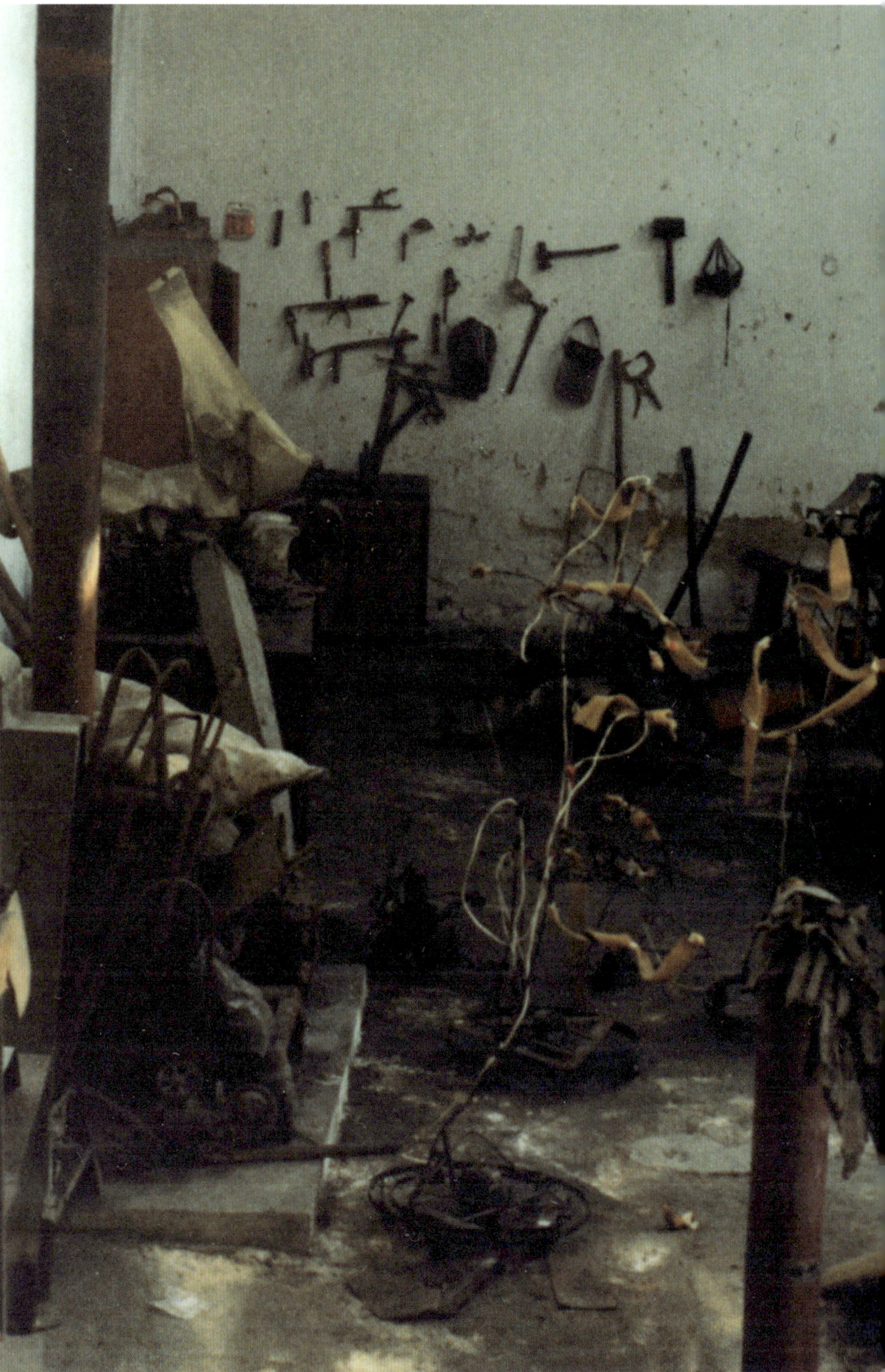

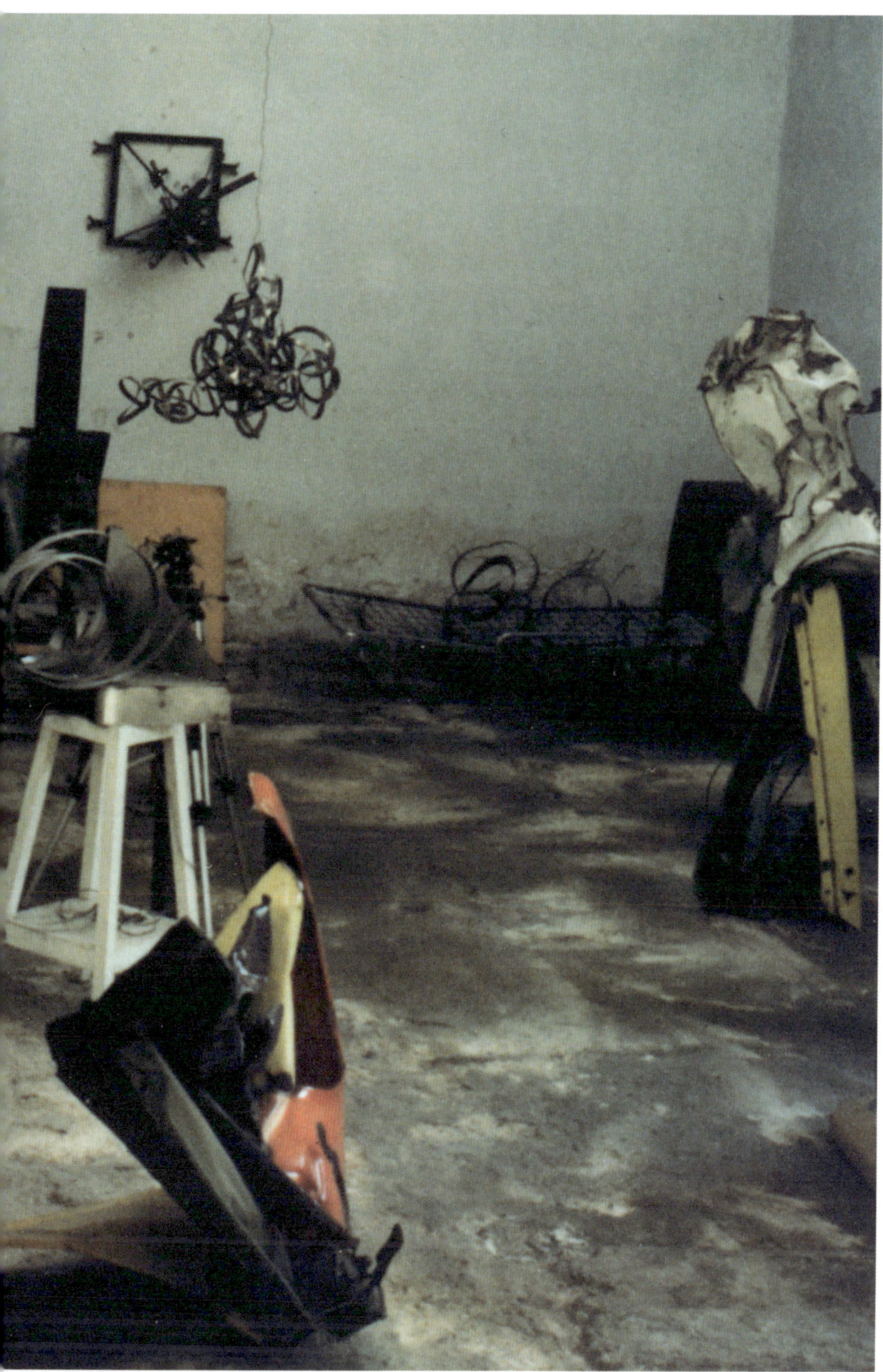

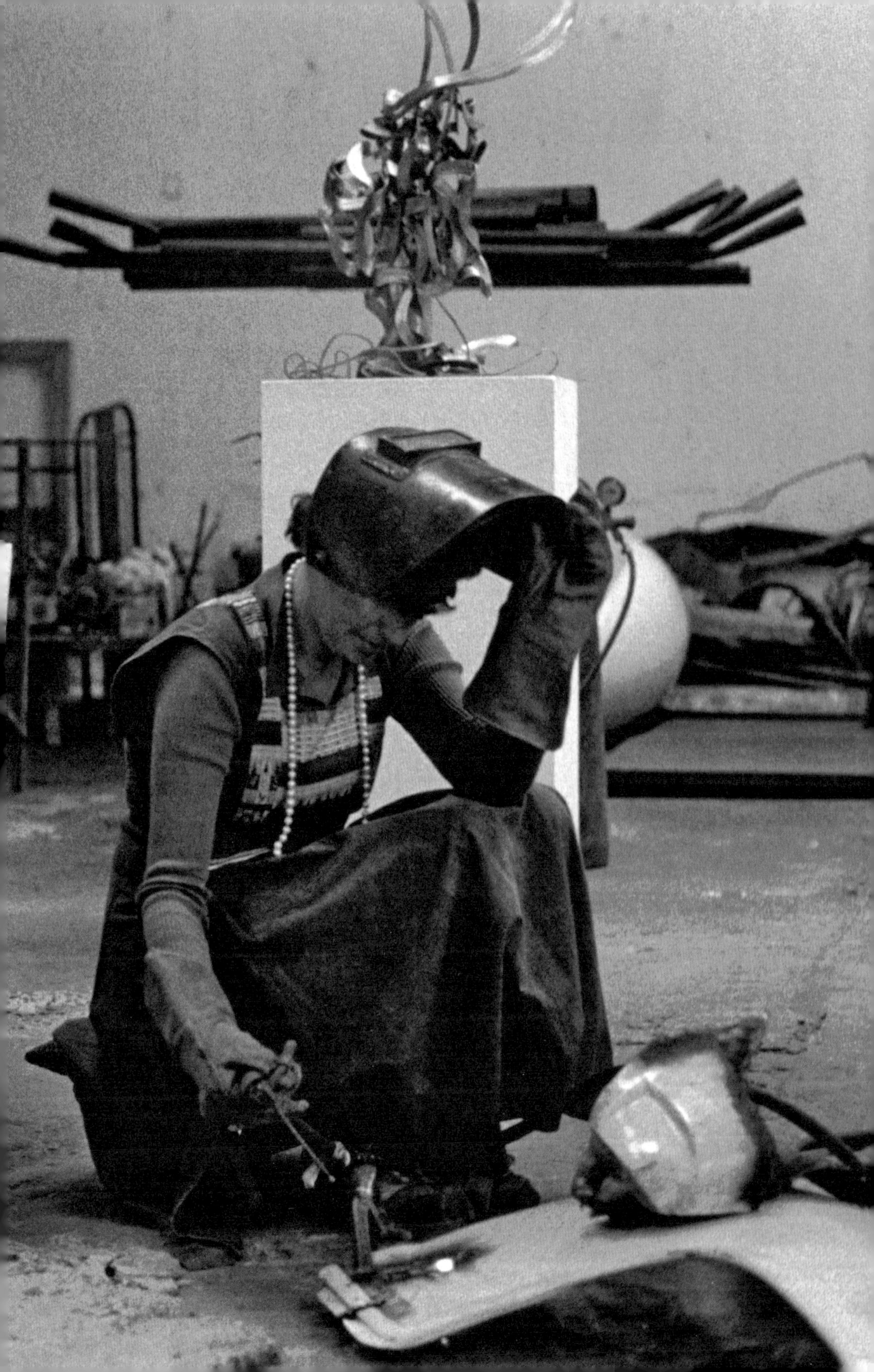

Feliza Bursztyn: Welding Madness

Marta Dziewańska

"I, too, overflow; my desires have invented new desires, my body knows unheard-of songs. Time and again I, too, have felt so full of luminous torrents that I could burst – burst with forms much more beautiful than those which are put up in frames and sold for a fortune. And I, too, said nothing, showed nothing; I didn't open my mouth, I didn't repaint my half of the world. I was ashamed. I was afraid, and I swallowed my shame and my fear. I said to myself: You are mad! What's the meaning of these waves, these floods, these outbursts? Where is the ebullient infinite woman who … hasn't been ashamed of her strength? Who, surprised and horrified by the fantastic tumult of her drives (for she was made to believe that a well-adjusted normal woman has a … divine composure), hasn't accused herself of being a monster? Who, feeling a funny desire stirring inside her (to sing, to write, to dare to speak, in short, to bring out something new), hasn't thought that she was sick? Well, her shameful sickness is that she resists death, that she makes trouble."

Hélène Cixous, "The Laugh of the Medusa", 1976[1]

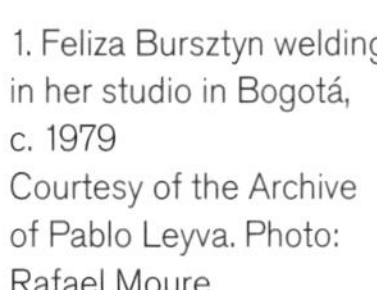

1. Feliza Bursztyn welding in her studio in Bogotá, c. 1979
Courtesy of the Archive of Pablo Leyva. Photo: Rafael Moure

2. Pile of scrap metal in Feliza Bursztyn's studio in Bogotá, c. 1978
Courtesy of the Archive of Pablo Leyva. Photo: Pablo Leyva

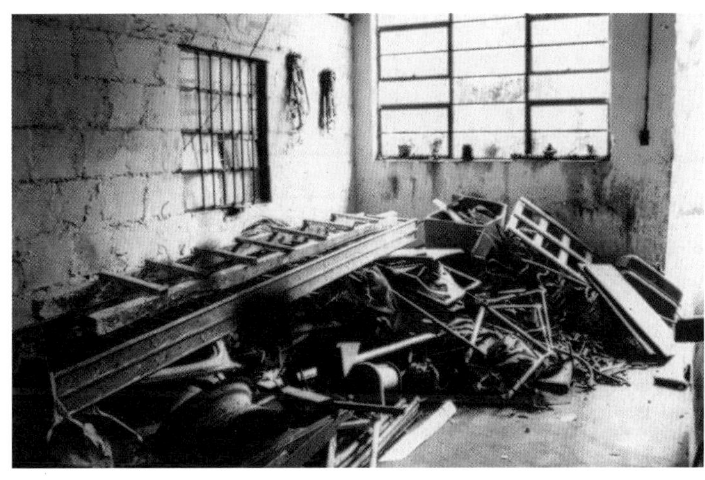

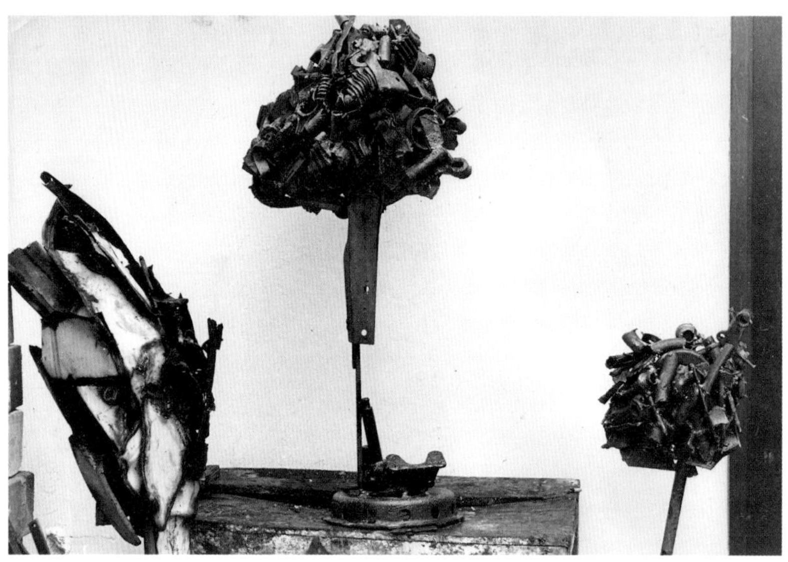

Feliza Bursztyn is a troublemaker. A very troublesome one. She does not create as one *should*. She does not respect the set rules and the status quo; she mixes low art with the high; instead of "creating", she assembles her sculptures from industrial debris that she has found or bought from factory workers, turning her exhibitions into curious spectacles with an abundance of protagonists but no narrative, no focus, no punchline (fig. 2). Her works – strange hybrids of kinetic abstractions, semi-realistic more or less grotesque figures, with suggestive titles – build no coherent story; it is difficult to link them, to define them unambiguously, to encapsulate them in some kind of *-ism*. And at the same time, they all belong to some strange, eccentric family, in which one work or series refers to the next or the previous one, without, however, creating any final connections, meanings, or clear sequences. The artist herself says little about them: she does not explain, makes no attempt to tell a story, does not elaborate. She puts them on pedestals, mounts them on walls, hangs them from ceilings, puts them on imaginary stages, dresses them up, plugs them in, makes them dance and gives them dramatic lighting – while incessantly being ironic towards them.

Another issue with Bursztyn is that her artistic modus operandi is not feminine. Rather than a brush, she uses a welding torch; rather than a bone china teacup (since women should stick to "feminine" art), she works with industrial pipes and factory scrap, which she assembles into somewhat obscure, abstract forms. Her preferred colour is metallic silver or aluminium and rust; her sculptures are rough and bulky, often asymmetrical, and openly erotic (some might call them vulgar). From the outset, the critics' opinions did not augur well for her future. Walter Engel, the most influential art critic at the time, wrote that "her works lack plastic value" and that the only artistic problem they address is "assuring equilibrium", since Bursztyn composes her works of bits of junk around a vertical axis. He concluded with the utterly patronising tone that Bursztyn should give up being a sculptor, and that developing her *Chatarras* (Junk Sculptures) into viable works of art would require a miracle (fig. 3).[2] The artist seems not to be affected by these criticisms: she does not explain herself nor does she make any attempt to rise to the criticism, to improve herself or to raise her game. On the contrary: she works with conviction, drawing from some mysterious source, with passion and laughter – as if she had not the slightest doubt (a woman artist… having no doubts?) about the value and stakes (both visible and hidden) of her art.

But Bursztyn not only creates as a woman artist would not or *should not* create; she also does not live as one would *expect* a woman to live. Her provocative art goes hand in hand with an extravagant, wild life-style, its rhythm set by the pulse of work, endless parties, and late-night discussions in the waft of her cigarette smoke – about art, politics, being engaged, theatre, music, literature, the working class – and her more or less spontaneous travels. As a Jewish woman, Bursztyn breaks the ban by divorcing her husband, which makes her excluded not only from her religious community but also from her family. As a mother, she decides to break the greatest of taboos: she will leave her children in the care of their father for the sake of her work and passion. As a partner, she will talk openly about her love affairs and fascinations with both men and women. In the Catholic, patriarchal Bogotá, she proudly flaunts her mini-skirts, high-heeled shoes, colourful nails, and strong make-up. There are anecdotes about how she and Marta Traba roamed the night-time city in a Vespa, without any underwear but sporting dark glasses. The neighbours are familiar with her thunderous laughter, and can occasionally hear her falling down the steep stairs of her studio after too many glasses of her favourite rum. Bursztyn will not be silenced – she is unstoppable. Fuelled by gusto and contrariness, she creates enthusiastically and with obvious enjoyment, living and thinking according to her own rule book. She does not shy away from bending or breaking the rules or creating new ones. She *profanes* constantly and at every step.[3]

The energy of this multi-layered and playful scandal brings to mind the image of a laughing Medusa, conjured up in Hélène Cixous's famous – and controversial – essay-cum-manifesto *The Laugh of the Medusa* (1976).[4] According to Greek mythology, Medusa, the youngest of the three

Gorgons, should have nothing to laugh about. Punished by Athena for her affair with Poseidon, from a beautiful girl, a protective, and caring figure, she has been transformed into a monster with venomous snakes instead of hair.[5] Her gaze turns all who look at her to stone. Deprived of her own body and revolting, robbed of pleasure and crying out for revenge – what reason would Medusa have to laugh, as posited by Cixous?

In a contrarian manner, Cixous tampers with the classical myth, yet presents it à rebours, she also reclaims it and re-writes it. She creates a singular pamphlet which twists the myth, tearing it out of the confines of the familiar opposites – beauty versus ugliness, reason versus chaos, passive versus active, before versus after – and in the process re-invents it. The philosopher takes as her starting point Freudian notions related to female sexuality, as manifested in the metaphor of the "dark continent" which appears in his essay *Femininity*.[6] The term encapsulates the projection of irrepressible wildness and hostile terrain, while conjuring up unexplored mystery, buoyed by the promise of control and domination. Cixous defies these perceptions. Exposing Medusa's unrestrained and unrestrainable, unconventional and abnormal body, rather than covering it up and making it retreat into the shadows, she gives it a voice. And it is not a voice pleading for understanding and protection, acceptance or identity. It is liberating laughter that breaks Medusa out of oppressive clichés, out of an absurd fear of stereotypic evaluation, criticism or rejection.

Cixous writes: "We're stormy, and that which is ours breaks loose from us without our fearing any debilitation. Our glances, our smiles, are spent; laughs exude from all our mouths; our blood flows and we extend ourselves without ever reaching an end; we never hold back our thoughts, our signs, our writing; and we're not afraid of lacking".[7] Not afraid of lacking? It is as if Cixous were describing the impossible, as if she were bringing to life a completely new – or perhaps simply hitherto unheard of – language, as if she were entering some forbidden territory, appropriating and insulting the rules that reign there. Her sacrilege seems to make her – like Medusa – euphoric. Cixous writes with verve, as if transported by laughter, energetically pressing on without paying attention to unfinished thoughts, or sentences that break up or stretch into infinity. She will not be channelled into the ruts of sequences of cause and effect, stylistic imperatives, or self-congratulatory pronouncements that end with a triumphant point. No way. She greedily multiplies questions, metaphors, and games of association; she is not afraid of sudden turns, and constantly ironic. "Write!", she commands. "Writing is for you, you are for you; your body is yours, take it. I know why you haven't written. (And why I didn't write before the age of twenty-seven.) Because writing is at once too high, too great for you, it's reserved for the great – is, for 'great men'; and it's 'silly'. Besides, you've written a little, but in secret. And it wasn't good, because it was in secret, and because you punished yourself for writing, because you didn't go all the way; or because you wrote, irresistibly, as when we would masturbate in secret, not to go further, but to attenuate the tension a bit, just enough to take the edge off. And then as soon as we come, we go and make ourselves feel guilty – so as to be forgiven; or to forget, to bury it until the next time. Write, let no one hold you back, let nothing stop you."[8]

There is no denying that, more than as a form of discovery or even revelation, Cixous should be read as a kind of retrieval: it is a statement of fact, a cleansing of prohibitions, and a return of what has been thrown outside the realm of the norm, of everyday life, of language. And more than that, Cixous not only describes – shamelessly – but also embeds female pleasure into the very structure of her text. She refuses to be decapitated and excluded from language – whether by the mythical Perseus or by submissive silence – thus restoring balance: she disarms taboos, snatches the female body away from its paradoxical materiality (opposed to reason and at the same time somehow detached from itself), mocks dualisms, and profanes the border of the (in)expressible.[9]

Without doubt, the art of Feliza Bursztyn is an open, multi-layered provocation, bordering on iconoclasm. At the same time, playing with her art, in addition to the courage of formal experimentation, with each of her works, the artist seems to question and invalidate: the existing orders, the valid canons, the reductive, inclusive-exclusionary binarisms. Working with scrap metal, factory waste, rusty cables, and corroded wheels and welding them into sculptural forms, she not only creates compositions that significantly mock the dominant ideals of beauty and refinement, but also undermines the distinction between the old and the new. The new in Bursztyn's work is never completely new – it is a transformation and critical variation on what had been. On the other hand, in the old, the artist seems to find ever new potential: as if by welding, twisting, and juxtaposing, she were constantly searching for new meanings inherent in and conveyed therein. Her *Chatarras*, inspired by the works of Nouveau Réalisme artists, or the later *Color* (Colour Series), which critically reference César[10] but which are also in a contrarian dialogue with the Groupe Panique (Panic Group),[11] on the one hand recall the old, glamorous life of these materials, but also point to their coarseness, impermanence, and inherent decay. Apparently, Bursztyn is incapable of treating the given as simply given. For her, it poses the task of constant reinterpretation.

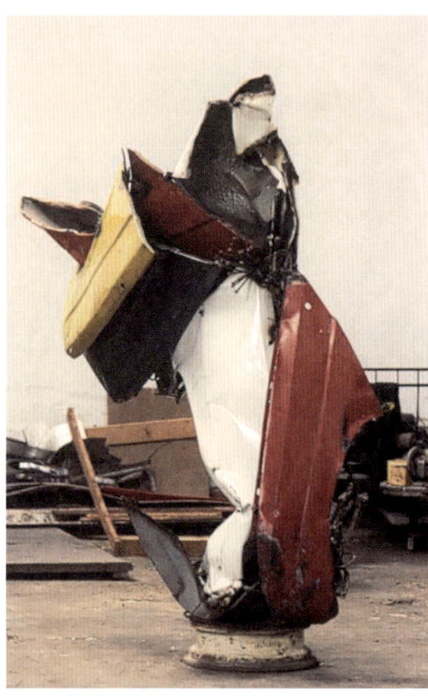

It is worth mentioning another dimension of these works, which the artist herself seems to accentuate, disqualifying (laughingly perhaps? This is not clear, but certainly with enjoyment) yet more dualism. Namely in her assemblages she uses materials that point not only to industrial waste (intended to be circulated by art institutions) and the ingenuity of the poor, but also, by inference, to the working class. For is not her favourite technique of welding with an oxy-acetylene torch associated with the toil of workers who, unlike artists who autonomously make decisions about their work, are part of an anonymous production chain and alienated from the result of their work? Are these workers not usually men? And isn't this why Bursztyn deliberately wears necklaces or floral silk kimonos every time she welds? (figs. 4–5)

The most important, Medusa-related, aspect of her work, however, is the perverse way that Bursztyn embeds her own, female body into her art. Within the context of literary art, Cixous wrote that a "Woman must write her self: must write about women and bring women to writing, from which they have been driven away as violently as from their bodies – for the same reasons, by the same law, with the same fatal goal. Woman must put herself into the text – as into the world and into history – by her own movement".[12] Thus far, both in literature and in art, the female body had been adorned, denuded, ogled, dressed up, and exploited, while simultaneously at all times passive and voiceless. It is as if it was in a paradoxical

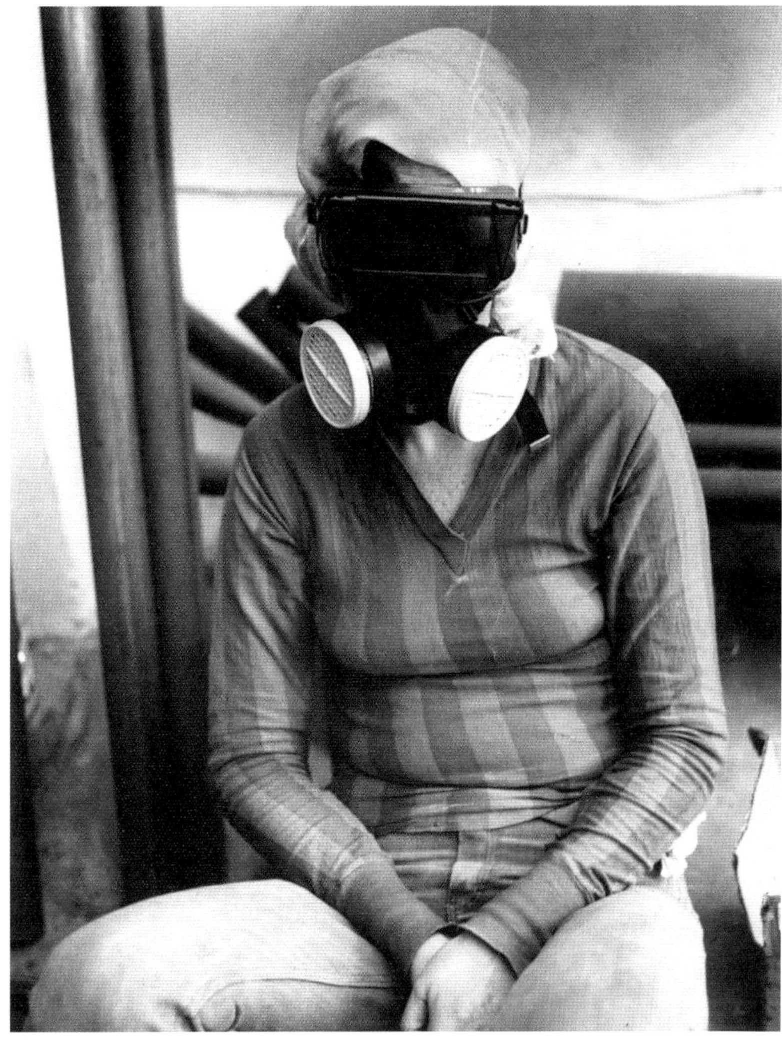

state of brutal cessation and suspension somewhere between being the object of the language and its speaker, but never its subject.[13] And just as Cixous returns to Medusa her voice and subjectivity, so does Bursztyn work with evident, active (rather than passive) pleasure. And more than that: she obliges us to admire her hysteric's beauty.

Bursztyn's art seems to be playing out along the very thin line between social/cultural/artistic discourse and the question of female expression. The artist openly defines this relationship as a collision when she says that in a patriarchal, "sexist country", the only way for her to have creative freedom is to "pretend to be the mad one".[14] Her intuition resonates with that of Cixous, for whom the problem lies in the language in which women are *The Other*, a language that, through omitting and dominating women's articulation of themselves, often pathologizes it, thus excluding their desires, their pleasure and their *jouissance*. In *The Laugh of the Medusa*, Cixous writes that the "woman has always functioned 'within' the discourse of man" as an object locked in a negative semantic loop. According to the philosopher, this loop annihilates a woman's "specific energy and diminishes or stifles her very different sounds". The only form of resistance is to "dislocate this 'within', to explode it, turn it around, and seize it; to make it hers, containing it, taking it in her own mouth, biting that tongue with her very own teeth to invent for herself a language to get inside of". Cixous cunningly exploits the duality inherent in the French term "voler", which means both "to fly" and "to steal". And it is precisely this precarious vagueness (which points to deriving pleasure from the play on words) that is the site of possible modification, displacement, and resistance.[15]

Feliza Bursztyn seems similarly incapable of confining herself to existing language, as her *Las histéricas* (The Hysterical Ones) clearly demonstrate: employing the hitherto masculine language of sculpture, the artist not only represents those who are usually considered beyond the pale, but with this representation she alludes to madness – and hysteria, historically considered a female form of madness – as a starting point and a specific strategy of her work. What is this supposed to mean?

Las histéricas were created between 1967 and 1968 in stainless steel, which the artist sourced in a factory producing heaters, so as to yet again link her work to industry (figs. 6–8). Unlike most motor-powered industrial machines, however, her creations produce nothing but

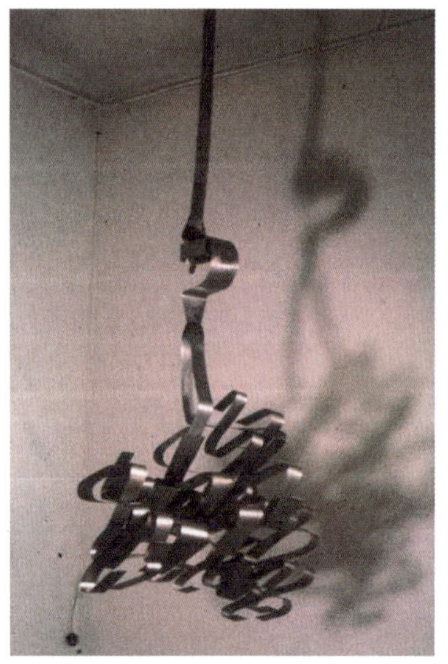

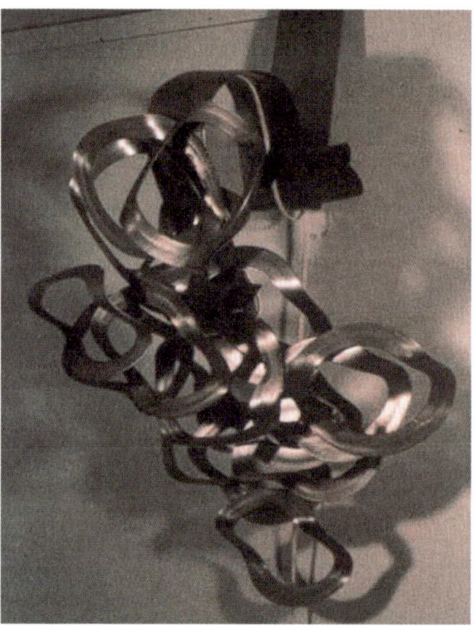

6. Feliza Bursztyn, *Histérica* (The Hysterical One), 1968 Courtesy of the Archive of Pablo Leyva

7. Feliza Bursztyn, *Histérica* (The Hysterical One), 1968 Courtesy of the Archive of Pablo Leyva

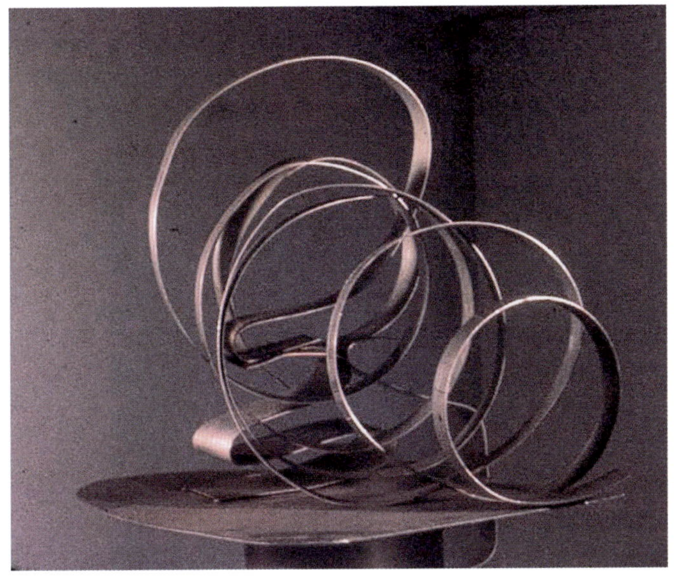

convulsive, jerky movement that appears possessed, as well as irritating noise. Their uselessness, their clumsiness, and the peculiar dissonance of the sound they emit produce a strange cacophony, irritating to the viewer. For their first presentation at the Museo de Arte Moderno de Bogotá (MAMBO) in 1968, Bursztyn placed them on all three floors of the institution, intending their noise to reach and shrilly penetrate every corner of the building. That same year she showed three of her *Histéricas* in the exhibition *Espacios ambientales* (Environments) in one small space, mounting them at different heights and illuminating them with dramatic spots that lit up and went out in irregular sequences. The artist arranged a specific situation for their reception: by entitling her installation *Siempre acostada* (Always in Bed) and mounting her mobile, moaning sculptures in a darkened bedroom-like setting while repeatedly turning on the peeping light, Bursztyn clearly builds an atmosphere of erotic tension. However, despite the fact that she was not the only artist taking up this subject in Colombia at the time, critics completely ignored all these pointers – evident, despite being abstract.

The momentum of Bursztyn's work, however, seems to be much greater than merely the boldness of a woman artist taking up the subject of (her?) pleasure.[16] By exhibiting her *Las histéricas*, and not just one, but a whole crowd of them, Feliza Bursztyn shows not only women at the moment of their (pleasurable) disobedience, but also points to what they themselves most often conceal, what they are always most afraid of, and what most frequently makes them remain silent: being labelled as maladjusted, sick, or abnormal, in a word – crazy. With her creative work, the artist steps

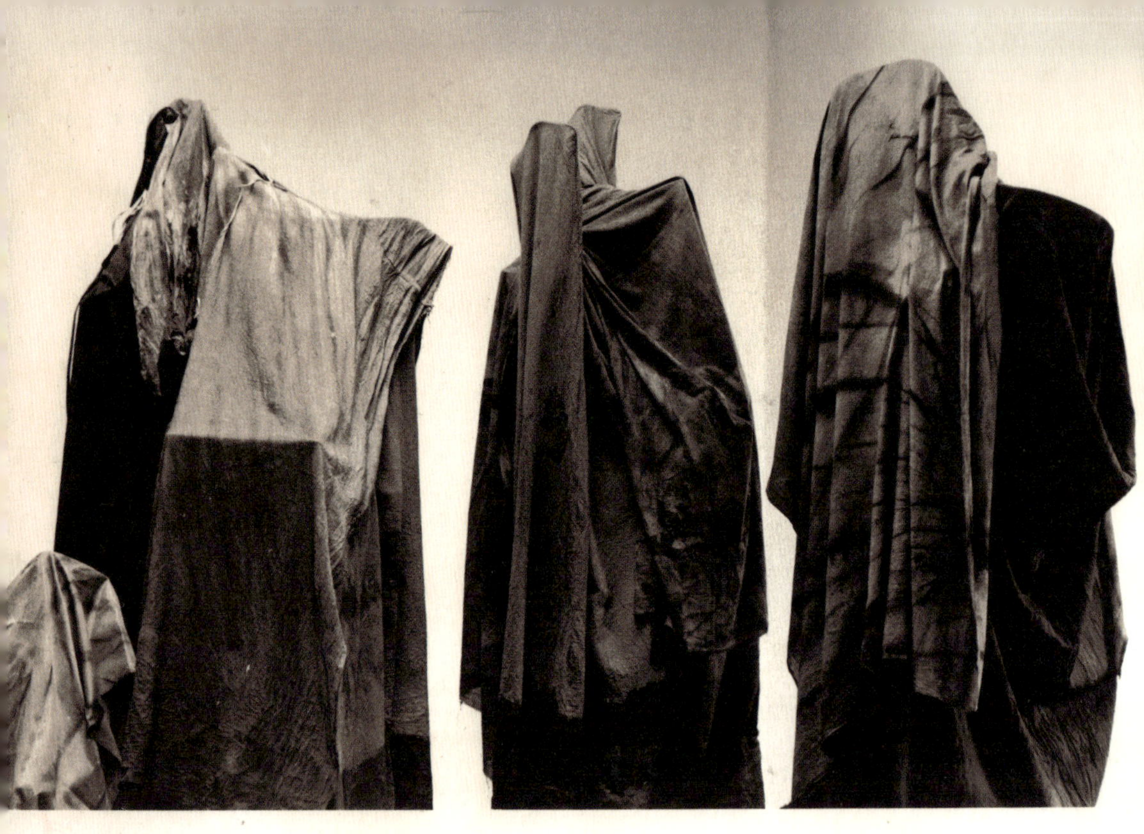

outside this exclusionary curse; she debunks it and ridicules it, while proudly turning hysteria into a starting point for her work.

Her strategy in this respect is twofold. Firstly, she no longer keeps hysteria concealed, no longer fears or sublimates it, but illuminates it spectacularly instead, ennobling it as worthy of admiration. And more than that: since the hallmark of hysteria is silence (as Cixous maintains, "having lost speech, the hysterics' tongues are cut off"), with Bursztyn, this aphonia seems to directly confront her ramshackle, shouty works.[17] After all, the artist seems to suggest, silence involves the same risk as the courage to speak out.[18] She chooses the latter, and her imperfect, eccentric and deliberately chaotic *Las histéricas* are, on the one hand, an articulation of the impossibility of verbalising one's desires (within the framework of the given syntax and, with it, the social dictates and prohibitions, templates of desire, processes of domestication, fetishization of femininity), and, on the other, a perverse moment of disagreement with this top-down brutally programmed inertia.[19] Even more than that: her *Las histéricas* are taking the floor on their own terms and they do it with a contrarian, impetuous metamorphosis from speaking objects (or, rather, talking ones, since they emit language that fails to express them) into speaking *subjects*.

This is an important moment – indeed, crucial. Because just as Medusa's laughter liberated her from absurd fear, so Bursztyn's *Las histéricas* seem to mock this fear and replace it with liberating and *eloquent* laughter. "Write your self", urges Cixous. "Your body must be heard. Only then will the immense resources of the unconscious spring forth." She continues: "To write. An act which will not only 'realize' the decensored relation of woman to her sexuality, to her womanly being, giving her access to her native strength; it will give her back her goods, her pleasures, her organs, her immense bodily territories which have been kept under seal; it will tear her away from the superegoized structure in which she has always occupied the place reserved for the guilty (guilty of everything, guilty at every turn: for having desires, for not having any; for being frigid, for being 'too hot'; for not being both at once; for being too motherly and not enough; for having children and for not having any; for nursing and for not nursing…) – tear her away by means of this research, this job of analysis and illumination, this emancipation of the marvellous text of her self that she must urgently learn to speak". Hysteria turns out to be a language that enables the woman, expelled from the language – in which Bursztyn functioned as an artist, a daughter, a wife, a mother – to articulate her displeasure. "Now women return from afar", enthuses Hélène Cixous, "from always: from 'without', from the heath where witches are kept alive; from below, from beyond 'culture'; from their childhood which men have been trying desperately to make them forget, condemning it to 'eternal rest'. The little girls and their 'ill-mannered' bodies immured, well-preserved, intact unto themselves, in the mirror. Frigidified. But are they ever seething underneath! What an effort it takes – there's no end to it – for the sex cops to bar their threatening return. Such a display of forces on both sides that the struggle has for centuries been immobilized in the trembling equilibrium of a deadlock."[20] Hysteria is thus not only a sign of repression but, if used subversively (and with laughter), can be a place of liberation and resistance.

Feliza Bursztyn, with no direct allusions or even feminist declarations (which she avoided or treated evasively), seems to practise an artistic version of *écriture féminine*.[21] Her impulsive, polyphonic, and iconoclastic art is not only the source of extremely daring and innovative artworks, but also seems to be a deliberate project of reclaiming language. It seems as if work after work – one *Histérica* after another, followed by the also provocative *Las camas* (The Beds), or the painfully perverse *La baila mecánica* (The Mechanical Ballet) (fig. 9) – all pointed out that it is not detachment or exclusion from language that is madness, but the awareness that language does *not* exhaust reality; that there are regions beyond it (as yet) unnamed, which does not mean they are non-existent. Madness is the conviction that there is *always* a beyond. Madness is the recognition of the limitations, shortcuts, reductionism, and painful exclusions of language: it is the conviction that language is imperfect and that it must be constantly re-invented, questioned, renewed. Madness is the lack of illusions that something is given once and for all. It is the certainty of the instability and fragility of language, of divisions, hierarchies, and canons. It is the courage to push the boundary between the utterable and the ineffable. Madness, Bursztyn appears to suggest, is also the courage to speak from the margins and speak from it in the first person (not necessarily with laughter, to start with; at first it may be a trembling, stuttering little voice that keeps losing its thread). Madness, by the same token, is a synonym for a wide-ranging project of profanation.[22]

Bursztyn's assessment and strategy are clear, their consequences are supposed to be radical and immediate: "Because she arrives – vibrant, over and again", Feliza Bursztyn seems to echo Cixous in a long but powerful monologue, "we are at the beginning of a new history, or rather of a process of becoming in which several histories intersect with one another. As subject for history, woman always occurs simultaneously in several places. Woman un-thinks the unifying, regulating history that homogenizes and channels forces, herding contradictions into a single battlefield. In woman, personal history blends together with the history of all women, as well as national and world history. As a militant, she is an integral part of all liberations. She must be farsighted, not limited to a blow-by-blow interaction. She foresees that her liberation will do more than modify power relations or toss the ball over to the other camp; she will bring about a mutation in human relations, in thought, in all praxis: hers is not simply a class struggle, which she carries forward into a much vaster movement. Not that in order to be a woman-in-struggle(s) you have to leave the class struggle or repudiate it; but you have to split it open, spread it out, push it forward, fill it with the fundamental struggle so as to prevent the class struggle, or any other struggle for the liberation of a class or people, from operating as a form of repression, pretext for postponing the inevitable, the staggering alteration in power relations and in the production of individualities … The new history is coming; it's not a dream."[23]

Madness understood in this way must not be hospitalized, must not be repaired, must not be silenced, must not be combated. Nor does it need to be feared.[24] Such madness must be constantly reinvented, constantly rewelded. And this is exactly what Feliza Bursztyn does: she keeps on welding madness.

Translation from Polish: Anda MacBride

1 Hélène Cixous, "The Laugh of the Medusa", trans. Keith Cohen and Paula Cohen, *Signs* 1, no. 4 (Summer 1976): 876.

2 Walter Engel, "Feliza Brustyn [*sic*] y Gloria Daza: Divagaciones sobre crítica, mentira y honradez en el arte", *El Espectador* (Bogotá), 2 September 1961.

3 See Giorgio Agamben, *Profanations*, trans. Jeff Fort (New York: Zone Books, 2015).

4 "Ceci est un scandale!" Monique Wittig to Hélène Cixous, cited in Ann Rosalind Jones, "Writing the Body: Toward an Understanding of l'*Écriture féminine*", *Feminist Studies* 7, no. 2 (Summer 1981): 247. Wittig's resistance marks the key moment of split (between essentialism and constructivism) within the second wave of feminism in the 1970s.

5 According to Ovid's account, Medusa impressed Poseidon with her beauty so much that he raped her on the marble floor of Athena's temple. Athena, however, did not tolerate such a desecration of her domain and, as a result, decided to transform Medusa into a terrible monster. Fitting punishment for getting raped, isn't it? (see Ovid, *Metamorphoses*, Book IV).

6 Sigmund Freud, "New Introductory Lectures on Psycho-Analysis. Lecture 33: Femininity" (1933), in *The Standard Edition of the Complete Psychological Works of Sigmund Freud*, vol. 22 (London: The Hogarth Press, 2001), 136–57.

7 Cixous, "The Laugh of the Medusa", 878.

8 Cixous, 876.

9 We remember how Perseus killed Medusa. He strategically placed his shining shield so that Medusa would see herself reflected in it. That way he could avoid looking her straight in the face, since the gaze of Medusa turned all who looked at her to stone. As soon as she came into view, he cut off her head. Interestingly, Perseus used Medusa's head to defeat his enemies – for the severed head did not lose its power. Every time he faced monsters he confronted them with Medusa's head to turn whoever saw it into stone.

10 The artist met him through Ossip Zadkine in 1959.

11 *Groupe Panique* was a collective formed by Fernando Arrabal, Alejandro Jodorowsky, and Roland Topor in Paris in 1962. The original idea, which came from Roland Topor, was to produce "art of monstrosities and panic fears". Inspired by and named after the god Pan, and influenced by Luis Buñuel and Antonin Artaud's *Theatre of Cruelty*, the group concentrated on chaotic and surreal performance art. As early as 1965 Bursztyn worked on scenography for *El Cementerio de Automóviles* written by Fernando Arrabal, directed by Kepa Amuchastegui, at Theatro La Candelaria. The set consisted of an elongated structure that resembled a car scrapyard. The actors could move through the space and move pieces of the set to create sound.

12 Cixous, "The Laugh of the Medusa", 875.

13 "[The] woman *cannot*, is unable, hasn't the power. Not to mention "speaking": it's exactly this that she's forever deprived of. Unable to speak of pleasure = no pleasure, no desire: power, desire, speaking, pleasure, none of these is for woman." Hélène Cixous, "Castration or Decapitation?", trans. Annette Kuhn, *Signs* 7, no. 1 (Autumn 1981): 45. Emphasis in original.

14 Maritza Uribe de Urdinola, "En un país de machistas ¡hágase la loca!", *El Tiempo: Revista Carrusel* (Bogotá), 30 November 1979: 15.

15 "If the imagination is to transcend and transform experience it has to question, challenge, to conceive of alternatives… You have to be free to play around with the notion that day might be night, love might be hate; nothing can be too sacred for the imagination to turn into its opposite or to call experimentally by another name. For writing is re-naming." Adrienne Rich, "When We Dead Awaken: Writing as Re-Vision", *College English* 34, no. 1 (October 1972): 23.

16 See Lucas Ospina's text in this book page 182: "I: What's your favourite pastime? FB: Sex! Ah, I've got another: cooking". See also Cixous, "The Laugh of the Medusa", 880: "A woman without a body … can't possibly be a good fighter. She is reduced to being the servant of the militant male, his shadow".

17 Cixous, "Castration or Decapitation?", 49.

18 Cixous speaks with a spirited and rousing voice: "The Dark Continent is neither dark nor unexplorable. It is still unexplored only because we've been made to believe that it was too dark to be explorable. And because they want to make us believe that what interests us is the white continent … And we believed. They riveted us between two horrifying myths: between the Medusa and the abyss. That would be enough to set half the world laughing, except that it's still going on". Cixous, "The Laugh of the Medusa", 885.

19 Cixous provocatively speaks of "stupid sexual modesty". Cixous, 887.

20 Cixous, 887.

21 See Lucas Ospina's text in this book, in particular pages 171–72.

22 Interestingly, the Italian edition of Giorgio Agamben's *Profanations* carries a wrapper that reads "Istruzioni per la felicità", or "Instructions on how to be happy".

23 Cixous, "The Laugh of the Medusa", 882–83.

24 "You only have to look at the Medusa straight on to see her. And she's not deadly. She's beautiful and she's laughing." Cixous, 885.

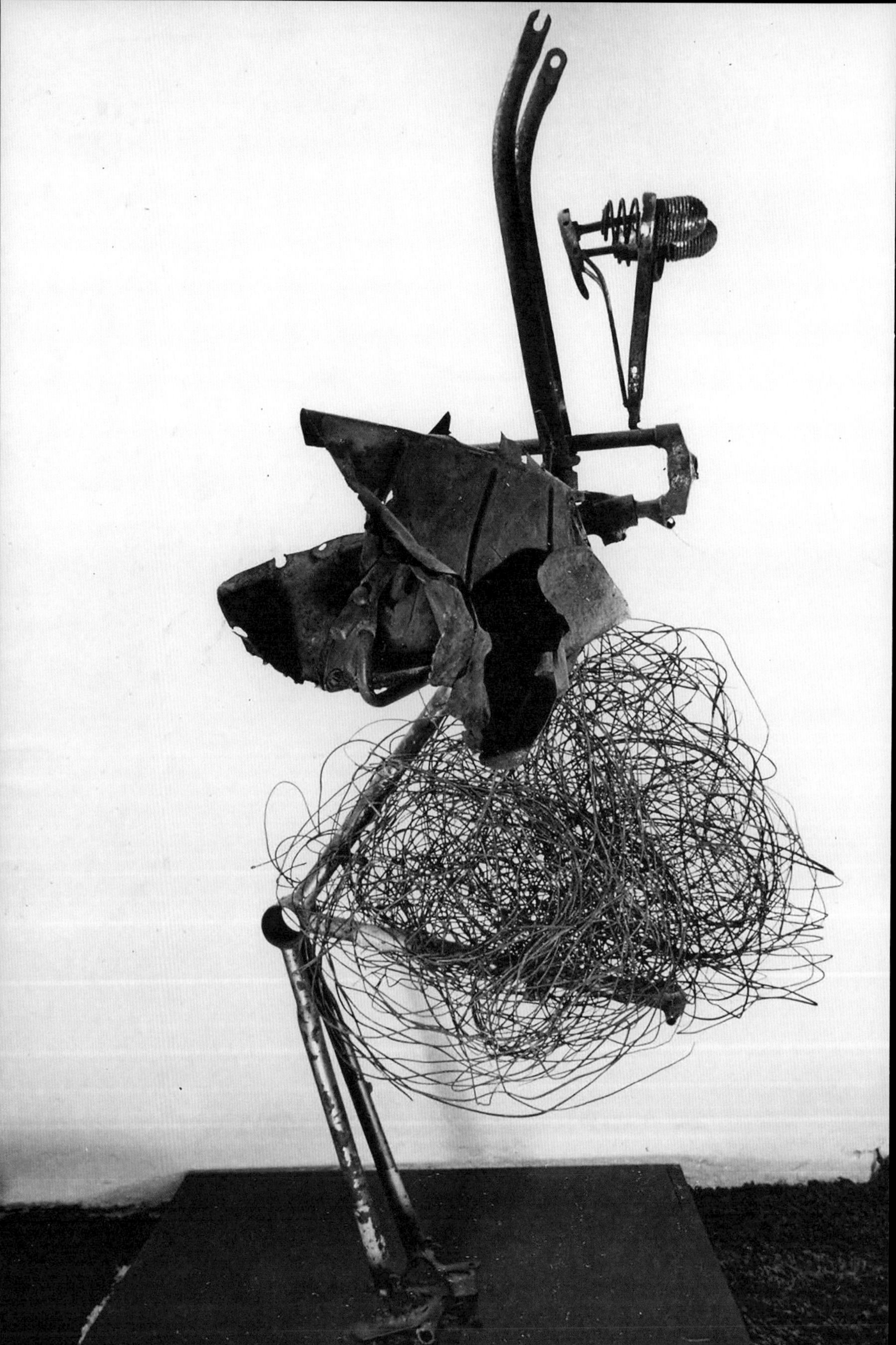

Suffering into Truth

Abigail Winograd[1]

Helmer: It's shocking. This is how you would neglect your
most sacred duties.
Nora: What do you consider my most sacred duties?
Helmer: Do I need to tell you that? Are they not your duties
to your husband and your children?
Nora: I have other duties just as sacred.
Helmer: That you have not. What duties could those be?
Nora: Duties to myself.

Henrik Ibsen, *A Doll's House*, 1879[2]

Feliza Bursztyn died for the first time in 1957. She was a twenty-four-year-old mother of three in an abusive marriage and she had decided to divorce her husband. She wanted to be an artist and she planned to leave Bogotá for Paris with her lover, the poet Jorge Gaitán Durán.[3] She wanted to end her conventional life.[4] Divorce was illegal in Colombia so the official decree was granted by a civil authority in New York. This, Bursztyn said, made her the first Jewish woman in Colombia to be granted a divorce. For Bursztyn's parents, leaders in Bogotá's minuscule Jewish community, this was a scandal they were not prepared to face so they severed their relationship with her by declaring her dead.[5]

Bursztyn's description of the split from her parents included a staged funeral complete with coffin and headstone. However, it is unlikely to have taken place precisely how she described it. Divorce was not uncommon among Latin American Jews, and rabbis across the Americas granted religious divorce decrees even when they were civically illegal. It

1. Feliza Bursztyn,
Chatarra (Junk
Sculpture), c. 1964
Courtesy of the Archive of
Pablo Leyva

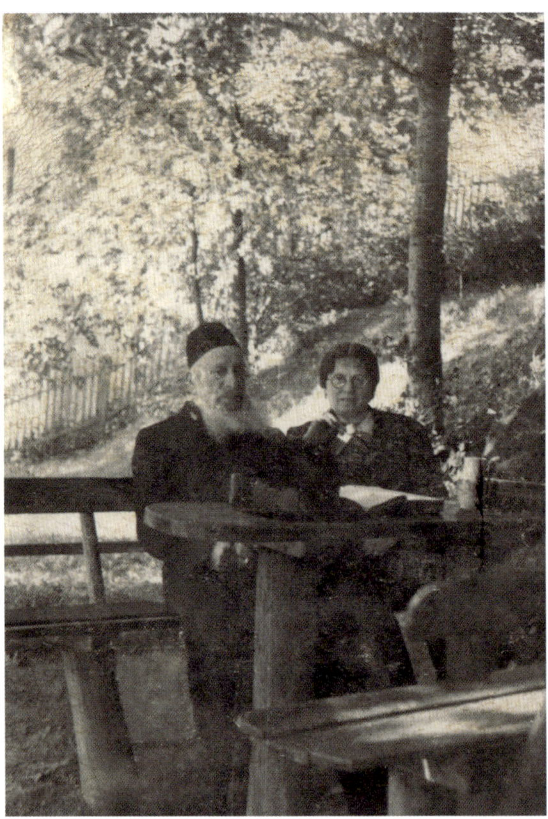

2. Bursztyn's grandparents, Yitzhak and Lente Bursztyn, Poland, 1937
Courtesy of the Archive of Pablo Leyva

was also not unusual for those who pursued relationships outside the faith to be ostracized from the community. In these instances, families would mourn the apostate child as if they were dead.[6] Bursztyn's father, Yaakov, was the son of the rabbi of Ostrołęka, a small town on the outskirts of Warsaw, and had himself trained to follow in his father's footsteps (fig. 2).[7] Remarkably, Feliza's mother, Chaja, had also studied in a religious school, an unusual practice for women at that time. Bursztyn's father was a religious and learned man who, upon his arrival in Bogotá, served as a de facto rabbi for the community. Given his position, she must have been fully aware of the consequences of her actions.

It is unclear whether it was the divorce or Bursztyn's relationship with a non-Jewish, married man that precipitated the rift between Bursztyn and her parents. Either way, there is no prescribed Jewish ritual for disowning a child. Jewish tradition does, however, provide a structure and a time-frame for mourning the dead. The bereaved are commanded to sit shivah for seven days. Following a funeral, the family of the deceased remain at home. During that time, they dress in black and refrain from work. They receive family, friends, and members of the community who bring food, offer prayers, and console the bereaved. On each day, services are held within the home and the Mourner's Kaddish, the Jewish prayer for the dead, is recited.[8] The Kaddish is a doxology, a hymn of praise, that does not mention death but rather proclaims the greatness of God in the face of unfathomable loss. Whatever the circumstances, it is difficult to imagine the depths of devastation this event must have occasioned in the artist's life and the incredible mettle Bursztyn exhibited in choosing to follow her passion regardless.

Over the years, Bursztyn's relationship with her parents would mend. Upon her return from Paris in 1960, Yaakov gave her an empty garage next to one of his factories. She would turn it into her home-cum-studio with the help of architects Rogelio Salmona and Carlos Valencia.[9] The duo transformed the garage into a long, narrow living quarters that occupied multiple floors connected by steep ladders, created a capacious kitchen, as well as the workspace in which she first began to tinker with scrap metal and produced her first *Chatarras* (Junk Sculptures) – composed of junk and industrial detritus (fig. 1). She bolted and welded discarded scrap metal, corroded tires, and rusted cables together into rough, abstract compositions. The artist gave each assemblage a feminine, organic name such as *Una Flor* (Flower) or *Niña alegre* (Happy Girl), mocking traditional gender roles and the perceived masculinity of art itself. She would occupy the home until the night she fled Bogotá for Mexico City seeking asylum. It remains more or less as she left it. After her father's death in 1962, she would continue to visit her mother, who moved to the United States to live with Bursztyn's sister Hela in San Francisco.[10] Bursztyn would likewise remain proudly Jewish and a fierce supporter of the state of Israel, frequently visiting her family there, and mounting an exhibition of the *Chatarras* in Jerusalem in 1961.[11]

In all things, Bursztyn was an unreliable narrator. She loved the theatre and her flair for the dramatic was evident in the evasive and exaggerated answers she provided in interviews. Throughout her life she gave conflicting accounts of events, reported fluctuating numbers of husbands, and gave cryptic responses to basic questions. She intentionally cultivated a public persona that eluded easy categorization and flew in the face of existing norms. Therefore, her somewhat hyperbolic description of the events surrounding her first funeral were in keeping with the brash, confrontational, and unapologetically feminist version of herself she presented in the press. Bursztyn's divorce was her first public act of rebellion, and it carried enormous consequences. With the dissolution of her marriage she lost not just her family, but her children

as well. We will never know the specifics, as there is no person left alive
to consult and, in the end, the "truth" does not matter. What matters is
that this first death was the foundational myth of the life of the artist
Feliza Bursztyn – a birthing of sorts.

—

> During my first night in Bogotá, I made my great decision:
> Colombia would be my eternal home, this great country would
> be the land of my children and my grandchildren. For this great
> country with my family, I keep the deepest and sincere feelings
> of gratitude. And to the beautiful Colombian land we have given
> our efforts and hopes with love and faith, and she and her people
> have reciprocated with generosity and nobility.
>
> Simón Guberek, *Yo vi crecer un país*, 1974[12]

Bursztyn was born to Polish Jewish immigrants in Bogotá on 9 September
1933. Her parents, Yaakov and Chaja Bursztyn, were new arrivals to
Colombia, having disembarked from a transatlantic voyage earlier that
year. They were ardent Zionists and spent time in Palestine in the early
1930s. Prior to their Atlantic crossing, a friend of the couple fled Palestine
for Colombia after running into trouble with the British authorities and
sent word to Warsaw. The Bursztyns decided to visit. The couple initially
intended to return to Poland, but after learning about Hitler's election to
the chancellorship in Germany and seeing the storm clouds of coming
war amass over Europe, they decided to stay put.

It is in keeping with the idiosyncrasies of the artist's life that the Bursztyns
should arrive in Bogotá in these unique circumstances. Jewish immigration to Colombia in 1933 was nearly non-existent. It was so insignificant
that in 1933 Colombia was not included in the annual census published by
the American Jewish Yearbook – an accounting that registered the three
hundred Jews living in Peru at the time.[13] Unlike many of its South American counterparts (Argentina, Brazil, Chile, Cuba), Colombia did not court
Jewish immigration at the end of the nineteenth and beginning of the twentieth century.[14] The Jewish communities that did exist in Colombia were
older and mostly comprised of Sephardic merchants situated in the commercial capitals of Cali or Barranquilla. They were remnants of the Jewish immigration to Central and South America that began with the conquest of the
New World. Like their counterparts in Brazil, the Caribbean, and elsewhere,
these historical Jewish communities were established around the time of the
arrival of the Dutch, Spanish, and Portuguese in the Americas.[15]

The Bursztyns were joined by a small number of co-religionists when a trickle began to arrive after 1936.[16] The Jewish community in Colombia was never large. It reached its peak in the 1960s when some 14,000 Jews called the country home. It remained small because Colombia enacted restrictive immigration laws in the 1920s that became more stringent in the late 1930s. In 1939, Jewish immigration was completely outlawed, and Colombian citizenship denied to all Jewish residents who were stateless, a burden disproportionately borne by those stripped of their German nationality by the Nuremberg Laws. The law was passed in response to rising middle-class resentment over growing competition with Jewish businessmen. These tensions resulted in open expressions of antisemitism and gave Colombia the unenviable distinction of having the second-largest number of registered members of the Nazi Party in South America.[17] The vast majority of the Yiddish-speaking Ashkenazi community (as Polish Jews, the Bursztyns would have been associated with this group rather than their German-speaking or Sephardic co-religionists) would not arrive until later in the 1930s and 1940s. As was the case for Jewish emigrants across Europe, these later arrivals increasingly found their way to Central and South America as their traditional destinations further north started to shut their doors to those fleeing the terror unfolding across the old continent.

Bursztyn was an outsider many times over: born Jewish in a Catholic country, the child of immigrants from Eastern Europe, and a feminist in a country dominated by the conservatism of the church. Even if she had wanted to hide who she was, her name made that impossible. Despite her fame, the press never seemed to be able to spell it correctly. She was sometimes called Felisa, the consonants at the centre of her name frequently jumbled or swapped. She seemed to bristle at the suggestion that she was an outsider nonetheless, frequently stating: "I am Colombian. I was born in the Marly Clinic".[18] It was from this position that she would tell the story of her life, knowing full-well that she would always be misunderstood.

—

> Awful things happen in every apartment house.
> Rosemary Woodhouse, *Rosemary's Baby*, 1968

In 1973, Bursztyn produced *El bebé de Rosemary* (Rosemary's Baby). The work, its title borrowed from Roman Polanski's eponymous film (1968), consisted of a crib painted black, covered in a black satin sheet and outfitted with a motor. It was an outlier in her series of *Las camas*

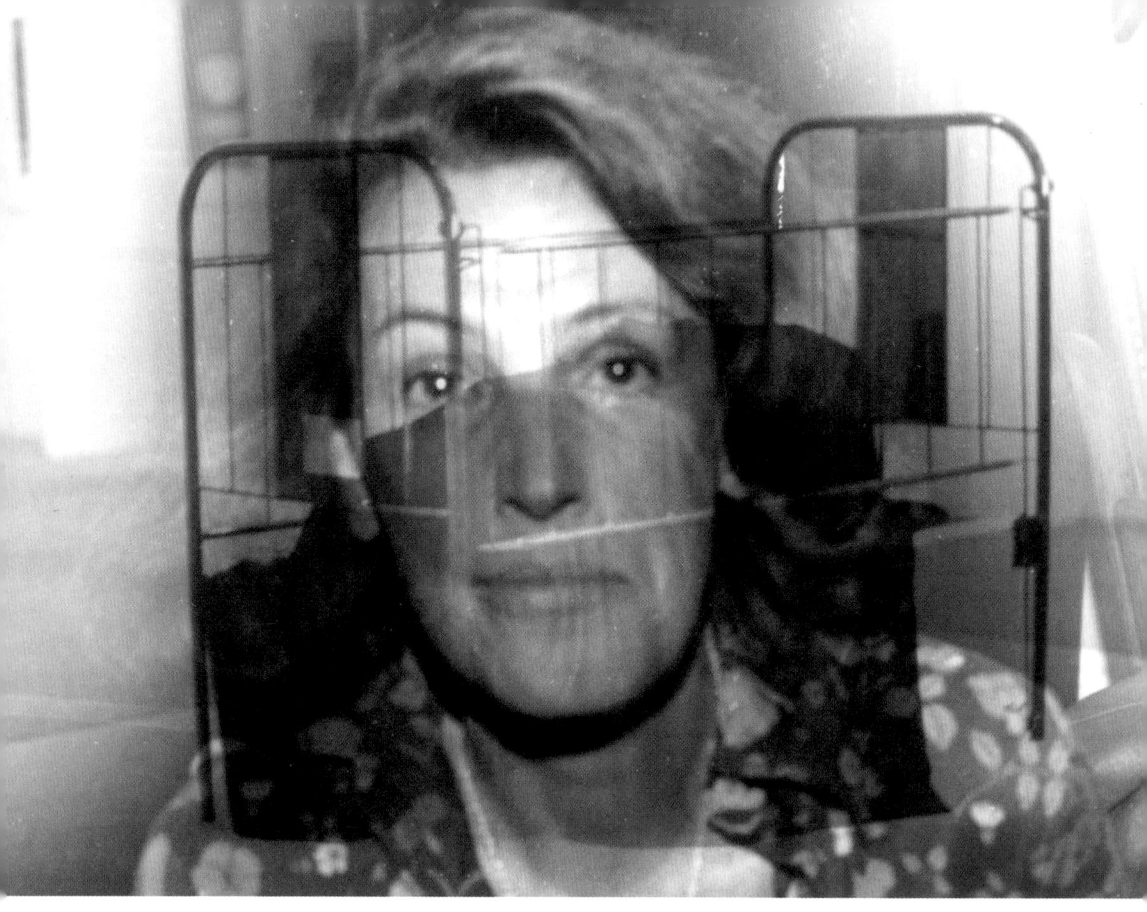

(The Beds), the only one to utilize a crib. Like the rest of the works in the series, *El bebé de Rosemary* periodically and unexpectedly vibrated producing an uncanny sense of presence in the empty gallery. The plot of *Rosemary's Baby*, based on Ira Levin's novel of the same name, centred on the pregnancy of Rosemary Woodhouse and her growing suspicion that her elderly neighbours are members of a Satanic cult. The tension of the film is located in the uncertainty of whether Rosemary is indeed at the mercy of demonic forces or is "just" having a nervous breakdown. Over the course of the movie, the Woodhouses' seemingly happy marriage devolves into a living nightmare. The film focuses on the home, which reveals itself to be a house of horrors. The disturbing nature of Bursztyn's work, no doubt part of the artist's intention, was reinforced by an extant double-exposure photograph of the work with a ghostly self-portrait floating above it (fig. 3). *El bebé de Rosemary* seems to be a bitter reflection on the circumscribed roles for women in a Catholic country, but also a critique of the normalized brutality so deeply rooted in an aggressively patriarchal culture. Given Bursztyn's predilection for Freudian analysis, it is impossible to look at these works without thinking of Bursztyn's life: like Rosemary's, her journey of domestic discord began in New York.

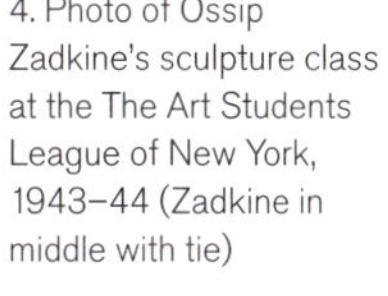

3. Double exposure
of Feliza Bursztyn and
El bebé de Rosemary
(Rosemary's Baby),
c. 1972
Courtesy of the Archive
of Pablo Leyva. Photo:
Pablo Leyva

At eighteen, Bursztyn moved to New York, a city that would play a prominent role in her short life. At the time, Bursztyn's father had already established himself in the textile industry, joining the ranks of successful Jewish industrialists in Bogotá.[19] The financial success achieved by the family afforded Bursztyn the ability to travel and gave her access to educational opportunities. Political tensions in Colombia erupted after the assassination of the liberal presidential candidate Jorge Eliécer Gaitán in 1947, and her parents thought it best to send her away. She moved to New York to finish high school.

Bursztyn stayed with an uncle who worked as an engineer for IBM building computer prototypes. She spent hours in his workshop watching him weld. (One wonders how this formative experience may have influenced the series *Minimáquinas* (Minimachines) produced in the 1970s.) Following her graduation, Bursztyn officially began her artistic training studying for two years at the Art Students League from 1948–50. Perhaps it was in New York that Bursztyn first learned about the Russian-born sculptor Ossip Zadkine, who had taught at the Arts Students League from 1943 to 1945 (fig. 4). While there, she would have overlapped with Monir Farmanfarmaian, Marisol, and Donald Judd, among others.

It was in New York that Bursztyn met her first husband, Larry Lawrence Fleisher. Fleisher was a mechanical engineer and former US Air Force pilot who had served in World War II. They married in 1952 when she

4. Photo of Ossip
Zadkine's sculpture class
at the The Art Students
League of New York,
1943–44 (Zadkine in
middle with tie)

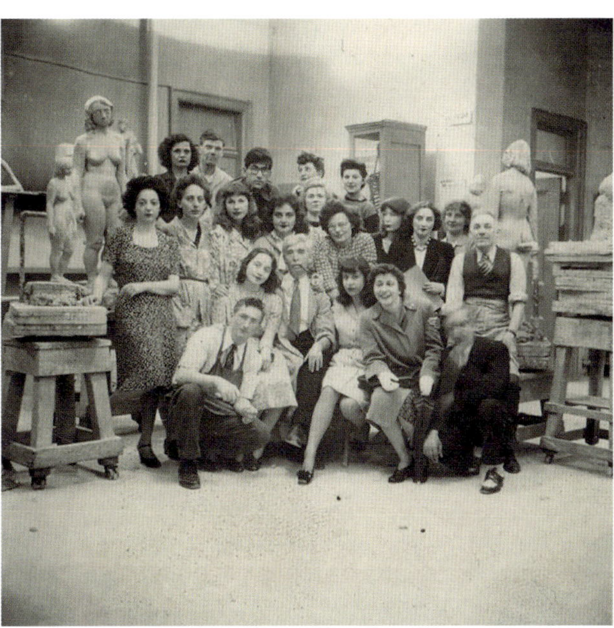

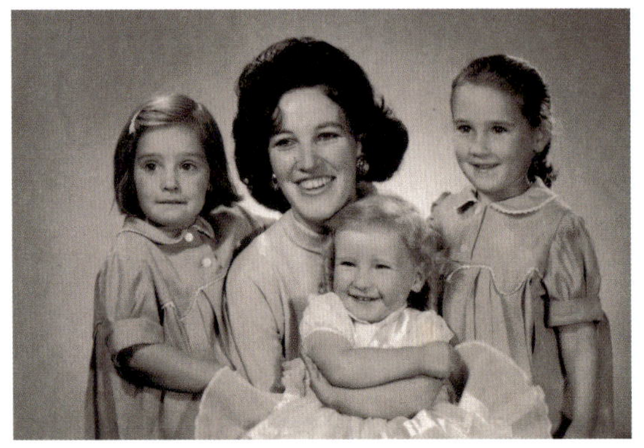

was barely into adulthood. The couple had three daughters in rapid succession: Jeannine (1954) and Bethina (1955) were born in New York, and Michelle (1956) after the couple moved back to Bogotá (fig. 5). Theirs was an unhappy marriage and Bursztyn suffered abuse at Fleisher's hands throughout their relationship. He violently objected to her desire to be an artist and in their final argument attacked her hands to prevent her from becoming a sculptor. Following the fight that ended their marriage, Fleisher took the girls and left Bogotá. The four moved to Texas, and Bursztyn only ever got to see her children when she could scrape together the funds to purchase a ticket. At her first exhibition in Bogotá at the Galería de Callejón in 1958, Bursztyn showed a series of watercolours painted on cardboard, one of which depicted a faceless woman, head bowed, holding the hand of a child (fig. 6).

—

> There is a time when terror helps
> the watchman must stand guard upon the heart.
> It helps, at times, to suffer into truth.
> > The Furies in Aeschylus' *Eumenides*, 458 BCE[20]

In Greek mythology, Clytemnestra was the wife of Agamemnon, King of Mycenea and Argos. Agamemnon commanded the Greek army during the siege of Troy launched to avenge the seduction of Helen by Paris. Before laying siege to the city, Agamemnon sacrifices Iphigenia, his daughter with Clytemnestra, to appease the goddess Artemis who has made bad weather appear to prevent the army's ships from sailing. In Agamemnon's absence and because she believes him dead, Clytemnestra takes a lover. When he returns, very much alive, Agamemnon brings his own lover Cassandra home to meet his long-suffering wife and report the murder of her child. In an act of rage, vengeance, and an alleged bid for

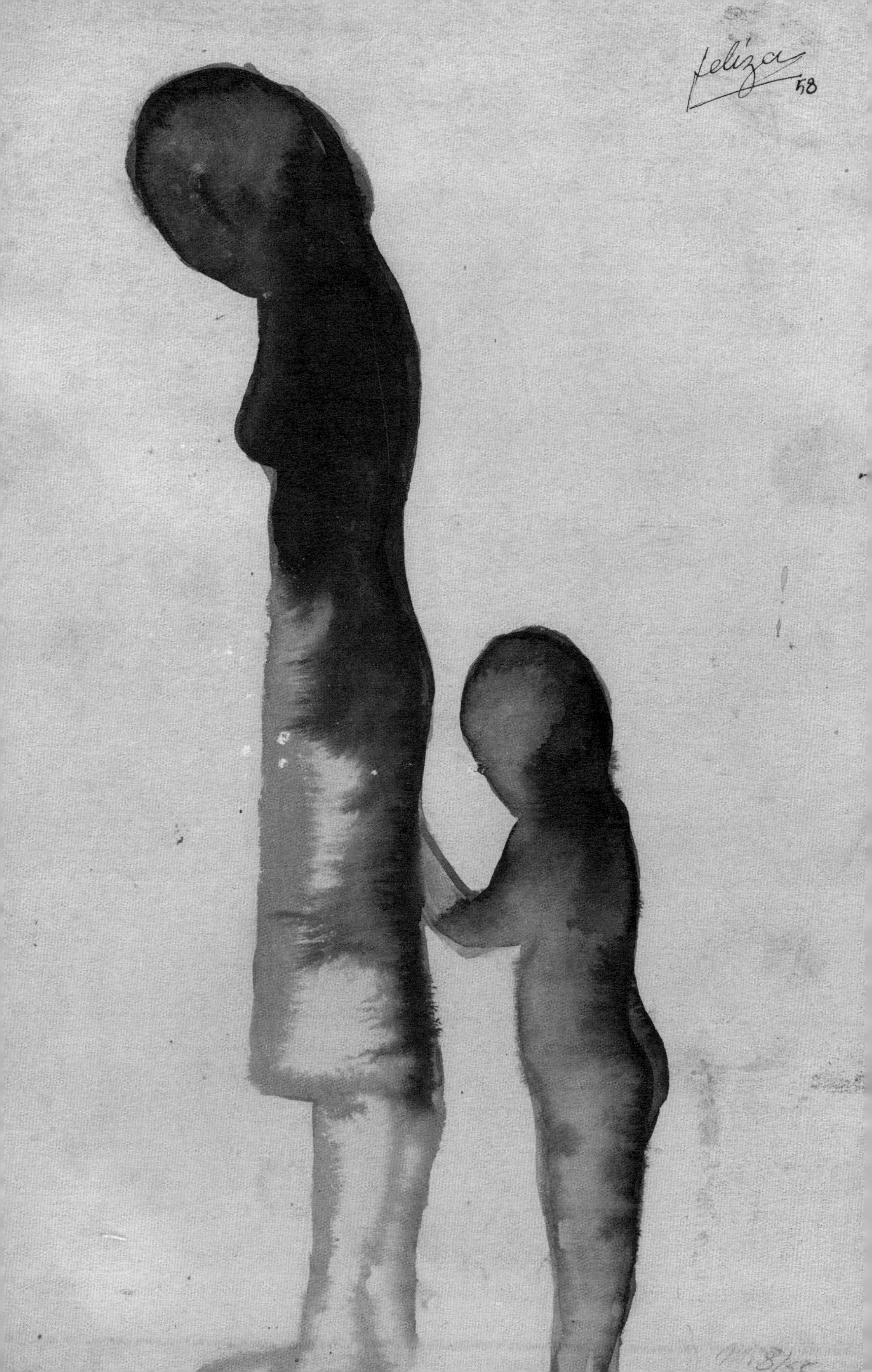

power, she murders Agamemnon by hacking him to death in a bathtub with an axe. She is, in turn, murdered by Orestes, her son, to avenge the death of his father. This story of the house of Atreus is recounted in Aeschylus' *Oresteia*, the only surviving ancient Greek tragic trilogy, written in 458 BCE. Aeschylus positions Clytemnestra as a crazed and unfaithful woman whose murder, ultimately, becomes the basis for the establishment of a system of law based in justice rather than vengeance.[21]

In 1980, the Belgian-born French feminist scholar Luce Irigaray offered a reassessment of Clytemnestra in a lecture titled "Body against Body: In Relation to the Mother", given at a conference in Montreal. Irigaray revisited Clytemnestra's legacy arguing that Orestes' murder of his mother and the mythic structure underlaying the tragedy represents the historical victory of patriarchy over matriarchy. The fear of women run amok, Irigaray argues, and the need to contain that energy is rampant in Aeschylus' cycle. For Irigaray, the killing of a mother (Clytemnestra) is the condition and the symptom of the patriarchy's operation: the matricidal paradigm, as established by Aeschylus, is the deepest source of women's banishment from Western culture.[22] She argued,

> Our urgent task is to refuse to submit to a desubjectivized social role, the role of mother, which is dictated by an order subject to the division of labour – he produces, she reproduces – that walls us up in the ghetto of single function. When did society ever ask fathers to choose between being men or citizens? We don't have to give up being women to be mothers.[23]

It is fitting that in 1963, Bursztyn participated in her first national competition, the XV Salón de Artistas Colombianos at the Museo Nacional de Colombia in Bogotá with a work titled *Clitemnestra*, from the series *Chatarras* (fig. 7). Bursztyn would subsequently go on to achieve mythic cultural status in her home country, a figure shrouded in myth herself. Bursztyn sacrificed everything to be an artist. For her efforts, the local press dubbed her "La Loca" (the Madwoman), a mantle she proudly accepted.[24]

By any measure, Bursztyn's life resembled a Greek tragedy. The end of her first marriage and subsequent separation from her children was preceded by the murder of many members of her maternal and paternal family by the Nazis. Her relationship with Gaitán Durán ended in 1962 when he died in a plane crash. Her friend and confidant, the artist Beatriz Daza, lost her life in a car crash in 1969. Bursztyn was in the vehicle with Daza and suffered serious injuries from which she would never

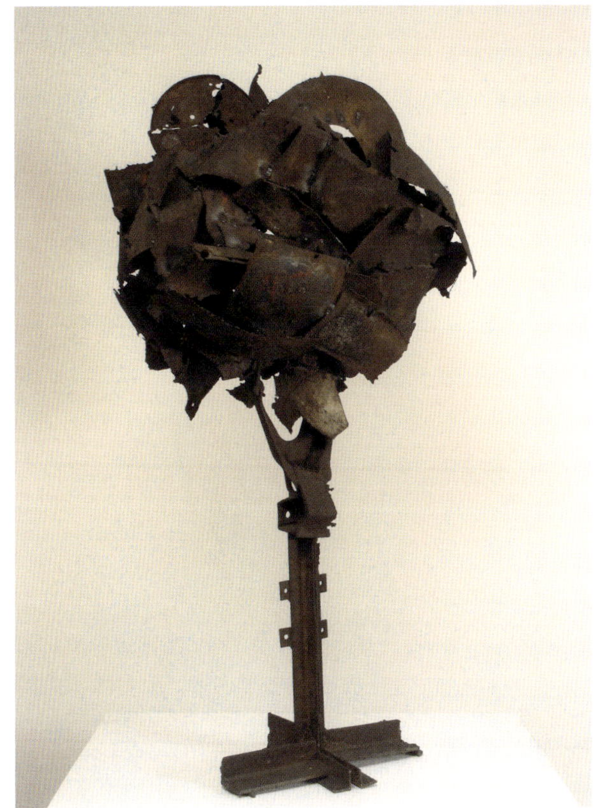

fully recover. Her collaborator, the experimental composer Jacqueline Nova, died of bone cancer at the age of forty in 1975. During her lifetime, Colombia was gripped by violent conflict that spread from the country-side to the cities and back. The conflagration brought political upheaval, repression, and limitations on various freedoms. Bursztyn would witness the harassment, arrest, and exile of her friends and confidants, among them Gabriel García Márquez.

It was García Márquez who interceded on her behalf when she was arrested at her home in 1981 after returning from mounting an exhibition of her *Color* (Colour Series) in Havana. In the early morning hours of 24 July 1981, Feliza was taken from her home by the Colombian military police and detained for two days. No specific reason was given for her arrest but Feliza was a person of interest for years. Her support of left wing causes and the Cuban Revolution, specifically, placed her under suspicion. In 1978, newly elected President Julio César Turbay Ayala (1978–1982) introduced the Security Statute. The law was, putatively, passed in response to an increase of guerrilla activity on the part of the 19th of April Movement (M-19) and the Revolutionary Armed Forces of

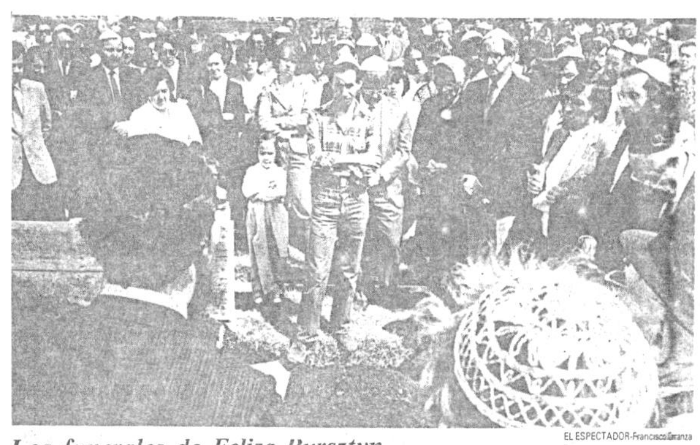

8. Feliza Bursztyn's funeral, *El Espectador* (Bogotá), 21 January 1982
Courtesy of the Archive of Pablo Leyva

Colombia (FARC). The Security Statute gave the military the sweeping power to question, detain, and charge individuals and ushered in the most repressive atmosphere since the dictatorship of Gustavo Rojas Pinilla (1953–1957).[25] During her detention, Bursztyn was bound, blindfolded, questioned, and tortured, all the while hearing others suffering a similar fate through the prison walls. This was the last straw. On 5 August, Pablo Leyva, Bursztyn's second husband, drove to the Mexican Embassy while she lay on the floor in the car's backseat. She was granted asylum and on 8 August boarded a plane to Mexico City. She stayed in García Márquez's home, and it was there that she made her final sculptures. Ultimately, Bursztyn and Leyva elected to move to Paris. She hoped to create a life for herself in the city of her first exile. At dinner with García Márquez, his wife Mercedes Barcha, Enrique Santos Calderón, María Teresa Rubino, and Leyva on the evening of 8 January 1982, Bursztyn suffered a heart attack and died in the restaurant 166 days after departing Bogotá. She was forty-nine years old.

Bursztyn's death – like her life – captivated the Colombian press (fig. 8). García Márquez penned her obituary. She was buried in Bogotá's Jewish cemetery. Her family and friends sat shivah, once again. The woman who so careful cultivated her own mythology passed into legend.

[1] I want to thank Pablo Leyva, Bursztyn's second husband and widower, for trusting me with her story. Bursztyn married him in Copenhagen in 1970. Leyva, an environmentalist and chemical engineer, was Bursztyn's partner until her death in 1982. He would lend his expertise to the artist's work, helping her construct the systems that made her sculptures move. The details of her life as they are relayed here, unless otherwise noted, have been conveyed in conversation with Pablo and his son Camilo Leyva over the past four years. Much of the information here was first published in Camilo Leyva, Manuela Ochoa, and Juan Carlos Osorio, "Cronología", in *Feliza Bursztyn: Elogio de la Chatarra* (Bogotá: Museo Nacional de Colombia, 2009), 73–83.
[2] Henrik Ibsen, *A Doll's House* (London: Stage Door, 2013), 59. First published 1879.
[3] Jorge Gaitán Durán (Pamplona, 1925 – Guadeloupe, 1962) was a writer, critic, journalist, and the founder of *Mito* magazine,

one of the most important literary journals on the continent.

4 Juan Gustavo Cobo Borda, "Entrevista trunca con Feliza Bursztyn", *Cromos* (Bogotá), 8 March 1983.

5 Anxiety about intermarriage and assimilation ran high throughout Latin American Jewish communities and the Colombian capital, Bogotá, was no different. A controversy about interfaith couples erupted in 1981, the same year of Bursztyn's exile, and reports of this debate circulated widely in the local Jewish press. Given the tensions around the topic nearly twenty-five years after Bursztyn's divorce, one can only imagine the scandal she must have caused. These arguments had a distinctly gendered dimensions, and there was particular angst about relationships between Jewish women and non-Jewish men tied to the matrilineal principle of Jewish descent. See John Dizgun, "Rights of Passage: The Struggle over Jewish Intermarriage and Conversion in Colombia", *Shofar* 19, no. 3 (Spring 2001): 41–55.

6 Maritza Uribe de Urdinola, "En un país de machistas, ¡hágase la loca!", *El Tiempo: Revista Carrusel* (Bogotá), 30 November 1979: 15.

7 Yitzhak Bursztyn was murdered by the Nazis in 1943. He is listed along with eight other Bursztyns from Ostrołęka who met the same fate in the Central Database of Shoah Victims' Names maintained by Yad Vashem, the World Holocaust Remembrance Centre in Jerusalem. Members of Bursztyn's maternal family were also lost.

8 I have had several conversations with rabbis, among them Rabbi Marc Berkson and Rabbi Victor Mirelman, trying to pin down the details of this event in Bursztyn's life. Neither rabbi knows of an instance in which a mock funeral was held to commemorate the "death" of a child. In the course of his research on Latin American Jewry, Rabbi Mirelman reports that it was not uncommon for children to be ostracized by a family after entering into a relationship, typically marriage, with a non-Jewish partner.

9 Rogelio Salmona (Paris, 1929 – Bogotá, 2007) was perhaps the most significant Colombian architect of the twentieth century and a close friend of the artist. Salmona, like Bursztyn, was the child of Jewish immigrants, a Spanish father and French mother, who moved to Bogotá in 1934. Salmona was a protégé of Le Corbusier for whom Salmona served as translator when the French architect came to Bogotá in 1947. Following an outbreak of violence and repression in Colombia, Salmona went to Paris in 1948 to work in Le Corbusier's studio.

10 Hela Bursztyn was born in 1929 in Warsaw. She became a celebrated biochemist and professor at Stanford University. Bursztyn's remained close with her sister throughout her life. It was Pablo Leyva who walked Hela down the aisle when she in turn married outside the faith.

11 Camilo Leyva, Manuela Ochoa, and Juan Carlos Osorio, "Cronología", in *Feliza Bursztyn: Elogio de la Chatarra* (Bogotá: Museo Nacional de Colombia, 2009), 73–83.

12 "Durante mi primera noche en Bogotá tomé mi gran decisión – Colombia sería mi hogar eterno… este gran país sería la tierra de mis hijos y mis nietos. Para esta gran patria con los míos, guardo los más hondos y sinceros sentimientos de gratitud. Y a la bella tierra colombiana hemos entregado con cariño y con fe nuestros esfuerzos y esperanzas, y ella y sus gentes nos han correspondido con generosidad y nobleza." Simón Guberek, *Yo vi crecer un país* (Bogotá: Fundación Simón y Lola Guberek, 1987). First published 1974. My translation. Simón Guberek was a Polish Jewish émigré to Colombia. He arrived in Bogotá in 1928. Guberek was a writer, journalist, and active member of the Jewish community. In 1974, he published his reflections on Jewish immigrant experience in a two-volume memoir.

13 "The Statistics of Jews", in *The American Jewish Year Book*, vol. 35 (September 21, 1933 to September 9, 1934 / 5694), 235–71.

14 Dizgun, "Rights of Passage", 41–55.

15 Judith Laikin Elkin, *The Jews of Latin America* (New York: Holmes & Meier, 1998). See also Adelaida Sourdis Nájera and Alfonso Velasco Rojas, eds., *Los judíos en Colombia: una aproximación histórica* (Madrid: Casa Sefarad Israel, 2011).

16 Gerhardt Neuman, "German Jews in Colombia: A Study in Immigrant Adjustment", *Jewish Social Studies* 3, no. 4 (October 1941): 387–98.

17 Claudio Lomnitz, *Nuestra América: My Family in the Vertigo of Translation* (New York: Other Press, 2021), 238.

18 *El Espectador - Diario de la Mañana* (Bogotá), 25 July 1967.

19 Dizgun, "Rights of Passage", 47.

20 Aeschylus, *The Oresteia*, trans. Robert Fagles (New York: Penguin Classics, 1977), 254.

21 Robert Fagles, "A Reading of 'The Oresteia': The Serpent and the Eagle", in Aeschylus, *The Oresteia*, 13–97.

22 Laura Green, "Myths, Matricide and Maternal Subjectivity in Irigaray", *Studies in the Maternal* 4, no. 1 (January 2012): 1–22, https://doi.org/10.16995/sim.48

23 Luce Irigaray, "Body against Body: In Relation to the Mother", in *Sexes and Genealogies*, trans. Gillian C. Gill (New York: Colombia University Press, 1993), 18.

24 It was common for Bursztyn's close friend and collaborator, the theatre director Santiago García, to help the artist name her work. Santiago García (b. Bogotá, 1928) was a pivotal figure in the history of Colombian theatre and the local post-war avant-garde more generally. A student of Bertolt Brecht, García was the founder of Teatro La Candelaria, which remains one of the most important theatre groups in Latin America.

25 Marco Palacios, *Between Legitimacy and Violence: A History of Colombia, 1875–2002*, trans. Richard Stoller (Durham: Duke University Press, 2006), 197–200.

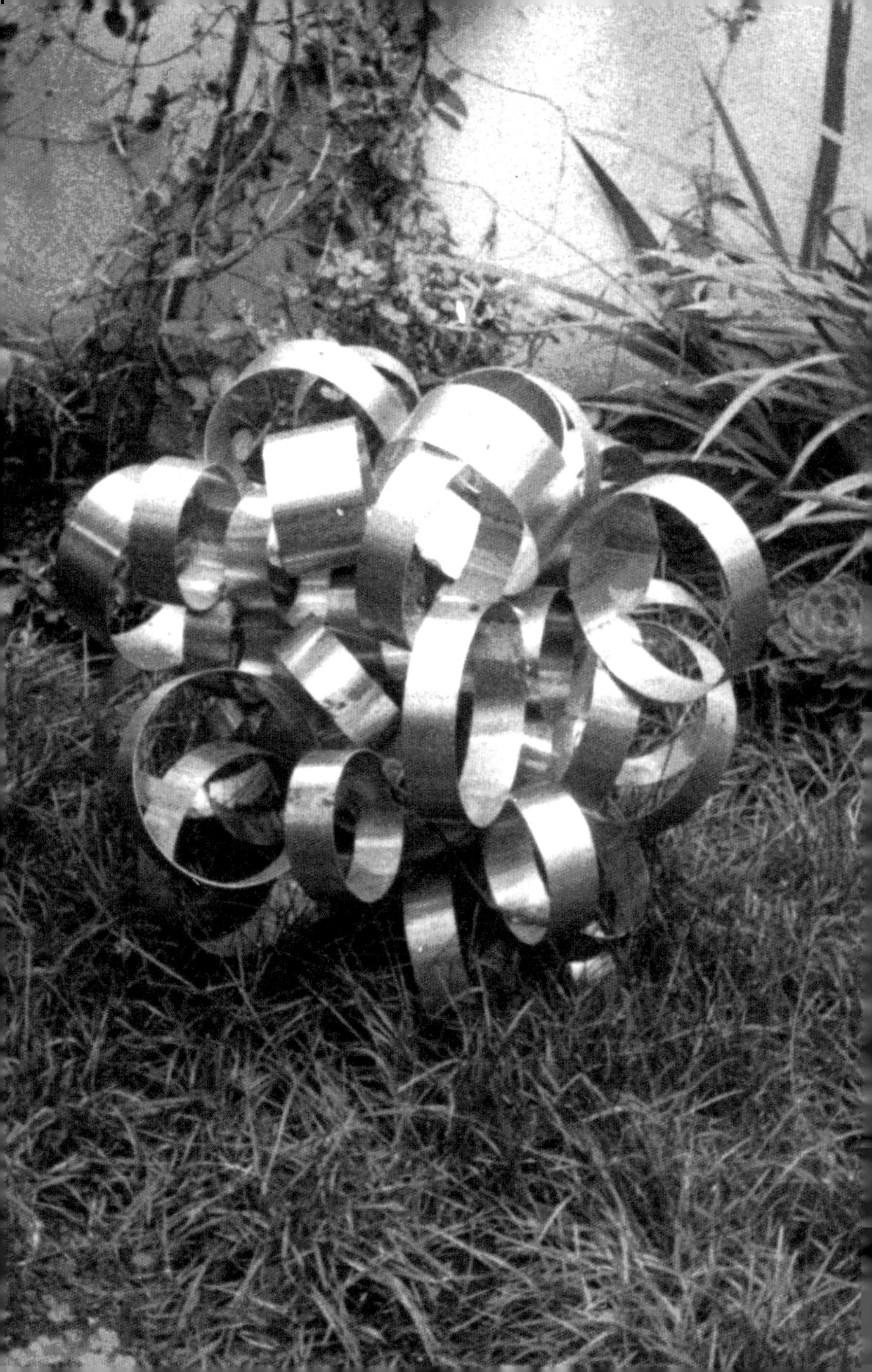

"Under this cloth and on this bed… there is a sculpture by Feliza Bursztyn"

Sylvia Suárez

A Miracle

Feliza's Bursztyn artistic career in Colombia took place, almost in its entirety, during the National Front (1958–74). This means that her work arose in the context of a restricted democracy, with authoritarian practices that grew exponentially from the beginning and reached their apotheosis under the government of Julio César Turbay Ayala, extending into the 1980s. Bursztyn's exile and death occurred precisely under that government and were directly related to the implementation of the Security Statute, by which *habeas corpus* was legally abolished, precipitating one of the greatest human rights crises in the recent history of Colombia. In his "Brief farewell note to Feliza Bursztyn's smell of guava", García Márquez described it as "an open war on intellectuals and artists who have the temerity to think, and whose solidarity with the most just causes troubles the sleep of a president who once claimed to have read a complete library of five thousand volumes" (fig. 3).[1]

1. Feliza Bursztyn, *Acero sobre acero* (Steel on Steel) sculpture in the artist's studio garden, c. 1976 Courtesy of the Archive of Pablo Leyva. Photo: Pablo Leyva

2. "Debajo de esta tela y sobre esta cama… hay una escultura de Feliza Burzstyn" (Under this cloth and on this bed… there is a sculpture by Feliza Burzstyn), *La República*, April 1974

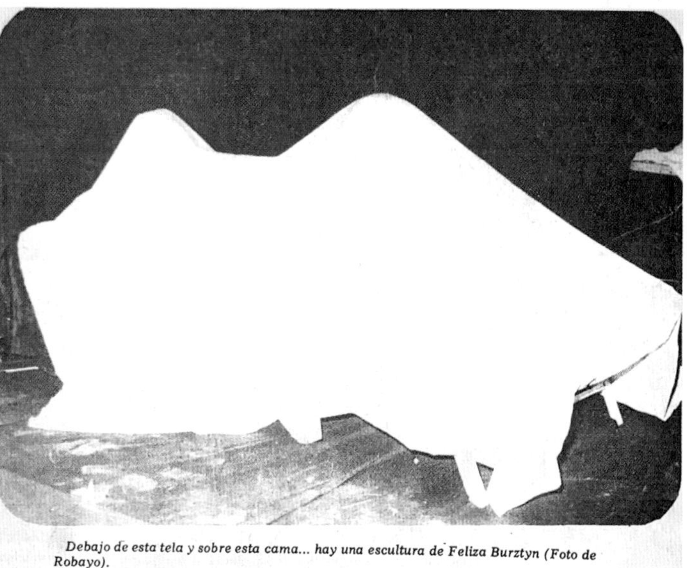

Debajo de esta tela y sobre esta cama… hay una escultura de Feliza Burztyn (Foto de Robayo).

Bursztyn returned to Bogotá from the United States, where she had studied art, got married, had three daughters, and divorced, a decision which, in her own words, caused her father to "wish her dead". At the time of her first exhibitions in Colombia, in 1958 and 1961, her work polarized critical opinion, with the highest and most positive note being struck by the glowing words of the Argentine writer and critic Marta Traba, while others with long experience in Colombia dismissed her work, such as Walter Engel, who in one of the most widely circulated newspapers in the country pronounced that "the only artistic possibility for her lies in simple techniques on two-dimensional surfaces … it would take a miracle for her to make a career as a sculptor".[2]

In cultural journalism, Bursztyn was assigned to the worst category, as a laughing-stock, placed on that timeworn, antediluvian shelf to which the most risky or avant-garde works, those that dared to dissent on artistic, cultural, and political matters, were consigned, one after another, for almost the whole of the twentieth century. Despite cultural conservatism, or "Colombian elitism", as Marta Traba calls it, the sixties were years of profound environmental, political, and cultural changes, processes of growing modernization planned by the developmentalist system of the second post-war period, years of growth and mutation of urban environments in the country, set against expansion and diversification of intellectual and cultural communities at a national level (fig. 4).

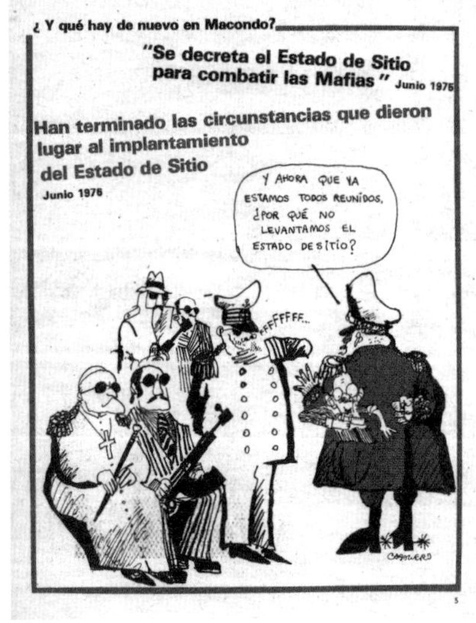

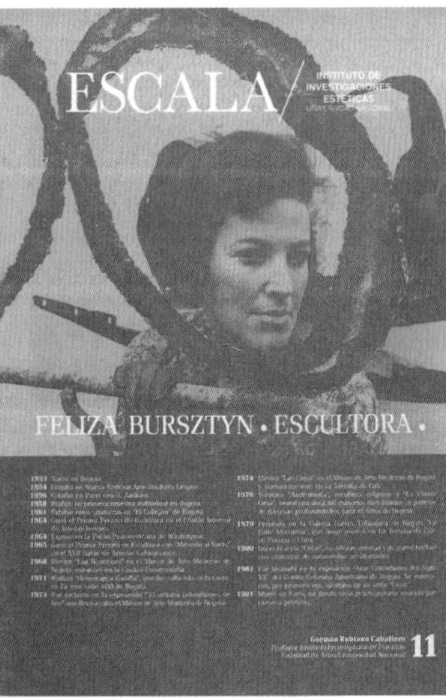

3. "¿Y qué hay de nuevo en Macondo?" (So what's new in Macondo?), caricature by Antonio Caballero, *Revista Alternativa*, date unknown

4. "Feliza Burzstyn Escultora", cover of the magazine *ESCALA / IIE*, no. 11, Universidad Nacional de Colombia, Bogotá, November 1986

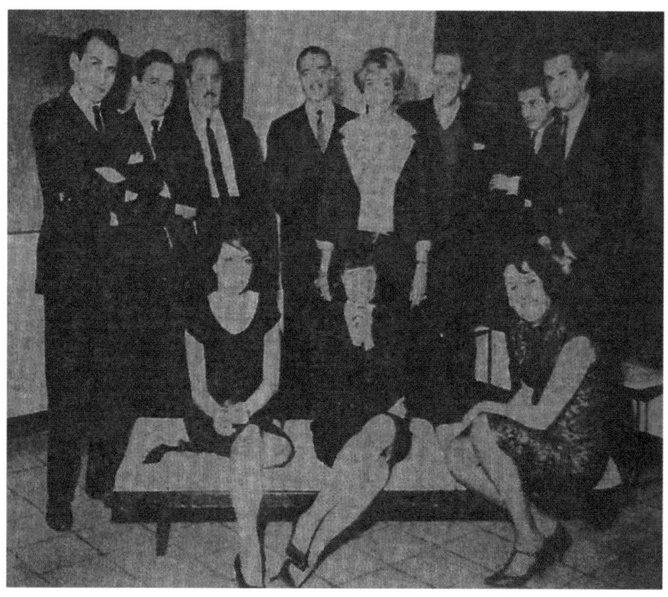

The avant-garde of avant-garde

Starting in the dictatorship of General Gustavo Rojas Pinilla, the main cities in Colombia, and Bogotá in particular, had been undergoing an expansion of spaces for female participation in academic, artistic, and cultural institutions, although women were still very far from attaining equal access to full citizenship. In 1954, in the context of the National Constituent Assembly formed under the government of Rojas Pinilla himself, female suffrage was recognized, but not until the last year of the dictatorship, in 1957, were the first elections held in which women exercised their right to vote.

In the visual arts, this movement was manifested in the growing participation of women artists on equal terms in various national and international competitions, and although they were certainly a minority, they played a prominent and even leading role in various artistic and cultural spaces in that period. The first two magazines devoted exclusively to publicizing the visual arts in Colombia, *Plástica* and *Prisma*, were run by women, the first by the painter Judith Márquez and the second by Marta Traba, and were spaces for raising awareness of the careers of women artists who had been increasingly coming to the fore, including Márquez herself, Lucy Tejada, Cecilia Porras, and Alicia Tafur. They were joined a few years later by the artists Beatriz Daza, Beatriz González, Nirma Zárate, Sonia Gutiérrez, and Clemencia Lucena, all of whom left a deep mark on Colombian art in the transition from the 1960s to the 1970s (fig. 5).

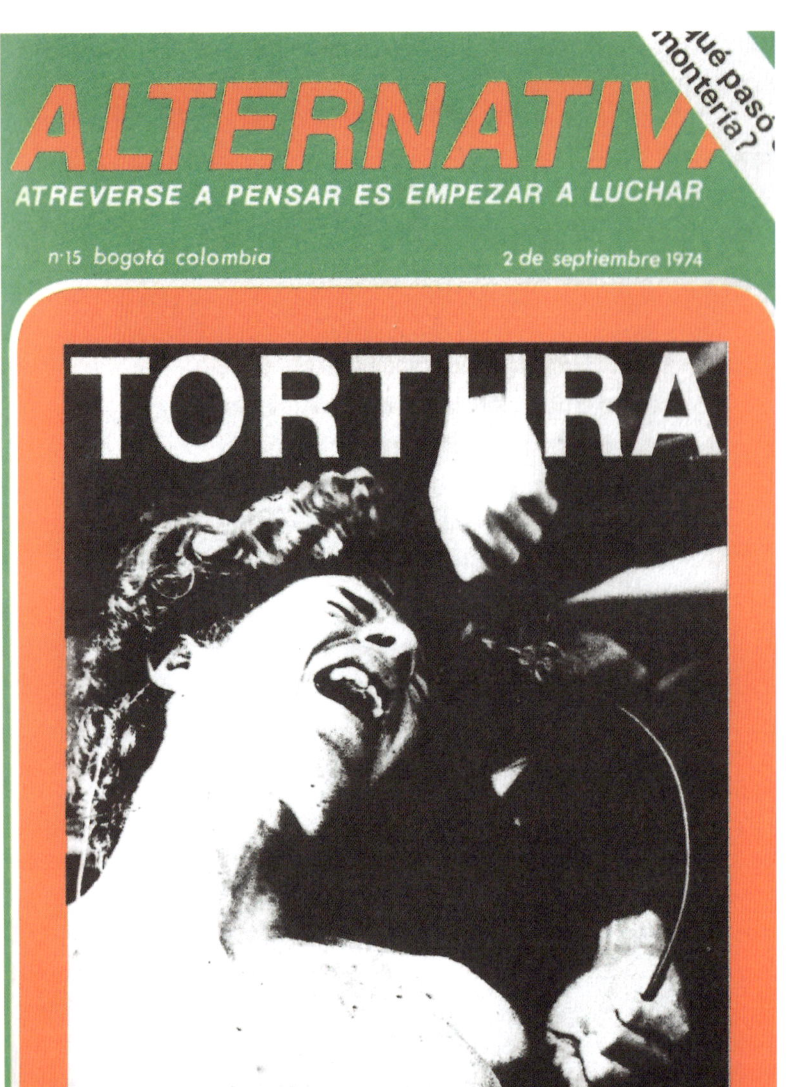

6. Taller 4 Rojo, "Gobierno del terror", cover of *Revista Alternativa*, no. 15, 2 September 1974, Archive of Jorge Mora

Similarly, the presence of women as cultural administrators, proto-curators, exhibition organizers, museum directors, and so on increased, forming that constellation of women at the head of the main Colombian art institutions, a constellation that orbited for several years around Marta Traba and included Emma Araújo Ortiz, Mireya Zawadzki, Maritza Uribe de Urdinola, and Gloria Zea, among other important women artists, intellectuals, and cultural administrators who were leading lights in the Colombian cultural scene from the 1960s.

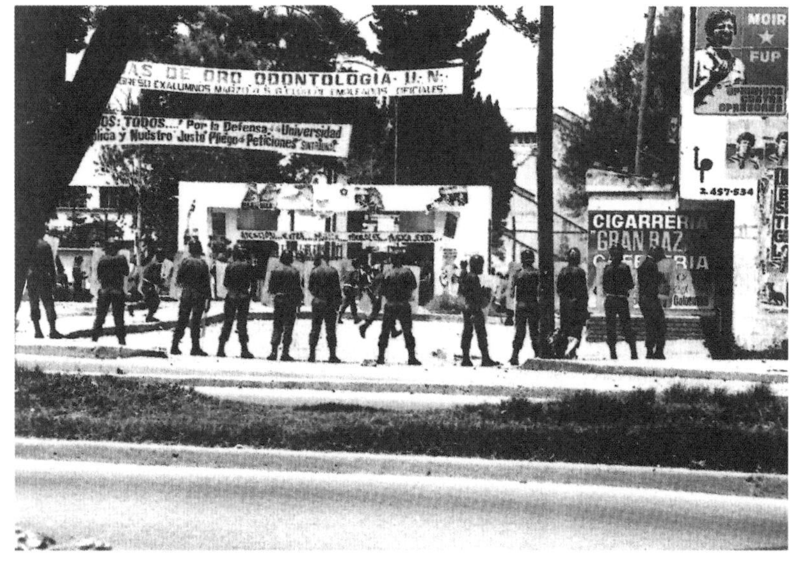

These women could certainly be said to have occupied the avant-garde of Colombian art for several decades, and although they did not get politically involved in the fight for gender equality, they adapted and took a pro-active part in the most critical cultural currents of their time. Among them, Bursztyn occupied the extremely lonely position of someone who is in the avant-garde of the avant-garde, belligerently disregarding prominent trends, even within the most critical artistic movements, and remaining faithful to the designs of her own creative process, which on several occasions led her to violate the boundaries of fixed genres and subgenres and to express herself beyond the borders of established practices.

Traba, who had herself experienced the bitterness of exile through her deportation from Colombia, ordered in 1968 but put into effect in 1970, said that Bursztyn was unintentionally avant-garde:

> In 1968, I myself suggested that Feliza's work (along with Norman Mejía's and Luis Caballero's painting and Pedro Alcántara's drawings) represented a profound breach of Colombian "landlordism" … I still think that this suggestion was valid, and that in a backward, stagnant country like Colombia, the disruption of "elitism", the loss of hierarchical fear, which is so clearly evident in Feliza Burzstyn's sculpture and embodied in an uninhibited and unbridled form in *Las histéricas* (The Hysterical Ones) and *Las camas* (The Beds), dents the apparently immovable surface of society. All the traumas of Colombian life, all its immutable, quasi-Tibetan hierarchies, thrive on resistance to change: what is

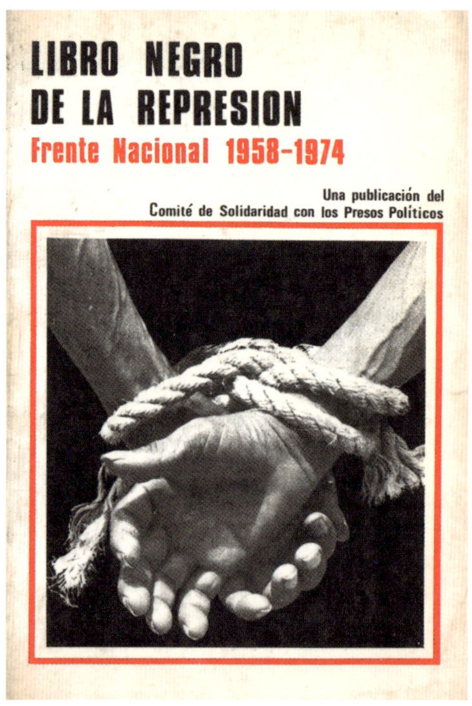

8. Cover of *Libro Negro de la Represión: Frente Nacional 1958-1974* (The Black Book of Repression: National Front 1958–1974), Comité de Solidaridad con los Presos Políticos, Bogotá, August 1974

more, they could not survive without the absolute, monolithic impermeability of that society and the top-down nature of hierarchies. When something, like Feliza's work, opens a rift, taking advantage of the momentary disruption it produces, the whole building is shaken: this disconcerting effect, admittedly limited and transient, is what I call artistic subversion.[3]

From the beginning of her artistic career in Colombia, Bursztyn rapidly aligned herself, emotionally, poetically, and politically, with the most experimental and avant-garde artistic and intellectual circle in the country. In particular, it is clear from many biographical details that she formed deep and lifelong friendships with the artists and writers of the Barranquilla Group, especially Alejandro Obregón, Gabriel García Márquez, and Álvaro Cepeda Samudio, with the founders and joint editors of *Mito*, Hernando Valencia Goelkel and Jorge Gaitán Durán (she was the latter's last romantic partner until his early death in 1962), and with the founders of the Casa de la Cultura (and later of the Teatro La Candelaria), Patricia Ariza and Santiago García.

This roll call of artists, writers, dramatists, actors, and activists could be greatly extended; it is important to note that the sixties and seventies in Colombia were years in which much movement was stirring in the field of culture and politics, years of enthusiasms and rebellions, years in which cultural change was brewing not only in the small number of exhibition rooms, theatres, auditoriums, and universities – crucial spaces for the country's intellectual, cultural, and political development – but also behind closed doors, in artists' apartments and houses, because right from the start Conservative Restoration Bogotá was a highly militarized and oppressive city, kept in check by the exercise of strict political control (figs. 6–7).[4]

From those years of enthusiasm, the country travelled along difficult paths, through increasingly blatant practices of censorship and repression by the National Front and subsequent governments, within the continuing sharing of power among the most reactionary elements of liberalism and conservatism, towards a gradual escalation of the war, severely polarizing the country's artistic and intellectual community, and giving rise to great waves of forced migration internally and to other countries, a phenomenon that has not yet been delineated in the history of art and cultural history in general in Colombia. Within this context, Feliza remained ideologically left-wing, without subscribing to party militancy or other forms of political organization, though openly displaying her affinity with the course of socialist Cuba, an affinity that she paid for, as has already been made clear, by being tortured and driven into exile (fig. 8).

Machines that laugh

If it comes to identifying Bursztyn's position in the context of Colombian art, we can point out that she tailored her activity to that of the country's young museums of modern art, especially Bogotá's Museum of Modern Art and the La Tertulia Museum of Modern Art in Cali, where over the years she exhibited her *Las histéricas*, *Las camas*, and *La baila mecánica* (The Mechanical Ballet). She took part in the main events that made up what was known as the most experimental visual art scene in Colombia, from the National Artists' Salons to the Avant-Garde Art Festivals in Cali and the Coltejer Art Biennials in Medellín. On every one of these occasions, she moved the boundaries of the experimental sculptural field through the execution of each component of her extended series and through the metamorphoses that her "exhibition" offered. Bursztyn always approached her exhibitions as opportunities to perturb the nervous systems of artistic and cultural institutions, turning each of her solo shows into a matrix for the event, in which sculpturality, scenography, and, since *Las histéricas*, cybernetics join forces to ensure disruption of the living in art spaces.

Analysis of Bursztyn's works regarded scrap metal mainly as a material to which she had easy access in a city with fragmentary and limited modernization processes like Bogotá. But the status of scrap metal in her work is not just a question of material and form, but of *poiesis*, given that from her first incursions into the use of scrap metal, in the mid-1960s, Bursztyn's creative work accommodated everything it entailed: the memory of a lost function, the trace of the detachment of a thing or a machine, and its entry into a different body. In her *Chatarras* (Junk Sculptures), *Minimáquinas* (Minimachines), *Las histéricas*, and even the *Color* (Colour Series), Bursztyn recontextualized the nuts, bolts, washers, buttons, bodies, casings, and motors in an order that altered their functional mechanical principles, so as to connect with the inexhaustible uniqueness of a presence.

Anyone who looks closely at Bursztyn's sculptures will see the filigree work, the countless spot welds that keep small parts and pieces together, and will be able to deduce the pleasure of forming a new life cycle out of what has been rendered obsolete, discarded, destroyed. Nor, moreover, will they fail to perceive the obvious fact that all these fragments and parts were brought from predominantly masculine worlds and recoded, in most cases, with nouns that are feminine in Spanish: "happy girl", "woman with horns", "Clytemnestra", "Andromeda", "junk" (*chatarra*), "hysteric" (*histérica*), "bed" (*cuja*), "mechanical ballet" (*baila mecánica*). Generally, Feliza's Bursztyn works are presences conjugated in the feminine, taken to museums and galleries from metal workshops and flea markets to "misbehave", make a noise, exhibit an impudent sensuality, attract attention, corrode and demolish the solemnity of the temple of the muses, disobey and be, as she once described herself as a child, "horrible, impertinent, rude, awful".[5] Over the course of her life, Bursztyn suffered harsh losses and terrible accidents, in which she fractured her hands and face and injured her back and neck, and she undoubtedly knew this process of resilience, this persistence of the life force and the creativity of disobedience, in her own flesh.

On countless occasions, commentators and critics of her work highlighted, for better or worse, the use that Bursztyn made of her sense of humour; as she herself put it, "the humour they produce depends on who is looking at them".[6] On the positive side, the more penetrating commentators on her work understood the joke as a critical force, with the dual content of happiness and sadness characteristic of irony. On the negative, the interpretation of humour in Bursztyn's works was nothing more than an exercise in simplistic ideological control, intended to ward off its critical force by relegating it to the realm of the absurd; but her works push in the opposite direction: what they relegate to that realm of the absurd is social reality itself revealed in pseudo-civilizing routines, in the judgements of double moral standards, and above all in the irrepressible chains of associations that made her viewers laugh.

So who was the machine? The vibrating hysteric? The creaking bed? The imperfectly choreographed dancers? Or the laughing automata?

[1] Gabriel García Márquez, "Breve nota de adiós al olor de la guayaba de Feliza Bursztyn", *El Espectador* (Bogotá), 2 August 1981.
[2] Walter Engel, "Feliza Brustyn [*sic*] y Gloria Daza", *El Espectador*, 3 September 1961.
[3] Marta Traba, "Feliza Burztyn [*sic*]: hizo la vanguardia a su pesar y sin proponérselo", *Semanario Cultural* (Bogotá), 20 March 1977.
[4] In a reminiscence of the cultural life of the Colombian capital in the 1960s, Italian artist Umberto Giangrandi remarked: "Bogotá was a city where parties were held at home, not like now where there are thousands of public places to go and have a drink, listen to good music, and talk to friends at night. La Macarena was the favourite district because a lot of artists lived there. There was one block where Hernán Díaz, Beatriz Daza, Enrique Grau, and Dora Franco lived. It was known as 'the hill of dishonour' because of all the crazy parties held there. The most famous were the ones organized by Enrique Grau. He had incredible happenings, where people dressed up, the music was really good, and Grau often produced film scripts starring himself as lead actor, filmed by the directors Luis Ernesto Arocha and Diego León Giraldo. At the time, these two filmmakers, Arocha and Giraldo, also made films of Feliza Bursztyn's work and put together visual productions for the openings of her exhibitions; this was very new and attractive back then. At the parties back then I met many writers, especially the Nadaists. Some Jewish intellectuals and art collectors also used to attend. Always present were Bernardo Salcedo, Carlos Rojas, Hernán Díaz, David Manzur, Manolo Vellojín, Arturito Velásquez, Alonso Garcés, and Momo del Villar, as well as all the members of the Belarca Gallery, Feliza, Álvaro Cepeda, Alejandro Obregón, Beatriz Daza, Dora Franco, Estrellita Nieto, Santiago García and Patricia Ariza, Miguel Torres, Alí Humar, Eddy Armando, Consuelo Luzardo, Vicky Hernández, Carlos Perozzo, Kepa Amuchastegui, Carlos Duplat, Dina Moscovitz, José Urbach, Juan Manuel Luguito, Margalida Castro, and the whole theatre and television combo, and all sorts of people!… It was a very complex group, very representative of the country's cultural world; they were conceptually, culturally, and politically nonconformist, with different sexual orientations. They contributed a great deal to changing ways of thinking. This was really valuable, because Colombian society was still very prudish and conservative, violently prudish. In those years, artists took very important steps towards breaking up that deep-rooted and highly exclusive social structure, to provide a new, broader, and freer perspective. The thing is that one tends to forget is that in Colombia, in the sixties, everything was still to be done and subverted, in the best sense of the word, from every point of view: political, conceptual, cultural, sexual, and so on and so forth, using the languages of writing, theatre, visual art, music, film, and others." Cited in David Gutiérrez Castañeda *et al.*, *Arte y disidencia política: Memorias del Taller 4 Rojo*, Taller Historia Crítica del Arte (Bogotá: La Bachué, 2015), pp. 446–62.
[5] "Felisa [*sic*] Bursztyn", *Diario del Caribe* (Barranquilla), 26 April 1974.
[6] *Diario del Caribe.*

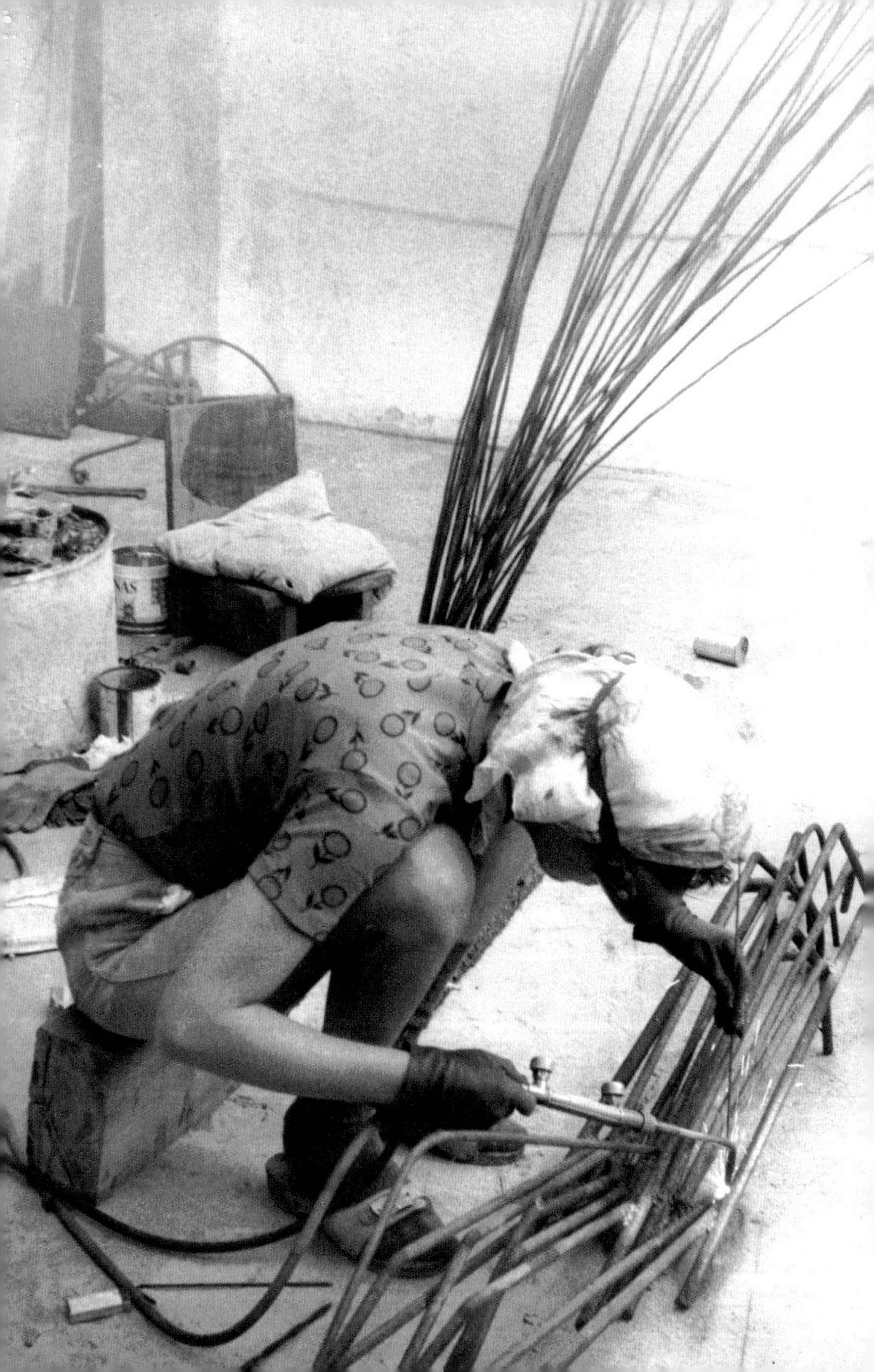

We Must Fight: Feliza Bursztyn and Colombian Women in the Arts

Gina McDaniel Tarver

[I am a] feminist and violent liberationist. Because I believe that there is a political and social difference between men and women, and it's that we women are not able do what we want with peace of mind. The problem is that you were raised in that way. You were raised "differently" since you were born … Moreover, there are no other possibilities, by tradition and by culture … Progress has been made, but not enough. We must fight and ensure that an equally skilled woman is paid the same salary for the same job as a man. And at this time, that's not the case.

Feliza Bursztyn[1]

1957 is a significant year in Colombian women's fight for equal rights: it was the first time they voted in a national election. It was also pivotal on a personal level for Feliza Bursztyn. Bursztyn was twenty-four years old, married with three children, and living in Bogotá. That year she left her husband and children, a radical and heartbreaking decision. She did it in order to become a professional artist, a goal her husband did not support. He wanted her at home with the kids, a common expectation in the United States, where he was from, and standard in Colombia. But scandalously, Bursztyn left her home to pursue her dream of studying art in Paris, and she left with another man![2] Her husband moved back with their children to the United States; they got divorced there, since divorce was illegal in Colombia.[3] This small part of her story reveals some of the difficulties that Bursztyn faced as a woman, and the strength and audacity of her commitment to art. It shows that her fight for women to be able to "do what we want with peace of mind" was personal as well as political.[4] Bursztyn was not alone in the struggle.

1. Feliza Bursztyn working in her studio in the 1970s Courtesy of the archive of Pablo Leyva. Photo: Pablo Leyva

During this period when changes swept across the globe, the hippie movement, miniskirts, the contraceptive pill, and sexual liberation arrived even to extremely conservative, Catholic Colombia. Bursztyn was part of

2. Marta Traba at the opening of Museo de Arte Moderno de Bogotá, 1962

a wave of change that opened new social, professional, and creative possibilities for women. She and her friends helped to propel Colombian art into a new era and also contributed to women's emancipation. Bursztyn's work is one of the best examples of artistic innovation in the 1960s and 1970s; she proved that women could lead the way in a field previously ruled by men. In this essay, I consider how her career intersected with those of other successful Colombian women in the arts, highlighting how these women complemented, supported, and inspired one another.

Famously sociable, Bursztyn was friends with many intellectuals and artists, so this brief account is far from comprehensive. I focus on just three key relationships: with art critic Marta Traba, artist Beatriz Daza, and musician Jacqueline Nova. As an art historian working from a cultural and temporal distance, I rely on published evidence, which is sometimes scarce, so my reflection on how Bursztyn influenced these women and vice versa, and how their work impacted others, contains elements of speculation based on what can be gleaned from both artworks and texts.

When Bursztyn burst into Colombian art, it was overwhelmingly dominated by men. The most famous artists were Alejandro Obregón, Edgar Negret, Eduardo Ramírez-Villamizar, and Fernando Botero, and, judging from participation in the annual National Salons, about three times as many men as women became professional artists.[5] Art education through universities was available to women. However, women were inculcated in notions of what was "proper" for them to do, and the main expectation was to marry and have children. Furthermore, women who studied art were encouraged to go into applied arts, like interior design.[6]

Notions of appropriate gender characteristics were also projected onto judgements of style. Art critic Casimiro Eiger's review of a Salón de Pintoras (Salon of Women Painters) in 1959 makes that clear. In arguing against separating women's art from men's, he writes that the label "feminine painting" usually indicates a "certain mixture of grace and charm, of soft harmonies and of slight insinuations, together with a certain sentimentality in the subject", whereas "masculine painting" connotes vigorousness, courageous formal solutions, audacious motifs.[7] He expressed his belief that these were socially constructed and invalid categories that should be discarded, since all good art exhibits the so-called "masculine" traits. However, as art historian Ana María Reyes shows, in the 1960s, art criticism continued to betray a deep sexism embedded in its formal analysis, and double-standards on the basis of gender were common.[8]

Despite this situation, women during Bursztyn's time had a great impact on the art scene and drove the promotion of new art forms. For example, the first specialized art journal in Colombia, *Plástica* (1956–60), which was dedicated to supporting abstraction, was created by the artist Judith Márquez and Rita de Agudelo (a friend of Bursztyn's), who ran the Galería San Diego (1969–85), which consistently featured the most radical tendencies.[9] No woman – arguably no person – did more to renovate Colombian visual arts in the 1950s and 1960s than Bursztyn's close friend Marta Traba (1923–1983). Traba was a prominent art critic who even had a popular TV show dedicated to art. She was a driving force behind the opening of the Museo de Arte Moderno de Bogotá (MAMBO), which she led from 1962 to 1969 (fig. 2).[10] She also taught art history at universities, served on admission and prize juries for art competitions, and organized exhibitions of Colombian art for foreign museums.

Bursztyn and Traba's friendship and careers were deeply intertwined. Traba enthusiastically supported Bursztyn's art, as a critic, exhibition organizer, juror, and close friend. The overlap of these roles, and consequent potential for conflict of interest, is notable.[11] For example, Traba was the main organizer of the I Salón Intercol de Artistas Jóvenes in 1964. She likely wrote the call to artists, which specifically encouraged the submission of "the latest tendencies" including junk art (*chatarra*), language seemingly tailored to include Bursztyn's work.[12] Traba was one of three members of the prize jury, which awarded Bursztyn first prize in sculpture (fig. 3). Traba also wrote a review of the salon in which she praised Bursztyn, a "genius of the junk", for her ability to create beauty out of base materials.[13] These facts show the degree of Traba's involvement in Bursztyn's career and her influence within the Colombian art scene.

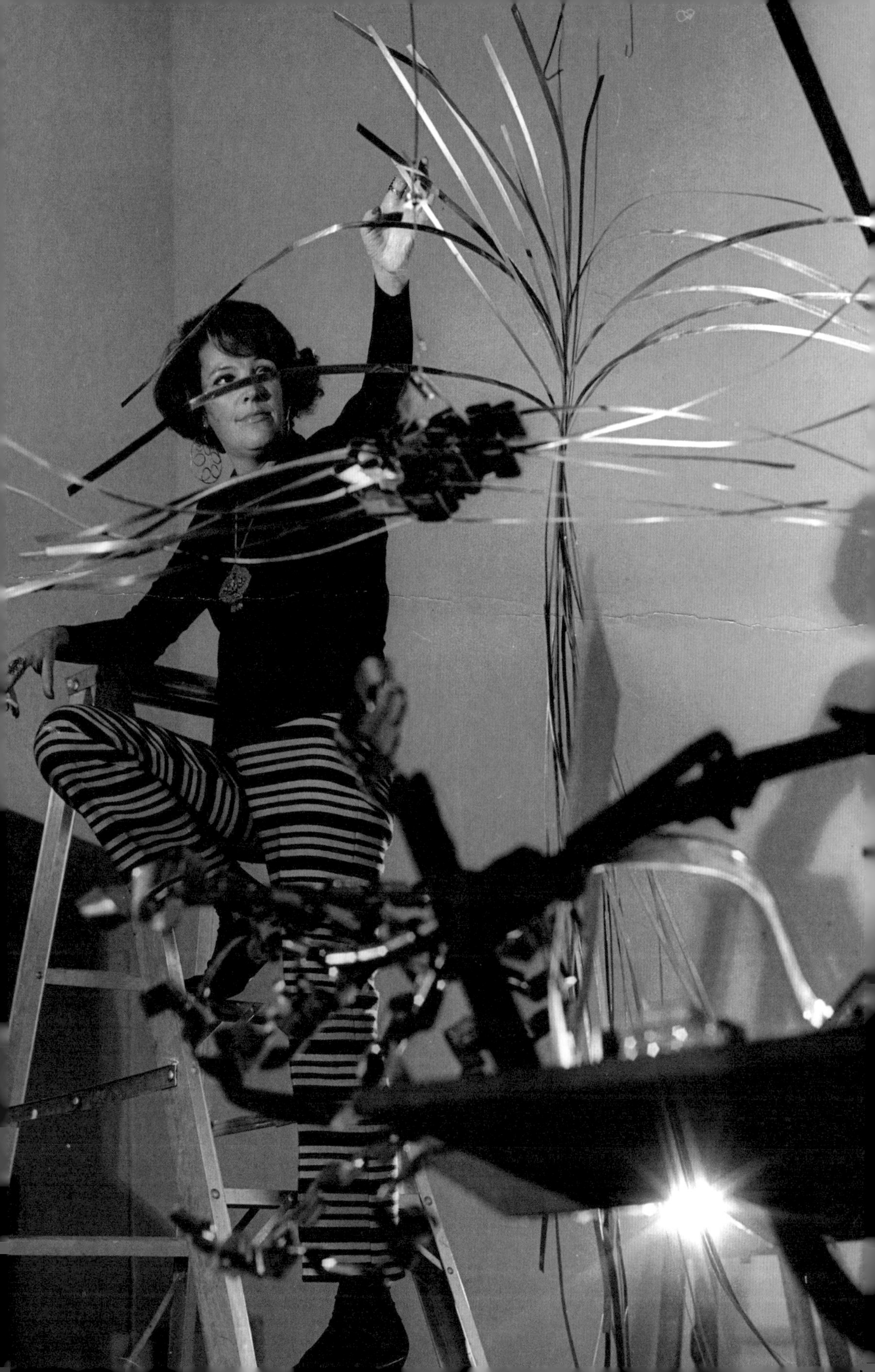

Traba did not hesitate to use her positions to promote Bursztyn's art because she strongly believed in its validity and power.[14] As the director of MAMBO, Traba organized some of Bursztyn's most important solo shows: *Chatarras* in 1964 and *Histéricas* in 1967. She was on the National Salon prize jury that awarded Bursztyn's *Mirando al norte* (Looking North) (fig. p. 13, bottom) the first prize for sculpture in 1965, and was a member of the committee that awarded her the commission for the monument to Colombian President Alfonso López Pumarejo in 1967. Both of these awards enveloped Traba and Bursztyn in controversy. When the radically new art that Traba supported – including Bursztyn's – caused outrage, as it often did, Traba went to battle to defend it.[15] That she did not shy away from polemic made her a role model for women's assertiveness. Traba surrounded herself with innovative artists like Bursztyn, forming a circle that became a powerful locus of change.

Another innovative artist whom Traba supported was ceramicist Beatriz Daza (1928–1968). Of Bursztyn's female artist friends, she was closest to Daza. Contemporary critics mostly perceived their artworks in opposite ways, but their similarities as well as differences make them complementary. Bursztyn's work was seen as extreme and associated with masculine practices. Hernando Valencia Goelkel wrote: "there is nothing 'feminine' in that confrontation with the inexorable stubbornness of iron".[16] Daza's, in contrast, was consistently described in terms related to ideals of feminine restraint. Critics wrote that Daza's art displayed "smooth and concentrated serenity",[17] that she followed "a sure, responsible, and measured path".[18] Nevertheless, Daza also dealt with prejudice not only as a woman but because her preferred means of expression was associated with utility and craft, therefore not considered art.[19] Like Bursztyn, Daza came to be respected for pushing material, technical, and aesthetic boundaries in ways that changed Colombian art.

Daza experimented with glazes and textures, with increased scale and ceramic "paintings", creating clay works that critics felt represented a new form of artistic expression,[20] which earned her prizes at the National Salon.[21] Around 1966, however, she had to stop making pottery since the toxic materials she used for glazes damaged her lungs. (Bursztyn would have similar health problems from welding fumes.) Daza began to make still-life compositions by embedding broken crockery and other items in plaster. These reliefs, now her most famous contributions to Colombian art, relate in multiple, fascinating ways to other modern art, including Bursztyn's *Chatarras* (Junk Sculptures).

Daza showed the reliefs in the 1966 exhibition *Testimonio de los objetos* (Testimony of the Objects) at MAMBO. Full of ceramic shards – much of which appear to be from her own pottery – the reliefs very literally mark a break with her earlier work. They exhibit a new antagonism that may well have been inspired by her friend Bursztyn's aggressive approach to art. Their broken crockery calls to mind domestic outbursts, uncontrolled rages expressed through destruction. As assemblages of found objects, they relate to Nouveau réalisme, as do Bursztyn's sculptures.[22] For example, Daza's *Hace mucho tiempo* (It's Been a Long Time, c. 1966) (fig. 4), freezes in time a real tea setting, similar to Daniel Spoerri's picture-traps of the early 1960s. Spoerri's works appear less mediated, captured as-is on a table-top, whereas Daza's are compressed and shattered. Daza's object-testimonies seem to trap moments of convulsion.

In the lower part of *Hace mucho tiempo*, refined objects – including a nineteenth-century porcelain tea cup and saucer, silver tea strainer, and lace doily – are embedded in a pale background. The dark upper part slides like a tectonic plate under the lower section, creating a fault line. Along this rift are broken pieces of rougher ceramics (likely of Daza's own production) as well as pieces of rusted metal gears that could have come straight out of Bursztyn's workshop. The mechanical parts seem to threaten to crush the fine porcelain. The cup itself has already been broken and glued back together, evidence of its fragility. Daza's assemblages, like Bursztyn's, give material testimony on the changing state of Colombian society. While Bursztyn's *Chatarras* draw from mechanical materials and evoke work spaces designated as male, Daza's reliefs relate to the physical space traditionally allocated to women, the private home. Spatial compression in Daza's assemblages shows the restrictiveness of "women's place".

Bursztyn's disorderly *Chatarras* implicitly challenged gender stereotypes because Bursztyn made them with materials and techniques associated with male labour.[23] Daza's assemblages, on the other hand, more explicitly refer to gender within Colombian society, particularly *Hace mucho tiempo*, since it contrasts objects from "feminine" domestic space with an encroaching modern world. Julian Serna points out that the dishes and silver here belonged to Daza's grandmother, who was the First Lady of Colombia (her grandfather Ramón González Valencia was President from 1909–10). This inheritance, in speaking of the role assigned to women within the country's conservative structures, points to a family lineage that aims to maintain among its members patterns of behaviour to safeguard a certain kind of social distinction. That is why this gesture

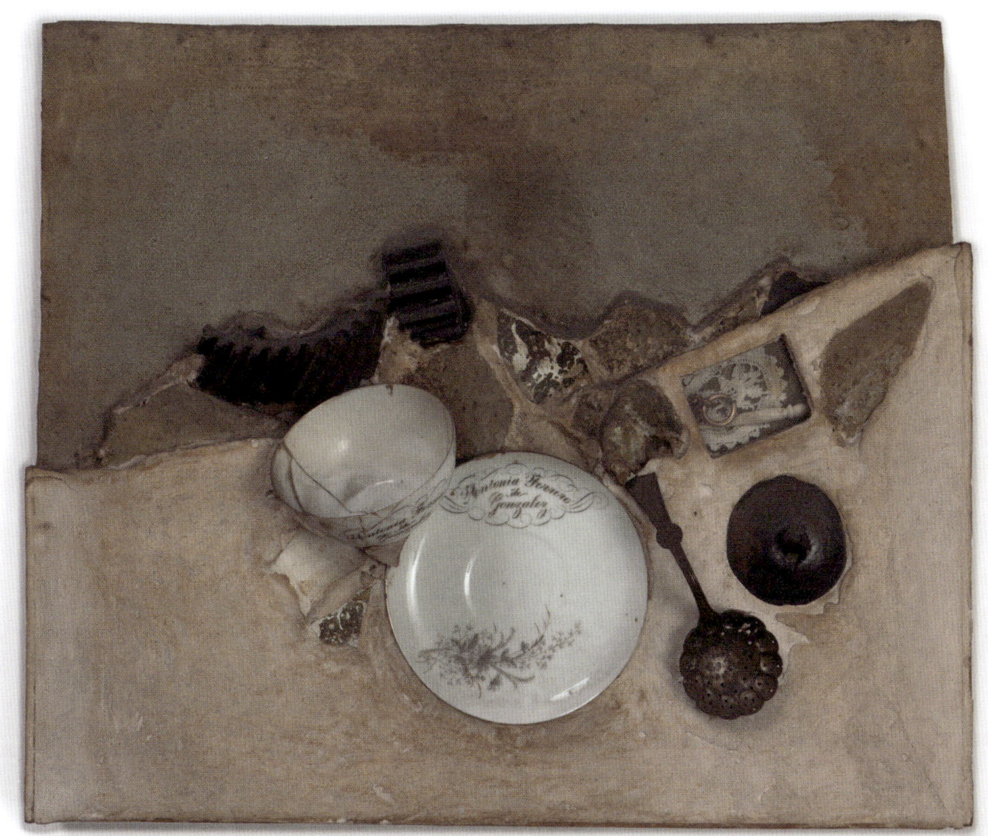

4. Beatriz Daza, *Hace mucho tiempo* (It's Been a Long Time), c. 1966, fragments of ceramic and diverse materials on plaster, 42 × 51 cm, private collection, Bogotá
Photo: © Ernesto Monsalve

is so strong: breaking those dishes is an act through which Daza gives permission to detach herself from the family tradition and the role that was imposed on women in Colombia up to that time.[24]

Daza's object-testimonies record her own "crazy" actions – smashing dishes, breaking with social expectations in her own life.[25] These are strikingly different from her earlier "serene" artworks; we might even say that they channel the mad power of her dear friend.[26] With these assemblages she, like Bursztyn, used material fragments to wreck social and artistic standards and forged new ones out of the remains.

On 23 June 1969, Daza and Bursztyn were together in Cali, participating in the VIII National Festival of Art, when they were involved in a car crash. Bursztyn recovered from serious injuries; Daza was killed. Bursztyn wrote a tribute to Daza for an exhibition of her work that MAMBO held in her memory, saying: "we can only honour her and somehow thank her for having been a friend and having given us so much".[27] With little documentation to rely on, we can only speculate as to how their friendship impacted Bursztyn's art, or Daza's for that matter. It appears that, around 1965–68, their artistic paths, which had seemed so different, converged, that they exchanged or shared ideas. With the reliefs of 1965–67, Daza embraced the fragment, assemblage, and the power of madness, all important aspects of Bursztyn's *Chatarras*. And Bursztyn began to create *Las histéricas* (The Hysterical Ones) in 1967, which deal more directly than her previous art with gender stereotypes, through the idea of female madness.[28] Furthermore, *Las histéricas*, and later *Las camas* (The Beds), produce an associative spatial shift in Bursztyn's art: leaving the mechanic's workshop, we move into the intimate zone of the bedroom, still a mechanized space, but now domestic.[29]

When Bursztyn exhibited *Las histéricas* in February 1968 at MAMBO, one aspect that jarred many critics was their noise.[30] Perhaps it was their clanking that led Traba to write, in the exhibition brochure, that *Las histéricas* were "as irritating as the music of Jacqueline Nova".[31] It turns out that this linking of Bursztyn's work with Nova's was prognostic. Bursztyn was fascinated with how sound added to the work and its space, and this interest led her to seek a collaboration with Nova.[32]

At the time when Bursztyn debuted *Las histéricas*, Nova (1935–1975) was in Buenos Aires studying avant-garde music, having received a scholarship in 1967 to the CLAEM – Centro Latinoamericano de Altos Estudios Musicales (Latin American Centre for Advanced Musical Studies) at Instituto Torcuato Di Tella. The scholarship was awarded

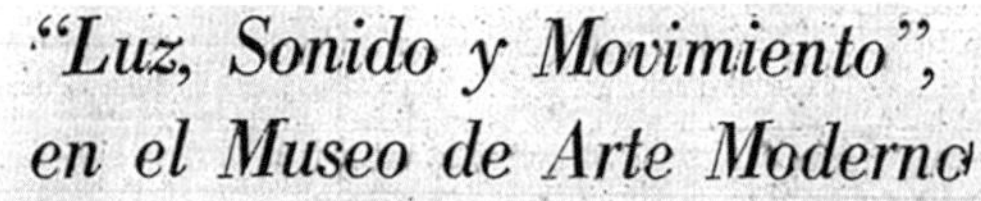

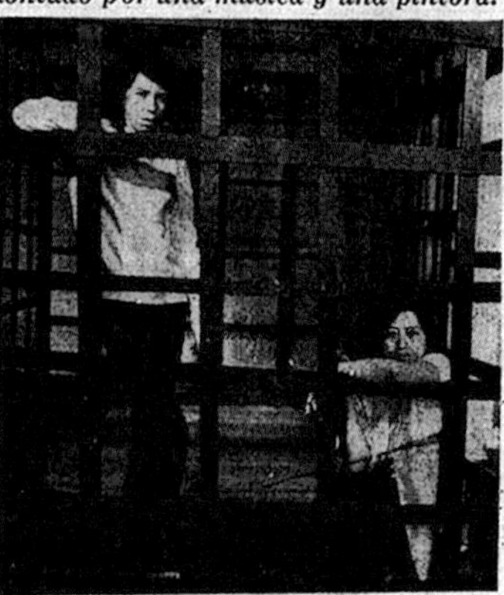

"Luz, Sonido y Movimiento", en el Museo de Arte Moderno

Es un espectáculo montado por una música y una pintora.

Por Gloria Valencia Diago

El Museo de Arte Moderno se ha visto asaltado durante los últimos días por elementos extraños a una institución de su índole; láminas metálicas, equipos de grabadoras, potentes reflectores, tríplex, tablones de distintos tamaños y hasta una gran máquina afiladora, materiales básicos para el espectáculo "Luz, sonido y movimiento".

Sin embargo, la materia prima solo llegará esta tarde a las 6.30, cuando se abrirán las puertas para inaugurar esta nueva modalidad de exhibición artística. Porque el personaje central será el mismo público. Así lo han querido sus organizadoras, Jacqueline Nova y Julia Acuña, compositora la primera y pintora la segunda, que, con la colaboración de ingenieros técnicos en las ramas electrónica y de iluminación y numerosos voluntarios, vienen trabajando a marchas forzadas en el montaje de una función jamás vista en Bogotá.

En qué consiste

Jacqueline y Julia explican que la idea consiste en la simultaneidad, signo de nuestro tiempo, de los efectos sonoros, luz y movimiento, con la participación directa del espectador, consciente o inconscientemente.

En un momento dado los haces de luz de los grandes reflectores caerán sobre una persona o grupo en particular, cuyas reacciones serán, en ese instante, cen las hojas metálicas al chocar y rozarse entre sí.

Tema para sicólogos

trayectoria con cinco exposiciones individuales y participación en numerosas colectivas.

Jacqueline Nova y Julia Acuña en la jaula, una de las sorpresas que ofrecerá el espectáculo "Luz, Sonido y Movimiento", del cual son autoras. (Foto de Enrique Benavides).

5. Jacqueline Nova (right) and Julia Acuña (left) in the exhibition *Luz, sonido, movimiento* (Light, Sound, Movement), Museo de Arte Moderno de Bogotá, *El Tiempo* (Bogotá), 20 March 1969
Photo: Enrique Benavides

on the basis of her explorations in aleatory and serial music, which had already established her reputation in Colombia as a radical composer.[33] CLAEM offered Nova the chance to work with the latest technology for recording and modifying sound, and there, Nova composed electronic music for the first time. She also began incorporating sounds from the everyday environment, particularly mechanical noises, into her compositions. Electronic music allowed her to explore "the marvellous world of machines".[34]

In March 1969, having returned to Bogotá, Nova and visual artist Julia Acuña created a multimedia installation at MAMBO, which they called *Luz, sonido, movimiento* (Light, Sound, Movement) (fig. 5).[35] It was a series of specially built spaces that contained found items such as a large cage and a knife grinder, illuminated by colourful lights and filled with the sound of Nova's music. *Luz, sonido, movimiento* brought attention to Nova's new electronic music and demonstrated its relationship to visual art. *Luz, sonido, movimiento*, Bursztyn's *Las histéricas* exhibition, and MAMBO's *Espacios ambientales* (Environments) (fig. 6) stand out as the earliest forays into multisensorial installation art in Colombia and evince the pioneering role of women.

Bursztyn began to create works that eventually became *Las camas* once she finished *Las histéricas*.[36] Adding the element of music was important to her, so she sought out Nova. As Bursztyn explained, they collaborated closely "to give the necessary tone to each bed and to objects that surround each", since *Las camas* "require a total environment".[37] Many reviews of *Las camas*, exhibited in Colombia in 1974, do not mention the music or name Nova as collaborator, but Bursztyn gave her credit for creating the ambiance that makes *Las camas* effective, saying they do not work without the music.[38]

Even more than *Las histéricas*, *Las camas* suggest human bodies, confusing or conflating machine and human. Bursztyn surrounded the beds with dark curtains, and lit them with spotlights, similar to how she had shown *Las histéricas*. But the metal armatures and motors in *Las camas* are hidden under great swaths of satin in bright colours that evoke the Colombian flag, bishop's vestments, and Colombian folk costumes.[39] Traba described the "cloth sliding over the bed like an ambiguous banner – sexual, patriotic, erotic".[40] The sexual connotation was clear; some critics compared the space to a bordello.[41] Nova's soundtrack consisted of "electroacoustic sounds created with metallic sheets and other sources that were unconventional for the time".[42] The music complimented the sound of the beds

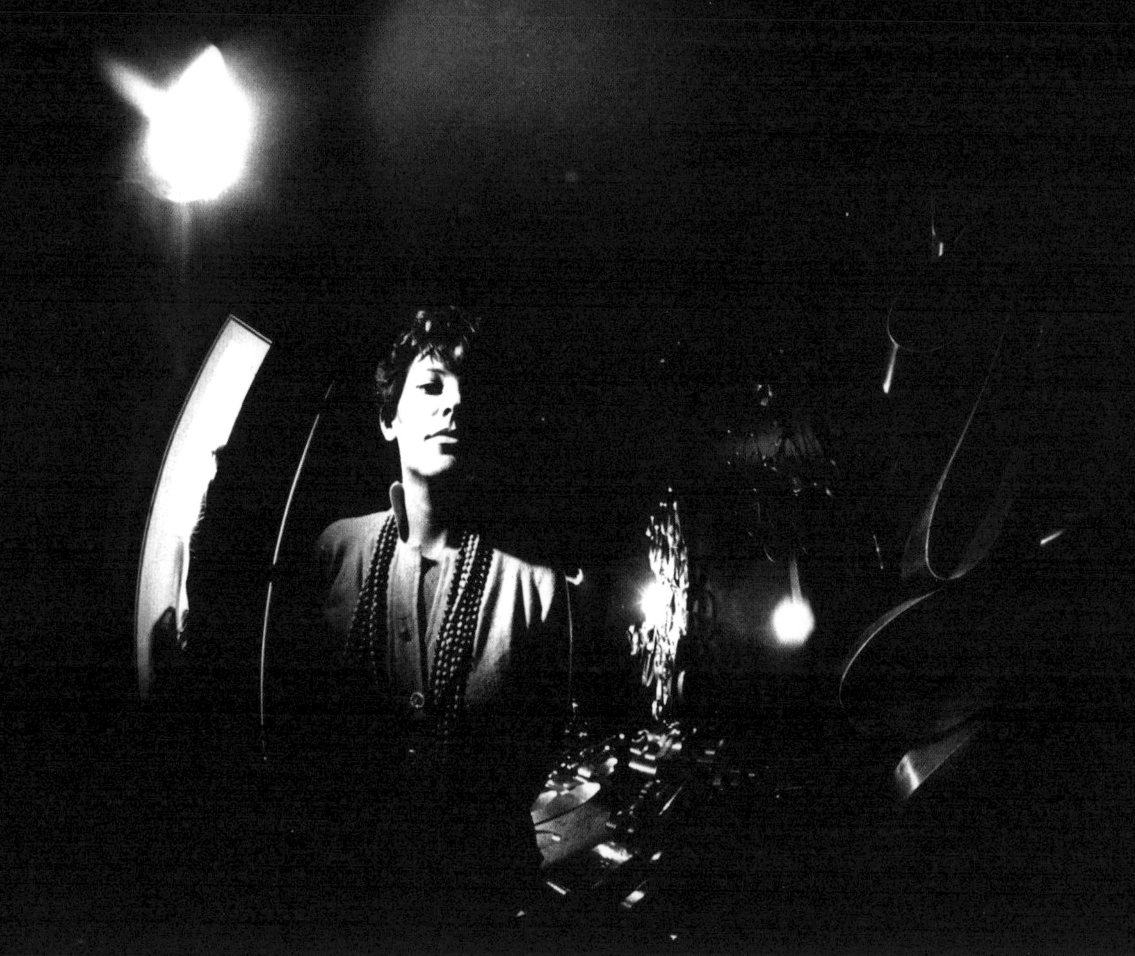

themselves and complicated the scene, adding to the absurd spectacle. It was not just the media of *Las camas* that was astonishing: for women artists to make such blatant references to sex, in all its physical exuberance and awkwardness, was revolutionary.[43]

This collaboration between Bursztyn and Nova was a perfect meeting of creative minds, as both women audaciously pushed the boundaries of their fields through their explorations of new means of expression and use of materials from the world of modern machines. Both women challenged gender roles in the process, since they literally entered spaces normally occupied by men (junkyards and industrial workshops and the CLAEM) and took up "male" practices (welding and musical composition and sound engineering). Artist Álvaro Barrios, Bursztyn's friend, noted that her work as a radically experimental artist was made even more difficult by being "in a society in which art made by women is more related to painting on porcelain than to autogenous welding",[44] and, similarly, musical historian Ana María Romano observed of Nova:

"her determination to be a composer went against class norms, because it conflicted with the 'good manners' of old-fashioned bourgeois guidelines in which, by tradition, the female incursion into the world of music was confined to the judicious interpretation of the piano".[45] Bursztyn and Nova considered their collaboration so successful that they immediately began to work on a new joint project, a mechanical ballet, which Bursztyn realized in 1979 as *La baila mecánica* (The Mechanical Ballet). Sadly, Nova died of cancer in 1975 at just forty years old. Without Nova, Bursztyn used very different music, a twelfth-century chant, not wanting to work with any other modern musician.[46]

Through bold endeavours such as these, Bursztyn and other extraordinary women in Colombian art worked against the kind of cultural and social conditioning that historically kept women subordinated to men. The fight for equality was hampered, as Bursztyn recognized, by psychological inhibitions; therefore, the work of these women must have had a profound impact on other women as examples of what was possible. Bursztyn, Traba, Daza, and Nova were not the only women working at this time who shaped Colombian art, but they are outstanding as examples of women who insisted on their own judgement, took the lead in action, developed their own means of expression despite strong social resistance, and decisively rejected socially designated roles to challenge "masculine" and "feminine" categories and make them less important in the realm of art. The fight for women's equality continues, and progress has been made, but not enough. Remembering these achievements, and how women *together* accomplished them, can inspire continued solidarity and work.

1 Margarita Vidal, "Feliza Bursztyn",
Vanidades, 21 August 1973, cited in Camilo
Leyva, Manuela Ochoa, and Juan Carlos
Osorio, *Feliza Bursztyn: Elogio de la chatarra*
(Bogotá: Museo Nacional de Colombia, 2009),
97. Unless otherwise noted, all translations
from the Spanish are the author's.
2 The man was Jorge Gaitán Durán, a famous
poet. They were lovers until he died in a plane
crash in 1962.
3 Divorce was only legalized in Colombia in
1991.
4 Vidal, "Feliza Bursztyn".
5 See lists in Camilo Calderón Schrader,
50 años Salón Nacional de Artistas (Bogotá:
Colcultura, 1990). Percentages of women artists
have improved, and some of the most famous
contemporary Colombian artists (like Doris
Salcedo) are women, but still there are more
men than women in the art world, in Colombia
as elsewhere.
6 Bursztyn's friend Beatriz Daza, for example,
earned her art degree from Universidad
Javeriana, a Jesuit institution, where an Art
& Decoration degree was offered just for
women. Julian Serna, "Si las paredes hablaran",
in Fundación Gilberto Alzate Avendaño, ed.,
Beatriz Daza: Hace mucho tiempo 1956–1968
(Bogotá: Alcaldía Mayor de Bogotá D.C.,
2008), 23.
7 Casimiro Eiger, "Salón de pintoras" (1959), in
Fundación Gilberto Alzate Avendaño, *Beatriz
Daza*, 180.
8 Ana María Reyes, *The Politics of Taste: Beatriz
González and Cold War Aesthetics* (Durham,
NC: Duke University Press, 2019), 62–63.
Beatriz González, along with Bursztyn, stands
out as the most important artist to emerge in
the 1960s.
9 The gallery showed Bursztyn's *Minimáquinas*
for the first time in 1969 and hosted solo
exhibitions of her work in 1972, 1974, and 1977.
10 Bursztyn helped Traba organize the museum;
they were among the 85 who signed the
museum's 1962 Act of Constitution (see Leyva,
Ochoa, and Osorio, *Feliza Bursztyn*, 78). Traba
directed the museum from 1962 to 1967, and
continued to run it as president of its board of
directors until June 1969.
11 One art historian maintains, "[T]he conflict
of interests that this practice represented was
not perceived as such in these days, perhaps for
the unusual critical spirit with which she wrote
her own reviews". Florencia Bazzano-Nelson,
"Cambios de margen: Las teorías estéticas de
Marta Traba", in *Dos décadas vulnerables en
las artes plásticas latinoamericanas, 1950–1970*
(Buenos Aires: Siglo Ventiuno Editores, 2005), 15.
12 This point is made in Nadia Moreno Moya,
*Arte y juventud: El Salón Esso de Artistas
Jóvenes en Colombia* (Bogotá: Instituto
Distrital de las Artes, 2013), 128.
13 Marta Traba, "El primer salón de artistas
jóvenes un éxito", *La Nueva Prensa*, no. 122
(1 September 1964): 60.

14 That Traba did not praise Bursztyn's
Chatarras when first exhibited in 1961 or when
included in the 1962 National Salon suggests
that Bursztyn earned Traba's subsequent
support through her work.
15 Marta Traba, "La Batalla No. 17", *La Nueva
Prensa*, no. 138 (25 September 1965), cited in
Calderón Schrader, *50 años*, 135–36. On the
controversy surrounding the monument, see
Héctor Muñoz, "El monumento a López es
un horror", *El Espectador*, 16 June 1967, and
Gina McDaniel Tarver, *The New Iconoclasts:
From Art of a New Reality to Conceptual Art
in Colombia, 1961–1975* (Bogotá: Ediciones
Universidad de los Andes, 2016), 57–63.
16 Hernando Valencia Goelkel, *Bursztyn*,
exhibition brochure, Museo de Arte Moderno
de Bogotá, 1974, Archives of the Museo de Arte
Moderno de Bogotá.
17 Elisa Mujica, "Una exposición de cerámica",
El Tiempo, 6 September 1959, cited in
Fundación Gilberto Alzate Avendaño, *Beatriz
Daza*, 74.
18 Walter Engel, "Beatriz Daza", *El Espectador*,
3 September 1961, cited in Fundación Gilberto
Alzate Avendaño, *Beatriz Daza*, 67.
19 "On sculpture there were heated
controversies. It was not acceptable to give an
award for a work made of tinplate, some said. It
was not tolerable to give an award for ceramics
as sculpture, others said." Walter Engel, "XII
Salón de Artistas Colombianos", *Plástica*, no.
15 (1959), cited in Fundación Gilberto Alzate
Avendaño, *Beatriz Daza*, 191. The critique of
tinplate applied to Alicia Tafur's work, but it
foreshadows how Bursztyn's media would be
questioned.
20 See for example Jorge Moreno Clavijo,
"Cerámicas de Beatriz Daza", *El Tiempo*,
September 1961, cited in Fundación Gilberto
Alzate Avendaño, *Beatriz Daza*, 224.
21 She won a second-place sculpture award
for a figurative work in 1959 and took a new
ceramics prize (probably added due to her
work) in 1962 and 1963.
22 On Bursztyn's art and Nouveau réalisme,
see Tarver, *The New Iconoclasts*, especially
chapter 1.
23 Tarver, *The New Iconoclasts*, 13–14.
24 Serna, "Si las paredes hablaran", 25–26.
25 Daza, like Bursztyn, transgressed socially as
well as artistically: both lived, for a time, with
men to whom they were not married, a bold
choice in their strictly Catholic country.
26 Bursztyn embraced "madness" as a strategy:
Maritza Uribe de Urdinola, "En un país de
machistas, ¡hágase la loca!", *El Tiempo: Revista
Carrusel* (Bogotá), 30 November 1979: 15.
27 Daza, exhibition brochure, Museo de Arte
Moderno de Bogotá, 1968, cited in Fundación
Gilberto Alzate Avendaño, *Beatriz Daza*,
233–34.
28 Gina McDaniel Tarver, "Antagonistic
Environments: Gendered Spaces in the Kinetic
Installations of Colombian Artists Feliza

Bursztyn, Jacqueline Nova, and Julia Acuña", in *New Geographies of Abstract Art in Postwar Latin America*, edited by Mariola V. Álvarez and Ana M. Franco (New York: Routledge, 2019), 208–24.

[29] "I deduce that [Bursztyn] has some connection to a mechanic's workshop." Walter Engel, "Felisa Brustyn [*sic*] y Gloria Daza", *El Espectador*, 2 September 1961. The association was raised by others, too.

[30] Betha Beatrix de Fernández de Soto, "Esculturas con sonido exhibe Feliza Bursztyn", *El Tiempo*, 29 February 1968.

[31] Marta Traba, *Histéricas*, exhibition brochure, Museo de Arte Moderno de Bogotá, 1968, Archives of the Museo de Arte Moderno de Bogotá.

[32] Manuela Ochoa, "Movimiento", in Leyva, Ochoa, and Osorio, *Feliza Bursztyn*, 18.

[33] Carlos Barreiro Ortiz, "Jacqueline Nova, la nueva música", *Lámpara* 24, no. 100 (1986): 39–40.

[34] Jacqueline Nova, "El mundo maravilloso de las máquinas", *Nova*, no. 4 (July–August 1966), cited in Carlos Barreiro Ortíz, *A Propoito de Jacqueline Nova* (Bogotá: Centro Colombo Americano, 1983), 17.

[35] Not much documentation of the work exists, aside from *Luz, sonido, movimiento*, exhibition brochure, Museo de Arte Moderno, March 1969, Archive of the Museo de Arte de la Universidad Nacional, Bogotá. My description comes from Gloria Valencia Diago, "'Luz, sonido y movimiento', en el Museo de Arte Moderno", *El Tiempo*, 20 March 1969.

[36] R. Ramírez Heredia, "Feliza Bursztyn, habla de camas y otras cosas", *Lecturas Dominicales*, 24 August 1975.

[37] Cited in Ramírez Heredia, "Feliza Bursztyn".

[38] Heredia, "Feliza Bursztyn".

[39] Miguel González, "Análisis de la obra de Feliza Burstyn [*sic*]", *El País*, 25 September 1974.

[40] Marta Traba, *Camas*, exhibition brochure, Museo de Arte Moderno La Tertulia, Cali, 1974.

[41] González, "Análisis de la obra".

[42] Juan Carlos Osorio, "Espacio", in Leyva, Ochoa, and Osorio, *Feliza Bursztyn*, 21.

[43] On the taboo against women's sexuality in Colombia, see Reyes, *The Politics of Taste*, 78.

[44] Álvaro Barrios, *Orígenes del arte conceptual en Colombia* (Bogotá: Alcaldía Mayor de Bogotá, D.C., 1999), 64.

[45] Ana María Romano, "Jacqueline Nova y el maravilloso mundo del ruido", *Revista Arcadia*, 19 July 2013, www.revistaarcadia.com/impresa/ especial-chicas-afuera/articulo/jacqueline-nova-maravilloso-mundo-del-ruido/32439.

[46] Pilar Tafur, "Feliza Bursztyn puso a bailar sus esculturas", *Nueva Frontera*, 16–22 April 1979.

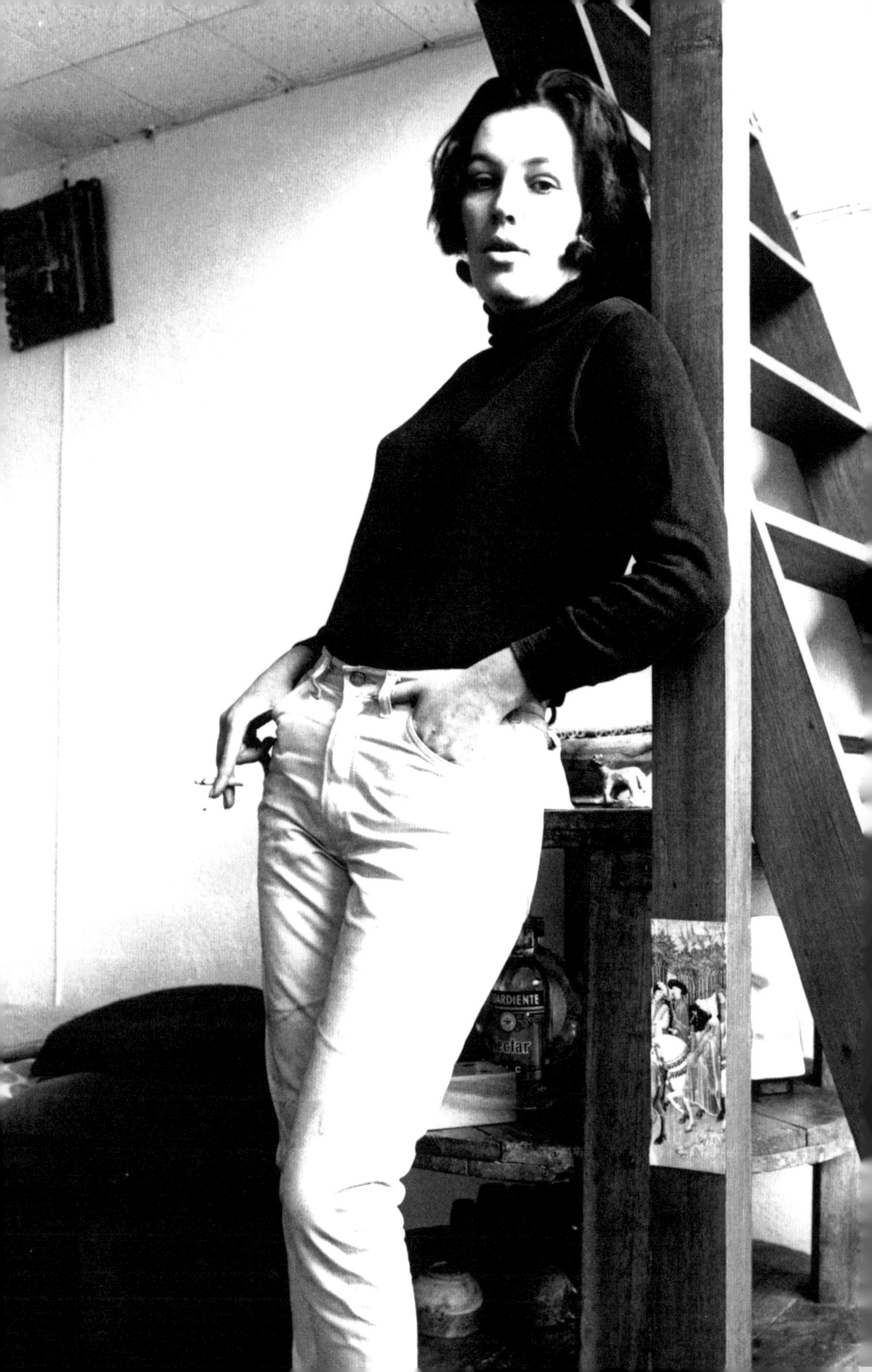

The Gendered Political Embodiment of Feliza Bursztyn's Work

Cecilia Fajardo-Hill

> I believe my work currently belongs to what we might call "Motorized Romanticism".
>
> Feliza Bursztyn[1]

Feliza Bursztyn declared herself as openly left-wing and also a feminist, and this should be understood as central to her work and life, though neither literally nor as reflecting an institutionalized view of these terms. While in most interviews she played down and avoided explaining the meaning and possible context of her work, when asked about her political views, she stated her deep interest in politics and also pointed out that her work may be interpreted in social and political terms.[2] Because we are not used to thinking of abstraction – the language that posthumously dominated the interpretation of her work – as rooted in a rich dialogue with existence, and we tend to separate her more objectual base work from the abstract, it is easy to minimize how political and meaningful Bursztyn's work is in embodying a profound and liberating relationality between life and art, as well as a critical positionality both in regards to political and gender regimes of existence.

Throughout her existence, Feliza Bursztyn did not conform either to social norms – always living an unconventional life – or to canonical principles about art, good taste, traditional tenets about sculpture, the role of the spectator, materiality, craftsmanship, etc. Bursztyn was so free that, as an artist, she was not bogged down by the harsh criticism of art critics and the press; as a woman, she was not circumscribed by the traditional roles of mother and wife; and in her political views, she was left-wing but didn't become entangled with the dominant Colombian Maoist and Trotskyist faction's outlook on politics that also saw feminism as an imported ideology which was both bourgeoise and imperialistic. Fellow artist Clemencia Lucena

1. Feliza Bursztyn in her home, Bogotá
Courtesy of the Archive of Pablo Leyva.
Photo: Rafael Moure

(Bogotá, 1945 – Cali, 1983), for example, transformed her early unconventional, incisive, and satirical work criticizing social standards and women in high society into a didactic pro-Maoist art, which subsumed women to a second plane. Bursztyn was both political and a feminist, in ways that transcended Colombia. If anything, she looked towards Cuba as a model of societal freedom and equality. In fact, the Cuban constitution contemplated that women had the same opportunities as men, and many of them participated actively at every level of society. However, it is important to recognize that what she understood by political and feminist is not defined by convention, and it certainly did not come across in any way possible as a narrative or obvious commentary. Her work and her persona were simultaneously hermetic – as she did not feel compelled to explain or justify anything – and absolutely open, in that she had a profound commitment to life and art and was intent in communicating on a personal level with her many friends and through her work.

On separate occasions, when asked if she was a feminist, she responded affirmatively, but the explanation given was of very different nature. She once replied: "Yes, of course, I love men".[3] A year later, in 1973, she stated that she was a "feminist and a violent liberationist" because of what she saw as the political and social differences between women and men, and the fact that women were not allowed to do whatever they pleased in peace. According to Bursztyn, women were born and raised within a series of taboos that limited their opportunities, and for this reason it was necessary to fight for equality. She did not think that this was achieved by going against men, and stressed that the problem was social, cultural, and political, not sexual.[4] Her assertion not to make men the enemy, and that the problem was not sexual, is clearly reflected in her work, coming across in the erotic undercurrent of series such as *Las histéricas* (The Hysterical Ones, 1967–69) and *Las camas* (The Beds, 1972–74). Her responses bring to mind fellow performance artist María Evelia Marmolejo (Pradera, 1958), who attempted to affiliate herself to a feminist organization in Cali in the early 1980s, but was asked to go against men. She refused to do so, claiming that she loved men and loved making love with them.[5] The issue for artists such as Bursztyn and Marmolejo is that feminism meant to fight against a patriarchal society without going against their personal freedom. Bursztyn was born into a traditional Jewish family and suffered a great deal when she divorced against her family's will and was separated from her children, but she maintained her right to freedom of existence. She had to fight to be a woman artist in a context that was not favourable to an unconventional artist like her.[6] When asked if she was not afraid of being seen as a madwoman, instead of an experimenter of new artistic languages, she responded: "I took advantage of the whole 'madness' thing, and played it up, so that I could really do what I wanted. Because I do believe that we're living in a male chauvinist world. And to be a sculptor and not be a man is very difficult. I resorted to this trick so that people would take me seriously, because they thought, 'maybe that crazy woman does interesting things'. And I think it worked".[7]

Between the 1960s and 1980s Bursztyn was not alone in maintaining a leftist position while fighting for her rights as a woman and an artist, as contemporary women artists throughout Latin America were either affiliated, sympathized, or were militant leftists while struggling for their role as women without being openly feminist.[8] What is unique about Bursztyn's art during this period is the aesthetic language and specific form of "conceptualism" of her work, ranging from abstraction to object-based sculpture and complex environments, that involved both a gendered and political positionality. I understand here conceptualism not as a cartesian notion based on the "dematerialization" of the object and art, but to describe a work that is embodied, gendered, performative, critical, experimental, while concerned with societal and political realities, even when these were not articulated as or reducible to discourse.

In this essay I am concerned with a group of works that involve forms of embodiment of aspects such as hysteria, sexuality, and the existential condition of human beings in society. As we read in an earlier quotation, Bursztyn engaged with the "strategy" of being crazy in order to exercise her artistic freedom, and she was renowned for her sense of humour and wit, as well as a refusal to easy explanations, which often irritated interviewers. This sense of humour, often dark, percolated in her series *Las histéricas*, *Las camas*, and *La baila mecánica* (The Mechanical Ballet, 1979), both in the conceptualization and materialization of the work's specific aesthetic qualities, and for the ways her art performed disobedient and perplexing actions through motor-generated movement. To this we need to add her staging of the works with dramatic lighting, sound, and dark backgrounds as in a theatre, which propitiated strong reactions in the spectator who could not help but laugh, scream, feel surprised, shocked, challenged, annoyed, or inspired. I would like to think of Bursztyn's sense of humour, personal and artistic (fig. 2), in terms of Mikhail Bakhtin's idea of the "culture of popular laughter" and the "carnivalesque", which is not merely celebratory, but subversive of

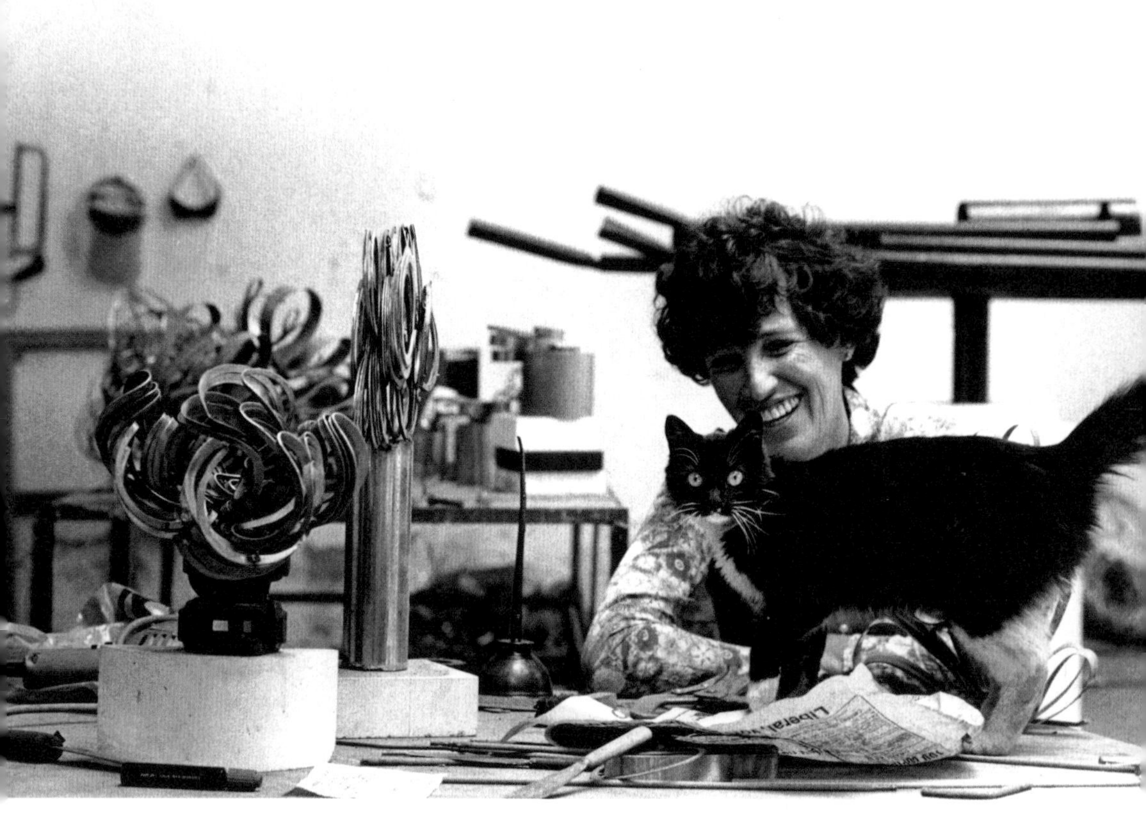

2. Feliza Bursztyn in her studio in Bogotá, c. 1980 Courtesy of the Archive of Pablo Leyva. Photo: Rafael Moure

dogmatism and social norms, and propitiates the release of stress and constraints within a given social order, in this case Colombian traditional society.⁹ Furthermore, the carnivalesque presupposes that the division between spectator and artist, and the officialism of the institution, is erased through a collective experience which is both eccentric and liberatory. By no means am I implying that the artist's work was understood or accepted in her own time, but rather that her provocations and the challenging nature of her art was independent from its reception, and that it was radical and inclusive. I refer to Bakhtin's notion of the "culture of popular laughter" also in relation to Bursztyn's socialist ideas, where the popular emerges as a cultural and social force, and where the spectator is given freedom, and a possibility of emancipation, as opposed to the conformism of an elitist traditional role of art.

Gina McDaniel Tarver argues that Bursztyn's widespread practice of recycling and using scrap materials followed a popular tactic for making do in a poor country such as Colombia, and that her reusing materials was also a way to celebrate the creativity of poor people, and therefore of the proletariat, as opposed to promote the country's elite desired progressive modernity. Tarver goes on to explain that the artist was proud that her working methods were proletarian and quotes Bursztyn affirming that she was "a worker and a solderer", as the definition of herself as an artist.[10]

Even though the *Las histéricas* series was mostly not made with recycled metal scrap, the works were produced from stainless steel and motor. These were motorized kinetic sculptures, in which the different components moved and made non-harmonious and clattery metal scraping noises when their engines were activated. As Tarver points out, the steel in *Las histéricas* had connections to industries, and because they left the work's motor visible, they emphasized a relationship to the world of machines more than aesthetics, thus activating a dialogue between her art and the working-class world. What is most remarkable, is the way that Bursztyn collapses the relationship with mechanics, the industrial, craft, the working class, and art, with the idea of mental and emotional excess associated to hysteria, a term popularly used to describe the over-emotionality and excitability of women. This confluence is one of the key proofs of the artist's independence and non-cooperation with the modernist progressive agenda of Colombia. Firstly, we do not associate modernity and progress to women, and secondly, we certainly do not relate it to the complex, unruly, and unpredictable nature of the female mind, in this case Bursztyn's.

When associating the unruly movement of the metal sculptures to the title *hysterical*, their abstractedness becomes disturbing: not only does it concern the spectator on a personal level, but it also reminds them of the fragility and irrational nature of modernity. Any spectator would relate to the pejorative term "hysterical", then and now, as it embodies the often uncontrollable, sometimes absurd nature of our mind and emotions. I trust that, for these reasons, the public often felt attacked by the unrestrained expressiveness of these sculptures. In this sense, the artist aptly and absurdly described her work as "Motorized Romanticism".[11] The romanticism of her project has nothing to do with the traditional or academic notion of the romantic, but with the celebration and embodiment of sensuality, freedom, and vitality without the repressive demands of rationality, perfection, modernity, and the control over the feminine.

In 1968, the artist staged a theatrical environment of twelve *Las histéricas* at the Museo de Arte Moderno de Bogotá (MAMBO), for the seminal group exhibition *Espacios ambientales* (Environments). The title of her installation was the suggestive *Siempre acostada* (Always in Bed), and for it she painted the space black and installed the sculptures on the floor, wall, and ceiling and lit them with spotlights that came on and off intermittently. The noise of the activated pieces overflew the space beyond their material presence. The ambiance has been described as multisensorial, with sexual connotations that recalled the bedroom. The sensuality embodied by the installation was highlighted by the simultaneous agitation of multiple sculptures, suggesting lack of control, and a collective overflowing of life, a sort of unrestrained orgy of the senses. More overtly erotic were her series *Las camas*, that she exhibited as an installation of thirteen beds at the MAMBO in 1974. *Las camas* were assemblages made with stainless steel scrap, cots, coloured satin sheet, and motors, and as in the case of *Las histéricas*, they were also staged in a dramatic setting of contrasted darkness and spotlights, and accompanied by an original score created for the occasion by experimental composer Jacqueline Nova (Ghent, 1935 – Bogotá, 1975). Large anthropomorphic sculptures, the satin was draped over volumes that suggested the presence of human beings lying on them, moving and shaking as if they were making love. The spectators were cast in a voyeuristic role, and while nothing was truly happening, everything insinuated a grand act of sensual celebration.

Marta Traba, who organized the exhibition and was a close friend and defender of Bursztyn's work, described it as "a liberating experience [that] could well illustrate the great theme of our century: eros and civilization".[12] Traba was clearly influenced by Herbert Marcuse's book *Eros and Civilization: A Philosophical Inquiry into Freud* (1955), which conflated Karl Marx and Sigmund Freud's ideas, as the basis for a non-repressive society, and thus she saw in Bursztyn's exhibition a grand liberatory proposal. The artist had two copies in her library – Spanish and English versions – and it is likely that her *Las camas* were influenced by Marcuse. Furthermore, it is plausible that, given the closeness between Traba and Bursztyn, they discussed this influential book. At this point this is only a conjecture, but it is not a far-fetched presupposition that Marcuse may have been in Bursztyn's mind when making *Las camas*, and that this installation materializes the centrality of sexuality both in life and culture by presenting the beds as a staged performative, immersive, and unescapable experience that overwhelmed the spectator to challenge their societal taboos. The centrality of sexuality to human freedom embodied in *Las camas* recalls the early notion by Teresinha Soares (Araxá, 1927) (fig. 3) that "free sexual exercise demands social and political freedom", which was in part informed by Marcuse.[13] Cecilia Vicuña (Santiago de Chile, 1948) also upheld that sexual pleasure and the erotic should be central to Salvador Allende's political revolution (1970–73).

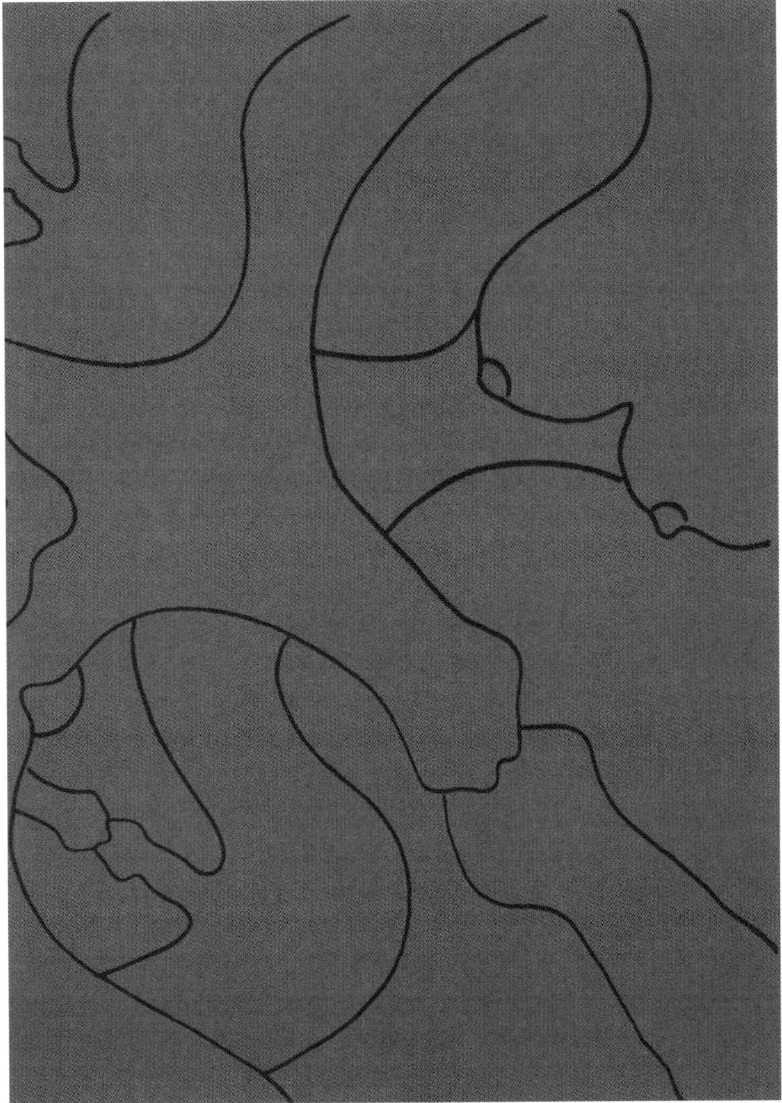

In an interview about *Las camas*, Bursztyn declared, making fun of the interviewer, that the role of the pieces was didactic and cultural.[14] To another author she jokingly affirmed that her favourite hobby was the bed, and when asked what her suggested solution to the problems of the country was, she replied: "My beds".[15] Miguel González interprets *Las camas* for their critical content, not solely for their overt eroticism in an installation that was reminiscent of a great brothel, but for the beds covers in bishop purple, yellow, blue, and red (the colours of the Colombian flag), and neutral mauve colour that he saw as "The State, the church, and the people". He highlights the interest of this work in a Latin American context by "presenting and proposing humour, eroticism, mysticism, and

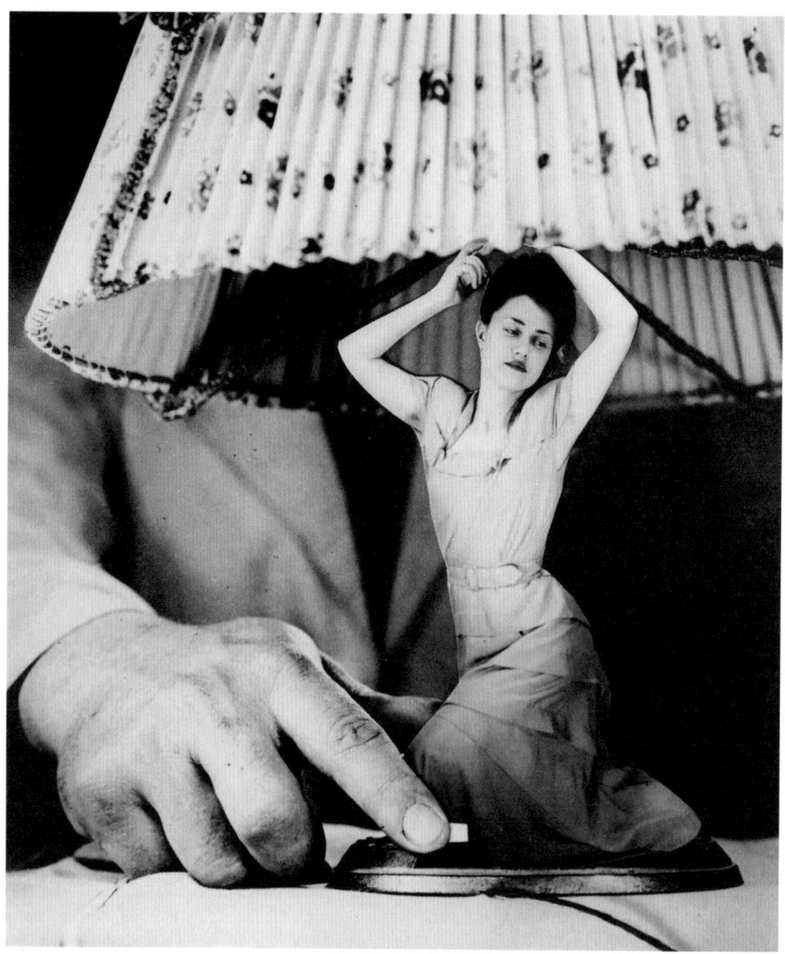

4. Grete Stern, *Articulos eléctricos para el hogar* (Home Appliances), 1949 © The Estate of Grete Stern, Courtesy Galería Jorge Mara – La Ruche

criticism – at the same time".[16] Gonzalez's interpretation is interesting because it adds a direct political dimension to the work that hasn't been emphasized but was most likely intentional – although Bursztyn would not explicitly admit to it. This points further to the multidimensionality of her art. The Colombian critic Eduardo Serrano points out that these works comment on one of the biggest taboos: sex, and consequently Bursztyn acknowledges the social role of contemporary art, providing a new consciousness about life and art.[17] This last comment is important because Serrano reads a social and visionary dimension into the artist's work, which is exactly why it was rejected: its reference to sexuality and its experimentalism.

It is interesting to relate Bursztyn's work to other women artists of a close generation that promoted the freedom of women, the body, the sensorial, and sexuality within artistic experimentalism. Many artists could be discussed in relation to this subject, but I will limit myself to mention only a few given the length of this essay, also to emphasize forms of embodiment that may be understood as abstracted.[18] Exceptionally, I would like to mention pioneer photographer Grete Stern (Elberfeld, 1904 – Buenos Aires, 1999), who realized her series of photomontages *Sueños* (Dreams, 1948–51) to go with a column titled *El psicoanálisis le ayudará* (Psychoanalysis Will Help You) for the Argentinean women's magazine *Idilio*. In works such as *Artículos eléctricos para el hogar* (Electrical Items for the Home, c. 1949) (fig. 4), Stern creates "dreams" – the object of study in psychoanalysis – to touch on the objectification and domestication of women through the surreal superposition of consumerist domestic items and the female figure. These pieces create an interesting dialogue with Bursztyn's appropriation of domestic and common objects in her work, as in *Las camas*, to transgress them and surface what is repressed. For example, her mural *La última cena* (The Last Supper, 1976) at SENA (Servicio Nacional de Aprendizaje) (fig. 5), a building in the centre of Bogotá, was made with twelve thousand pieces of pressed silverware that were adhered to square panels of steel. This strikingly beautiful mural both highlighted and paid homage to silverware, a central object in daily life, while making them unserviceable.

The *Bichos* (Critters or Creatures, 1960s) by Lygia Clark (Belo Horizonte, 1920 – Rio de Janeiro 1988) (fig. 6) are abstract hinged metal sculptures that are activated by the manipulation of the viewer. Though these works do not possess the same erotic references as Bursztyn's work, they

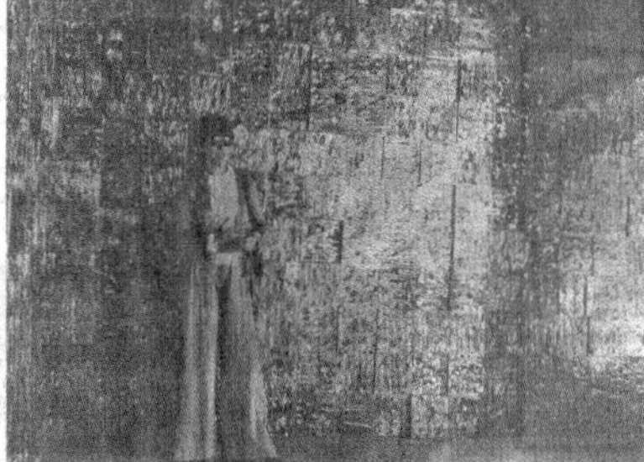

LUNES 16 DE AGOSTO DE 1976   ● EL TIEMPO ● -   3-B

De Felisa Burztin

Mural con 12 mil cubiertos

El otro día Feliza Burztin nos llevó a ver su "mural" del SENA. El SENA, nos explicó a tiempo que nosotros (el fotógrafo Angel y yo) nos metíamos en su diminuta Wartburg amarilla, le comisionó la decoración de un muro en su nuevo centro hotelero de la 30 con 14, y ella, por supuesto, se había puesto soplete a la obra, y había soldado un mural de seis metros por tres. Había aceptado el reto con alegría, puesto que ahora se dedica cada vez más a hacer obras de grandes proporciones, esculturas aptas para que sean alabadas, vilipendiadas (cosa que a menudo sucede con las obras de Feliza), escupidas, golpeadas (¡ojo, que son de metal y generalmente tienen puntas y filos!), o, cosa rara, disfrutadas.

Mientras la Wartburg, evidentemente enguayabada, se abría paso con dificultad entre buses, camiones y carros, nosotros pensábamos en el género de sorpresa que nos deparaba nuestra chatarrista favorita. Feliza siempre nos ha sorprendido. Lo que no quiere decir que su obra carezca de unidad ó de sentido. Feliza siempre ha sido una original, desde cuando empezó a soldar sus erizadas flores de chatarra, cuando la mayor parte de los escultores colombianos se dedicaban a un escuálido realismo o a una gélida construcción geométrica. Desde entonces sus obras, incluidas sus histéricas y sus camas, hechas con el optimista propósito de interrumpir el monótono letargo de nuestras artes plásticas, han tenido una originalidad difícil de encontrar en cualquier parte.

La invención

La invención es una necesidad en todo artista. Y Feliza tiene esta facultad en abundancia. Casi que ha agotado las posibilidades plásticas de las más heterogéneas muestras del detrito metálico de nuestra sociedad. Con paciencia (Feliza es una gran trabajadora), ha soldado infinidad de tuercas, anillos, arandelas, bielas, cadenas, manivelas, piñones, válvulas, resortes, virutas de acero, láminas inservibles, rotas, oxidadas y ha hecho con todo esto poéticas esculturas que, a veces (la soldadura no es eterna, pero nada lo es), se deshojan c o m o árboles en el otoño...

En esto, a Dios gracias, habíamos llegado a la moderna y amplia instalación del SENA. Entramos por la amplia cocina y subimos al hall (todo el edificio está construido como un hotel). Al fondo vimos una pared que reverberaba como el papel plateado de un Pielroja (dijo el fotógrafo). Pero al acercarnos aquella iba descomponiendo en mil fragmentos nuestras siluetas y el gran tapete rojo que adorna el vestíbulo. Una gran mancha de un rojo más pálido se concentraba al lado derecho de la pared y mil destellos rojos aparecían sobre... ¡ah, esa era la sorpresa!, miles de cuchillos, tenedores, cucharas, cucharitas y utensilios de cocina, de acero inoxidable. Feliza había soldado, la cosa le llevó seis meses, cerca de doce mil cubiertos. Los había apachurrado en distintas disposiciones, sobre doscientos y pico de paneles de reluciente acero, que luego había empotrado en la pared a distintas alturas, formando así un luminoso relieve metálico.

Girasoles

Y mientras el fotógrafo trataba (le llevó tiempos y un teleobjetivo) de captar el detalle de los utensilios, nosotros pudimos ver a nuestras anchas el hermoso muro. Los cucharones parecen girasoles. Los paneles hundidos se reflejan en los que sobresalen, creando una ilusión de transparencia. Y el todo posee una extraña opacidad (debida a la multitud de planos recortados), pues to que no refleja sino los colores. De cerca también se pueden ver los puntos de la soldadura que Feliza nunca trata de esconder, para que quede huella visible de sus manos, y además, la firma, excéntrica como ella, diagonal y ascendente y, claro, soldada.

El mural de Feliza era, en suma, una felicísima decoración a la altura de obras suyas más libres, más caprichosas. Cada cosa, en fin, tiene su lugar. Y nadie mejor que un artista para saberlo.

Satisfechos, colmados con la sorpresa y con un enorme apetito (¿algo qué ver con la obra?), nos metimos, como pudimos, otra vez en la Wartburg, y la interrogamos.

Bueno, primero la chatarra, luego el movimiento, después el **shock,** ahora los cubiertos y mañana, ¿qué?

Ah!, que ya veríamos, nos dijo, y admitió con una risa alegre, tener una que pesa cuatro toneladas... y otra que combina todo lo que acabábamos de mencionar: el metal, el movimiento, la irreverencia y además, otra cosa: el espectáculo. ¡Un ballet!

¿¿Un ballet? No creímos haber oído bien. Pero sí. Una de las próximas sorpresas, afortunadamente inagotables, de Feliza, es ni más ni menos que un ballet. ¿Un ballet por una escultora? Bueno, pues iremos a verlo, aunque no nos guste el ballet y aunque sea en Wartburg. Porque este va a ser diferente, va a ser otra sorpresa de Feliza!

Nicolás Suescún

Mural "La Ultima Cena", realizado por Felisa Burztin. (Foto del Archivo.)

5. Feliza Bursztyn, *La última cena* (The Last Supper), 1976, published in *El Tiempo* (Bogotá), August 1976 Courtesy of the Archive of Pablo Leyva

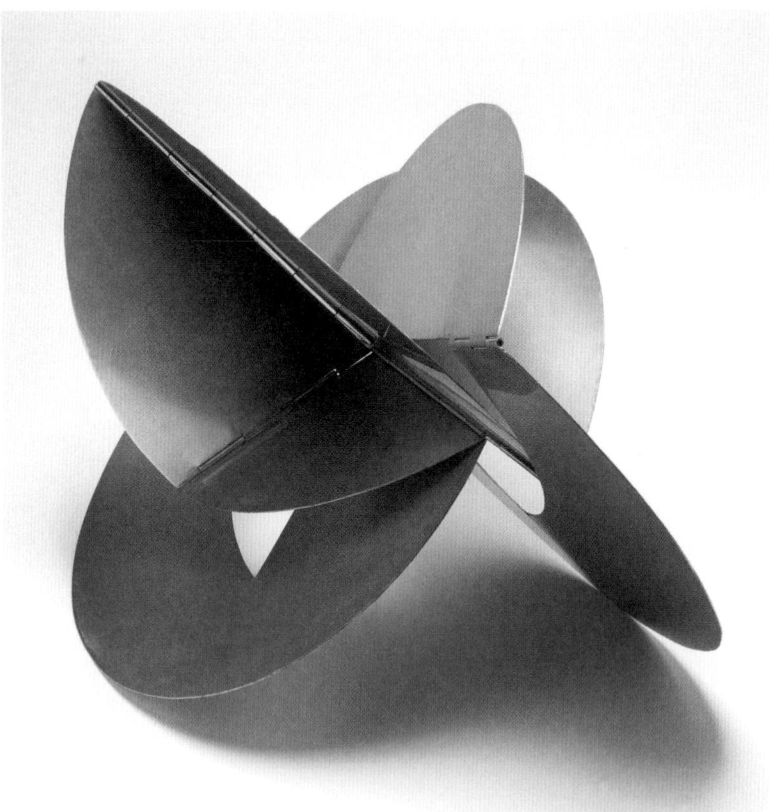

are conceived as "living" forms that exist relationally between abstraction and the performative, and between their creator and the viewer who manipulates them, while embodying the idea of an unstable and changeable living creature. The animation of matter and form, and the active role of the spectator, bring Clark and Bursztyn closer together.

As Bursztyn refers to hysteria in *Las histéricas*, a big topic in psychoanalysis, it is meaningful to refer to the *Mapas mentais* (Mental Maps, 1971–76) by Anna Maria Maiolino (Scalea, Italy, 1942) (fig. 7), a series which charted the complex nature of her mind and memory, in random arrangements of language and sometimes colour within grids. These works question logical genealogies, psychoanalysis, and oppositional divisions both within the picture plane and in relation to her own life, thus escaping an easy definition of the mind, in the same way that Bursztyn's *Las histéricas* escape the control of hers and the spectator's.

In dialogue with Bursztyn's embodied spatial interventions is Marta Palau's (Albesa, Spain, 1934) *llerda* series from 1973, composed of large-scale abstract sculpture installations made with woven Spanish jute. These

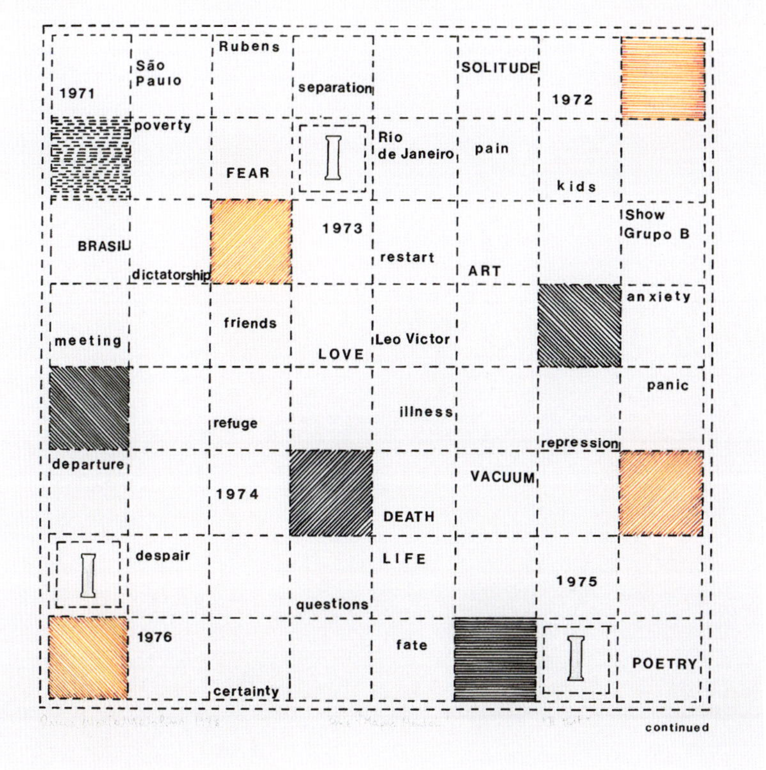

pieces transform and embody space with their monumentality and disobedient feminine forms, suggestive of gigantic vaginas. As in the case of
Bursztyn, these sculptures' relationship to the architecture transforms the
space into a feminine one.

There is something not only intimate but eschatological about Bursztyn's suggestive hysterical sexuality, although the body per se is absent
from her works, and it is only made present by the spectator who reacts,
willingly or unwillingly, to them. In the case of Nuyorican artist Sophie
Rivera (New York, 1938–2021) for her series of colour photographs
Rouge et noir (Red and Black, 1977–78), she photographed close-ups of
the toilet bowl with bloodied tampons. When seen from afar, the works
appear to be abstract oval forms suffused in a soft reddish pink. It is only
when you come up close that you realize what they actually represent.
Usually, the public is disgruntled and even ashamed by these images. A
reaction not at all dissimilar to the one that audiences and critics alike
experienced when looking at Bursztyn's work, although, in both cases,
they were simply confronted with something commonplace that involves
all humans, their sexuality, and bodily functions.

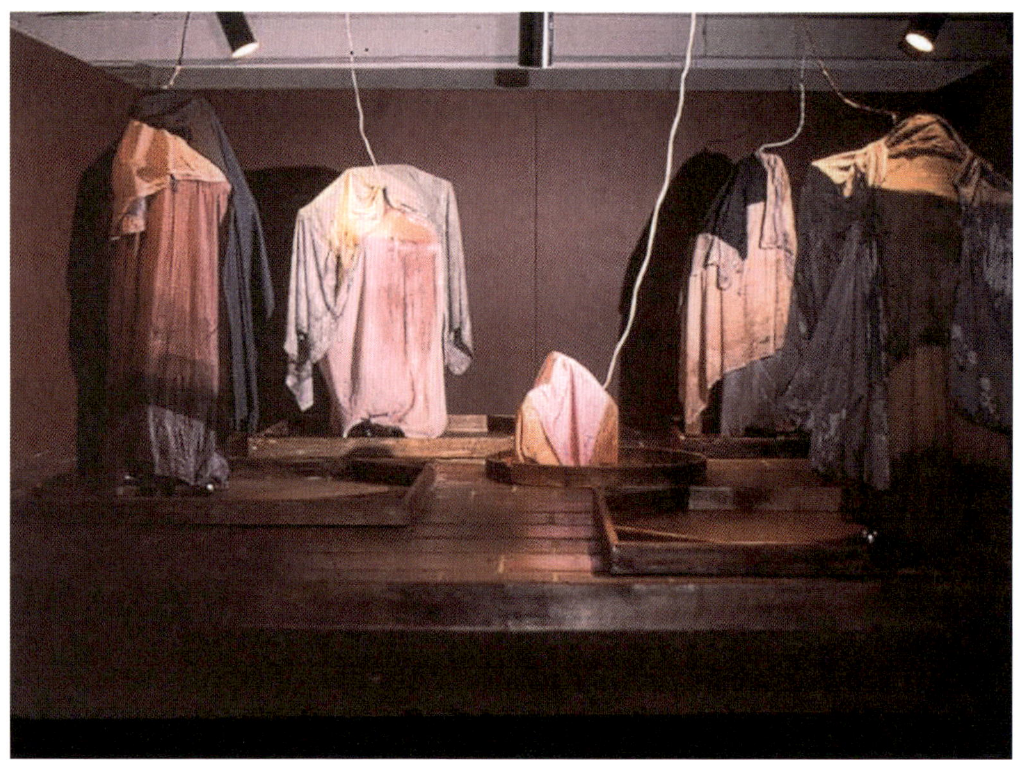

The final work I want to mention here is the series *Glu glu* (1960s) by Amelia Toledo (São Paulo, 1926 – Cotia, 2017), particularly the work *Peso* (Weight, 1970), a glass container filled with water, red pigment, and foam which, when stirred, produces long durational bubbles creating the impression of seeing blood activated by a life of its own. Whereas most of her *Glu glu* pieces involved colourless bubbles inside an hourglass like shape, which are ultimately abstract works, the mysterious liveliness of the bubbles, and the faint reminder of laboratory test tubes and our body, have always suggested that these works also pay homage to bodily fluids such as human saliva.

Feliza Bursztyn exhibited the environment *La baila mecánica* (fig. 8) at Galería Garcés Velázquez, Bogotá in April 1979. It included seven characters called Pechuga, Fragata, Pipa, Enano, Piolín, Gordillo, and Bailón, which danced to the solemn choral music of 12th-13th century French composer Perotinus Magnus. According to Germán Rubiano Caballero, Bursztyn had long wanted to create a mechanical dance and had proposed to Jacqueline Nova to write the music for it, but Nova died before this was possible, so the artist chose an obscure music that was not contemporary.[19] Bursztyn spent more than five years working on these sculptures and their technology. The figures could be taken apart and

8. Feliza Bursztyn, *La baila mecánica* (The Mechanical Ballet) installed in the Museo La Tertulia, Cali, 1979 Courtesy of the Archive of Pablo Leyva

reassembled for other venues, and never looked exactly the same once put back together.[20] The artist dyed and stained with "dirty" colours such as ochre, brownish grey, orange, and pale purple, the fabric that covered the headless anthropomorphic figures. She presented daily performances of twenty minutes each, where the lights went out and spotlights would focus on the figures rotating and vibrating to the rhythm of the music. Their movement activated by an engine was sombre and spasmodic, creating a general mood of melancholy. The festive character of *Las histéricas* and *Las camas* was replaced by a sense of solemnity and gravity. Furthermore, the movement of the figures was circumscribed by individual wooden floor ridges and cables attached the upper section of the figures to the ceiling, creating a strange sense of the robotic and lack of freedom. It should also be remembered that in 1978 Julio César Turbay Ayala was elected President of Colombia and that same year he created the Security Statute decree by which he gave the military the freedom to interrogate, detain, and torture individuals suspected of being involved with leftist guerrilla activity. It is my interpretation that the darkness and gravity of *La baila* were a direct response to the increasing levels of political repression in Colombia. Bursztyn's herself was taken from her home and interrogated in 1981, upon her return from exhibiting *La baila*

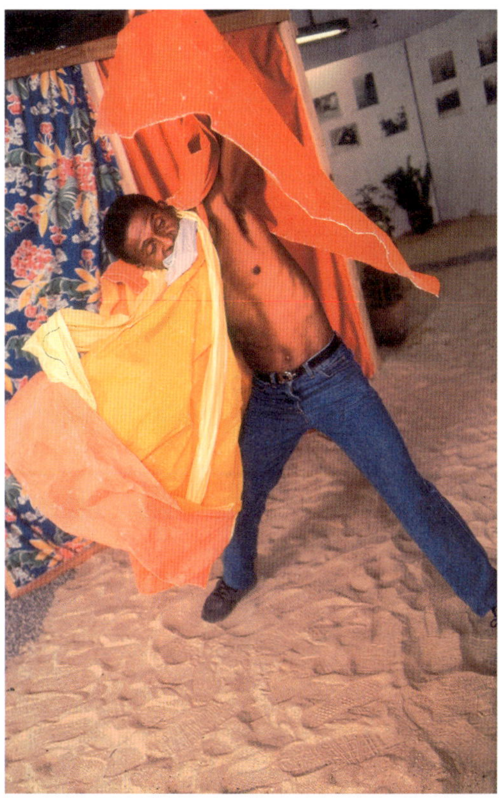

9. Nildo da Mangueira wearing Hélio Oiticica's *Parangolé P4 Cape 1*, 1964
Photo: Andreas Valentin

in Cuba, which lead to her exile the same year. The anthropomorphic figures in *La baila* were described by critics as beggars, sad, monstruous, flagellants, thus introducing marginalization into the museum. This specific moment in the social and political life of Colombia carried with it the crisis of much that was important to Bursztyn: her ideals for a just society, culture, and her personal freedom, and this is clearly reflected in the strange sadness and uncanniness of this work.

In the chronology of Bursztyn's first retrospective exhibition catalogue by Camilo Leyva, Manuela Ochoa, and Juan Carlos Osorio, it is suggested that the staging of the dancers in *La baila*, who moved accompanied by music, bears a close relationship to Hélio Oiticica's (Rio de Janeiro, 1937–1980) *Parangolés* (1964–79) (fig. 9), a series of portable capes, flags, banners, and tents made of painted fabric, ropes, plastics, and diverse materials, that the artist and other participants wore to dance to the rhythm of samba.[21] Beyond the direct notion of embodiment in their work, perhaps the strongest connection is the social underpinning in the work of both artists. Whereas Oiticica created *Parangoles* in dialogue with the people of Mangueira Hill, a shanty town of Rio de Janeiro dominated by marginalization and state violence, Bursztyn created *La baila* to embody a social and political crisis.

Perhaps an even closer connection can be found with Carmela Gross's (São Paulo, 1946) *A Negra* (The Black Woman, 1997) (fig. 10), an imposing, larger-than-life headless figure covered with many layers of black nylon tulle. The sculpture-like body is supported by a platform on wheels that allows for the piece to be moved. This urban mobile sculpture was originally installed on the busy Avenida Paulista in São Paulo. In a conversation with Douglas de Freitas, Gross explained:

> It only speaks of the great veil, of the great set of overlays of fluid matter, of a negative of the bride, of the widow … This work was done for the street, but even now in the museum, the rod and handle are present. It points to the cart, to the machine. And even if on another scale, there is still an allegorical car residue, an extraordinary monument on wheels, in the parades of the samba schools – a social machine, a collective work, simple and complex at the same time.[22]

Although not motorized like Bursztyn's figures, *A Negra*, too, refers to the machine, to dance, and to the body, and both artists bring a strong social dimension to their work. Paulo Miyada interprets *A Negra* as "replacing the exotic body of African origin with the massive volume

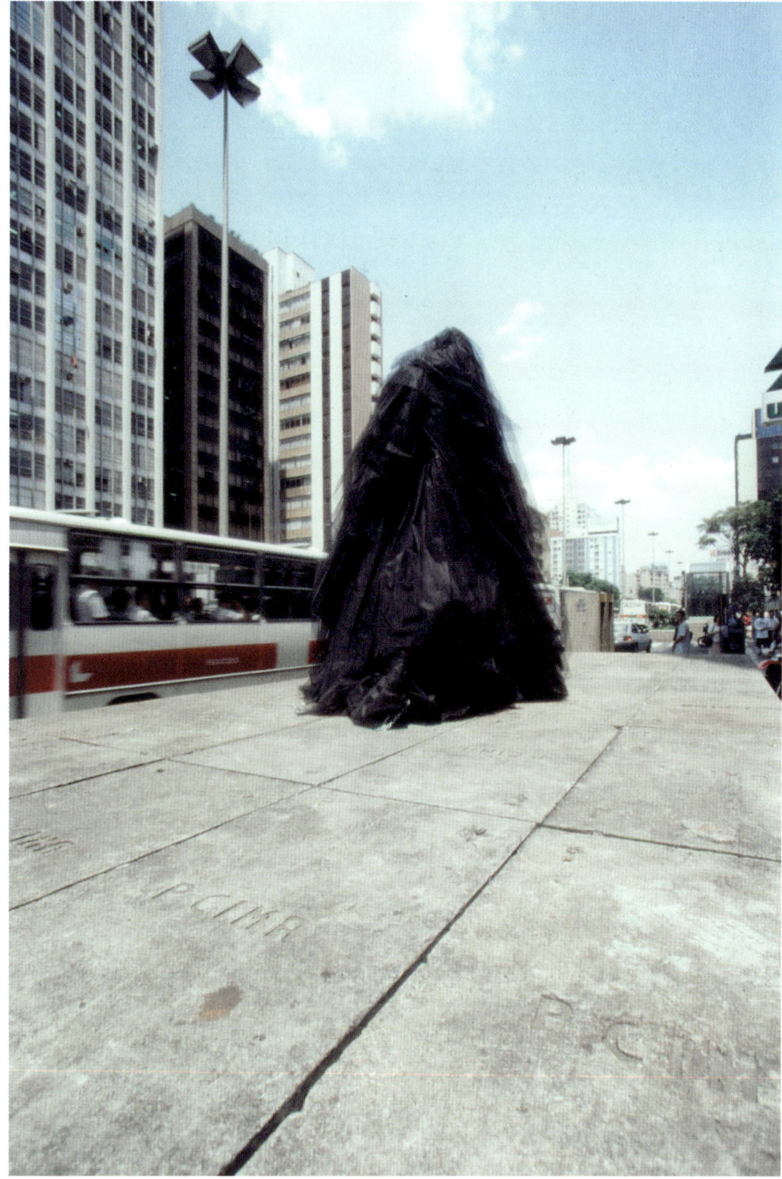

of invisible bodies", and in this he recalls the phantasmagorical presence of Bursztyn's headless "beggars", those members of society that were marginalized and/or repressed.[23] In the case of Bursztyn, *La baila* related both to the working class, the politically persecuted, and human existence, while Gross's *A Negra* embodied the marginalized and invisibilized Afro-Brazilians, specifically women, and popular life in the streets – and, in the case of Oiticica, the marginalized people in the favelas. In both cases the figures have a phantasmagorical presence and, to borrow Ivo Mesquita's description, they "float like a shadow".[24]

In this essay I have explored how Feliza Bursztyn's work, far from being abstracted and detached from life and the social and political realities of Colombia, embodies a profound criticality and relationality with her time which is both political and gendered. Her leftist leanings and feminist stance permeate her work, particularly *Las histéricas*, *Las camas*, and *La baila*, giving urgency to her invitation to interpret her art in social and political terms.

The making of her art was embedded in a notion of labour that brought her closer to the working class and the "proletariat", and away from progressive conception of modernization and bourgeois traditional ideas of beaux arts and good taste. The ways in which Bursztyn challenged the public to participate in performative situations were unconventional and unpalatable, involving not only a rupture with the traditional role of passive spectatorship, but promoting a more horizontal and participative stance for the spectator that could be potentially emancipatory. The sexual connotations, vitality, and uncontrollability of her motorized sculptures, as well as the multisensoriality of her environments, countered rationality and the subordination of women, and encouraged freedom of expression. Finally, her unconventional motorized sculptures and performative installations were ways to provoke and activate the spectator and challenge society's taboos and lack of imagination. Ultimately, Bursztyn's transgressive, creative, and freeing humour that I have associated with Bakhtin's notion of the "culture of popular laughter" and the carnivalesque, morphed in *La baila* – her last public project in Colombia before her untimely death – in the context of a growing repressive situation in the country, into a sombre spectacle of a ghostly reality where it was no longer possible to celebrate and be free.

1 "Yo creo que mi trabajo actualmente está dentro de lo que podríamos llamar 'Romanticismo motorizado'." "Entrevista telegramática con Felisa [*sic*] Bursztyn", unsigned, *El Tiempo* (Bogotá), 28 May 1972. Unless otherwise noted, all translations from the Spanish are the author's.

2 See Margarita Vidal, "Feliza Bursztyn", *Vanidades* (Bogotá), 21 August 1973.

3 "Sí, claro, me encantan los hombres". Beatriz Zuluaga, "Feliza Bursztyn. La mujer de las camas", *Mujer* (Bogotá), October 1975: 68–72.

4 Vidal, "Feliza Bursztyn".

5 Personal conversation with the artist, New York, 2015.

6 Many women artists in Colombia were marginalized, especially if they transgressed taboos of sexuality and political criticism, but also for the simple reason of being women, such as Debora Arango (Medellin, 1907-2005), Sonia Gutiérrez (Cucuta, 1947), Karen Lamassone (New York, Colombian, 1954), Maria Evelia Marmolejo, Rosa Navarro (Barranquilla, 1955), and many others.

7 "Aproveché lo de loca, e insistí en ello, para hacer realmente lo que quería. Porque yo sí creo que vivimos en un mundo machista. Y ser escultor y no ser hombre, es muy difícil. Para que la gente me tomara en serio, recurrí a ese truco, porque pensaban: 'a lo mejor esa loca hace cosas interesantes'. Y creo que esto funcionó." Maritza Uribe de Urdinola, "En un país de machistas, ¡hágase la loca!", *El Tiempo: Revista Carrusel* (Bogotá), 30 November 1979: 15.

8 On this subject see Julia Antivilio Peña, Mónica Mayer, and María Laura Rosa, "Feminist Art and 'Artivism' in Latin America: A Dialogue in Three Voices", in Cecilia Fajardo-Hill and Andrea Giunta, eds., *Radical Women: Latin American Art, 1960–1985* (Los Angeles: Hammer Museum, University of California and DelMonico Books/Prestel, 2017), 37–41.

9 Mikhail Bakhtin, *Rabelais and His World*, trans. Hélène Iswolsky (Bloomington, Indiana: Indiana University Press, 2009). First published 1965.

10 Gina McDaniel Tarver, "The Art of Feliza Bursztyn: Confronting Cultural Hegemony", *Artelogie* 5 (October 2013), http://cral.in2p3.fr/artelogie/IMG/article_PDF/article_a273.pdf (accessed 9 October 2021).

11 "Entrevista telegramática".

12 "Experiencia liberadora, bien podría ilustrar el gran tema de nuestro siglo: eros y civilización." Marta Traba, *Camas* (Cali: Museo de la Tertulia, 1974), n.p.

13 Cited in Sofia Gotti, "Eroticism, Humour and *Graves*: A conversation with Teresinha Soares", *n.paradoxa: international feminist art journal*, vol. 36 (July 2015): 72.

14 *Las Camas de Feliza: Una Obra didáctica*, 1974.

15 Nicolás Suescún, "Las Camas de Feliza en el Museo de Arte Moderno el 26", *El Tiempo* (Bogotá), 24 March 1974. In 1979, when interviewed for the *La baila* exhibition in Cali, she indicated that her favourite hobby was sex. Maritza Uribe de Urdinola, "Feliza 'baila en Cali'", *El Pais*, 18 November 1979, 5–6.

16 "planteando y proponiendo humor, erotismo, misticismo y crítica – al mismo tiempo." Miguel González, "Análisis de la obra de Feliza Bursztyn", *El Pais* (Cali), 25 September 1974.

17 Eduardo Serrano, "La intuición artística de Feliza", *La Patria Revista Dominical* (Bogotá), 7 April 1974. Reprinted in *Demonstraciones: Bursztyn y Salcedo* (Bogotá–Medellín: Fundación Gilberto Alzate Avendaño and Museo de Antioquia, 2007), 91–92.

18 Some of the most radical artists in tackling the issue of female sexuality are Karen Lamassonne (New York, 1954), with the series *Baños* (Bathrooms, 1978–81); Maria Evelia Marmolejo (Pradera, 1958), with performances such as *11 de marzo - ritual a la menstruación, digno de toda mujer como antecedente del origen de la vida* (11 March - ritual in honour of menstruation, worthy of every woman as a precursor to the origin of life, 1981; Cecilia Vicuña's 1960s-1970s performative erotic poetry; Teresinha Soares' performances, paintings, and her album of prints *Erótica*, 1970; and Paola Weiss (Mexico City, 1947–1990) pioneering videos such as *Ciudad Mujer Ciudad* (City Woman City, 1978) and *Mi Corazón* (My Heart, 1986), amongst many others. In 2017 Bursztyn was included in the exhibition *Radical Women: Latin American Art, 1960–1985*, which I co-curated with Andrea Giunta, in the themes Erotics and Mapping the Body. In addition to those mentioned here, Bursztyn was also in dialogue with such artists as Zilia Sánchez, Delfina Bernal, Kati Horna, Ana Mendieta, Lygia Pape, Sandra Llano Mejía, and others.

19 Germán Rubiano Caballero, "Feliza Bursztyn: Escultora", *Escala* 1, no. 11 (1968), 2–14.

20 She presented *La baila* at the Museo de Arte de la Tertulia in Cali, 1979; Rzezby Gallery, Warsaw, 1979; and Casa de las Américas, Havana, 1980.

21 Camilo Leyva, Manuela Ochoa, and Juan Carlos Osorio, *Feliza Bursztyn: Elogio de la chatarra* (Bogotá: Museo Nacional de Colombia, 2009–10), 89.

22 Douglas de Freitas, *A conversation with Carmela Gross*, https://carmelagross.com/a-conversation-with-carmela-gross/ (accessed 10 October 2021).

23 Paulo Miyada, *The Geographer, the Bad Proofreader and the Speleologist*, https://carmelagross.com/the-geographer-the-bad-proofreader-and-the-speleologist/ (accessed 10 October 2021).

24 Ivo Mesquita and Thaís Rivitti. "Carmela gross: a body of works", a discussion. In: Carmela Gross: Um corpo de idéias. São Paulo: Pinacoteca do Estado de São Paulo, 2010.

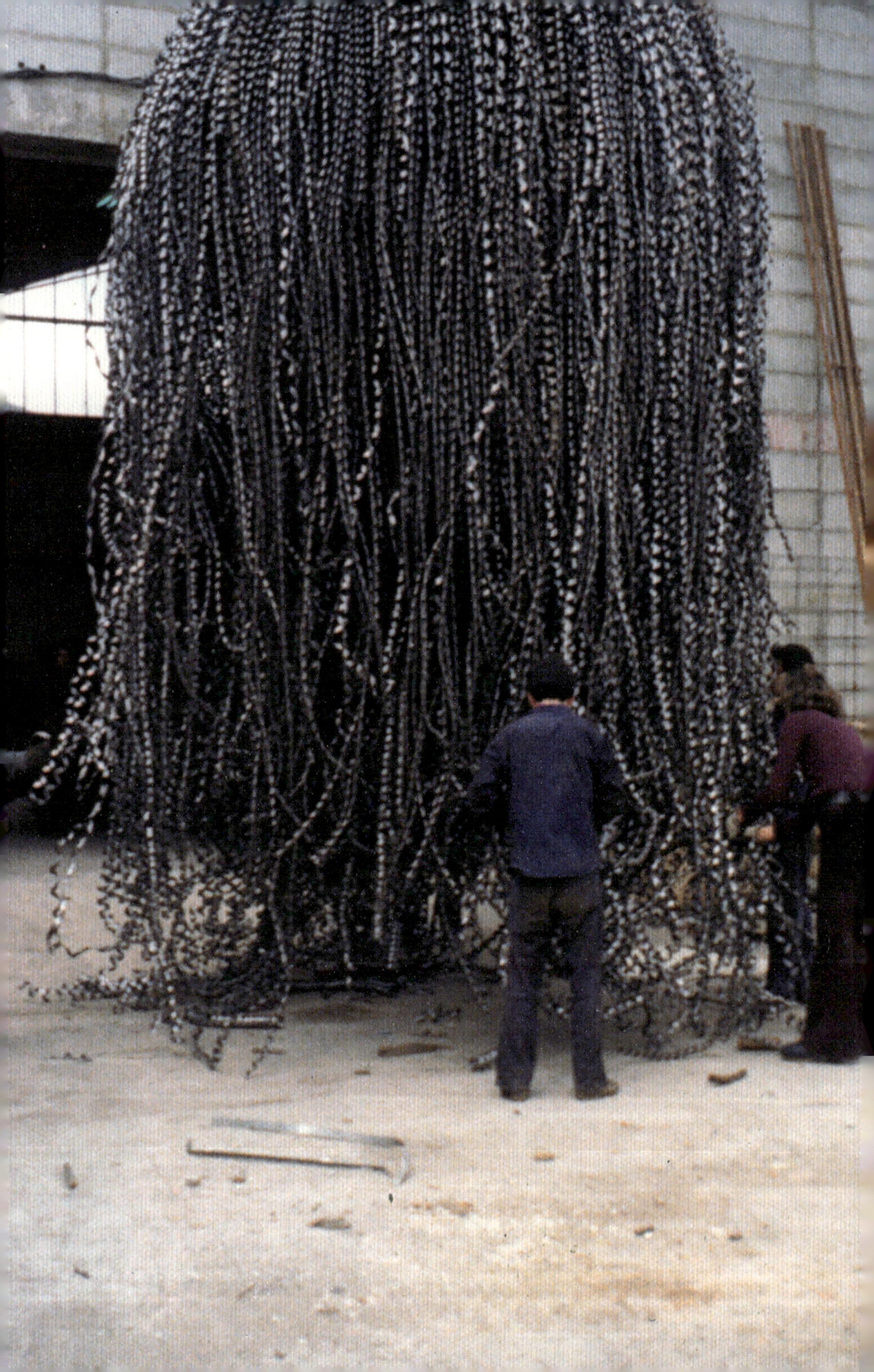

Feliza Bursztyn: Medusa in Colombia

Lynn Zelevansky

"Sex" . . . is also said to be a natural thing, a thing that exists outside politics. Feminism shows that this too is a fiction, and a fiction that serves certain interests. Sex, which we think of as the most private of acts, is in reality a public thing. The roles we play, the emotions we feel, who gives, who takes, who demands, who serves, who wants, who is wanted, who benefits, who suffers: the rules for all this were set long before we entered the world.

Amia Srinivasan[1]

In 1968, the Colombian artist Feliza Bursztyn mounted the exhibition *Las histéricas* (The Hysterical Ones) at the Museum of Modern Art in Bogota (MAMBO). It covered three floors and was packed with kinetic sculptures. They were hanging off the ceiling and the walls, sitting on pedestals and on the floor, shaking and creating a clanging, and in some cases a shrieking, noise.[2] Dramatic light enhanced the reflective qualities of the works' stainless steel and cast powerful shadows. The sound of metal touching metal was inescapable.[3] The show simulated, and perhaps induced, an encounter with hysteria. This was a shocking exhibition for the average Colombian museum-goer at the time. Bursztyn maintained that she didn't create her work to send messages beyond its formal impact, but it's hard to imagine that the implications of the term "hysteria" escaped her.[4] Indeed, the physical and emotional experience of the exhibition was its most impactful aspect, but there were also the implications of, and associations with, the word itself.

Since ancient Egypt, hysteria was considered a female disease. That notion travelled through the centuries, appearing in Greece and Rome, and making its way into modern Europe. Most often the cause of the "disease" was thought to emanate from a "wandering" uterus, an organ foreign to men with the awesome power to give life. It needed to be controlled and for centuries the most common cure was thought to be

1. Feliza Bursztyn,
Medusa, 1974, c. 4 m
high × 2.4 m diameter
Courtesy of the Archive of
Pablo Leyva. Photo: Pablo
Leyva

more sex and more children. That, doctors believed, would bring the uterus back into line, and not incidentally, it would keep women in their place, which was at home serving the family. Mark S. Micale, who specializes in intellectual history and the history of medicine, notes that hysteria has been "a dramatic metaphor for everything men found mysterious or unmanageable in women",[5] and according to the historian and theorist, Cecily Devereux, it was also used as "evidence of the instability of the female mind and body".[6] Bursztyn's exhibition gave visitors a taste of hysteria as men had imposed it on women for millennia.

Today, Bursztyn is respected and admired in Colombia as a pioneer of post-World War II art, but in her lifetime she was a Jew working in a very conservative Catholic country, far removed from the international art world. She was harassed by the government for her leftist views, and her art, which often freely invoked sex as a "public thing", in Srinivasan's terms, drew antagonistic and sometimes aggressive responses.[7] She was worldly, having studied for four years in Paris and lived in New York. She travelled often to the United States and Israel to see family members, to Cuba, where she admired the values of the revolution, and to Paris, where she had many friends, but she always returned to Colombia. She said it was because she loved the Colombian people.[8]

Bursztyn's films show her as unconventional and daring, with a theatrical nature. She seemed to enjoy flaunting her difference. Asked to explain her occupation, she once replied: "I'm a labourer and a welder".[9] A woman defining herself in those terms was unheard of in Colombia at the time; these were men's occupations. Bursztyn was shattering established gender roles, and people didn't take it well. They thought she was mad, and her response was: "In a sexist country, pretend to be the Mad One!".[10] She explained: "I took advantage of the whole 'madness' thing, and played it up, so that I could really do what I wanted. Because I do believe that we're living in a male chauvinist world. And to be a sculptor and not be a man is very difficult. I resorted to this trick so that people would take me seriously, because they thought, 'maybe that crazy woman does interesting things'. And I think it worked".[11] Being strange was the best way for her to live and work in Bogotá.

Bursztyn was among a group of women artists internationally who, in the 1960s, took on the dynamic between sex and power in their search for agency. Making art at the cusp of second wave feminism, before there was a theory and a movement to support them, they were harbingers of things to come. In each country, they fought for recognition on a level with their

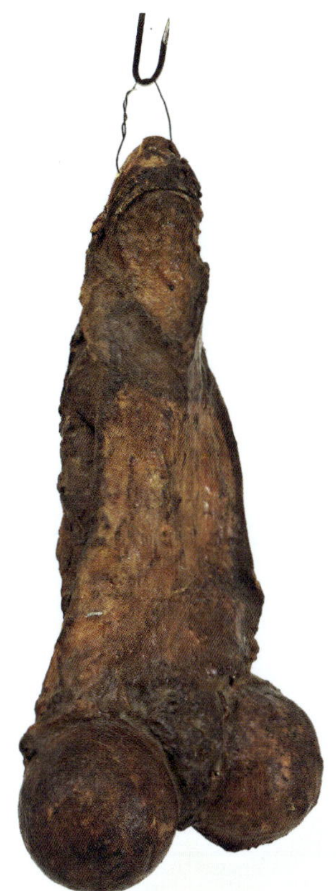

male counterparts. Like Bursztyn, they made unorthodox, subversive, and often fascinating work, powerful expressions of their condition. They investigated their own alienation in their exploration of sexual dynamics.

Working in New York in 1968, Louise Bourgeois created *Fillette* (Little Girl) (fig. 2), a two-foot-tall penis with testicles wrapped in a protective blanket and made of Latex covered plaster. Hanging from the ceiling on a large meat hook, it is essentially a castration. The title of the work, *Fillette*, further undermines male genitalia.

Yayoi Kusama was born in Matsumoto City, Nagano Prefecture, Japan into an environment that she describes as "exceedingly conservative".[12] Eager to escape it, she flew to Seattle, Washington in 1957 and had her first US exhibition there.[13] She moved to New York City the following year, determined to gain recognition. By 1962, having garnered some renown for her "Infinity Net" paintings, she turned to sculpture, working with found objects. Her first three-dimensional piece was a discarded armchair that she covered with stuffed phallic-shaped forms and then painted white. The fringe at the bottom of the armchair remained. It is a surrealist object not dissimilar in conception from Meret Oppenheim's fur lined teacup;[14] each makes the familiar strange by imposing alien materials on a household object. She followed *Accumulation No. 1* (fig. 3) with many pieces of furniture, ladders, and cooking utensils similarly covered with phallic projections.

A burlesque of male sexual obsession, these works are both compelling and amusing, but for Kusama, who was phobic about sex, they were an expression of her need for control over male desire. That concern is more baldly expressed in a collaged photograph that she had taken of herself lying naked on *Accumulation No. 2*, a couch covered with phallic protrusions.[15] Like a pin-up, she poses on her stomach, knees bent, wearing only high heels and the polka dots that cover her body. The message is: "This is my world. You can look but you can't touch".

A related but more aggressive expression of the desire for control is *Action Pants: Genital Panic* (1969) (fig. 4) by the Austrian artist Valie Export. It is a set of six screen prints baring identical images that were made to commemorate a performance that she did in a Munich art cinema the year before, just as second wave feminism was emergent. In the poster she is sitting outside on a bench. Her feet are bare, which connotes both danger and vulnerability; who but a mad person would go barefoot on city pavement? She sprawls on the bench, her legs apart, wearing a tight leather jacket and a pair of crotchless pants that expose her genitals, and

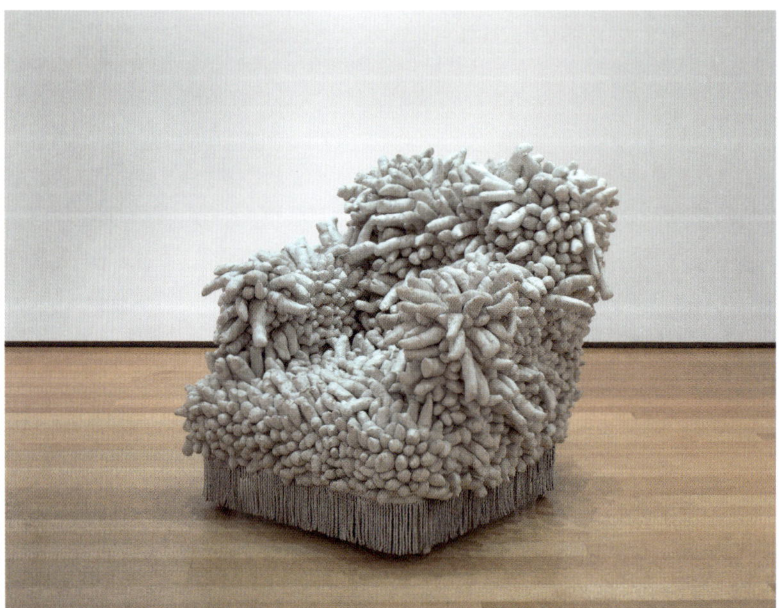

3. Yayoi Kusama, *Accumulation No. 1*, 1962, padded and sewn fabric, upholstery fringe, 94 × 99.1 × 109.2 cm, Museum of Modern Art (MoMA), New York, inv. 1182.2012 © 2022. Digital image, The Museum of Modern Art, New York/Scala, Firenze

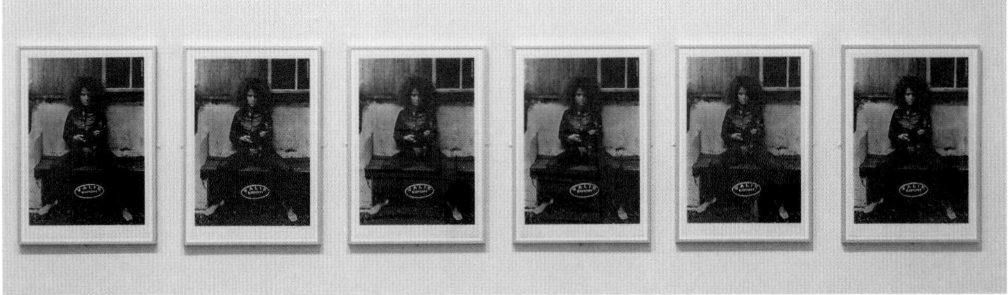

4. Valie Export, *Action Pants: Genital Panic*, six screenprints on paper, 658 × 459 mm each, Tate Gallery, London © Tate, London

she holds a machine gun. This is a bare-faced challenge to the notion of "woman as icon, displayed for the gaze and enjoyment of men".[16] It says: "Just try and take me". A dare that no one is likely to take.

Like Kusama and Valie Export, Bursztyn performed for the camera, though not nude. The art historian Gina McDaniel Tarver published a newspaper clipping from 3 August 1964 showing Bursztyn in an attractive dress, standing by one of her *Chatarras* (Junk Sculptures), which was made of rusted steel and old machinery. She slouches, with a cigarette dangling from her lips. With both hands she holds a hammer below her waist. The "unusual accessory" and casual pose, apparently captured mid-shrug, together with her fashionable dress, create dissonance.[17] She looks as though she is about to smash her sculpture, or already has. Either way, there is the sense of rebellion and maybe even incipient violence.

In the photograph, Bursztyn is of course defying norms in a way that probably seemed comical to her friends but was designed to provoke. According to Marta Traba, the director of MAMBO when Bursztyn showed *Las histéricas* there, people were not so much against the art as they were against the woman who made it. Years after the *Chatarras* were first exhibited, she would recall: "From the first moment, a moral sanction, much more than an aesthetic sanction, weighed upon junk".[18]

Bursztyn used film as well as photography as a performance medium. *Las camas de Feliza Bursztyn* (Feliza Bursztyn's Beds, 1974), for example, though directed by someone else, is obviously a manifestation of her vision.[19] It is an expressionistic piece, named after Bursztyn's kinetic sculptures, *Las camas* (The Beds) (1970–74), although the works only appear towards the end of the film. The lighting is dramatic, the images and sound repeat and superimpose on themselves. A voiceover tells us that she is the most important sculptor in Colombia. She walks through the house and garden naming objects, as well as the cat and dog. She laughs a lot, for no apparent reason.

Her installations with kinetic sculpture constituted her primary form of performance. Her sculptures were actors in full mise en scènes. Movement encourages the human tendency to anthropomorphize and it made Bursztyn's objects seem alive. The definition of kinetic is "the motion of material bodies and the forces and energy associated therewith", and her installations were filled with that energy.[20] The theatrical potential in kinetic art perfectly matched Bursztyn's theatrical nature.

Her art could be disturbing and subversive, but also funny. *Las camas* comprised her second solo exhibition at MAMBO in 1974, and it was more explicitly sexual than *Las histéricas*. It included thirteen sculptures that used life-sized beds as supports. Unlike *Las histéricas*, the moving parts of the sculptures were hidden beneath large swaths of fabric, many of which were brightly coloured with a satiny sheen. The beds shook or undulated in ways that made sexual references unescapable. Clearly, coitus was going on under the covers. This time, instead of the metal sculptures making their own noises, the works were accompanied by an original electronic music score by the Colombian composer, and friend to Bursztyn, Jacqueline Nova.

Las camas pushed the boundaries of what was acceptable in Colombia. Traba described it as "an attack on the passivity of the public", and they responded negatively.[21] In making her art in conservative Bogotá, Bursztyn affirmed the strength of women and bore witness to their potential for independence, but she also knew that her kind of provocation could be problematic in her country. She joked around when asked about the meaning of *Las camas*, but the exhibition's message clearly was that a liberated woman was entitled to express herself sexually as much as any man.[22]

In the early to mid-1960s in the United States, it was possible to push the limits further in order to send a related message, and a few women expressed their independence through nudity and eroticism. Carolee Schneemann was prominent among them. Her work has been called "kinetic painting" because she mixed her movements with expressionist art.[23] The first work in which she used her own naked body was *Eye Body: 36 Transformative Actions for Camera* (1963) (fig. 5), in which she created "a series of physical transformations" of her body within her installation. A photograph shows her lying naked on the floor of a large painted structure. She is covered in paint, grease, chalk, ropes, and plastic. A protest against the way women were treated in the art world, the work was meant to "challenge and threaten the psychic power lines by which women were admitted to the Art Stud Club, so long as they behaved enough like the men, did work clearly in the traditions and pathways

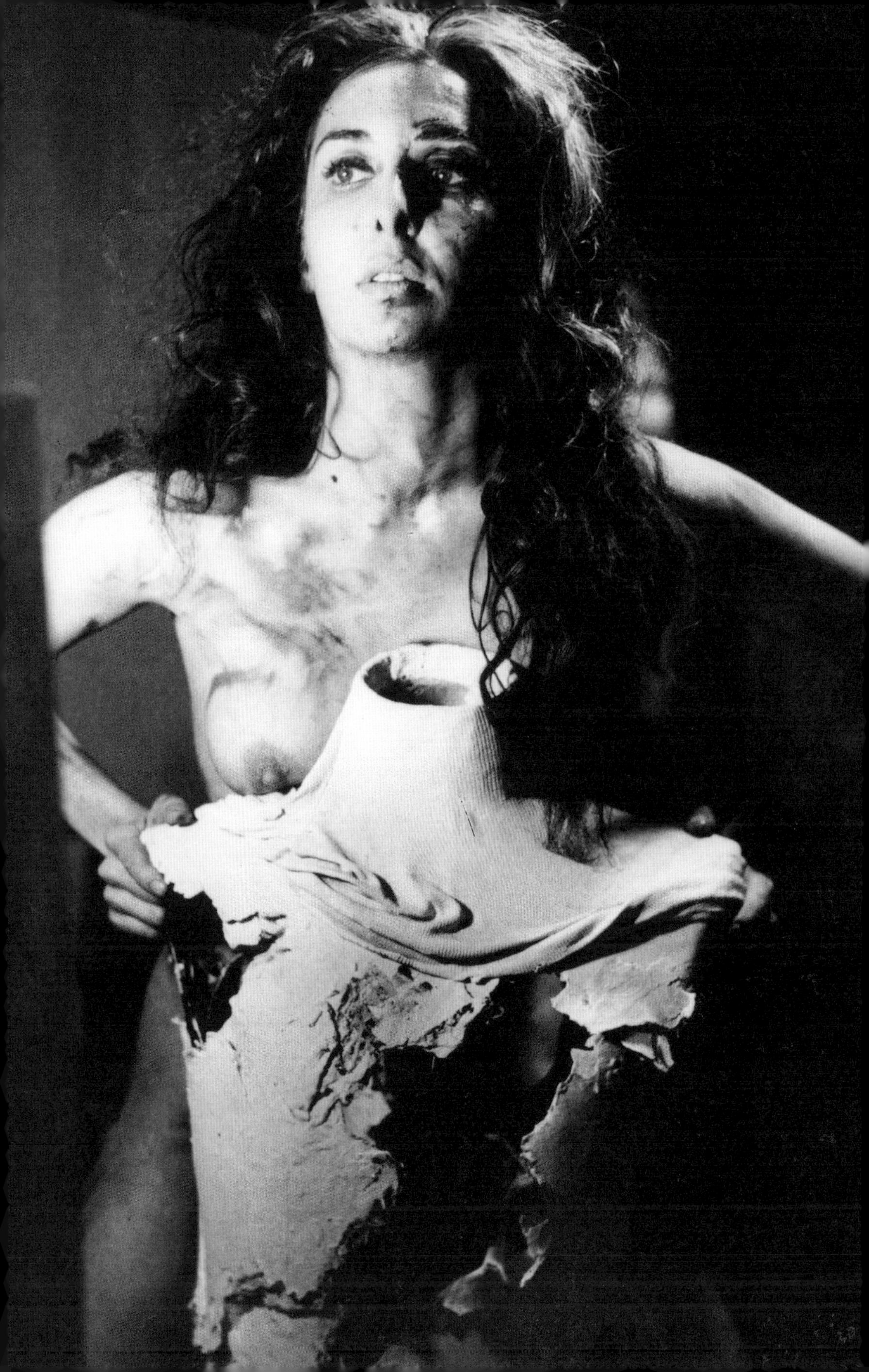

hacked out by the men".[24] Like Bursztyn, Schneemann was creating art that was indisputably and even aggressively female, and it was powerful.

Bursztyn and Schneemann made extremely provocative art for their respective environments. Schneemann later realized that making her work before there was a fully formed and widespread theoretical underpinning to support it was profoundly difficult. The same goes for her willingness to appear nude in a performance by a man. In an ode to the artist Robert Morris, written after his death in 2018, she explained the problem to him, recalling her experience of playing Manet's *Olympia* naked in his famous 1963 performance piece, *Site*: "There has been too much retroactive criticism of *Site* as lacking in feminist principles", she wrote. "In 1963, such principles were barely emergent – the immense gender transformations were just ahead of us." But she also wrote: "*Site* both historicized and immobilized me".[25] This was the price of being objectified, treated as an ideal rather than a functional, intelligent, and creative human being.

The objectification of women impacted Bursztyn in the opposite way. Having been placed on a list of the ugliest women in Colombia, she fought her enemies with awareness and humour. Acknowledging the stupidity of the list, she responded: "I have a petition with a thousand signatures that claims that I am NOT the ugliest woman in the country".[26] Women who are threatening to men suffer this kind of offensive characterization. In the United States, Betty Friedan, the author of the groundbreaking book, *The Feminist Mystique* (1963), was frequently called unattractive. The inference is always that only women who can't get a man would be feminists.[27] Despite this treatment, Bursztyn did not hesitate to rub her critics' noses in the fact that she lived freely, and welded scrap metal, insisting that there was nothing anomalous about that. Among the ways she delivered this message was a photograph of herself soldering (an activity she loved) wearing a dress with pearls, and welding in a fur coat in the film *Las Camas de Feliza Bursztyn*. These images, like the picture of her in a party dress with a hammer, are amusing, but they also created discord.

She reaches out to the public, however, with her *Minimáquinas* (Minimachines, 1969–74). Made from welded scrap metal and parts of disassembled typewriters and other machines, these sculptures can be as small as four inches and as large as twelve. Some of the *Minimáquinas* look like insects while others resemble prehistoric creatures. One walks on tall skinny legs, which support a square body made from a machine part with rows of small buttons sticking upward. Having chided the public on its passivity with her major installations, these works have a lightness and humour to them, and they can engage viewers directly, as some have moving parts that can be manipulated by the public. They are an invitation to participate in art making, for by moving the parts the viewer creates something new. Countering the injunction that art can be seen but must not be touched, it makes viewers essential players in the creation of these works.

There are challenging aspects to the *Minimáquinas*, too. In one, a circular form with openings in it is mounted on a pole that sits in a base like a tiny shower head. Curly wires resembling hair frantically jut out of the circle in all directions. Perhaps it is a look back at the notion of hysteria. In another, a long, hollow, skinny poll leans at an angle out into space and spews metal threads, suggesting an ejaculation. Bursztyn must have enjoyed the reference.

The *Minimáquinas* also star in the 1971 film *Azilef* (Feliza spelled backwards), which has a trippy atmosphere.[28] The setting is dark and the objects shake and shiver before they take off, floating into view like celestial bodies and then floating away. Marijuana leaves float by, too. A Colombian rock band sings a cheerful song in English about a voyage into space, promising a "lovely trip". The film ends when a hand grabs one of the floating pieces, stops it in mid-air and locks it in a cabinet. It is Bursztyn. She is the wizard that makes everything go, but *Azilef* also expresses fear of being locked away.

In 1974, the same year that she is showed *Las camas*, Bursztyn made an extraordinary work of art, one that is wholly unique but was, unfortunately, ephemeral. It was made for La Feria Industrial de Bogotá in payment to a man who had helped her to create other works. About 4 metres high and 2.4 metres in diameter, it had a bell-like structure that supported long strands of curled tubing that covered the support and trailed below it. Hanging from a crane many feet in the air, with its curls blowing in the breeze, it closely resembled a disembodied head and quickly acquired the name, *Medusa* (1974) (fig. 6).[29]

As with *Las histéricas*, there is meaning to the title that impacts the work itself. Once beautiful, the mythical Medusa became a monstrous creature at the hands of a jealous Athena. She had venomous snakes for hair and could turn anyone she looked upon to stone. This was one powerful woman. Unfortunately, she was mortal and Perseus, who was a "hero," was able to behead her using a mirrored shield given to him by Athena that allowed him to see Medusa without actually looking at her. (The

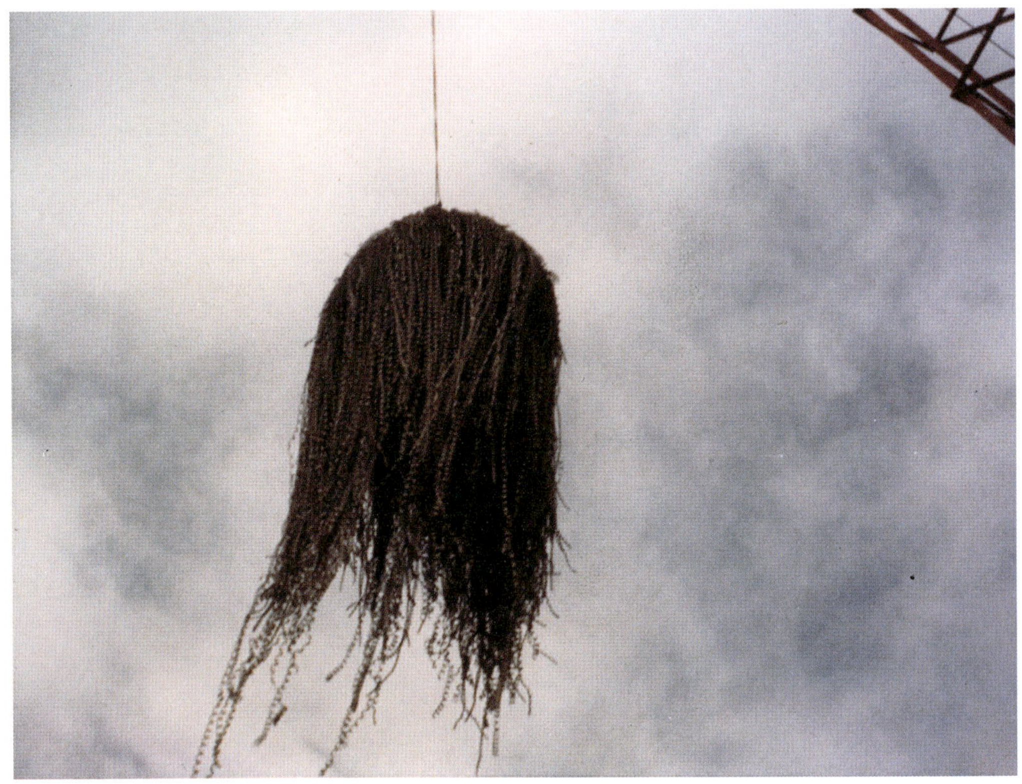

6. Feliza Bursztyn, *Medusa*, 1974, c. 4 m high × 2.4 m diameter Courtesy of the Archive of Pablo Leyva. Photo: Pablo Leyva

myth has different iterations but it always pits woman against woman.) Even in death, however, Medusa's power was such that Perseus had to keep her decapitated head in a special sack strong enough to contain it.[30] English professor Elizabeth Johnson notes that "in Western culture, strong women have historically been imagined as threats requiring male conquest and control, and Medusa has long been the go-to figure for those seeking to demonize female authority".[31] Bursztyn's *Medusa*, her head free of Perseus's sack is, in contrast, a statement in support of the strength and power of women.

Bursztyn's ability to move from very small works like the *Minimáquinas* to the enormously ambitious mise en scènes of her installations and to her huge sculpture, *Medusa*, shows the breadth of her talent and sophistication over the course of her short career. As much as any woman working anywhere at the time, she had a profound understanding of the power dynamics vested in sex. She fought a battle for her rights as a woman and for other Colombian women, as well.

Bursztyn created one last major installation work titled *La baila mecánica* (The Mechanical Ballet), which she showed at Galería Garces Velázquez in Bogotá on 5 April 1979. In it there were seven figures, each with a motor that attached to the ceiling and allowed it to dance, accompanied by twelfth century liturgical music. They were shrouded in fabrics that were old, stained, and wrinkled, giving the impression of poverty. The performance was very possibly a response to an election the previous year that brought a regime to power that was increasingly autocratic and guilty of human rights abuses.[32] In 1981, it would force Bursztyn into exile.

[1] Amia Srinivasan, *The Right to Sex: Feminism in the Twenty-First Century* (New York: Farrar, Strauss and Giroux, 2021), 12.

[2] José Roca, "Feliza Bursztyn 1933–1982", in Tate Americas Foundation Annual Report 2014 (London: Tate Americas Foundation, 2015), 11.

[3] Roca, "Feliza Bursztyn 1933–1982".

[4] See Lucas Ospina's text in this book page 175.

[5] Mark S. Micale, "Hysteria and Historiography" (320), quoted in Cecily Deveroux, "Hysteria, Feminism, and Gender Revisited: The Case of the Second Wave", *ESC* 40, no. 1 (March 2014): 20.

[6] Deveroux, "Hysteria…", 20.

[7] One evening Bursztyn and her husband, Pablo Leyva, were returning from a party when they saw some men with a tow truck trying to bring down her public sculpture, *Homenaje a Ghandi* (Homage to Ghandi). Leyva got out of the car to hit one of them but when they saw that the couple had stopped, they left. She was terrified. See Lucas Ospina's text in this book pages 176–77.

[8] Ospina page 173.

[9] Ospina page 170.

[10] Maritza Uribe de Urdinola, "En un país de machistas, ¡hágase la loca!", *El Tiempo: Revista Carrusel* (Bogotá), 30 November 1979: 15.

[11] Uribe de Urdinola, "En un país de machistas", quoted in Manuela Ochoa Ronderos, "The Uninhabited Stages: Stepping into Feliza Bursztyn's House", master's thesis, San Francisco Art Institute, May 2013, n.p.

[12] Yayoi Kusama, *Infinity Net: The Autobiography of Yayoi Kusama*, translated by Ralph McCarthy (Chicago: University of Chicago Press, 2011), 61.

[13] Kusama, *Infinity Net*, 14–15. Kusama's first US exhibition was at the Zoe Dusanne Gallery in Seattle. It included 26 watercolours and pastels.

[14] Meret Oppenheim, *Object*, 1936, fur-covered cup, saucer, and spoon, The Museum of Modern Art, New York, inv. 130.1946.a-c

[15] The photograph was by Hal Reiff. The collage is no longer extant.

[16] Laura Mulvey, "Visual Pleasure and Narrative Cinema", in *The Feminist and Visual Culture Reader*, edited by Amelia Jones (London–New York: Routledge, 2003), 49.

[17] Gina McDaniel Tarver, "The Art of Feliza Bursztyn: Confronting Cultural Hegemony", *Artelogie: Recherche sur les arts, le patrimoine et la littérature de l'Amérique Latine*, 17 October 2013: 2.

[18] Tarver, "The Art of Feliza Bursztyn", 5.

[19] The film was directed by J. M. Arguaga, with an original score by Jacqueline Nova.

[20] https://www.merriam-webster.com/dictionary/kinetic

[21] Quoted in Tarver, "The Art of Feliza Bursztyn", 5.

[22] See Lucas Ospina's text in this book page 177.

[23] Carolee Schneemann was trained as a painter and was always an expressionist. See Sabine Breitwieser, "Kinetic Painting: Carolee Schneemann's media", in Sabine Breitwieser, ed., *Carolee Schneeman: Kinetic Painting* (Saltzburg, Munich, London, New York: Museum der Moderne and Prestel, 2018), 13–25.

[24] Carolee Schneemann, "Eye Body: 36 Transformative Actions for Camera", in Breitwieser, *Kinetic Painting*, 116.

[25] https://www.artforum.com/print/201902/carolee-schneemann-on-robert-morris-78376

[26] See Lucas Ospina's text in this book page 182.

[27] See for example Cynthia Fuchs Epstein, "The Focus of Feminism: Challenging the Myths about the U.S. Women's Movement", *Amnis*, online, 1 September 2008, https://journals.openedition.org/amnis/634

[28] *Azilef* was directed by Luis Ernesto Arocha.

[29] Email from Carlos Leyva, 19 September 2021

[30] Madeleine Glennon, "Medusa in Ancient Greek Art", The Metropolitan Museum of Art, Department of Greek and Roman Art, March 2017, https://www.metmuseum.org/toah/hd/medu/hd_medu.htm

[31] Johnson brings Medusa up to date: when Hillary Clinton was running for US president in 2016, she was often equated to Medusa in right wing publications and online. Elizabeth Johnson, "The Original Nasty Woman", *The Atlantic*, 6 November 2016, https://www.theatlantic.com/entertainment/archive/2016/11/the-original-nasty-woman-of-classical-myth/506591/

[32] Tarver, "The Art of Feliza Bursztyn", 11–12.

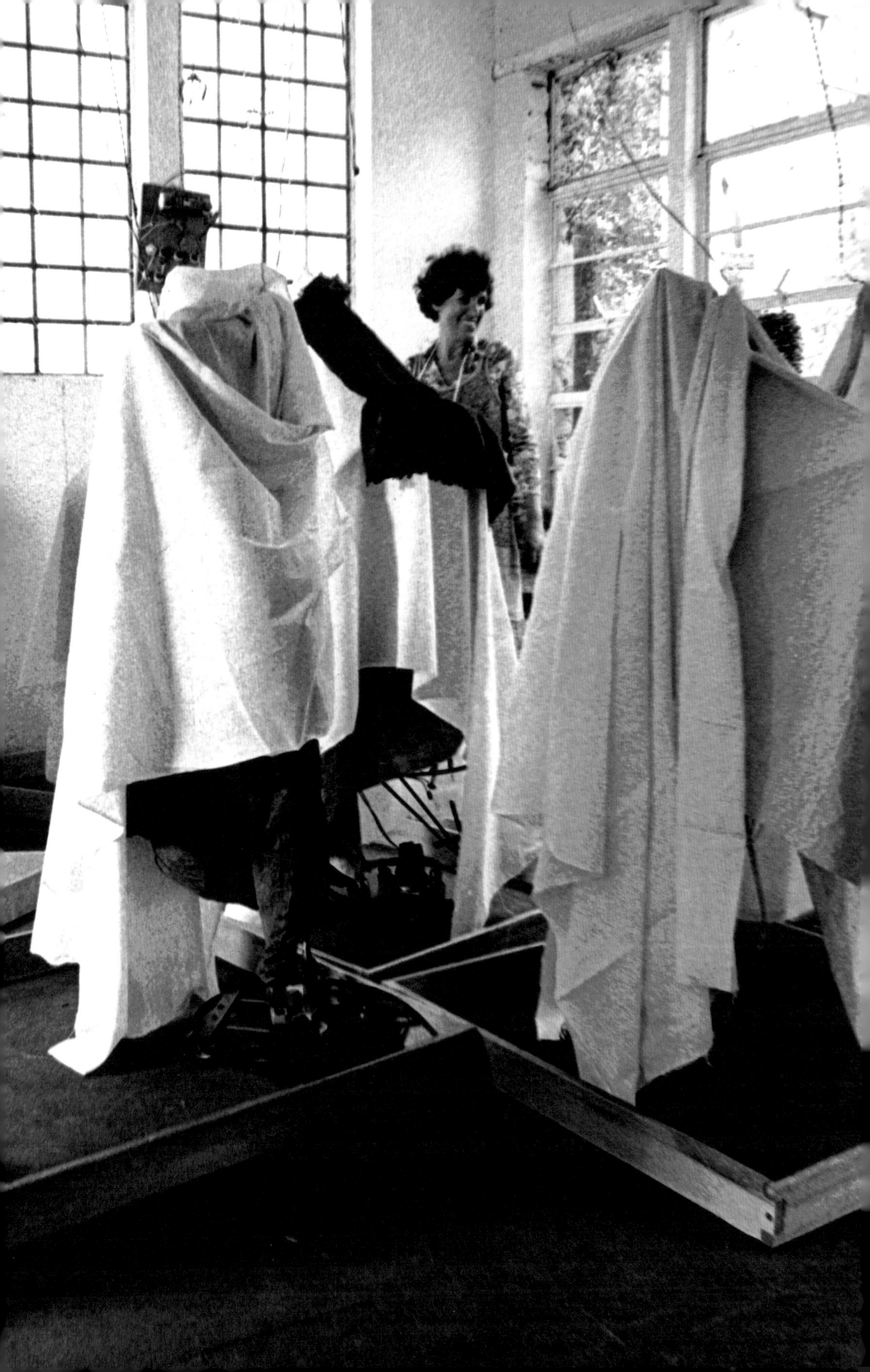

La baila mecánica

Julia Buenaventura

To Patricia Ariza
To Santiago García

In 1957, Feliza Bursztyn returned from Paris, where she had been studying sculpture with Ossip Zadkine, one of those artists who appear in the classic photograph of expatriates in New York in 1942, beside Roberto Matta and Yves Tanguy, just in the opposite corner to André Breton and below Piet Mondrian. In that photograph from 1942, they are all around forty or fifty years old, exiled, at the height of the Second World War. When Bursztyn met Zadkine, some time had passed; the teacher, back in Paris, had opened one of those workshop-schools where young people, far from chasing a qualification – because these places do not even award one – go to learn. Indeed, it reminds me of the workshop where the Brazilian painter Anita Malfatti became Anita Malfatti, the independent school opened by Homer Boss in early-twentieth-century New York. "How long did you study with him [Zadkine]?", Juan Gustavo Cobo Borda asked Bursztyn in a posthumously published interview:

> Four years. A whole lifetime. He had a wonderful studio. He would offer us a drink. It was my initiation. We used to arrive at school at seven in the morning, in the winter: imagine the cold. The old man gave us a glass this big full of brandy to warm us up and we set to work. At that time, he used to come once a week with a stick and knock over everything we'd done, saying: "*merde, merde, merde!*". And finally he said: "Why don't you go back and practise?", and the following week he came back and knocked everything over again.[1]

Back in Bogotá, Bursztyn was twenty-five, with three daughters and a marriage. In Paris she had made some small bronzes, human figures with thin legs and big bellies (fig. 2). Well, since there were no foundry workshops in Colombia, Bursztyn stopped exploring bronze and devoted herself to drawing and getting to know a city that was outside her restricted social circle (families of Jewish traders). It was in that very

1. Feliza Bursztyn in her studio with *La baila mecánica* (The Mechanical Ballet), c. 1979
Courtesy of the Archive of Pablo Leyva. Photo: Raphael Moure

period that she came into contact with two figures who, in different ways, were to be essential to her artistic career. The first of them was the poet Jorge Gaitán Durán, who had founded the legendary magazine *Mito* in 1955. In Bursztyn's words, from the same interview:

> You know, if I'm a sculptor, it's thanks to Jorge. You never do things for someone, they just happen. My marriage was going badly, I was fed up and I wanted to separate. One day I met Jorge at the Excelsior, a café that was a tunnel where 200 people crowded in on top of each other. He invited me to lunch, I accepted, and hey

presto! A week later we were already living together! He could do eighteen things at once. He had an extraordinary capacity for work. That was a great help to me, for making sculptures, which is real hard work.[2]

In October 1958, two press articles appeared about Bursztyn's first exhibition at the El Callejón gallery in Bogotá, a series of figurative watercolours on paper. The first, featured in *El Tiempo* of 5 October, complete with photograph, was by Marta Traba; the second, in *El Espectador* of 12 October, was by Jorge Gaitán Durán. I have found no traces of that 1958 show, but the picture published in *El Tiempo* and other watercolours by Bursztyn, painted in the sixties, give us some clue to how it was as a whole. In that short article, entitled "The Dense Cloud of Being", Gaitán Durán reports two elements that are striking, since in a way they were to pervade the future sculptor's work. On the one hand, there is the constant presence of human figures with no particular features, indistinct splotch-figures that refer to specific personalities, without revealing identities; on the other, there is the variety of supports. Gaitán Durán says: "We should not be surprised that these works executed with humble materials, on pieces of cardboard or yellow card, sheets torn at random from some workbook, are solid and rich. The point is that presence contains all human possibilities".[3] These supports are in tune with the use of scrap metal and ignoble materials used in the construction off her future works.

After that very first show, almost in the twinkling of an eye, Bursztyn and Gaitán Durán travelled together to Paris. There, Bursztyn sought out Zadkine to talk to him about her dilemma: there were no foundry workshops in Colombia. Zadkine's reply was, let us say, eminently practical: "Change country". However, faced with Bursztyn's flat refusal, he had the idea of sending her to visit César, who worked with self-produced welding and scrap metal. Bursztyn and Gaitán Durán returned to Colombia, and she began to look for the materials and tools that would enable her to work with old iron, while the poet Gaitán Durán, together with the composer Luis Antonio Escobar, began the process of writing and producing *Los hampones* (The Thugs), a three-act contemporary opera for soloists, chorus, and percussion, shot through with influences from Bertolt Brecht, Alfred Jarry, Samuel Beckett, and Eugène Ionesco. It is a strange, remarkable piece, produced just once at the Teatro Colón in Bogotá, in October 1961, with a cast of musicians and artists who were to be figures of prime importance on the art, music, and intellectual scene in Colombia over the following decades: from Remo Giancola to Olav Roots and Carmiña Gallo. It was directed by the young Santiago

García, who, at the age of thirty-three, had just arrived from the former Czechoslovakia, having immersed himself in Brecht's total theatre.[4] After participating in *Los hampones*, García was appointed to coordinate the Studio Theatre of the Universidad Naciónal (National University) until the presentation of Brecht's play *Life of Galileo* a year later, in 1965, at the same Teatro Colón. He was dismissed in turn and departed to found the Casa de la Cultura (1966), which was to become Teatro La Candelaria, one of the main laboratories for Collective Creation in Latin America.[5]

The theatre director Santiago García is the second of the crucial figures Bursztyn met in those early years of her career. When I interviewed him in 2005, García told me that when Bursztyn returned to Colombia to start working with scrap metal, he introduced her to Televisora Nacional (National Television), where she was hired to produce sets and stage machinery for the programmes on that incipient Colombian television, which was treated as theatre. From that first meeting, around 1959, until 1979, when García invented the names for *La baila mecánica* (The Mechanical Ballet) – the last great work produced by Bursztyn before her fateful exile – the bond between Bursztyn and García, as friends and collaborators, ran deep. They were jointly engaged in shaping a type of artwork – theatre or sculpture – that abandoned the limits of art and questioned the authorship and originality of the modern Romantic genius, the genius as creator versus the ordinary citizen – worker or employee – as repeater. A type of work capable of dismantling social hierarchies, breaking down the boundary with the public, including the public itself as a creator of meaning, an active participant in bringing the project into being, whether it be sculpture or theatre, since genres no longer matter here; what matters is art as liberation on a profoundly revolutionary path. Revolutionary, but anti-dogmatic. It must be said: despite the constant and furious attempts of her friends, Bursztyn always declined to join the Communist Party.

Julia: Was Feliza Bursztyn a member of the Communist Party?
Santiago: No.
Julia: No?
Santiago: No! *Never in the life.* She was a completely crazy, independent spirit, a very close friend of Patricia [Ariza], very friendly with people in the Party… but she wasn't a member … the thing is, she had very open, very democratic political opinions, you know? She didn't have the discipline to be a member of the Communist Party, she wouldn't even have lasted… she wouldn't have attended the second meeting of the cadre, go to hell… all that… very anarchic, so impossible.[6]

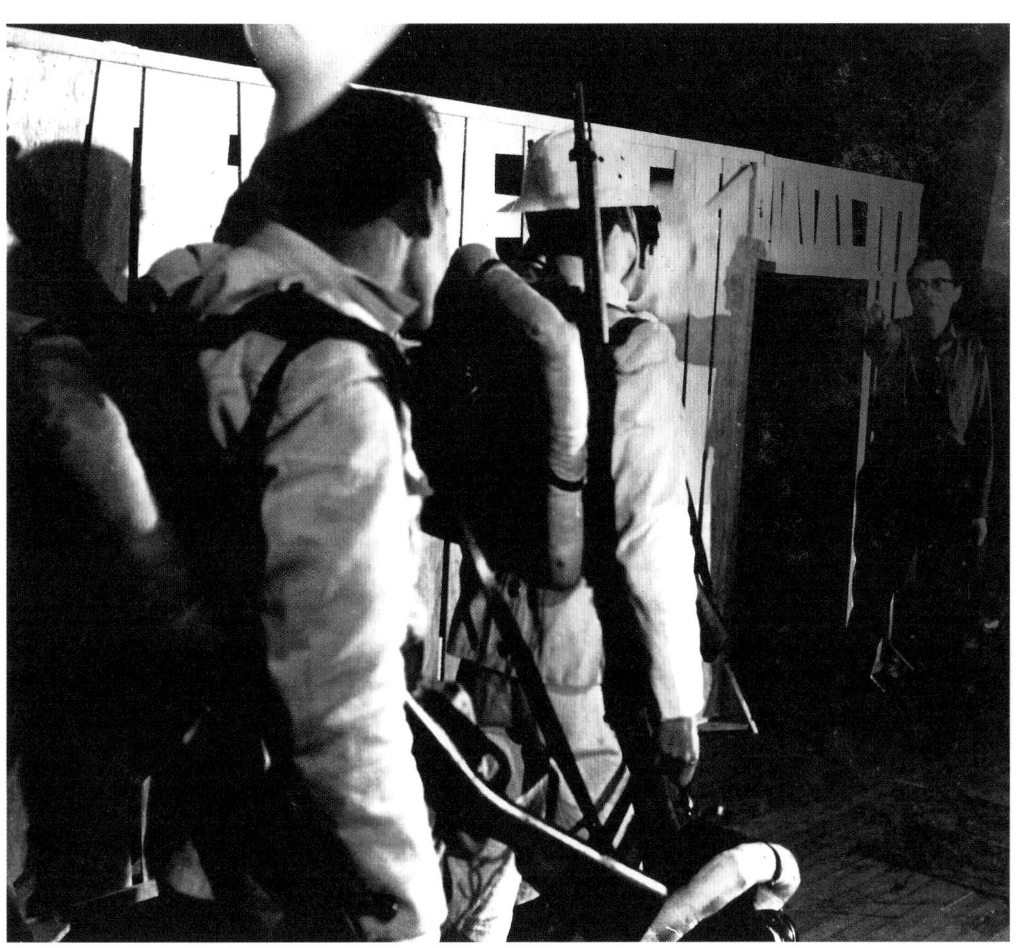

3. Staging of Bertolt
Brecht's *Man is Man*
(1926) at Teatro La
Candelaria, Bogotá, 1964.
Set design: Enrique Grau,
props: Feliza Bursztyn
Courtesy of Archivo
Teatro La Candelaria

After the presentation of the opera *Los hampones*, Gaitán Durán, who
had gone to Paris, died on the way back to Colombia, when his plane
crashed just after taking off from the French capital. It was 1962 and
Bursztyn had settled in Bogotá, with her self-production welding workshop going full steam ahead. Indeed, she had already had her first show
of *Chatarras* (Junk Sculptures), again in El Callejón, in 1961.

—

The relationship between Bursztyn's work and new Latin American
theatre is deep but not obvious. At that time, transgressing boundaries
between genres in art was not a matter of aesthetic experimentation but
of social liberation, from the Teatro do Oprimido and the experiments
of the Theatre of the Catholic University of São Paulo (TUCA), centres
of resistance during the Brazilian dictatorship, to Enrique Buenaventura's Teatro Experimental de Cali, and including, of course, Teatro La

Candelaria in Bogotá, among other centres that were to extend from Mexico to Argentina. After the production of *Los hampones*, García left the country to spend a year at the Actors Studio in New York, a city where he was received by Bursztyn's sister, Hela, and the painter Omar Rayo. Later, upon his return to Bogotá in 1963, as I noted previously, García was hired as director of the Studio Theatre of the National University.

> Santiago García: And then, at the National University, having returned from my wanderings in Europe, I decided to put on a play by our friend Bertolt Brecht called *Man is Man* [1964] (fig. 3), so she [Bursztyn] did all the staging part of this work for me as regards the apparatus, and Grau worked on the set design. Grau did the sets for me and Feliza worked on … [part of interview lost on recording] since *Man is Man* is a play about a guy who goes out to buy a fish and is put in the army out in India in the 1920s, I needed a load of apparatus and props: machine guns and cases for them, and since she worked in scrap metal, she did all that stuff for me…
> Julia: Machine guns made of scrap metal?
> Santiago García: The machine guns, the lorries, all those cases. We had a problem with the Army, because when we went to present the play in Ibagué, they stopped us, because since we were from the National University they thought the weapons were real, and they were made of car scrap, which was the way she worked… in scrap metal.[7]

After *Man is Man*, García undertook a production of *Life of Galileo*, a work in which Bursztyn did not collaborate, according to García, as she was busy making some new moving pieces. She had probably already started these experiments with *Las histéricas* (The Hysterical Ones) pieces in aluminium that moved and screeched, driven by small record-player motors. The fact is that between 1961 and 1965 Feliza made countless sculptures: *Homenaje a Copérnico* (Homage to Copernicus, 1962), *Clitemnestra* (Clytemnestra, 1963), *Flexidra* (1964), and *Mirando al norte* (Looking North, 1965), winner of the First Prize for Sculpture at the 17th National Artists' Salon. It was a period in which Feliza became a recognized sculptor, very close to the art critic Marta Traba, and with an exhibition at the Pan-American Union in Washington in 1964.[8]

So you could say that Bursztyn was between two worlds: abstract sculpture on the one hand and Latin American social theatre on the other, two worlds that have been separated in historical accounts. Marta Traba, at least at first, was an enemy of muralism and therefore of painters like Pedro Nel Gómez and Débora Arango in Colombia, staunchly defended by followers of the radical left, who considered abstract art a mere bourgeois self-indulgence with no commitment, and saw figurative art as something that the people could understand and that therefore constituted a tool of liberation. I know I am putting forward a caricature, sketching the period in very broad strokes. I also know that the communists were not stupid; they were generally born of bourgeois stock and aware that producing socialist realism in the second half of the twentieth century was a dead end. According to a story told by my father, Nicolás Buenaventura, who played an active part in the processes of the Teatro La Candelaria group and was for decades a member of the Communist Party Central Committee in Colombia, on a trip to Moscow he asked a comrade why they were still producing such low-quality social realism, and the *tovarishch* answered, more or less, as follows: "Comrade, if there were only Russian icons in painting when we came to power, what did you expect us to do?".[9]

What am I getting at? The point is that the historical narrative of the arts usually follows a division of the second half of the twentieth century in Latin America, presented as geometric abstract versus political figurative art (and, with the latter, committed theatre), and yet that division is complex, since each permeated the other. What is more, each was the other. Bursztyn was producing the staging of a work by Brecht directed by García, but at the same time Traba (that early Traba waging her crusade against muralism) was writing the first critical articles on Feliza's work.

In short, the encounter between visual arts and theatre is profound, and with it the encounter – sometimes in the sense of a clash, sometimes as a merging – between political figurativism and geometric abstraction. Feliza constructed the sets for Kepa Amuchastegui's *Cementerio de automóviles* (Automobile Graveyard) in 1964; Grau and Bursztyn, as I said, worked on Brecht's *Man is Man*, directed by García; Obregón did the staging for *El triciclo* (The Tricycle), by Fernando Arrabal, for La Candelaria; and in Cali, Pedro Alcántara, Óscar Muñoz, and David Manzur (who was abstract in that first period) worked hand in hand on the productions by Enrique Buenaventura and the Teatro Experimental de Cali. After the performance of Bertolt Brecht's *Life of Galileo* in 1965, owing to questions of political order and following a tremendous production which was a watershed in the history of Colombian theatre, García was expelled from the Studio Theatre of the National University;

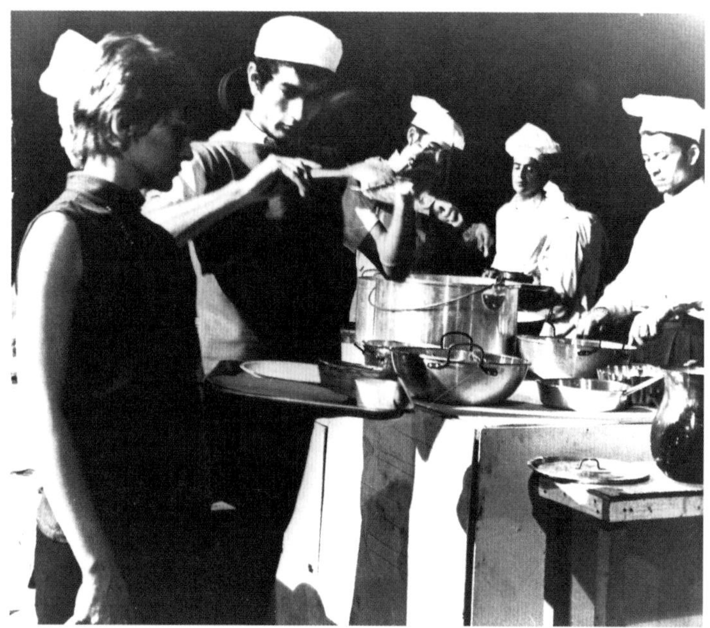

he then left with all his companions to found the Casa de la Cultura, which would subsequently become Teatro La Candelaria. This was a place where people from different disciplines converged, connected at a time when, as I have said, the boundaries between artistic genres were dissolving. So much so that in 1967 the Casa de la Cultura extended an invitation to Alejandro Jodorowsky to take part in a theatre festival with his ephemeral acts. I quote García again:

> … we began our work at the Casa de la Cultura with a play by Carlos José Reyes, *Soldados* [Soldiers], based on Álvaro Cepeda Samudio's novel *La casa grande* [The Big House]. A year later we invited Alejandro Jodorowski and did a chamber theatre festival, to which the Venezuelan dramatists Román Chalbaud and Isaac Chocrón also came. Jodorowski brought his project for "ephemeral" shows and "happenings". We then put together a series of performances of ephemeral acts and happenings at the Casa de la Cultura, which in my view was very important. Kepa Amuchástegui and Ricardo Camacho were there taking part. There were loads of people involved in that completely crazy experiment in Colombian theatre in the sixties, which was to do a one-month session of ephemeral events, happenings, unusual acts. I did a few amazing ones with the painter Omar Rayo. And that attitude of doing something so crazy drew in a lot of people. Although at the same time it was something that threw a lot of the

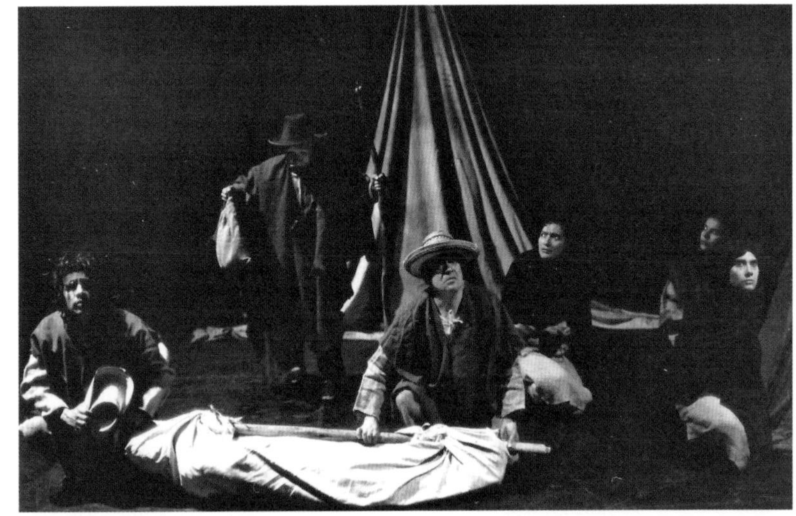

5–6. Staging of João
Cabral de Melo Neto's
Vida y muerte severina
(Life and Death of
Severino, 1956) at Teatro
La Candelaria, Bogotá,
1974. Set design: Feliza
Bursztyn
Courtesy of Archivo
Teatro La Candelaria

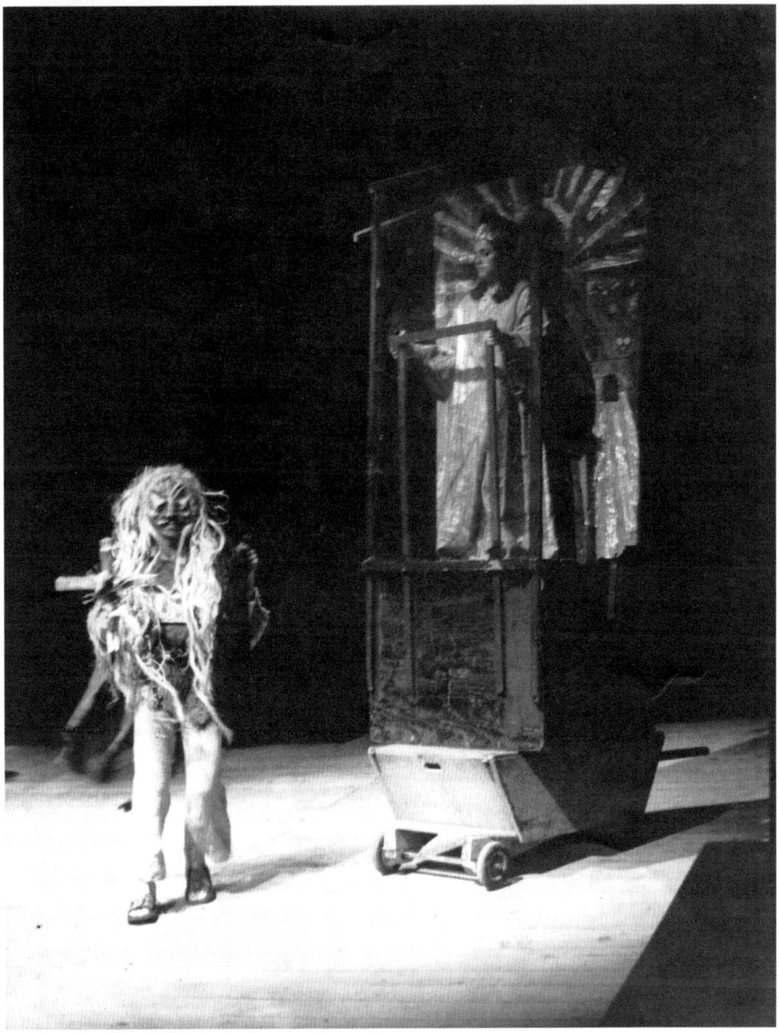

people who followed us off their stroke, especially people on the left, who were our most active followers and were characterized by being deadly serious.[10]

It is clear that many people on the radical left did not like happenings, just as they did not like geometric abstraction. And yet those same people were deeply committed to Teatro La Candelaria and the new paths being opened up from it towards shaping a revolutionary work, not in its content, please note, but in its form: a Collective Creation that broke with the figures of author and protagonist, a work that breached the frontier between representation and reality, profoundly questioning art as fiction.[11] In a world that has turned into fiction, art is the deep crack that opens to enter the real and listen to the sirens' song extrapolating the limits of applause. In 1968, the theatre group obtained La Candelaria's current building, through an agreement with the City Council. It was a large colonial house for which Feliza donated the flowerpots: fuel drums which she had cut in half with a blowtorch. That same year she also produced *Las histéricas*, the series of sculptures in aluminium which cry and screech, and the spectator can do no more than just put up with them.

And when it comes to *Las histéricas*, you have to ask yourself: what are they? Ladies screeching or abstract-kinetic art? Feliza always insisted, with a laugh, that she was not going to give any explanation on this subject. But these wailing women burst onto the national scene like a visual artwork that has turned into theatre, a set of hysterical women – and the label "hysterical" always refers contemptuously to a woman who has liberated herself from the first of all human subjugations, the subjugation of gender. One of the most important elements of the series *Las histéricas* is undoubtedly its name. This title, far from being merely ornamental or dispensable, constitutes the work itself, turning abstract pieces into characters. Each of *Las histéricas* is a woman, a hysteric. And there Bursztyn brings abstraction back to representation, but a type of representation completely different from visual mimesis, that is, from any revolutionary scheme imagined by David Alfaro Siqueiros or Pedro Nel Gómez. Bursztyn brings abstraction into the realm of politics, for the liberation of a subjugated person – be it a woman or a slave – is always a political question, just as Cildo Meireles turned the dematerialization of art into a way of resistance to the dictatorship, and later on, in the 1980s and 1990s, Félix González-Torres made his work like a virus that went through the market.

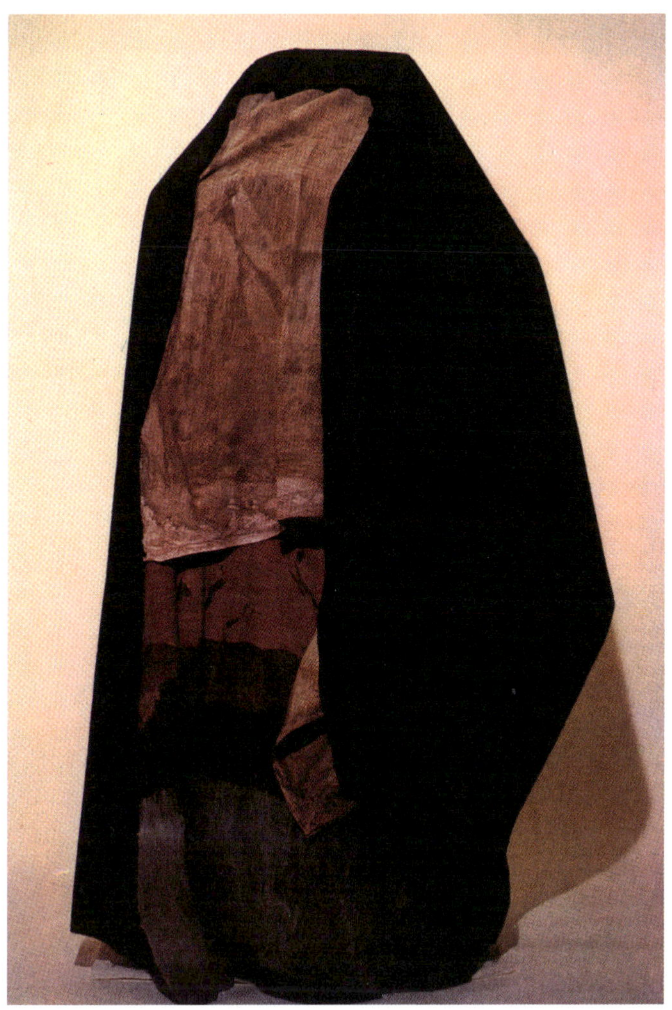

In 1968, Bursztyn built the set for the Candelaria group's next production, Arnold Wesker's *The Kitchen* (fig. 4). It was just around this time that she showed her sculptures in Santiago de Chile, where the politician and art critic Mário Pedrosa, exiled by the dictatorship in Brazil, was organizing the Museum of Solidarity with Salvador Allende. Bursztyn returned happy from Chile, firstly because, as she told Pablo Leyva, she had never seen so many sculptures together, and secondly because she had met a woman with whom she was to strike up a close friendship, Miria Contreras, "La Paya", a secretary who acted as a kind of interior minister during the Allende government: nothing moved in the cabinet without first passing through her hands. Allende – it must be said – was her lover.

We have now entered the 1970s. Allende was murdered or forced to commit suicide on 11 September 1973 by Augusto Pinochet's troops in a coup at the Casa de La Moneda, from which La Paya managed to get out alive; after many hazards and arrangements, she set off on the exiles' journey to Paris. In 1974, the year after the coup d'état in Chile, Bursztyn produced two essential works. First, the staging for *Vida y muerte severina* (Life and Death of Severino), an adaptation of the poem by Cabral de Melo Neto produced by the Catholic University of São Paulo (TUCA) Group, with music by the young Chico Buarque (figs. 5–6). Second, *Las cujas* or *Las camas* (The Beds), an installation with music by Jacqueline Nova, consisting of a set of thirteen beds covered with satin sheets in gaudy colours, under which structures representing two lovers having sex moved and squirmed, moaned and writhed. In Santiago García's words:

> It's a work very close, very much akin [to theatre]… it was now the period when ideas for installations came from performances, when the boundaries between dance and theatre and between these two and the visual arts were beginning to break down; in other words, the fixed borders between the different arts were beginning to be breached… Feliza was already a representative of that need to find hybrid expressive means, which were part theatre and part sculpture and part visual arts as well; there was a lot of visual art in them… and of what later became performance and installation art: they were installations.[12]

The boundary between sculpture and theatre has been subverted; in *Las cujas*, Bursztyn is figurative, allegorical, direct, and specific. She is talking about sex, about what is not talked about. It is a work, moreover, that ventures into vulgarity, into bad taste: an openly coarse, almost ridiculous work, which easily earned the disapproval of Traba. Later on, in 1977, Bursztyn travelled to Cuba to present her sculptures at Casa de Las Américas, the cultural centre that became a touchstone for Latin American art. It was a remarkable trip, during which she became very friendly with the revolutionary leader Haydée Santamaría, who participated with Fidel in the attack on the Moncada barracks in 1953.

—

One afternoon, in 1957, the painter Ignacio Gómez Jaramillo stood opposite the Café Automático in Bogotá, gun in hand, waiting for the art critic Traba, who had written an article describing him as something like an imitator of imitators (that is, of the muralists). Gómez Jaramillo was dissuaded by none other than Gaitán Durán from carrying out his attempt to kill a critic who, as we know, during her early years in Colombia, from

1954 up to 1966, when she began to change her perspective after meeting Ángel Rama, had viciously attacked painters who followed any line close to nationalism, to the point of completely excluding them from the scene. Indeed, Traba was particularly unfair to Débora Arango, a painter who, soon after escaping from the persecution of the Bishop of Medellín, attracted the critic's attention. So, it is not surprising that accounts of art in Colombia seem to involve a split between committed, figurative art and modern painting and sculpture, led by Traba and her so-called chosen ones: Obregón, Grau, Ramírez Villamizar, Negret, Botero, and of course Bursztyn herself. However, I insist, each group was mixed with the other: each was the other. In the *Graficario de la Lucha Popular en Colombia* (Graphic Portfolio of the People's Struggle in Colombia, 1977), produced to raise funds for the Communist Party, all of Traba's group and also those she excluded took part: from Obregón to Pedro Nel Gómez, from Roda to Luis Ángel Rengifo. This was at the height of the 1970s, when the problem of creating art of one's own, no longer nationalist but Latin American, took on acute importance in the agenda of both critics and artists.

Once again, what am I getting at? That Bursztyn's work, though acclaimed by Traba, must not be separated from the experimentation of committed theatre and art, which represented a political struggle, just as Bursztyn's work with García was decisive in their respective artistic creations. Bursztyn's last large-scale piece is *La baila mecánica* (fig. 7). Presented on 5 April 1979, it is a kind of play, and even had to be visited at specific times, as the Galería Garcés Velásquez's invitation shows: "Performances at 11.30 am, 3.30, 5.00 and 6.30 pm". The launch of *La baila* gave rise to some seven press notices between April and November 1979, added to which were the reviews in 1980, when it was taken to Cali, to the Museo La Tertulia, with a text by Marta Traba in the brochure.

Bursztyn, two decades into her career, was now a well-established figure, an authority in the art field in Colombia, so *La baila* was keenly awaited and widely acclaimed. The remaining parts of the work were donated to Tate London by Leyva in 2014 and were not put on view until 2021 after this piece had been completed, so we could only reconstruct it from accounts.[13] The press quotations create a vivid impression, but for reasons of space I will cite only one, by gallery owner Alonso Garcés, in an interview with the artist Álvaro Barrios, precisely about Bursztyn:

> In the middle of the room … she made a large wooden stage, roughly a metre high, with some steps to get up to the platform, all completely

dark, and a black light that illuminated just the figures on the platform. People came in; you had to get accustomed to the darkness to be able to move around within the gallery space. When you had got used to the dark, you began to discover these figures swathed in cloths … The sound of metal, of all these pieces of iron, scrap metal, mixed with the sound of the music and what you perceived visually, made up one of the beautiful works I have seen in my life.[14]

As I pointed out, after Valencia Goekel wrote the brochure for the Garcés Velázquez Gallery in Bogotá, Traba proceeded to write the text for La

Tertulia in Cali. Curiously, the two authors agree in relating Bursztyn's *La baila* to *The Threepenny Opera* by Bertolt Brecht. And I think they are right, for as soon as the parallel is suggested, the first act of the opera comes to mind, when Filch, the poor lad beaten for trying to beg for a little money in the streets of London, arrives at the office of Mr Peachum, who is to grant him a licence to beg and an "outfit", or suitable costume, in exchange for a sum of money and a contract for 40% of the earnings received.

Brecht's descriptions of the begging outfits are very funny, perhaps because they touch the depths of human suffering: "Outfit A: victim of vehicular progress. The merry paraplegic, always cheerful (*He acts it out*), always carefree, emphasized by arm-stump. Outfit B: Victim of the Higher Strategy. The Tiresome Trembler, molests passers-by, operates by inspiring nausea (*He acts it out*) attenuated by the medals. Outfit C: Victim of Advanced Technology. The Pitiful Blind Man, the Cordon Bleu of Beggary".[15] Faced with such outfits, the young man demands:

> FILCH. – What about my things?
> PEACHUM. – Property of the firm. Outfit E: young man who has seen better days or, if you'd rather, never thought it would come to this.
> FILCH. – Oh, you use them again? Why can't *I* do the better days act?
> PEACHUM. – Because nobody can make his own suffering sound convincing, my boy. If you have a bellyache and say so, people will simply be disgusted. Anyway, you're not here to ask questions but to put these things on.[16]

Filch changes his clothes and goes out to beg in the street he has been assigned.

—

La baila was a resounding success. As I said, it travelled from Bogotá to Cali, where it was packed up and sent on its way to Poland. Bursztyn herself went to Cuba to present some new junk sculptures, made, apparently, from Nescafé tins. However, on that new journey to Cuba, the outlook had changed; Haydée Santamaría, her friend and the director of Casa de Las Américas, had committed suicide on 28 July 1980. It was months after the beginning of the massive Mariel boatlift, following the request for asylum at the Peruvian embassy by over a thousand Cubans.

Let me recall that nearly 125,000 migrants left in that boatlift, between April and October, which is 1% of the Cuban population. This revealed, beyond a shadow of a doubt, that the Revolution had failed.

Soon after returning to Colombia from Cuba, on 24 June 1981, Feliza was captured and subjected to a lengthy interrogation, blindfolded, without food or water, in the National Army stables. Her capture was made possible by Turbay's Security Statute, of 1978, which granted the Army authority to carry out interrogations without a court order or oral hearings. After this, Bursztyn took refuge in the Mexican embassy, where she applied for political asylum. On Bursztyn's last night in Bogotá before she went into exile, Patricia Ariza called together a group of actors and artists in front of the embassy to serenade her with protest music. When they were ready to start, the Army arrived and formed a ring around them, which threatened to close. Patricia told them all to keep quiet, and exclaimed: "Mr Ambassador, on your saint's day, we've come to wish you a happy birthday". And in front of the disconcerted troops, the group began to sing the Mexican birthday song *Las mañanitas*. Then a member of the embassy staff appeared at the window and said loudly: "The Ambassador is very pleased with this expression of affection from the Colombian people on his birthday, but he has not been able to come out in person because he is very tired". With that, the Army and the friends began to disperse.

In Mexico City, where she stayed with Gabriel García Márquez, who had also had to leave Colombia after Turbay's purge, Bursztyn was refused entry to the United States, the country where her daughters were and which she had visited regularly. France, by contrast, offered her asylum. Feliza left for Paris, lodging with none other than La Paya, who was organizing the remains of the Museum of Solidarity that they had managed to get out of the country after the coup against Salvador Allende. The last portrait Feliza did, before her death on 8 January 1982, is of La Paya: a few odd lines, a small pair of glasses, and an outline in ballpoint (fig. 8).

[1] Juan Gustavo Cobo Borda, "Entrevista trunca con Feliza Bursztyn", *Cromos* (Bogotá), 8 March 1983.

[2] Cobo Borda, "Entrevista trunca".

[3] Jorge Gaitán Durán, "La densa nube de ser", *El Espectador*, 12 October 1958.

[4] The University of Pamplona researcher and lecturer Jesús Emilio González Espinoza has published an article compiling all the information on this work and its single production, https://repositorio.uca.edu.ar/bitstream/123456789/1130/1/hampones-medio-siglo-opera-colombiana.pdf (accessed 25 October 2021).

[5] Collective Creation has a long history in theater in general. In Latin America it was fundamental in the second half of the twentieth century as a form of political resistance against oppressive regimes and dictatorships. See Kathryn Mederos Syssoyeva and Scott Proudfit, eds., *A History of Collective Creation* (New York: Pallgrave Macmillan, 2013).

[6] Santiago García interviewed by the author, Julia Buenaventura, in 2005. Unpublished.

[7] Santiago García interviewed by the author, Julia Buenaventura, in 2005. Unpublished.

[8] One must not forget that the director of the Pan-American Union was Gómez-Sicre, who had been part of an extensive United States government programme to promote art that distanced itself from muralism-nationalism, a type of art that, far from being politicized, would be rooted in purely aesthetic issues; the foundation of modern art museums in Latin America was in line with this. Following this orientation, Marta Traba, who was a friend of Gómez-Sicre, promoted an uncompromising break with muralism, with artists like Diego Rivera or Siqueiros, who, in turn, were ready to take up cudgels against any new perspective in art. A classic example is her 1954 letter opposing the appointment of the geometric abstract artist Mathias Goeritz as a museographer at UNAM, a letter that did in fact lead to him losing the post.

[9] Obviously this is not true; there was the whole group of artists persecuted by Stalin: Malevich himself, who unded up painting peasants so as not to be murdered or deported; Bulgakov, condemned to ostracism; Mayakovsky, who committed suicide in 1930. The list goes on.

[10] Víctor Viviescas, "Pequeña enciclopedia de La Candelaria: entrevista a Santiago García", *Literatura: teoría, historia, crítica* 14, no. 2 (July–December 2012): 232–33.

[11] One need only recall the structure of the collectively created work *Guadalupe, años sin cuenta* (Guadalupe, Countless Years, 1975), in which the central character, Guadalupe Salcedo, never appears on stage.

[12] Santiago García interviewed by the author, Julia Buenaventura, in 2005. Unpublished.

[13] The sculptures are reconstructed in the exhibition *Feliza Bursztyn: Welding Madness* at Muzeum Susch, however, it should be noted that the installation presented by Bursztyn in 1979, more than a set of sculptures, was a staging in which the "characters" moved through the use of engines. In this way, the work lasted a specific period of time.

[14] Álvaro Barrios, *Orígenes del arte conceptual en Colombia: 1968–1978* (Bogotá: Alcaldía mayor de Bogotá, 1999), 66–67.

[15] Bertolt Brecht, *The Threepenny Opera*, in *Collected Plays: Two*, edited and translated by John Willett and Ralph Manheim (London: Bloomsbury, 2015), 99.

[16] Brecht, *Threepenny Opera*, 99.

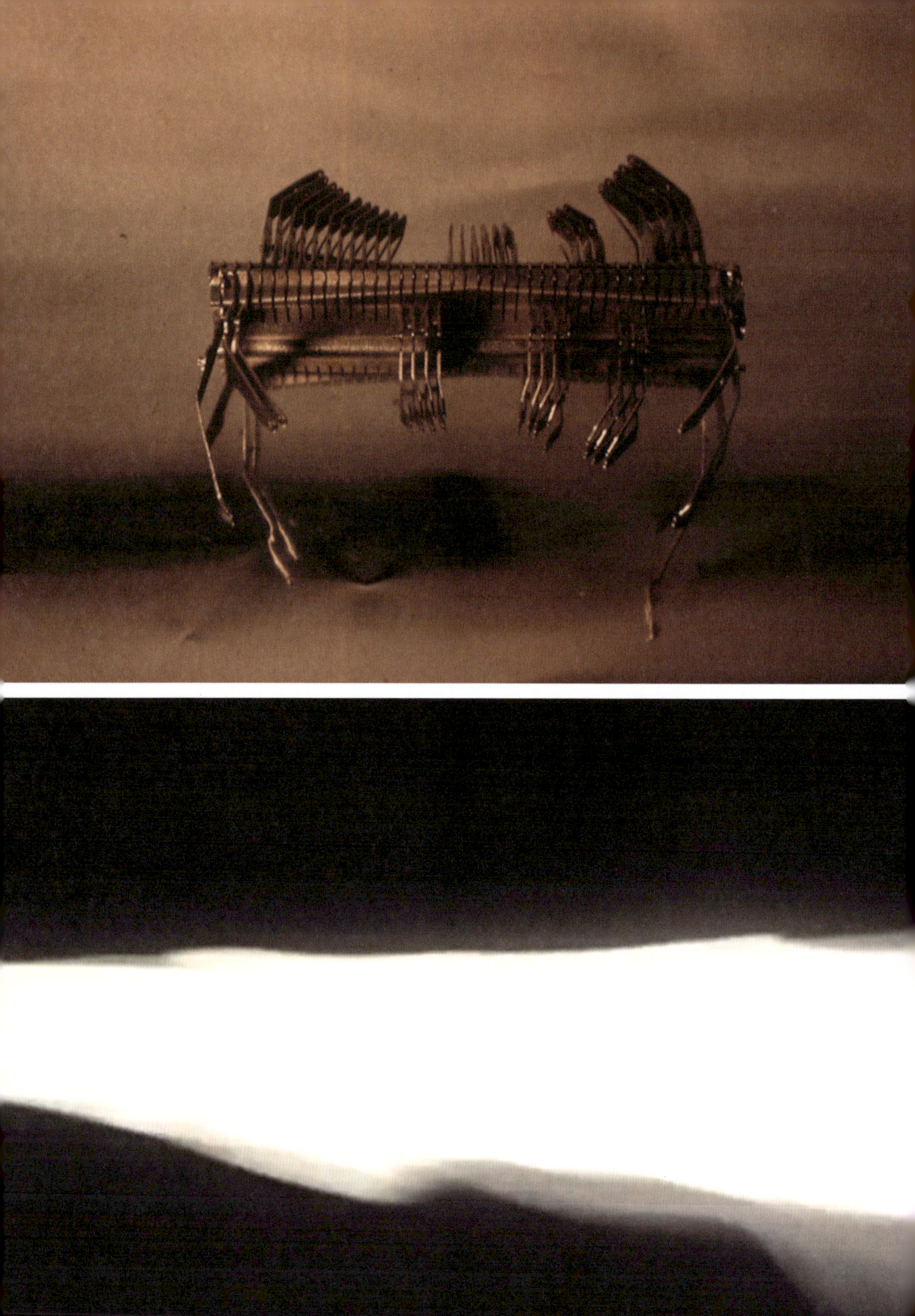

Azilef, *Minimáquinas*, and the Other Dimension of Feliza Bursztyn

Camilo Leyva

The gas flows through the blowtorch and the sound of combustion intensifies when the audio channel opens in *Azilef*, the experimental film by Luis Ernesto Arocha and Feliza Bursztyn. In a scene on a black background, the rocket, this time fuelled by acetylene, takes off from the sculptress' work surface: a piece of cast iron scrap which functions, in the context of the film, as the space exploration base for her imagination, to inhabit the planet called Azilef. Then a burst of flame travels across the screen from right to left; the flame grows, tracing a linear path, and gives way to the image of a glowing horizon, where an artificial light stands in for the ruling star. Simultaneously the music begins, with synthesized voices and electronic instruments, by the band Los Teipus, establishing the atmosphere of dawn on that exogenous planet. The light picks out ridges and troughs in the ground; we can see the impact marks of other objects on the surface. These cracks and scrapes are witnesses to the passage of time and the relationship to other objects and surfaces that leaves traces on the shining terrain.

The first thirty seconds of Arocha's film open up Bursztyn's world, that of the *Minimáquinas* (Minimachines), *Miniesculturas* (Minisculptures), or *Esculturas de bolsillo* (Pocket Sculptures), which play the leading role in this text and in *Azilef* (figs. 1–2). The first exhibition of this series of sculptures opened on 11 November 1969, and as well as several small-scale pieces it was accompanied by the experimental film made jointly by the artist and the director Arocha. This seven-minute work, on 16mm film, was entitled *Azilef*, reversing the letters of the sculptress' first name, just as the name of the group that provided the music for this short film, Los Teipus, reverses the syllables of the colloquial Colombian expression *Los putas* (roughly "the devils" or "the aces"). Azilef, according to Arocha, was the planet where the strange beings that hover in the film existed: Bursztyn's sculptures, made from discarded parts of typewriters and scrap iron of various origins. By that time, Bursztyn had

1. Feliza Bursztyn, *Minimáquina* (Minimachine), c. 1969 (photo c. 1973) Courtesy of the Archive of Pablo Leyva. Photo: Pablo Leyva

2. Film still from *Azilef*, c. 1969, directed by Luis Ernesto Arocha, Instituto de visión gallery, Bogotá

been working with scrap iron for nearly ten years and had found a new discarded material: the odd pieces of stainless steel she used to make *Las histéricas* (The Hysterical Ones) and the "environment" *Siempre acostada* (Always Lying Down), just a year before the *Minimáquinas*.

In the article published in the newspaper *El Tiempo* on 28 October 1969, entitled "'Minifeliza' Bursztyn Launches a New Style", the author comments that Bursztyn is in the hospital and that Arocha is presenting the short film of "the cinematic version of 'pocket' Feliza" for her. In the brief interview in this article, Bursztyn appears excited by the new possibilities of these small-scale sculptures, works that she made even after the surgery resulting from a tragic car accident in 1968. This admission to the hospital may have been part of the recuperation and recovery process. The *Minimáquinas* and *Miniesculturas* were easier to weld; the small parts could be held without the effort required for medium- and large-scale scrap metal sculptures. But this reading may contradict the intention of Bursztyn, who announces in the same article: "There is no capitulation at all in the 'Minifeliza', as you say. It's simply that in small pieces I find a better medium of expression to show how iron, fire, and I are equals, loving each other, but with a full-time love, a fully completed circle".[1]

There is indeed no capitulation; the answer is clear when she says that she was interested in entering this dimension of sculpture. Her work ethic is revealed: she was producing in spite of illness, tragedy, or accident. She allowed no excuses in her practice and that is why she made her works from what she had available: waste, scrap, parts of damaged and forgotten machines. The construction operations in the *Minimáquinas* series are simple and compelling. She makes the sculptures with articulated segments stripped to the bone, retaining special springs, bushings, and rivets so that movement is maintained (fig. 3).

In the decisions on how her work was constructed and exhibited there was an implicit need to change the way the public related to it. The initial shock caused by presenting a work of art made from pieces of metal waste welded together is obvious: critics' discussions and press reviews of Bursztyn's sculpture focused on this point. Moreover, her work involves a disruption, rarely covered at the time, of the art spaces created by modes of exhibition inherited from the discussions in the United States stemming from the works of Abstract Expressionists. After the middle of the twentieth century, white spaces were required which constructed a now suspect "neutrality", making it possible to differentiate between what was and what was not a work of art. Those white cubes have permeated

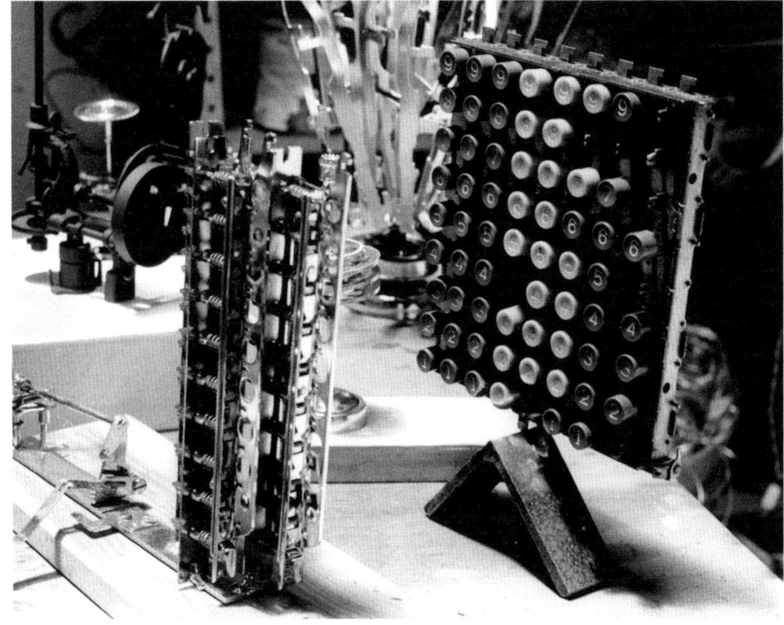

3. *Minimáquinas* (Minimachines) in Feliza Bursztyn's studio, c. 1973 Courtesy of the Archive of Pablo Leyva. Photo: Pablo Leyva

the ways of presenting art from that moment until now. Bursztyn's break with expectations goes beyond using scrap metal and waste material to make her sculptures. It is also revealed in the way she proposed that the visitor's body should explore and activate the sculptures in the exhibition space. And although she participated in exhibitions in the white cube, she took it as a site of experimentation and suggested a way of inhabiting it that was different from the canon mentioned above. Both in *Las histéricas* and in the *Minimáquinas* there is the intention to create a world more related to expanded theatre and the "environments" developed by the American artist Allan Kaprow in 1958–59, which blurs the traditional notion of conducting the exhibition in the white cube and is supplemented by the work Bursztyn did in collaboration with Arocha.

Azilef was screened on a window at the Bogotá headquarters of Galería San Diego.[2] At that time it could be seen from the street, so it invited the public to follow. It invaded the public space and formed part of the setup of the exhibition. Visitors saw the sculptures in conjunction with the images in the film, where they are characters in an imagined world and in the artist's studio; the rock music of Los Teipus invited viewers to "have a lovely trip through the Milky Way made of dreams and magic". This trip transported people out of the white cube, and at that moment they were in tune with the context of the counter-culture and space exploration, which, that same year, only a few months before, took the first humans to the moon, in July 1969 (fig. 4).

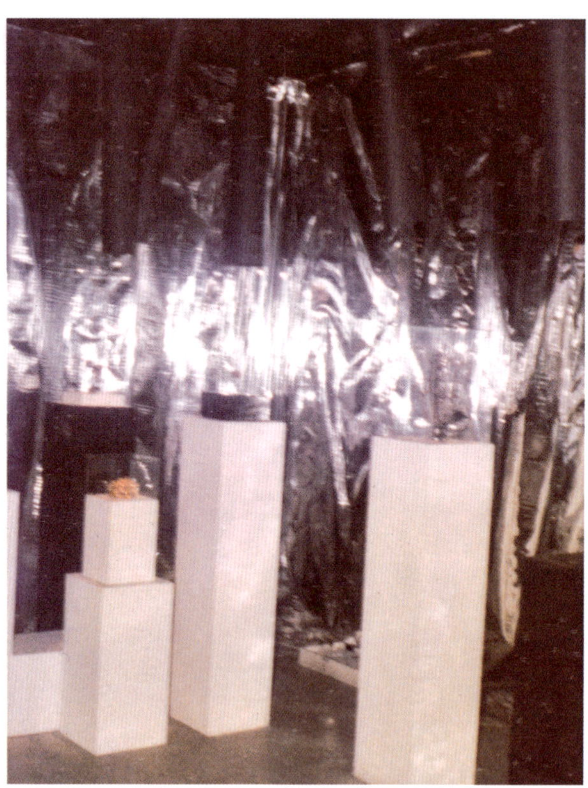

There is no record of the setup of that first exhibition of the *Minimáquinas*, but in the photo that does exist from the 1970s we can see that Bursztyn used white pedestals and urns to show the sculptures. This museological approach used in traditional exhibitions is subverted, as the walls of the space are lined with silver plastic sheeting, a material she also used in the film with Arocha, thereby creating the impression of being inside a spaceship. There is an allusion in these materials to the technological advances of the time: the prevalent use of aluminium, shiny stainless steel, and plastics or acetates and other petroleum derivates were among the developments that accompanied the imaginaries of progress in that period, the post-war space and arms races. These design choices reinforce the argument that Bursztyn meant to alter the experience of the white cube. This intention can be traced from *Las histéricas* and *Siempre acostada* (1968) onwards.

As well as proposing changes in the typical experience of the exhibition space when installing her work, there is a constant striving after movement in her sculptures: in the film *Las camas de Feliza* (Feliza's Beds, 1974) by José María Arzuaga, Bursztyn said that they "do move, unlike the country". The suggestion of movement in the sculptures starts in the early 1960s with the series *Chatarras* (Junk Sculptures), where the pieces that make up mobile systems in industrial equipment or motors and in water pipes and networks are part of the assemblage. In some cases, the sculptures are made with taps or pistons that have movement of their own and can be manipulated, although at that time there was no direct invitation from the artist to the public to move the sculpture, as there was in the *Minimáquinas*. Other objects trapped in the composition of the sculpture make unexpected movements: loose washers on lower-gauge bolts, nuts stuck on tacks and in gear mechanisms, metal plates and tin cans that vibrate because they are only welded at a single point and act as levers or suspended cantilevers.

In the series after 1967, such as *Las histéricas*, made from stainless steel waste, the encounter with movement is clear; the flexible nature of the material makes the millimetre-thick sheets flex or touch each other, squeaking and making waves that reflect the light in the space. Moreover, Bursztyn connected them to modified motors with masses welded to their shafts so that the movement would be uneven and eccentric. In those exhibitions she used switches with rudimentary timers that enabled her to create cycles of vibration and rest. At other times she included contact activation systems so that the people who were there caused the works to move frenetically.

There are two ways of approaching movement in the *Minimáquinas* that I want to highlight. In the first, Bursztyn uses the parts articulated by their original mechanisms in their machine state. Moving parts of typewriters are used so that the public, invited to interact with the work, will manipulate the sculpture: turning a cog, changing the position of a metal sheet, creating a vibration, or moving a part that returns to its initial state by means of a spring. When activating these mechanisms, we cease to anticipate what the machine does; it no longer imprints a letter on paper and the cylinder stops turning the sheet; a repeated movement is generated, which is disappointing because there is no result that satisfies the expectation of a functional action. This short circuit means that the small sculptures are perceived as discrete bodies which become creatures, strange, fractured beings separated from their initial use, which one can guess by examining their component parts. It is as if Bursztyn were placing viewers in a limited role on a Fordist assembly line. They only have to repeat an action that produces no more than a minimal perceptible result. The finished product can be seen in the window of a shopping gallery outside the factory (fig. 5).

The second way in which Bursztyn suggests movement for this series of sculptures is when they turn into animated bodies in the fantastic world

5. Film still from *Azilef*, c. 1969, directed by Luis Ernesto Arocha, Instituto de visión gallery, Bogotá

of Azilef. They come to life and play roles within the planet. Morning breaks in Azilef after the image of fire in the rocket. The intense star that lights up the metal surface moves by a special effect, in the manner of Michel Gondry, propelled by a human arm. The star-lamp makes the shadows change and dawn is over in a few seconds. A sculpture is seen imitating a bush in the inhospitable landscape of Azilef. This world appears punctuated by flashes of metal: amid the rebellious attitudes of 1960s youth who felt fervour for change running through their veins. Changes in fashion, access to the contraceptive pill, music festivals (now legendary), cold war tension, student movements, songs of revolution, and developments in science that enabled philosophy and the arts to envisage relationships between different beings and posit new worlds: utopias running in parallel.

Bursztyn created a complex, independent world. She laid claim to her space within the context of art in Colombia, separated from her first husband, she asked her father for a piece of land three metres wide to make her studio and be able to put together her sculptures. It was the conquest of a space of one's own, of imagination and freedom, following Virginia Woolf. The call to have a voice, celebrate, roar with laughter and make sculptures from the leftovers of society, things that were despised and looked at askance. That establishment of one's own world is a strong impulse which interests me in *Azilef* and in the *Minimáquinas*. The definition of creating worlds comes to my aid from a text by the artist and writer Patricia Reed, when she says:

> Every human lives in a world. Worlds are composed of contents, the identification of those contents, and by the configuration of

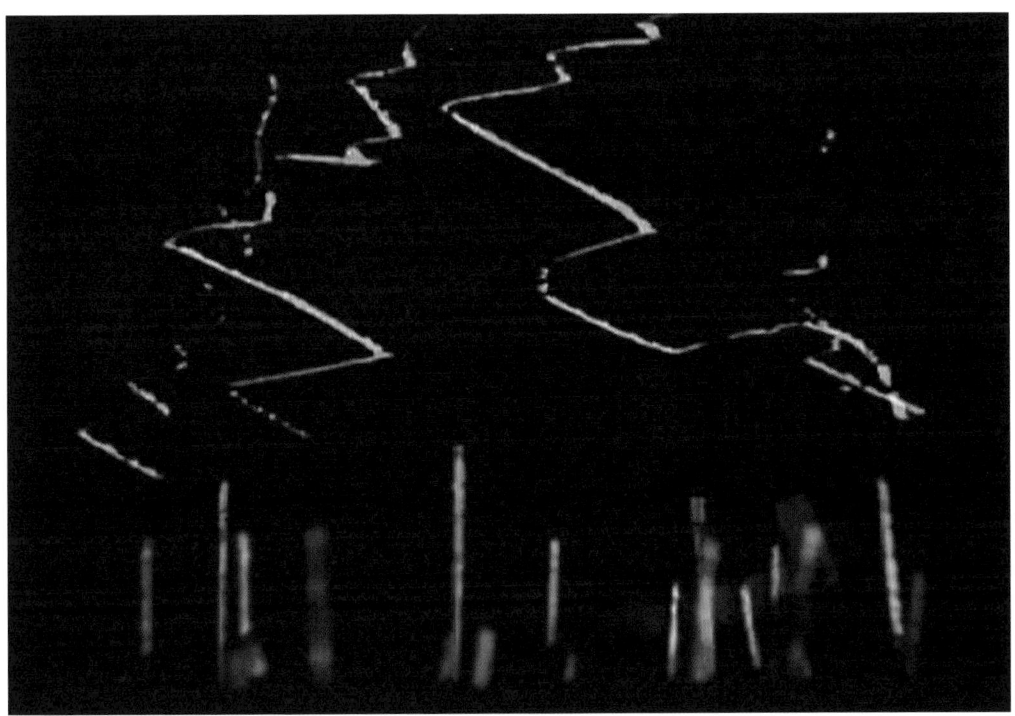

content-relations within – semantically, operationally, and axiologically. As spaces of inhabitation, worlds are made concrete through manners of doing and saying that affirm a coherence between its contents and the identities of its contents, as well as content-relations therein. The identification of the contents of a world and its relational configuration is what establishes frames of reference for *practical* orientation (fig. 6).[3]

In the film, these "other" beings live outside rigid definitions and notions of what ought to be; they are the articulating contents of the world: they creep and communicate through animated furrows, flying and spinning like satellites of Azilef. They land in the sculptor's hands and return to the studio, the shop shelves. However, restless to the end, they appear in the reflection from the special polarized goggles worn for protection from welding sparks, move in the space of the frame, and mix with marijuana plants. These little animated automata are a sample of what is potentially present in the machines they are spawned from. For instance, when a swarm of typewriter keys vibrates and is transformed into an alternative communication system, language is displaced from convention. Film editing makes it possible to dislocate time and the functions of objects as in Bursztyn's sculpture. Just like in the film *2001: A Space Odyssey* (1968) by the American director Stanley Kubrick, these machines communicate through light. HAL 9000, the film's artificial intelligence, with his fixed light, vibrates almost imperceptibly, increasing the intensity of his relationship with the main character, turning the slight changes of light, in the fixed image of his red and yellow bulb, into a language that supplements human language and places it under tension (fig. 7).

Bursztyn's *Minimáquina* entitled *Hal* is made from the insides of a matrix scalar calculator, probably by the Monroe company; it has two plates welded on its sides and a foot made of parts taken from a typewriter. This Hal could be a primitive version of the sophisticated HAL 9000 from Kubrick's film. It communicates through basic algorithms and turns, suspended in the airspace of Azilef. What intentions does Bursztyn's Hal have as a character? He does not seem to go against his creator like the 9000; there is an internal consistency between the nodes of the system and internal regulation processes in the creative world Bursztyn presents. This brings me close to the quotation from Reed. The formal decisions and actions in the *Minimáquinas* series of sculptures and the film *Azilef* deploy arguments that define a traceable state of the world. There is a synchrony between the sculptures and their parts, as well as iridescences that project meaning in many directions, and there is a generous quantity of transmission and receiver aerials that enable connections to be formed with various worlds. One of these worlds consists of the ideas

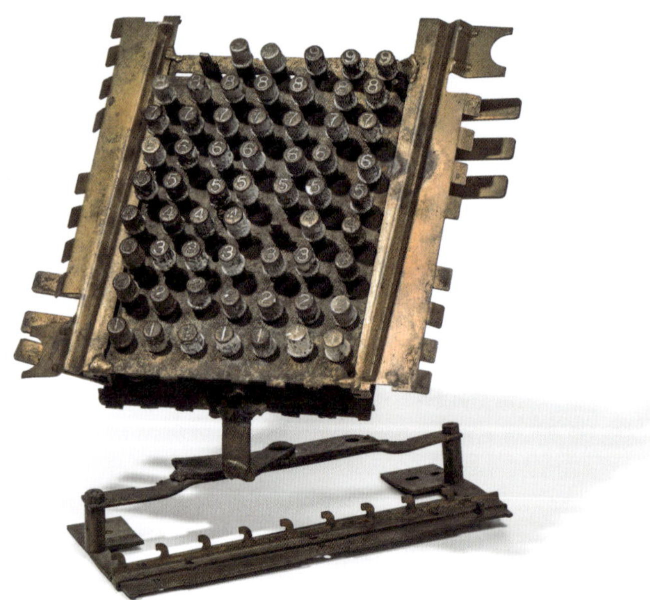

7. *Hal*, from the series *Minimáquinas* (Minimachines), 1969 (photo 2021) Courtesy of Muzeum Susch. Photo: Óscar Monsalve

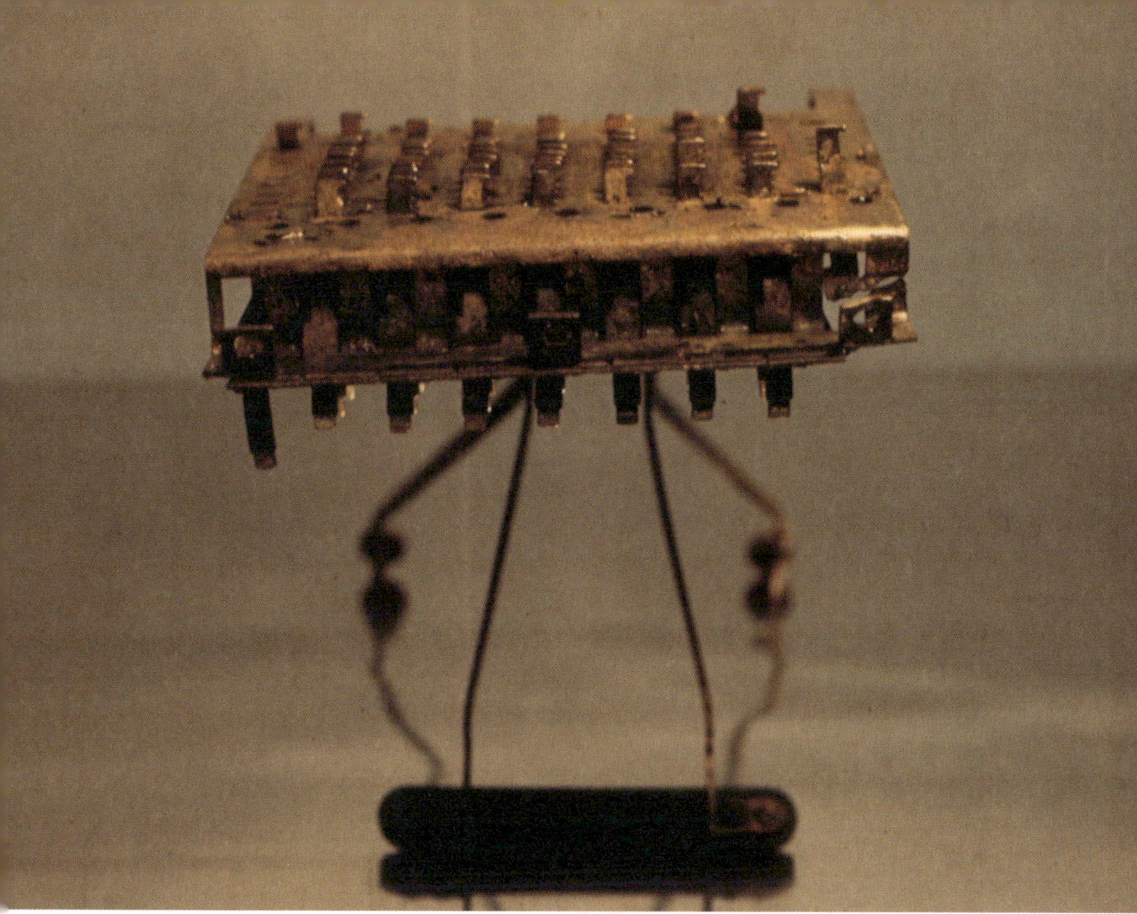

of Professor Donna Haraway, as part of the substance of cyberfeminism and the manifestos of the VNS Matrix and Laboria Cuboniks collectives.

Haraway anchors her theoretical endeavour from cybernetics, defining the cyborg as a "hybrid of machine and organism, a creature of social reality as well as a creature of fiction".[4] This hybrid is designed as "a blasphemous antiracist feminist figure useful for science studies analyses and feminist theory alike".[5] The cyborg, the hybrid, enables me to bring the worlds of Haraway and Bursztyn together, in the force of the creatures they create, both on the level of language and metaphor, as well as on the physical plane of the concreteness of scrap metal. Both set up experimental work platforms, laboratories to compose and decompose in vectors that escape towards reality, practice, interpretation, and language. Bursztyn's sculptures/creatures/cyborgs, as well as shunning the expected in the art context, are projected with the utopias of the period that nourished the intellectual worlds of Haraway, Shulamith Firestone, and beyond. In full awareness and freedom to name herself, Bursztyn took refuge under the mantle of a "crazy woman" to be able to live without having to bear all the weight of being categorized at various levels. The phrase, which has now become a motto, "In a sexist country, pretend to be the mad one!", is evidence that "crazy woman" or "magician" or "witch" served to let her position herself on the boundary of society so as not to be immediately rejected.[6] She maintained her field of action by carrying on for as long as her living machinery allowed her, just as the equipment that fed her work did.

The "crazy woman" could live in a liminal state, engaging in cross-overs, mixing and boundary transgressions, the favourite themes of twentieth-century commentators, according to Haraway.[7] These liminal entities are pursued, expelled, or admired, depending on each community. So "the magician is unsettling to people as a borderline creature and is never treated as a full member of their society, but he [she] is also a source of fascination and revered as a healer, diviner and rainmaker".[8] Liminal states cannot be maintained for long; some aspects turn into norms and others are banished. The light of the flares that these intellectuals set off in tune with their contexts are valuable and ephemeral stimuli for thought to action. How do we participate in that world of Bursztyn's? What roles can we have as viewers of that work? We need to maintain the force and concreteness of the objects and spaces this artist created, as well as her work ethic. Words dance and combine in dissonance or harmony with that world. Our hands can adjust a metal joint; we read her statements in the press and we can experience her work. This mass of content opens its floodgates and expands when it is mixed, hybridized, with us. How long does a day last on Azilef? (fig. 8)

[1] "'Minifeliza' Bursztyn lanza nuevo estilo", *El Tiempo*, 28 October 1969.

[2] There is another short film which accompanied the series entitled *Las Histéricas*, also made in collaboration with Luis Ernesto Arocha: they called it *Hoy Feliza* (Today Feliza). In the records of the Fundación Patrimonio Fílmico both films appear with production dates in the early 1970s, but as is clear in the quotation from the 1969 article in *El Tiempo*, Arocha showed her the final cut of *Azilef* for her exhibition in November that year.

[3] Patricia Reed, "The End of a World and Its Pedagogies", *Making & Breaking* 2 (2021), makingandbreaking.org.

[4] Donna J. Haraway, *Manifestly Haraway* (Minneapolis: University of Minnesota Press, 2016), 5.

[5] Donna J. Haraway, *Modest_Witness@Second_Millennium. Femaleman©_Meets_Oncomouse™: Feminism and Technoscience* (New York: Routledge, 1997), 295.

[6] Maritza Uribe de Urdinola, "En un país de machistas ¡hágase la loca!", *El Tiempo: Revista Carrusel* (Bogotá), 30 November 1979: 15.

[7] Donna J. Haraway, *Modest_Witness@Second_Millennium*, p. 52

[8] Minsoo Kang, *Sublime Dreams of Living Machines: The Automaton in the European Imagination* (Cambridge, MA: Harvard University Press, 2011), 35–36.

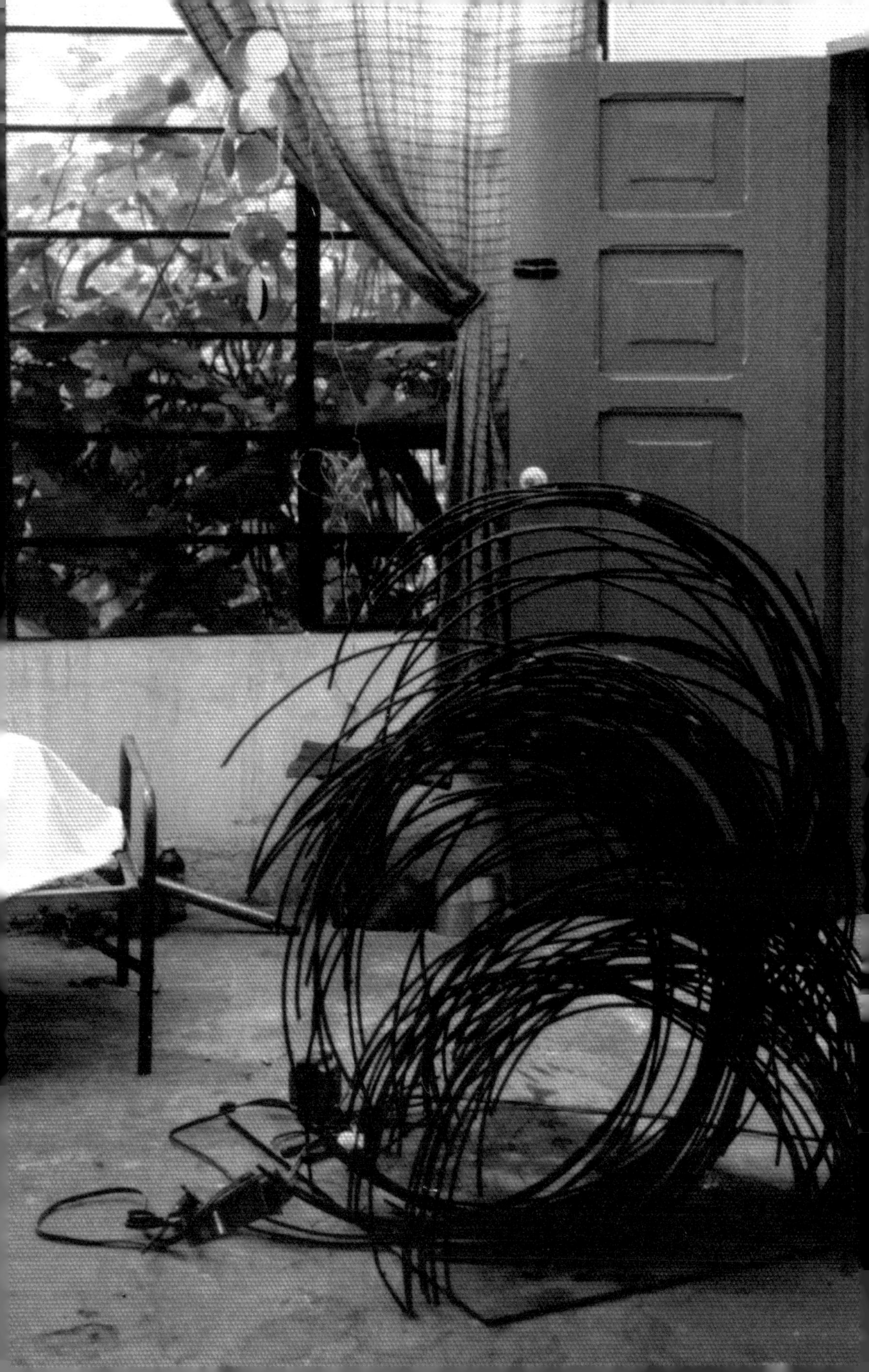

The Existence Written in Rhythm

Daniel Muzyczuk

> Just another existence. This existence was written in rhythm, in motion, maybe that's why it turned out to be so unusual? This movement belonged to an unknown world, which gradually, like a giant machine, stretched out, stretched one by one, unhooked all its hidden modes.
>
> Marta Traba[1]

The main purpose of László Moholy-Nagy's *Light Prop for an Electric Stage* (1930) was to present itself. The piece was constructed to be the sole actor in a theatrical piece. Watching it move in the specially designed interior is an experience that involves the viewer by the use of movement and the sound that the object produces while moving. One cannot be separated from the other. Just like other early kinetic sculptures, this piece was also an attempt at a construction of an object that would be a spatialisation of abstract painting. We can trace a whole kinetic movement that exploded in the 1960s to that model – a moving object that is the embodiment of constructivist faith in progress, objectivity, and rationalism. This model promoted in cities like Paris or New York dominated the common vocabulary for decades. However, the movement even at the time was clearly more diverse and the artists who were treated as representatives of the tendency had different stakes.

Positioning Feliza Bursztyn's work in the kinetic sculpture historical lineage is on the one hand easy and logical, but as soon as it gets there it begins to question the category itself. Her work is driven by different concerns than the progress proclaiming artists from the Denise René circle. We will more clearly see the differences by considering the theory behind the work of one of the paradigmatic artists of kinetic art: Nicolas Schöffer. His spatiodynamism was an attempt at using the field of art as a laboratory to design objects that would influence the way people experience space and time. Not unlike the theories of Władysław Strzemiński

1. Interior of the artist's studio
Courtesy of the archive of Pablo Leyva.
Photo: Pablo Leyva

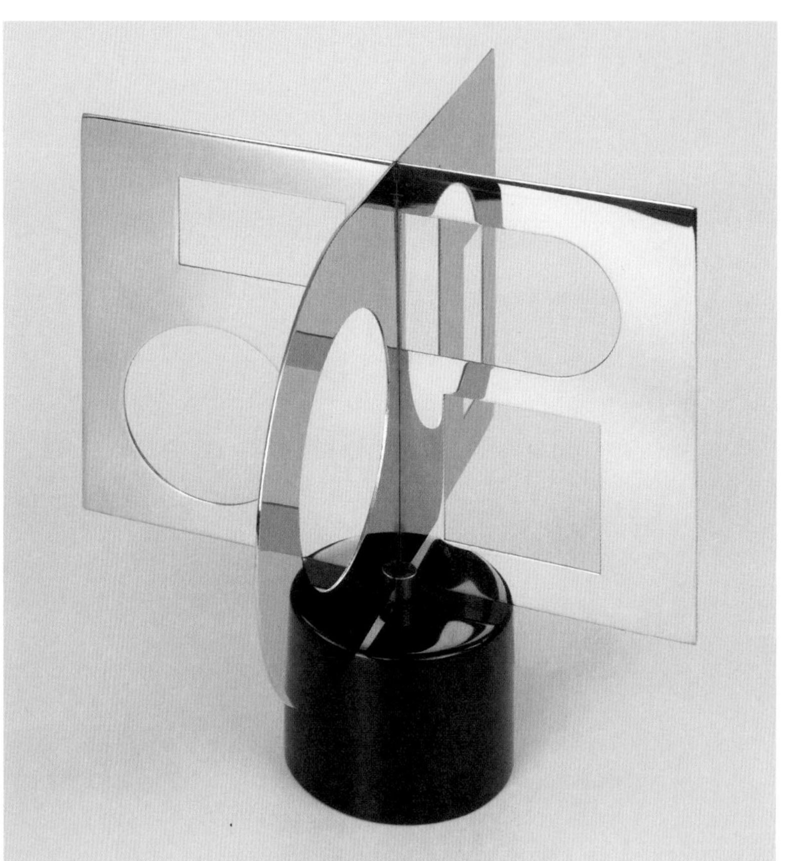

and Katarzyna Kobro in the 1930s, he believed that "calculated effects will bring about a dynamited visual condensation, will oblige man to react physically and psychically, they will act on the individual corporal expression and improve the quality of the collective corporal expression, by relieving the masses of their psychic as well as their physical tensions, and freeing them from their complexes".[2] Schöffer was deeply interested in the therapeutic aspects of new art. His thinking was not far removed from the classic of German Lebensreform philosopher Ludwig Klages, who, at the beginning of the last century, claimed that the machinic tempo of life as determined by the industrial revolution is the deep cause of suffering. The complex and flexible biological rhythms needed to be subsumed to a regular measure of the metronome and other time-regulating machines. The rescue can only come from a deeper understanding of the nature of rhythm and proposing new ways in which people can get synchronized again. Schöffer dreamt of a reconnection not by abandoning or moving out of the city. He saw rescue in repurposing the use of machines. Cybernetics offered a framework for kinetic work of art to become a machine for regulating the rhythms of everyday life.

Spatiodynamism was meant to heal the trauma of being thrown into an inorganic environment that demands efficiency. From today's perspective, it is not hard to see that this tendency was easily subordinated to the general idea of filling homes and workplaces with objects that are making existence more pleasant, be they a kinetic multiple or Japanese bells (fig. 2).

The tendency to see kinetic art as objects that tie the room together is of course a shortcut. Within the movement there were artists that were seeing their work quite differently. Schöffer was also interested in the darker areas, but he would never explore them. He saw works that were not sharing the constructivist genealogy as symptoms of disturbance that are worth studying, just like an illness that needs examining only to come up with a solution. These lines could have been written after seeing for example the work of another kinetic art pioneer, Jean Tinguely: "Eroticism, sexual obsession, often condition the productions of the surrealists, like those of mental patients, with the difference that the ones deliberately go out in search of such images, while the others undergo them. A mental ailment is in the first place a deep disturbance in the psychophenomenological field of the individual. This means that the temporal structuration oscillates or functions abnormally, in a broken, halting way, too fast or too slowly; the differentiation between dreams and the waking state diminishes, and even disappears on one or several planes at once, creating

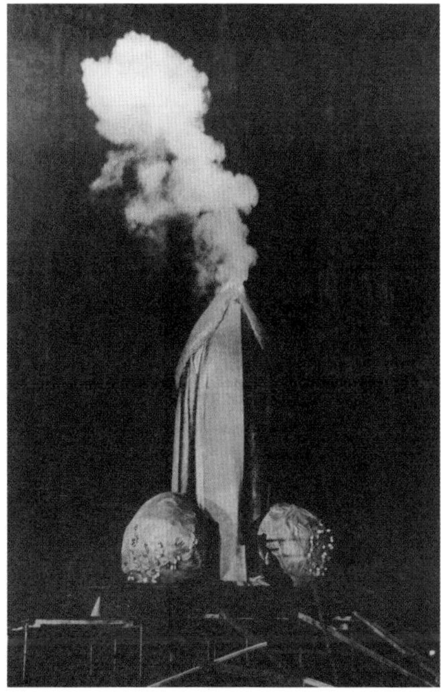

3. Jean Tinguely, *Victory*, 1970, 33 × 24.8 cm (page), print dimensions variable, Museum of Modern Art (MoMA), New York, inv. 282.1974.1-16 © 2022. Digital image, The Museum of Modern Art, New York/Scala, Firenze

a confusion and even a dangerous interpretation between the two states. The balanced oscillation between pleasure and anguish becomes fixed at the extremes, or alternates without transition by shocks; anguish and sexuality become dominant themes among the surrealists, and characteristic obsessions among mental patients. The study, the organization and the mastery of these oscillations in their temporal structuration, the defining of the role of the component elements and their movement, would make it possible to clarify many mysteries, which concern both artistic creation and man's mental equilibrium, two problems which are closely related" (fig. 3).[3]

Bursztyn's work is definitely more rooted in the surrealist sources. While sharing with Schöffer and Tinguely the interest in metal as the basic material, she is much closer to the latter in that she is not concerned with the shiny surfaces of brand new elements. The connection between them was noticed quite early. Marta Traba pointed out that both were referring to "organic situations".[4] The power of anthropomorphism is based on the suggestion of transformation. This is another trait of the surrealist provenance. A complex set of procedures involving montage, movement, and giving title is responsible for turning a piece of metal mechanism into something reminiscent of a living body.

Luis Ernesto Arocha's 1971 short film *Azilef* begins with the welder's flame acting as if it is a source of life. A lone light illuminates an abstract landscape on which some sculptures appear. They are animated and interact with each other with the help of "rays" scratched directly on the film. The soundtrack is composed of two music pieces. The first is a psychedelic rock song by Colombian band Los Teipus, which amplifies the oneiric surrealism of the animation.[5] But there is another, more interesting piece of music that is briefly introduced: *Atmosphères* by György Ligeti, written ten years earlier. This work is considered revolutionary as it was one of the first that blended the recent discoveries of electronic music with acoustic instruments. Ligeti chose to work with a large ensemble in order to create masses of sound that would appear stable in an attempt to induce the sense of timelessness. Arocha suggests that these objects are familiar and strange at the same time. They resemble living beings, yet their ontological status is questionable.

Scrap metal is a material that points to a less optimistic vision of the progress of technology and its influence on human beings. In this regard, Bursztyn's work resonates strongly with pieces of another artist from a peripheral modernism, Henryk Morel. Morel was a Polish sculptor who debuted in the early 1960s and developed a distinct style. Unfortunately, his career was disrupted by a suicide in 1968. His notebooks contain writings on earlier sculptors that played an important role for his own development:

> Moholy-Nagy: Because light is a spatiotemporal element, we can enter the regions of a new perception of space only by emphasising the problem of light ... Kobro: A sculpture is part of space, therefore links or relations with space are a sine qua non of its being organic. Sculpture should not be a formal composition, enclosed in its mass, but an open spatial structure, in which the internal space of the composition is linked to the external.[6]

While this statement might sound to voice a similar sentiment to those neoconstructivist texts of Schöffer, a glance at the work of Morel clearly positions him on a very different pole to that occupied by the proponents of cybernetics. The scrap metal sculptures are built as structures that divide the space. The series entitled *Domy* (Homes) is significant in the contrast between the solid metal structures that resemble architecture and rubber tires that are being pushed into these blocks. It seems like a statement on the work of Kobro, whose abstract structures saw the role of sculpture as a method of organizing space. The light metal pieces were placed in an abstract, bodiless space. Rubber hence becomes a metaphor of the disciplined body. It is nearly crushed by the forces that are beyond the control of the individual. It is easy to see these pieces as the outcome of the traumatic experiences with the machine. One piece from 1968 entitled simply *Kompozycja* (Composition) gives a slightly different feeling to these objects whose affective force is based on contrast. It is composed of blades of a mechanical plough and rubber tire crushed in between these sharp things. Existential in tone, this piece is also very graphic in suggesting violence. The affective work of the piece is based on the research of the artist into the psychological reactions to juxtapositions of different objects. In an essay describing the framework of these experiments he wrote: "My attention was drawn to research by Rubinsztejn, Kreutz and Rorschach, dealing with the laws of emotional action of forms and shapes on the awareness of recipients. I tried to show how people react to shapes that are not represented, e.g. rounded or sharp, and what kind of impressions they evoke in them thanks to the mechanism of associations. The experience of psychologists and psychoanalysts has shown that there are objective laws of these reactions. They are not contradicted by the fact that the recipient's individual predispositions (character traits, mood of the moment, experiences recorded in memory) contribute to the way of perceiving, and the nature of emotional reactions".[7] Morel's ways of perceiving were then deeply influenced by psychoanalytical methods. The primary conflict between two elements, one soft and the other solid, is a recurring motif of his visions. While the sculptural objects were staging of these juxtapositions and offering metaphors, Morel was constantly looking for ways to extend these visions by creating total installations and adding the musical element to his works. This is another aspect that connects his work with that of Bursztyn.

The series *Las histéricas* (The Hysterical Ones) (fig. 4) is an entry point to the realm of sound. Just like with the work of Morel or even Tinguely this moment might seem like a side effect of usage of specific materials. But the development and refinement of the tendency, seen here in the crude version, convinces me that it is in fact a crucial addition. A simple mechanism makes a piece of metal constantly oscillate causing it to produce rhythmical noise. This description places these pieces close to the works of Tinguely, but of course there are significant differences. The title of the work clearly introduces the notion of the female body. Instead of male bachelor machines, we are looking at the bride that suffers from the effects of the sexual trauma. The trembling is a characteristic element that might be easily traced back to the source in the images of hysterics available in the archive of Jean-Baptiste Charcot. However, the sound bears more connections to one of the most meaningful stories of female hysteria – the case of Dora. The symptom of the trauma that launches the analysis is the cough that the patient cannot get rid of. Freud connected the compulsion to the prohibition of a sexual intercourse, and eventually hysteria stands into a scene occupied earlier by masturbation: "But the conclusion was inevitable that with her spasmodic cough, which, as is usual, was referred for its exciting stimulus to a tickling in her throat, she pictured to herself a scene of sexual gratification per os between the two people whose love-affair occupied her mind so incessantly".[8] This is characteristic of Freud, and later used at length by Lacan, that a structure needs to be uncovered in order to understand the meaning of the symptoms. These appear instead of something else that remains hidden. This aspect is made even clearer by Elizabeth Grosz: "Dora's hystericization of the throat and breathing apparatus, her shortness of breath and tussis nervosa, Freud claims, exhibit an upward transposition from a genitally experienced set of sensations that must be repressed. Her throat and vocal cords take on the meaning of the phallus, for they are the heirs, as Freud suggests, to the whole of the patient's sexual life. Particular regions of the body image may take on the meaning of other repressed sexual zones of the body. This implies that there is a lability of meaning for the

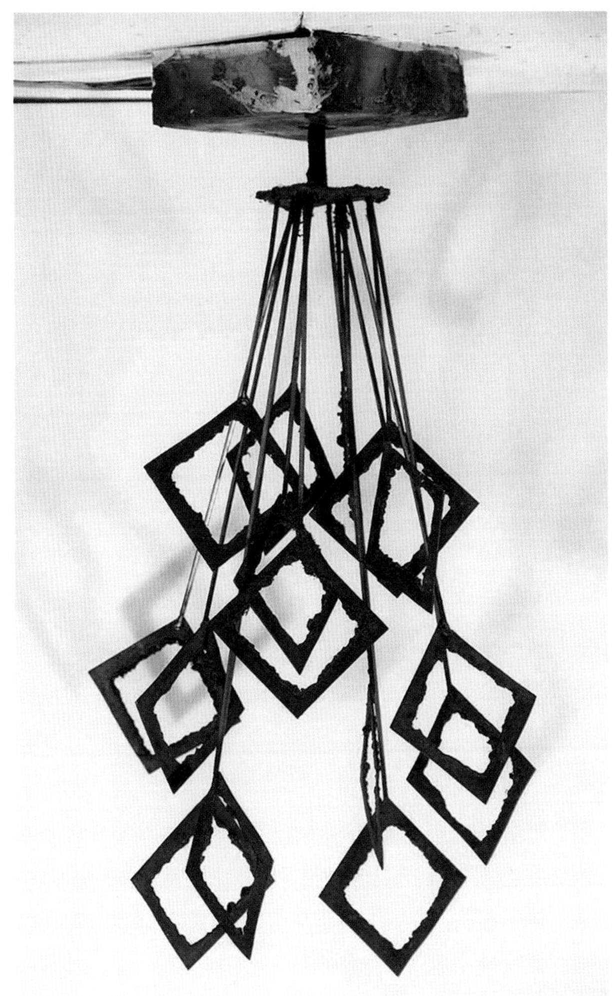

various bodily organs, zones, and processes. Any zone of the body can, under certain circumstances, take on the meaning of any other zone".[9] The organism is an assemblage of objects that can, under certain circumstances, replace each other in their symbolic function. In his delirious *Libidinal Economy*, Jean-François Lyotard saw something even more meaningful in this quid pro quo: "Dora the organic's respiratory system is jammed, Dora the hysteric's respiratory system works wonderfully, and there is no need to seek a secondary benefit for her troubles. The benefit is immediate, there is no benefit, there is a pulsional machinery put in place, which functions on its own account, and this machinery does not work according to death or according to Eros, but according to both, erotic as a regulated machine (a machine upon which discourse will try to produce a reasonable simulacrum in Freud and Lacan's texts), lethal as a deregu-latory machine (which the analyst wants to repair) – but also mortal as regulated (because it condemns Dora to a sterile repetition), and alive because of its deregulation (because it attests to the fact that the libido circulates and invests over the organic body, in its unpredictable displace-ability)".[10] Freud connected the sound with a motion, which, because it is a double for something else entirely, needs to acquire its own, machinic logic. It is reproductive and destructive at the same time. One movement becomes the sign of libido as it is a symptom of the death drive.

Why are all those things important while approaching one of Burszt-yn's mobiles? First of all, we see the work of displacement. After all the title, oscillation, and sound is enough to treat a piece of mechanism as a metaphor of something else. On the basic level the meaning is created by displacement. First, you need to reduce a human being to a medium of symptoms of trauma. Then it is easy to make way for a whole series of substitutions. Here comes in another parallel with the work of Tinguely as seen by Félix Guattari: "The grandmother who pedals inside the automobile under the wonderstruck gaze of the child-a non-Oedipal child whose eye is itself a part of the machine-does not cause the car to move forward, but, through her pedalling, activates a second structure, which is sawing wood … In all these examples (to which should be added narcotics functioning as a desiring-machine, the junky machine) there appears a properly machinic death drive that stands in opposition to the Oedipal regressive death, to psychoanalytic euthanasia. And there is really not one of these desiring-machines that is not profoundly de-Oe-dipalizing" (fig. 5).[11] Pontus Hultén also noted the displacement in the work of Tinguely that opened these machines to this kind of death drive: "The motion makes the pieces even more pathetic; they refuse to die, to lie still. The beautiful veneer of our civilisation is penetrated, and the depths of destitution hidden beneath make gestures at us. It is somehow obscene. The junk seems more real than the new and shiny, partly because it is so marked by life".[12] Isn't this the disruptive, anarchic, and subver-sive machine that both Grosz and Lyotard sensed in Dora's throat? Another type of death drive that leads to emancipation? The judgement depends on the relation of the machine with the viewer. Let us look at how Bursztyn created space for attention to be focused.

Las histéricas were presented originally in a mass – a hospital room with many patients. This must have been a terrifying sight. A certain attempt at the creation of a specific sense of theatricality needs to be acknowledged. It seems to be in relation with an even closer reading of the key Dora case. After all, we need to go from the molecular to the molar. It is not surprising that Dora's case opens another door – that of displacement.

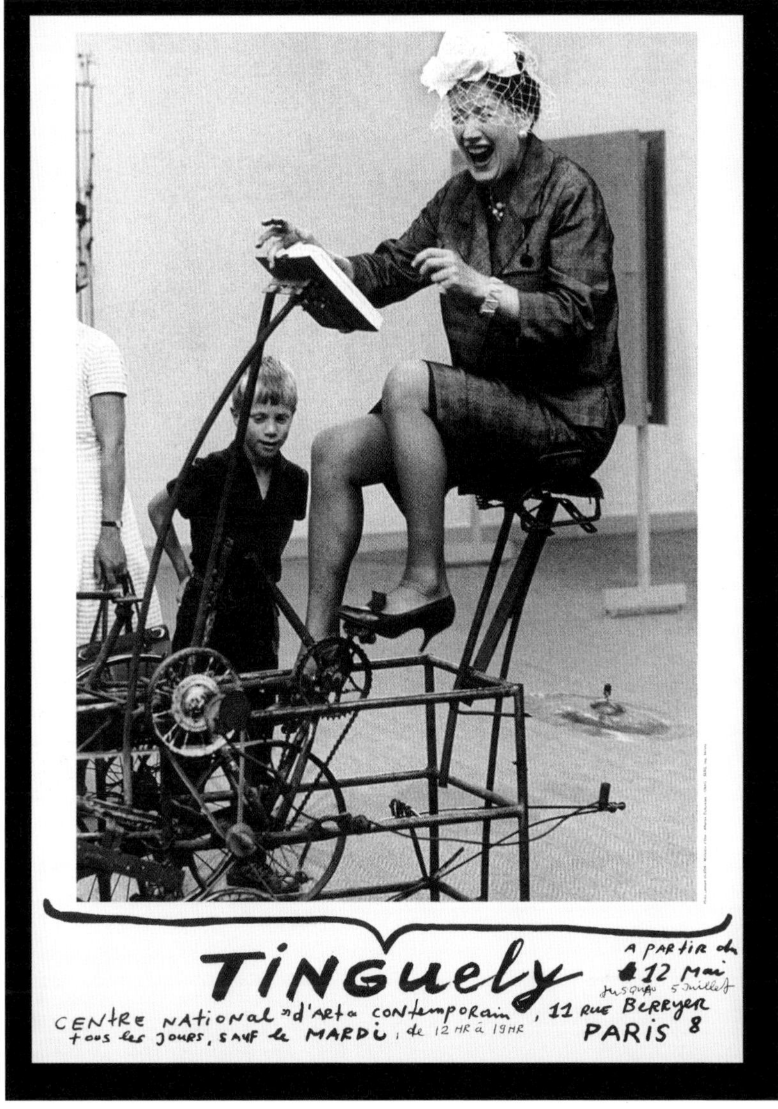

As the therapy develops and the structure is being discovered, it is also played out – performed if you will. The therapist is cast in the role of one of the characters of the original traumatic event. Bursztyn's works are beginning to be staged like theatre performances. This aspect also draws her closer to Tinguely. The visitor is invited into a space where different works are cast in different roles. Her next exhibition project was entitled *Las camas* (The Beds, 1974) (fig. 6) and seemingly represented a rendering of another, more concealed part of the case of Dora: "Dora's symptomatic acts and certain other signs gave me good reasons for supposing that the child, whose bedroom had been next door to her parents', had overheard her father in his wife's room at night and had heard him (for he was always

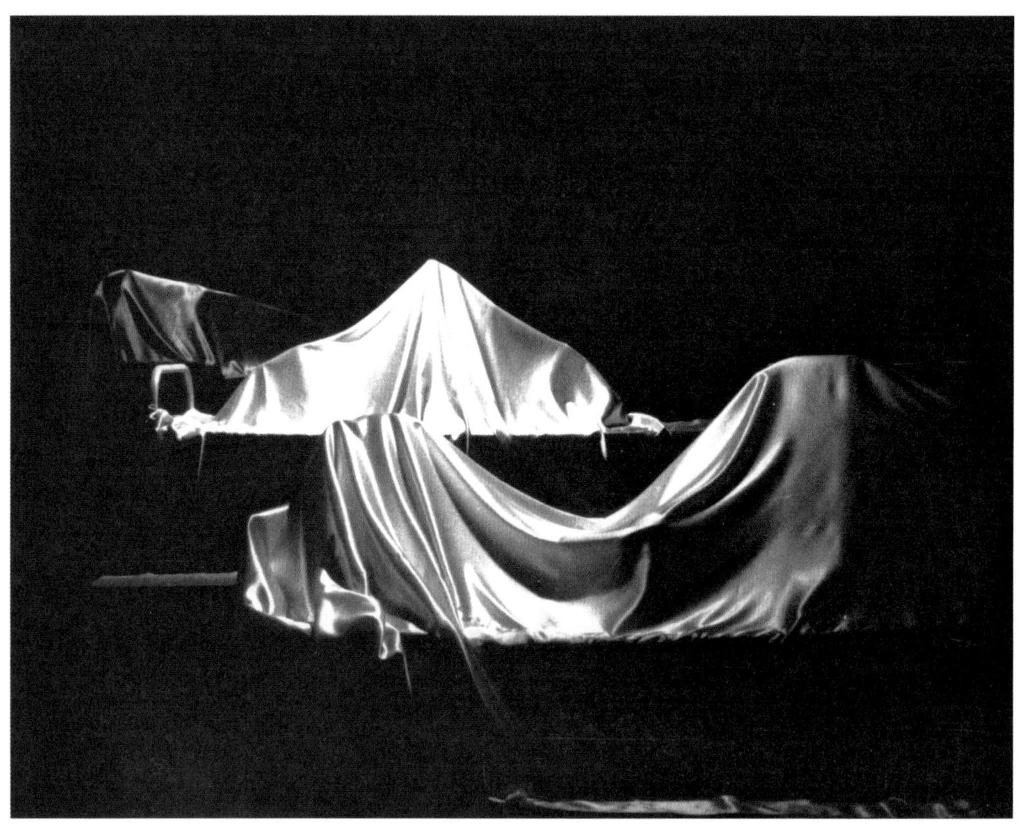

6. Feliza Bursztyn,
Las camas (The Beds),
1974
Courtesy of the Archive
of Pablo Leyva. Photo:
Pablo Leyva

short of breath) breathing hard while they had intercourse. Children, in such circumstances, divine something sexual in the uncanny sounds that reach their ears. Indeed, the movements expressive of sexual excitement lie within them ready to hand, as innate pieces of mechanism. I maintained years ago that the dyspnoea and palpitations that occur in hysteria and anxiety neurosis are only detached fragments of the act of copulation".[13] Again, just like in the case of cough, the aural element seems to be at the centre of the traumatic event. Thus, the kinetic beds of Bursztyn also needed a sound design that would amplify the theatricality of the spectacle, and she turned to electroacoustic music composer Jacqueline Nova. There were several reasons why this alliance was successful. In 1969, Nova was joined by a visual artist, Julia Acuña, to create an audiovisual environment at MAMBO entitled *Luz, sonido, movimiento* (Light, Sound, Movement). They were testing different sounding materials in order to create distinct affective spaces. Nova was also known as a composer who praised new sound worlds that were opened up by the usage of the machine. In her manifesto she wrote: "The earth is entirely submerged within a magnetic field analogous to that produced by a magnetized strip lying on its axis of rotation. Within that magnetic field is found, the world of machines, the world of the composer, of the artist who is concretely situated in the current moment. Outside that field is the fainthearted; the one who does not decide to participate in our fight. This repulsion of the inert world, towards the objects and machines that surround us, is a fixation on the past, as a means of protection; it is fear of the present. Even more, that world wants to try to forget that it lives – if it lives – in the second half of the 20th century; but what the conscious forgets, the unconscious brings out".[14] Nova was also interested in the archetypical. She had just finished a longer electroacoustic work entitled *Cantos de la Creación de la Tierra* (Songs of the Creation of the Earth, 1972). This was a piece where she used recordings of voices of indigenous people retelling the story of the origins of creation. They were heavily treated with electronic instruments until the words were unrecognizable. Nova focused more on the rhythm of the speech as if she were looking for something more perennial. The music she proposed for *Las camas* followed a similar trajectory. Again, the material for sound objects was quite limited. It is dominated by the dense mix of sounds sourced from different metal objects. There is another layer that is brought to the surface – the heartbeat. In a way we can view this montage of two distinct sounds, whose sources are easy to decode, perform a similar juxtaposition to that is apparent in the kinetic objects. Even if the mechanisms are hidden this time behind satin sheets, they are still recognizable by the oscillations. The movements and the beds are causing the viewer to identify the assemblages as anthropomorphic. The music was meant to make this sensation stronger and more grounded. Nova's music had one more effect. It was escalating the theatricality of the setup. The viewer needed to develop a critical distance to these objects, because they were not meant to produce identification of the person with the machine. At least not upon first glance. Bursztyn's work seems to be based on this careful balance between recognition and denial.

Yet, her approach to sound is even more complex. The theatricality of *Las histéricas* is based on the supposition of the presence of the viewer. Sound is the element that is creating an atmosphere that cannot be inhabited: "A noise that … appears as a contradiction in terms as it is carried by the hand by an artifact – the turntable motor – designed to spiral towards a destination. In this order, the *Histéricas* are given as a game of the senses, like a walk in which the roads diverge and turn back on themselves to find contradictions, never an end. Feliza builds her tapes, bends and moulds them, to subject them to an unfeigned noise, a real noise insofar as it is produced by the shock and convulsions, the movement is what creates the sound and the one that traces the bridge with the viewer. The noise,

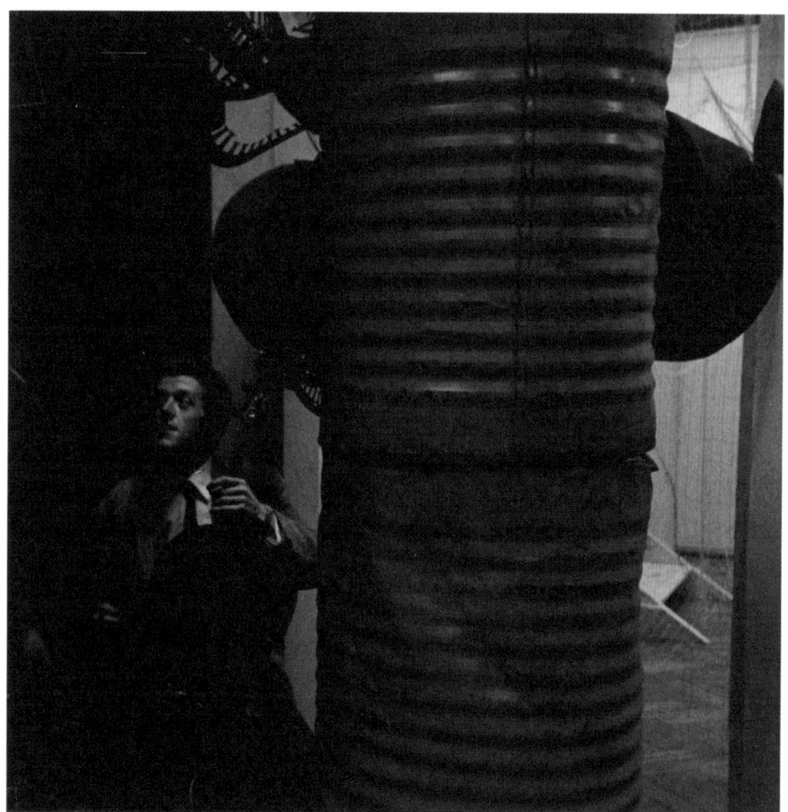

7. Composer Zygmunt
Krauze and artists
Henryk Morel, Cezary
Szubartowski, and
Grzegorz Kowalski,
*5x, an 'audio-visual
performance'*, 1966,
Galeria Foksal, Warsaw.
In the photo: Cornelius
Cardew
Courtesy of Galeria
Foksal. Photo: A. Zborski

in effect, ensures that such a spectator is not simply an entity alien to the
piece, but rather that he is forced to endure it or endure it until patience
overcomes him".[15] It discourages the viewer, scares them away. Noise is
the instrument for the creation of a scene of terror.

Once more Morel might be used as the marker of a certain tendency.
The pieces he realized after *Domy* were expanding into sounding environments. The viewer was placed there in order to be subject to different
processes that were triggering sensations. They were expected to become
active participants in an emancipatory experience (fig. 7). Audiovisuality
was introduced in order to create an immersive experience that would
release visitors from passivity. The oppressive side of his works was
significantly reduced. Bursztyn went in the opposite direction. Instead of
participation, she found the critical value in the theatricality and staging
of the mechanism of an anarchic death drive. While Morel moved closer
to the optimistic sentiments of Schöffer, Bursztyn continued exploring
trauma. The stakes are higher and they can be seen in the oscillation itself.
The therapeutic aspect of these spectacles can be seen in another aspect.
Philippe Lacoue-Labarthe performed a fundamental re-reading of a work

of one of the lesser-known students of Freud, Theodor Reik. For this psychoanalyst the subject is formed by rhythm and he is "calling upon biology and all the well-known phenomena of periodicity and alternance (waking/sleeping, activity/fatigue, etc.), in its primitive, archaic, primary character-going so far as to suppose a state of pure and simple rhythmic undifferentiation at the origin of human development (which would be identified with the achievement of a complex arrhythmic state). Consequently – and this is what interests Reik – the pulsional process subject to this rhythmic alternance remains infra-liminary, and thus only unconscious empathy is able to grasp it".[16] These works do not simply stage trauma and the machinic death drive. Their power also lies in their potential to reduce the individual to the most basic process of individuation. After all, as Traba wrote: "existence was written in rhythm".

[1] Marta Traba, *Słoneczne labirynty*, trans. Kalina Wojciechowska (Warsaw: Czytelnik, 1972), 39.

[2] Nicolas Schöffer, "The Three Stages of Dynamic Sculpture", in *Nicolas Schöffer* (Neuchâtel: Éditions du Griffon, 1963), 140.

[3] Schöffer, "The Three Stages", 140.

[4] Gina McDaniel Tarver, "Antagonistic Environments, Gendered Spaces and the Kinetic Installations of Colombian Artists Feliza Bursztyn, Jacqueline Nova, and Julia Acuña", in Mariola V. Alvarez, Ana M. Franco, eds., *New Geographies of Abstract Art in Postwar Latin America* (New York: Routledge), 2019, e-book.

[5] Gina McDaniel Tarver, "The Art of Feliza Bursztyn: Confronting Cultural Hegemony", *Artelogie* 5 (October 2013), http://cral.in2p3.fr/artelogie/IMG/article_PDF/article_a273.pdf

[6] Henryk Morel, *Rodin*, unpublished manuscript, quoted in Anna Maria Leśniewska, "Obszar znaczeń", in Anna Maria Leśniewska, ed., *Henryk Morel* (Warsaw: Galeria Sztuki Współczesnej Zachęta, 1996), 23.

[7] R. T., "Uczestnicy II Biennale: Henryk Morel", *Głos Elbląga* 172, 21 July 1967.

[8] Sigmund Freud, "Fragment of an Analysis of a Case of Hysteria", in *The Standard Edition of the Complete Psychological Works of Sigmund Freud. Volume VII (1901–1905)*, trans. James Strachey (London: Hogarth Press), 48.

[9] Elizabeth Grosz, *Volatile Bodies: Toward a Corporeal Feminism* (Bloomington, IN: Indiana University Press, 1994), 77.

[10] Jean-François Lyotard, *Libidinal Economy*, trans. Iain Hamilton Grant (Bloomington, IN: Indiana University Press, 1993), 53.

[11] Félix Guattari, "Balance Sheet for 'Desiring-machines'", in Félix Guattari, *Chaosophy: Texts and Interviews 1972–1977*, edited by Sylvère Lotringer, trans. David L. Sweet, Jarred Becker, and Taylor Adkins (Los Angeles: Semiotext(e), 2009), 104–5.

[12] Pontus Hultén, *The Machine as Seen at the End of the Mechanical Age* (New York: The Museum of Modern Art, 1969), 172.

[13] Freud, "Fragment…", 79–80.

[14] Jacqueline Nova, "El mundo maravilloso de las máquinas", *Nova* 4 (July–August 1966), https://www.scribd.com/doc/261298079/JACQUELINE-NOVA-El-Maravilloso-Mundo-de-Las-Maquinas

[15] Julia Buenaventura, *En primera persona: seis pasajes sobre Feliza Bursztyn* (Bogotá: Alcaldía de Bogotá, 2019), 73.

[16] Philippe Lacoue-Labarthe, "The Echo of the Subject", in Philippe Lacoue-Labarthe, *Typography: Mimesis, Philosophy, Politics* (Stanford: Stanford University Press, 1998), 198–99.

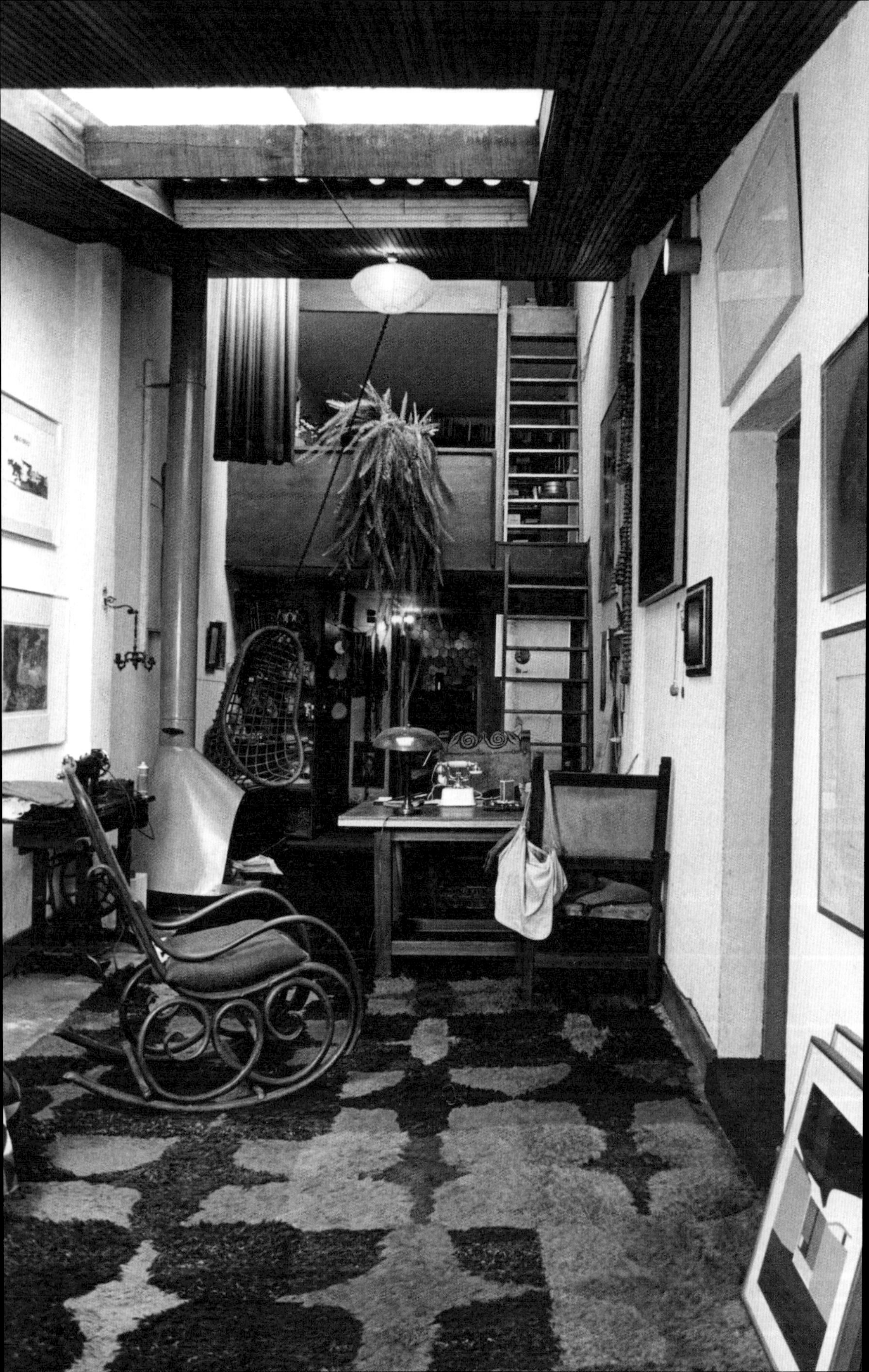

Feliza Bursztyn: "In a sexist country, pretend to be the mad one!"

Lucas Ospina

A few words

On 14 January 2019, the Colombian artist Lucas Ospina published "Feliza Bursztyn: 'En un país de machistas, ¡hágase la loca!'" (Feliza Bursztyn: "In a sexist country, pretend to be the mad one!"), a kind of literary biopic, put together from numerous articles and interviews published over the course of the artist's life and around the time of her death in leading Colombian magazines and newspapers of the period.[1] In his text, Ospina assembled an autobiographical narrative in the form of an interview. The fictional element in it is limited to constructing a space-time continuum in which statements made by Feliza at many different times converge, by creating a single interviewer who, in turn, is an amalgam of all the original interviewers and reporters. So, the fiction presented by Ospina does not extend to Feliza's voice (in other words, everything Feliza says in the text she said at some point in her life) but highlights the consistency of her acerbic, outspoken sense of humour, capable of taking shortcuts that left her interviewers panting and lost, at a turn in the path. Joining all these interviews and articles together allows us to hear Feliza's voice more clearly; we can imagine her eyes gleaming just before she leaps in a new direction, leaving so many journalists lying in her wake with their stupid, malicious questions; we can even hear her legendary peals of laughter. However, at the end of the text Ospina breaks the rules of his own game and introduces a magical, poetic and political twist of great significance, giving Feliza the opportunity to tell us something about her own exile and death, and to make her last joke, in the first person.

Sylvia Suárez

1. Feliza Bursztyn's home, Bogotá
Courtesy of the Archive of Pablo Leyva. Photo: Rafael Moure

___

A narrow street, a front door painted bright red, a garage. The house was a textile factory that belonged to Feliza Bursztyn's parents. The space has changed over the years but its industrial appearance – high ceilings, large windows, cement floors – still survives. In 1963, after the unexpected death of her lover, the poet Jorge Gaitán Durán,[2] and that of her father, the artist inherited a section of the factory: the garage area – a long, narrow space. The house and studio are located in the area of the mechanical workshops and her "colleagues", the neighbours who repair cars, supply her with much of her raw material. As you enter there is a kind of patio with a dusty blue sports car resting in it.

The interviewer knocked on the door and the serving woman led him to the hall, a room as unusual as the front door. It is the width of a large garage, but of considerable depth and contains, at the far end, a kitchen and three open floors connected by steep staircases without rails. The apartment is a narrow, cramped strip full of paintings and hand-made rugs; none of the furniture matches the rest; it is a delightfully well-ordered mess, the expression of people who know that a house is for living in, that it is movement; you cannot avoid the impression that Feliza Bursztyn is too busy living. Here, pliers, welding masks, motors, and mechanical waste are mixed up with artworks by her friends, literature in several languages, foreign magazines, and furniture designed by her. The interviewer is immersed in contemplation of the pictures on the walls and the weird construction which makes him think of the structure of a Mayan pyramid, when a strange being with the body of a woman and the head of a Martian appears through a door on his right. The creature, dressed in dirty, faded jeans, takes off the enormous welding goggles, a kind of diving helmet, and a white cloth to reveal a lively, smiling face. One, two, three storeys, but not conventional floors for conventional people. They are three levels that you have to reach by firemen's stairs. The interviewer, intrigued, asks her how she manages to make that climb after four Tres Esquinas rums. The sculptor explains that she has never fallen down those stairs, which look so hazardous, and offers him a glass of rum. She adds that she is not joining him because "I never start before sundown". The interviewer recalls that someone described Feliza Bursztyn's voice to him as that of a spoilt little girl capable of uttering the most high-calibre vulgarities. She wears high heels and platform soles, "whore's shoes", as she calls them (fig. 1).

The interviewer accepts a cup of tea and begins firing the questions, observed by two female cats, Dada and Wanda Landowska, and their four heirs. The sculptor takes out a jumbled pile of photos. Hundreds of sculptures made from scrap metal with tubes and metal sheets pass

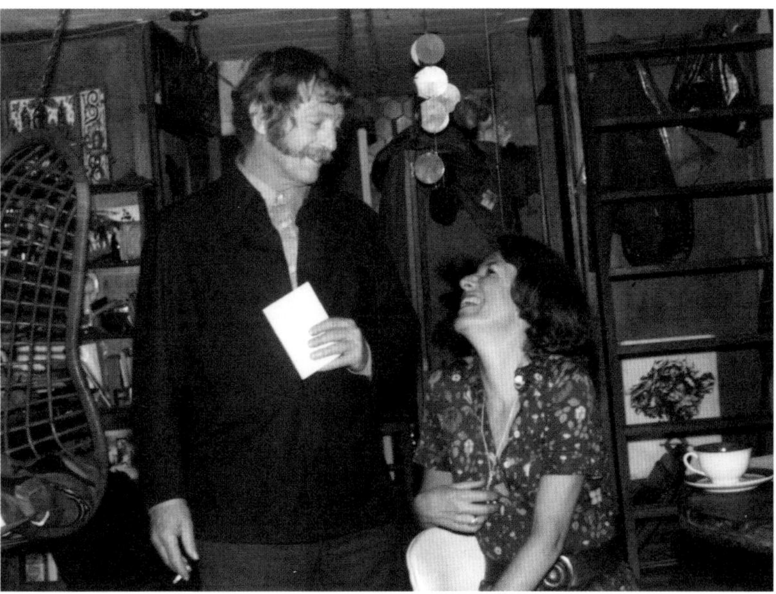

through the interviewer's fingers, while he mentally searches for the influences and parallels. Out of the corner of his eye he sees that Feliza Bursztyn's everyday bed is an anti-bed; it has no mattress. Every night the sculptor, who has nothing in common with a fakir, goes to sleep on a board stretched out between satin sheets, with a peasant-style woollen blanket and a red satin patchwork bedspread.

"And this is my house, full of old iron, spot welders, transformers, paintings, scrap metal, cats, dogs, flowers, seeds. Of course, there's also a kitchen…", she says. The interviewer recalls a conversation he had earlier that morning with one of the regular guests: "If you'd tried her hot pepper soup, a thin broth with pepper, a dash of pepper and more pepper, her sticky rice with tomato sauce and lots of parmesan, her dry – sometimes very dry – spaghetti with garlic or her solid stewed chickpea soup, you would never have believed that for more than twenty years painters, sculptors, politicians, critics, poets, and writers sat at her table. If as well as seeing her, hearing her, going to her house, spying on her, and trying her cooking, you had been her friend; if you had drunk Tres Esquinas rum with her, or vodka, or the whisky she bought by the box, served in glasses with awkward ice cubes and stirred with her finger; if you had talked to her about Cuba, Russia, Colombia, the Kabbalah, the pros and cons of *Revista alternativa*, the mysteries of *El Tiempo*, the covers of the *New York Review of Books*, the articles in *Time*, the art criticism in the *New Yorker*" (fig. 2).

The interview begins.

Interviewer: People call you Feliza perhaps because your surname is difficult to spell in Spanish. Where does Bursztyn come from?

Feliza Bursztyn: Two thousand Jews set off to walk to Palestine. My dad didn't go because he was a rabbi's son. My mother, the daughter of Polish timber merchants, also left for Palestine at the age of sixteen – the only woman on the boat. Dad worked in the socialist party and didn't believe in trade at all. One day the English captured a close friend of his. He took all his money out of the bank, paid it to some guards, they got the guy out and put him in a barrel, and the man arrived in Buenaventura. He wrote to dad from there, telling him about the bananas, the mangoes, and the journey, and he said to mum: "Stay here, I'm going to see what Colombia is like". I was born here.

I: What is your relationship with Jewish culture?

FB: My divorce was the first in the Jewish colony in Colombia. That's why my father wished me death, after I divorced my first husband; my family "killed" me with a Jewish ritual: they dug a grave and filled it with stones on top of each other. Later we got along well; I even inherited my grandfather's books. He was a Polish rabbi who died in the Holocaust. Paradoxically, when my eldest daughter Trié called me and told me she was marrying a goy, I replied that she couldn't have children with a goy. I behaved just like my father. Inheritance is a powerful thing…

I: What is your position on the Arab-Israeli conflict?

FB: My position on this war is difficult, because I'm left-wing, but I'm also Jewish. I'm a complete pacifist, but I think the Jews have a right to defend themselves. They were attacked and they defended themselves.

I: So they're in the right in this war?

FB: No war is right. Israel can repel attacks, but not occupy territory that doesn't belong to it. The root of the problem is that Israel – like all small countries – is a "piece" on the international chessboard at which the great powers play. Israel has no interest in making war.

I: Did you study art?

FB: I finished secondary education at a convent school in Teusaquillo and felt attracted by art. I was eighteen and I went to New York to study at the Art Students League. Then I went to Paris where I stayed for five years and studied with Ossip Zadkine at the Grande Chaumière.[3] It was the period of Brancusi, Giacometti, and a little later Tinguely and César.

I: How many times have you been married?
FB: Five. Some by a civil wedding and some with a blessing.

I: Why have you married so many times: is it love, habit, or addiction?
FB: After the third time I think it's an addiction.

I: Any children?
FB: Three daughters from one of my marriages.

I: And are you married now?
FB: Very much so.

I: What about your daughters?
FB: They stayed with their father; they went to Texas.

I: What was your life like in Paris?
FB: You know, if I'm a sculptor, it's thanks to Jorge. You never do things for someone, they just happen. My marriage was going badly, I was fed up and I wanted to separate. One day I met Jorge at the Excelsior, a café that was a tunnel where 200 people crowded in on top of each other. He invited me to lunch, I accepted, and hey presto! A week later we were already living together! He could do eighteen things at once. He had an extraordinary capacity for work. That was a great help to me, for making sculptures, which is real hard work.

Over in Paris, in 1960, I began welding. I studied classical sculpture. In clay. From clay you move on to plaster, make moulds, and so on. Zadkine did classical sculpture and that was what I studied. I made bronzes. These little men you see there are in bronze. They're what's left of that period. Late homages to the master. I came back from Paris to Colombia, and as there is not and never has been a foundry in Colombia, I had to go back and tell Zadkine: "In the country where I live there are no foundries". He told me: "Then change country".

I: And what was he like?
FB: Lovely, a lovely old man, seventy-odd, but completely crazy, raving mad. He gave a sculpture course at the Grande Chaumière for people who had finished fine arts. People who went there to "find a path", as he called it. There were about fifteen of us, from various countries. French, Japanese. I had already studied painting in New York. And he found it hilarious, because as I couldn't speak any French, he could talk to me in English, and he thought that was the greatest way to practice. He became

very fond of me. It was lovely. He spent the whole time saying: "Why is it that they don't get women pregnant anymore?". He was very distressed about it. He said that in his day they were always pregnant.

I: How long did you study with him?
FB: Four years. A whole lifetime. He had a wonderful studio. He would offer us a drink. It was my initiation. We used to arrive at school at seven in the morning, in the winter: imagine the cold. The old man gave us a glass this big full of brandy to warm us up and we set to work. At that time, he used to come once a week with a stick and knock over everything we'd done, saying: "*merde, merde, merde!*". And finally he said: "Why don't you go back and practise?", and the following week he came back and knocked everything over again.

I: Zadkine was important, wasn't he?
FB: Yes, those convoluted forms. In that period all the sculptors were Russian, all émigrés. Great people, very civilized. When I went back four or five years later, I heard gossip about the old man; he was about seventy by then. He left his wife and went off with a twenty-year-old model, and he got her pregnant! He managed it. Imagine his poor wife: she was going crazy.

I: And who else was around?
FB: Giacometti, no less. He went to the same café every day, at the same time, to get drunk. Did you realize that all Giacometti's sculptures are of the same face? It's his wife's face. He was obsessed with her. He had a wonderful studio; you went in and there was a layer of dust this thick over everything. And he asked people not only to please not touch the dust but not even to blow, because if they ever blew, everything would be messed up.

I: How long were you in Paris?
FB: Jorge and I were in Paris for four years. He was writing, I was studying. He even wrote on the paper napkins in cafés. It was the period of the essay on Sade, the poems of *Si mañana despierto* (If I Wake Up Tomorrow), his diary. He also ran the magazine [*Mito*] from there, and wrote letters to Hernando Valencia, scolding him because he had got drunk and hadn't done what he was supposed to.[4]

I: Did Jorge and the other Latin Americans lead a bohemian life?
FB: Yes, like students, very irresponsible. As soon as the cheque arrived from Colombia they spent it all, in the best restaurants, and the next day they didn't even have the money to buy bread for breakfast. Jorge,

as always, talked to everyone. He was very friendly with Octavio Paz and Juan Liscaro; they spent all their time talking about Latin America. Typical rich kids' bohemia. He read a lot, chatted, and screwed.

I: Meanwhile, what about you?
FB: I was with Zadkine, working in clay and plaster. Then I went to see César, the one with the crushed cars, the one with the scrap metal. A metal worker that size! Half as big as Hernando Valencia, and that's saying a lot. Napoleon must have been like that. He had a gigantic workshop. And he taught me to weld. Like a good Frenchman he was an out-and-out male chauvinist. Almost like the Mexicans. Pure macho. And when I learned to weld, I came back to Colombia to make those things, the first of them, which were round houses, with screws. I did my first show in 1960, at Casimiro Eiger's gallery.[5] Like everyone else, I started at Casimiro's place.

I: What did he think of your sculptures?
FB: I imagine he must have found them terrifying. And that was very nice because Casimiro was the guide, the modern man par excellence, and he was really a completely classical gentleman.

I: How did it go?
FB: Very well. Marta Traba launched a passionate defence of my iron-work, and it all turned out very well. Neither Luis Eduardo Nieto Calderón nor Germán Arciniegas, nor their attendants at the court of good taste, asked for the exhibition to be closed. And all Jorge's friends were there: Mother (Alejandro Obregón), Hernando, Gabo.[6]

I: What were they like back then?
FB: Gabo was a journalist on *El Espectador*. Very, very thin, dark, and extremely nervous. With a tiny moustache. He smoked like a chimney. Incredibly nervous. When he sent *No One Writes to the Colonel* from Paris via Germán Vargas, Jorge went crazy: he devoted a whole issue to it.

I: And what was Jorge (Gaitán Durán) like?
FB: First of all, he was a Santanderean to his fingertips. And one of the shyest people in the history of this country. That was Jorge. Morbidly shy, which made him terribly aggressive. He was the rich kid living among a load of people who were really fucked: Hernando Valencia, Pedro Gómez Valderrama, Gabo, Alejandro Obregón.[7] They were all poor back then, except Jorge. At that time, not even Alejandro was selling a lot of pictures. It was a bohemia of beer and brandy. We held parties in Jorge's apartment with Santanderean tamales, and Jorge bought boxes of wine.

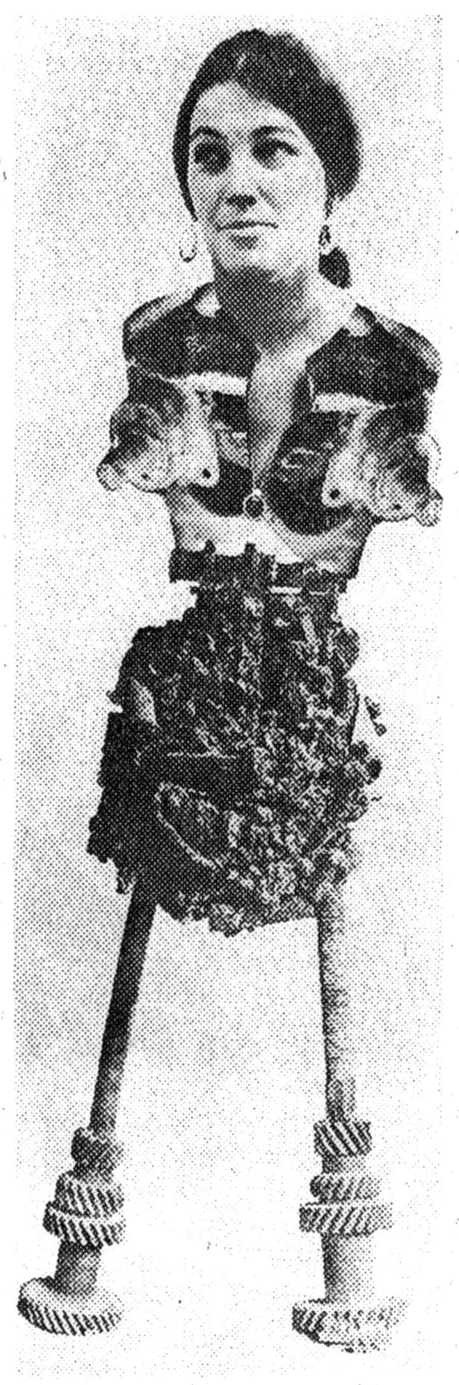

FELIZA EN CHATARRA.—Su amigo, el fotógrafo Federico Hecth, hizo esta foto-montaje de la escultora Feliza Bursztyn, autora del "Monumento a López", en una de sus obras.

It was an amazing luxury, as if they were boxes of champagne; people fainted. Also, everything was still more provincial. A totally small-town atmosphere. Everyone knew who was going around with who. Gossip, gossip. Just imagine: I came to think Jorge was a communist.

I: Why?
FB: Well, because everyone who was a rebel was called a communist. To be honest, I always thought Jorge was reactionary, but he wasn't considered to be. That phobia he had about the Church, priests, sexual repression; people thought all that stuff was horrible, and that's why they called him a communist, for opposing the priests. For the denunciations published in *Mito*.

I: And you lived with Jorge up to his death?
FB: No, I went to Israel to do an exhibition and Jorge wrote to me to tell me my father had died. While I came back, he went to Paris, and while he was returning from there for us to meet, he was killed. On his death the group broke up. He was the point of connection.

I: What about you?
FB: I carried on with my iron pieces, but as they were completely flat up till then, I began to make them fatter. In Colombia there was no possibility of casting or anything. I didn't want to be a lady of culture or follow the advice grandmothers in the capital gave well-to-do girls: "just play dumb" and marry well. They thought I was crazy, but I took advantage of the whole "madness" thing, and played it up, so that I could really do what I wanted. Because I do believe that we're living in a male chauvinist world. And to be a sculptor and not be a man is very difficult. I resorted to this trick so that people would take me seriously, because they thought, "maybe that crazy woman does interesting things". And I think it worked. I wanted to work in scrap metal, but I was so poor, so poor, that I didn't even have enough money to buy scrap metal. One day I found a room full of Nescafé tins at Rogelio Salmona's house.[8] I used them to do my first show, *Las Chatarras* (Junk Sculptures), at the Museo de Arte Moderno, Marta Traba's museum (fig. 3).[9]

I: Some have said that you use welding very badly in your works. What do you think about that?
FB: Maybe; actually, I'm sure, and I promise you that the day I master this job of welding I'll use screws.

I: On one occasion they said that your junk sculptures fell apart so easily that they seemed to be made with nail varnish…
FB: How strange; I wasn't painting my nails at that time.

I: Did you make a break with Colombian sculpture by looking for forms in scrap metal, as Alejandro Obregón also did with painting?

FB: I think I did make a contribution and that young people are looking towards scrap metal, in a country where we don't use wood, or bronze, or stone.

I: Do you think maestro Obregón is in decline?

FB: I don't believe any such thing… in any case, his alleged decline would be glory for others.

I: What's your opinion of the painter Botero?

FB: Botero is like García Márquez; they became so important, so very, very important, that they had to leave the country, perhaps to become less important.[10]

I: When you speak like that, are you driven by passion, by conviction?

FB: The most important thing of all is passion, passion while knowing what you're talking about. The problem of criticism is never a problem of justice, it's a problem of taste. An art critic can't be dispassionate. Passion is based on knowledge.

I: But if we consider that these critics are leaving records for the future…

FB: Records for the future are left by works of art, not by critics. A critic serves to show people certain paths that are his own, not necessarily the truth, because nobody owns the truth. And what is good today may be terrible five years from now.

I: What do you think of art critics in our country?

FB: Well, there are all sorts, from very mediocre to very bad, all with an erudition worthy of Bristol's *Almanac*.

I: How have critics treated you?

FB: They've said all sorts of things, from the best to the worst. For example, a critic who visited me in my workshop published this: "Eccentric so-called sculptress prepares serious assault on established art. A woman with outlandish clothes and manners is planning an inconceivable outrage against the art of Phidias, Michelangelo, and Arenas Betancourt. Luckily, there is still time to thwart the dark conspiracy. The Society for Improvements and Embellishment, the Board of Censors and all institutions and individuals who still love the fatherland must take the matter into their own hands before it is too late…".

I: Do you think religion is necessary for an artist?

FB: The most important thing is to believe in yourself. I don't believe in God, I believe in people. For Jews God has not arrived yet. Jehovah has not arrived. We're still waiting.

I: And what do you think about changing things through religion?

FB: I don't think that's the way. Changes must be political, not religious. We can't go back to the Middle Ages. All change has to be political.

I: How would you classify yourself within current art?

FB: I think my work currently belongs to what we might call "Motorized Romanticism".

I: What are you working on at the moment?

FB: On trying to answer you.

I: Some people think your work is an irreverent hoax. Others consider it serious and very well researched. What does Feliza Bursztyn herself think about her work?

FB: I've been working at this for many years. I'm not the kind of person to waste so much time on leg-pulling. It would be incredibly unprofessional. Besides, I have great respect for the public. I think a work is really important to the extent that people get something from it. The work ceases to exist if there is no one to receive it.

I: And how do you earn your living?

FB: By welding beds and other things.

I: And do you think you're going to sell these works?

FB: No, of course not, nobody would be that crazy: you'd have to be mad to buy them. You can't make a living from sculpture, but I live on sculpture. And I don't live so badly. But this type of sculpture is what I have fun doing, it's what I like. It doesn't matter that I'm never going to be an Onassis.

I: Has art made you money?

FB: I get by, which is already more than enough. I live a very contented life. I have what I need, nothing superfluous. And that's to live at ease with myself and other people. I'm happy.

I: Isn't sculpture useless? Isn't it just a pointless adornment bought by those who can afford it, merchandise available to those who have the money to spend on a decorative object?

FB: I've constructed works in scrap metal where the cost was reduced precisely because they were in that material. I've made sculptures for public squares and parks and schools. In some places, I've worked on a wall: in other words, made a mural with the scrap metal "left over" from the construction itself. Turning it into an aesthetic space, which serves to rest the eye or please the senses. I think that doing sculpture like this has profound social propensities. Not as a mere decorative object. I can tell you that there's a neighbourhood of very poor people in Colombia who asked me to make them a sculpture for their school. I asked them to give me objects. You can imagine what they gave me. Goodness knows: thousands of objects, tins, tubes, saucepans, old iron, masses of things, and with those objects we made the mural. They helped me; that's why I'm using the plural. In their school is our mural made from objects of no apparent value.

I: How would you define your job?
FB: I'm a labourer and a welder.

I: Did the Economic Emergency affect you?
FB: Not at all! I've always lived in a state of emergency.

I: Do you believe in so-called moments of inspiration for an artist?
FB: No, I don't! I think that as soon as you start working on something, there's a total integration of the artist and their work.

I: Can one speak of a sculptural movement in the Colombian school in the arts?
FB: No. In Colombia there's no tradition, there's no school… And it's a big advantage, believe me. There are few people making sculpture, but the phenomenon exists all over Latin America. Poverty. It's much easier to sit down and do little drawings on a napkin than to get a shed and welding equipment. That's a lot of work. Besides, all the people working in sculpture in Colombia are very similar. Let me tell you, when I was a teacher at Tadeo Lozano University – funny, isn't it? – I wanted to bring a Polish sculptor to teach the students how to work stone, which is the one thing we have plenty of in Colombia, and they wouldn't let me. And also, you have to question the teaching curricula, which rarely change because teachers occupy their posts for ever and go from young to senile practically without realizing. When I thought I'd finished my studies I found that the famous classic steps I'd learned in the academy had no justification. That business of making the figure first in clay, then in plaster, and finally casting it in bronze, in other words doing the same thing once, twice, three times, or four times, made no sense, especially since there were a series of things to be done.

I: But how can sculpture be taught?

FB: It can't. If anything, you can make suggestions on the material. All you can do is teach a few techniques. And let people get used to seeing sculptures around the place. Of course, they rush past and hardly notice them. Sculpture is strange, very strange; you never know what's going to happen with it, but it's such fun.

I: But influences do exist in the new generation of artists?

FB: I don't think they exist. And I would dare to go further: I don't think plagiarism really exists. I prefer to think of the millions of similar works as the result of chance.

I: Have you had any special satisfaction in your career?

FB: I consider that all satisfactions in life are small. Life is too important a thing to take it seriously. I make art with a laugh, which is quite serious, by the way.

I: Hence your *Las histéricas* (The Hysterical Ones) series, the beds.

FB: Yes.

I: When did that series begin?

FB: In 1968. They were in stainless steel, with a little motor. Then I set them to music, later I covered them with cloths, and finally I took them to bed.

I: Were you confronted with a lot of curious comments?

FB: Yes, from curious to very morbid.

I: They say you're an extremely liberated woman…

FB: How nice!

I: What is a liberated woman?

FB: Let me tell you: either we're born liberated or we never liberate ourselves.

I: Do you love someone?

FB: The mother.

I: Electra?

FB: Always.

I: Are you one of those feminists who complain and carry placards, down with men, etc.?

FB: No. I love men! I think they're a wonderful invention, which needs to be looked after [*laughs interminably*]; the problem, as I see it, is social, cultural, and political. Not sexual.

I: Would you go back in time?
FB: I like how things are today, but I have no regrets about yesterday…
I: Do you not like saying how old you are?
FB: That's got nothing to do with it; the facts are what counts.

I: How do you manage to keep so thin?
FB: I'm paid to.

I: Would you have plastic surgery?
FB: No, I like the marks of the passing years.

I: How many cavities?
FB: All the holes in the world.

I: Holes?
FB: Facts.

I: Big?
FB: Not very big.

I: Who do you get on better with, women or men?
FB: Men.

I: Did you enjoy the Witchcraft Congress you recently attended?
FB: It was great fun. It's the best symbol of the country. I think this and the National Planning Department represent us better than a picture by Alejandro Obregón.[11] I showed a sculpture there called *El bebé de Rosemary* (Rosemary's Baby) in the Visual Arts Room. A black cradle, with black drapes, on a white platform. The girls who cleaned the room were terrified and commented while looking at it: that must be something like death.

I: What is your highest aspiration as an artist?
FB: To make art.

I: And as a woman?
FB: To do everything artistically.

I: Do you feel different from other women?
FB: No, not at all.

I: Do you write?
FB: No, but I would love to have done so.

I: After the *Las camas* (The Beds) series, what came next?
FB: The Ballet, mechanical forms with music.

I: With humour as well?
FB: Of course; I'd die without it.

I: Do you give your sculptures names?
FB: Sometimes. This one [*pointing to a work*] is called *Pantófulo No. 4.*

I: Why? Were there previous Pantófulos?
FB: No, it's just that it's number four.

I: Why did you call your prizewinning sculpture in the Intercol competition *Reblakadaka*, the name of one of the pioneers of aviation in India?
FB: Because it had form, like air…

I: Did you name the work after it was finished?
FB: Yes.

I: What is Colombia to you?
FB: The *patria boba*.[12] In a country like Colombia, so poor in human and intellectual values, Marta's departure was a catastrophe. There is not and in the history of Colombian culture there never has been an intellectual who has done as much for art as Marta Traba. I am amazed that this event did not give rise to a more formal protest from Colombian intellectuals, but of course the thing is that talking about freedom and being free are two different things. Don't go telling someone they're not free; they'll be furious and want to kill you to prove that they are.

I: So why do you live here?
FB: Because of its people, the most beautiful and delightful in the world.

I: Was your monument to former President Alfonso López Pumarejo inspired by some physical or political feature of the ex-president?[13]
FB: No. It's a strictly visual artistic conception. I wanted something sober and very dignified. I completely left the character aside to search for forms,

I used tubes of all dimensions and sizes so that the materials would disappear and only the form would remain. I think Dr López is worthy of that tribute. I was asked for a monument in his memory, not a statue of López in an outdoor suit and a starched shirt, which I would not have done, because it would be disrespectful to him as a politician, as well as the fact that I consider him one of our most important men. Of course, it takes very little to be important in Colombia. Besides, statues are made so that pigeons can relieve themselves on them. I don't believe in monuments…

I: And why tubes, precisely?
FB: Because tubing is a very noble and very simple material.

I: Did you ever meet Dr López?
FB: No. I didn't even know his son Alfonsito, also former president; I have no political affinity with him.

I: Do you think yours is the best homage that could have been paid to President López?
FB: No. Why should I? I don't think my work is the best. But it was approved by people who know about art, such as Marta Traba, Fernando Martínez, and Rogelio Salmona.[14] In Havana they built a really beautiful monument with the remains of a boat that the anti-Castro people blew up in the port, some time ago. It is a tribute to the victims of that criminal attack. In Jerusalem they also built a very beautiful monument to the heroes of the 1948 war, out of tank gun barrels.

I: So what do you think the criticisms of your monument were due to?
FB: To the fact that we're an underdeveloped country. Besides, I don't want to defend my works. They defend themselves on their own.

I: To what do you attribute your attraction to sculpture?
FB: They are aberrations with which you make things.

I: So you consider sculpture an aberration?
FB: Naturally.

I: And what about your liking for scrap metal? Do you find beauty in those twisted Nescafé tins?
FB: Of course I do.

I: But the way you work is more concerned with the physical than the spatial, isn't it?

FB: What I love is the physical side: welding. Spending hours welding. But I can't do it anymore because my lungs have rotted. They were completely rotted by the welding, and I get tired and out of breath. I can't do it anymore.

This process of modelling scrap metal is the least delicate imaginable, twisting and crushing tins, iron, screws…

But that, in itself, is art: converting one thing into another. Like Michelangelo, when he turned a block of stone into a statue, the total transformation of matter is essentially that. Art has managed to open thousands of paths. Sculpture used to be understood as the representation of characters, and sculptors devoted themselves solely to portraits. Now, by contrast, a new boundless frontier has opened up before us, holding thousands and thousands of surprises in store. It can't be denied that we are living in a much more exciting period, as far as art is concerned, than any previous time.

I: And what's the deal with welding?

FB: Ahh, this business of casting metals is a real delight. With heat you can do whatever you want. Melt them like plasticine. Welding is really nice, with subtleties and textures. Very, very nice.

I: Do you give your sculptures a particular subject?

FB: No. I don't want to convey messages, either social or aesthetic. I sculpt because I like doing it.

I: Is there some reason why you chose scrap metal to work with?

FB: Of course: it's an aesthetic way of expressing yourself. Giving an aesthetic value to something that didn't have it before. Giving nobility to any material, not necessarily marble. The fabulous thing is that you're a worker at a factory where not just lorries are made, but delicate objects. I initially chose scrap metal because I felt it was important as a material, but then I got a bit bored with using it; also, I think art is an investigation and involves changing material, form, movement. I can tell you that the attraction of scrap metal for me is that it's a material that's already been used. It's already had its time of existence and then become refuse. Perhaps it's closing the great circle: making the object, using it and throwing it away. I close the circle by giving use again to something that was apparently dead. The world of forms is openly a kind of self-service restaurant where those who want something help themselves to what suits them, and what depends on each artist is the intelligent and sensitive use they make of that basic repertoire they've acquired.

I: In the text he wrote about you for the Museo de Arte Moderno,

Hernando Valencia spoke of how you left things lying around, in the workshop, at random, scattered, and then they began to talk to each other and paired up: this tube with that screw, this shapeless lump with that typewriter.[15] Pieces of scrap, junk, which joined together, composing something else, without you playing much of a part…

FB: Hernando's so nice, isn't he? I didn't really understand what he was saying, but it's the opposite of what everyone does, making drawings and sketches and getting things out of them. I work the other way around: I look for the material first, then, if I like the material, I make something with it, and normally, at first, you can't really tell what it's going to be. What I do depends on the material. It's the material that tells me what has to be done. Where to start.

I: And how do you look for it?
FB: Others go out whoring, I go out visiting workshops. Besides, people give me a lot of material for free.

I: Do you have a supplier?
FB: Exactly: like those drug dealers on motorbikes who come to your house bringing you big bundles of marijuana wrapped in the *El Tiempo* literary supplement, there are dealers who come and bring me scrap metal that they've kept because they thought it was wonderful.[16] Sometimes they're right. And other times I'm the one that goes out looking. Gigantic scrap workshops, over there in the south.

I: And what do they say?
FB: About the crazy woman?

I: Do any of them happen to have seen what the crazy woman does with their old iron?
FB: No. That would be terrible! I try to make sure they don't find out much, because the price depends on it. The only price those cases have is what they see in your face. I try to say that it's to fix something at home, a hole, a wall that's collapsed, things like that. Otherwise they start charging like crazy.

I: But didn't one of them recognize the *Homenaje a Ghandi* (Homage to Ghandi), that four-ton mass on the corner of Calle 100 and Carrera 7a?
FB: Yes, sure: they were going to steal it.

I: What? Themselves?
FB: Well yes, I think they were going to do it themselves, to resell it.

I: When was this?

FB: One night, very late, Pablo and I were coming from a party and we saw some guys with a crane, pulling the statue and trying to knock it over.[17] They were pulling and pulling. I was terrified. Pablo got out of the car, ready to hit them, but fortunately they realized we'd stopped and left. Thank God it was securely in place. Pardo set it up. Otherwise they'd have taken it. Can you imagine? That's why we gave it that monumental plinth which is now all covered with graffiti, and as soon as they introduce that red bus along Carrera 7a at the junction with Calle 100, no one knows where my sculpture will end up.[18]

I: But the big pieces must surely have been more thoroughly prepared – the SENA mural, for example.

FB: Yes, of course, that was with a design and durable materials. With 15 or 20 tons you can't take much of a risk. You have to consider that it might fall on us and kill everyone. It's terrifying.

I: Tell us about your beds…

FB: Very nice, but better in bed.

I: What's your favourite song?

FB: *La cama de piedra* (The Stone Bed).[19]

I: Your favourite book?

FB: *Los caballeros de la cama Redonda* (The Knights of the Round Bed).

I: Your solution for the country's problems?

FB: More beds. Remember: beds are good, if you can't sleep, rest!

I: And where are the beds now?

FB: In Mexico, in the Museum of Mexico City, in pieces. They finished them off. There was nothing left.

I: How many were there?

FB: There were thirteen.

I: Why thirteen?

FB: I don't know. That's as far as I got. There was no room for more in the museum gallery. I would like to have added more, but there was no room. So they stayed like that: thirteen.

I: First there were the *Chatarras* (Junk Sculptures), then *Las histéricas*, which you endowed with movement, straight after that came the *Pequeñas maquinitas* (Little Machines), made from old typewriters and transformed by hand, without motors. Then your great environment, *Las camas*, which had music, as well as movement. And now there's the *La baila mecánica* (The Mechanical Ballet). What's the idea behind this piece?

FB: I can't even remember. I work on three or four things at the same time, as a relaxation technique, and also to be able to see, because if you get deeper and deeper into just one thing, you can't see anything anymore. On the other hand, if you do something else, you stop and look. Then you can see. In this way I made the beds, minisculptures, and typewriters at the same time. I worked on the *Baila* for about four years. I made all the mechanisms something like eighteen times. I completely invented everything. Nothing worked; the cables blew. Dreadful things happened. It was like reinventing the wheel. Like the bumper cars in the Ciudad de Hierro funfair in the National Park. That came after the beds. From the theory of things moving. But they also move in themselves. I wanted to try it out, to see whether they themselves could move on their own. And it turned out to be great fun… the things they said. For example, Alejandro Obregón went crazy: he was convinced they were all women.

I: Everyone judges according to their position, don't they?

FB: Here, as in those stupid reports, we should add: "much laughter". And, of course, other people saw monsters, things like that. People see very strange things. It was nice, and sort of very theatrical.

I: What is *La baila mecánica*?

FB: In *Las histéricas* the sculptures were in stainless steel with motors and sound, and with their tick-tick-tick-tick-tick they drove you mad. Then *Las camas* had movement but no sound of its own. Jacqueline Nova had composed some music specially for them. Later we thought of doing the ballet. Jacqueline was going to write the music again. When she fell ill, she assured me that she had it all ready. Jacqueline died, the music didn't appear and then I put my mind to doing something totally different from what she would have done. I didn't think I should set my ballet to modern music. That's why I went for the twelfth century. I find mechanics fascinating. You'd be surprised how much I know on the subject. Of course I don't know as much as I'd like, but I do know enough to work in this type of sculpture. I see a piece of waste material and I die of happiness. Then I saw those little motors, I bought them and they worked brilliantly for me. *Las histéricas* had already had motors, but they were from record players and were very expensive for me. Starting from those motors I began to make my sculptures, with technical advice from Ramón Rodríguez to make the dolls dance and move as I wanted. People ask me why I didn't call the work *Baile mecánico*, in the masculine, as in normal Spanish, instead of *Baila mecánica* in the feminine. I put it in the feminine because it sounded horrible to me in the masculine. The day the parts of *La baila* arrived at the gallery it looked more like a battlefield than an art exhibition, but it soon started to take shape until it became that combination of scaffolding, ghostly music, and contortions that is the *mechanical ballet*.

I: How do you approach "dressing" your ballet?
FB: I always thought of those sculptures as people, perhaps sexless characters that move, dance, and sing.

I: Why did you give names to the seven characters who make up the group?
FB: I'm convinced that each sculpture has its own character, its personality, a different way of moving, a distinct tone, a world of its own. Exactly like people. So it seemed natural that they should have names: Fragata, Piolin, Pipa, Gordillo, La Fragata, Chiquito, and Bailón, hooded blind characters who dance singly or two or three at once, spasmodic and trembling, around an orange dwarf who never rests.

I: Why did you choose music by a composer from eight centuries ago for such a modern work?
FB: I looked for a composer who didn't remind me of what Jacqueline Nova would have done. "El Chuli" Fernando Martínez gave me the solution when he found me the music of Perotinus Magnus, from the twelfth century. He's a very interesting composer and was a revolutionary in his period, one of the most outstanding men of his time. It's sacred music with male-voice choirs. I know Jacqueline would never have done it like that.

I: How much did *La Baila* cost you?
FB: I don't know. A lot! Four years' work.

I: Where does the commercial sense of your work lie?
FB: Nowhere. Or perhaps in the lithographs I'm going to sell to those who come and see the performance of *La baila*.

I: If it's taken you eight days to set up the work and it had to be transported here by lorry, tell me, how are you going to manage when it has to travel?
FB: I don't even want to think about it. I refuse to touch that subject yet... And the most serious problem is that it's going to travel as far as

Poland and Havana, and of course all over Colombia.

I: And where is *La baila* now?
FB: Here, in pieces. But the thing is that there were three *bailas*. They're out there, around the world, moving.

I: But between *La baila mecánica* and *Las camas*, which moved, were there other things, apart from the small sculptures?
FB: Yes, large sculptures, in metal, such as that of *Andromeda*, which is at the SENA in Chapinero.[20] And the mural of the forks, which is at the SENA in the centre… such fun.

I: And what other large sculptures of yours are there?
FB: There's a big one at the Banco del Comercio, on 13 and 8a, on the fifth floor, which is like a patio but is the management gallery. A thing this big. Gigantic. With hoops, like *Andromeda*. One day it fell over and it looked great. I thought what had happened was wonderful, but the people at the bank didn't.

I: And what about these radical changes in your work?
FB: It's precisely a matter of changes; art is experimentation and all the changes have been very important to me; they connect with each other until it comes down to this. Every time you start something new you think it's your salvation, and sometimes it turns out to be just stupid. But at that moment you're convinced it's where the party is.

I: Have you ever done any other kind of sculpture, more traditional, let's say, or painting, or drawing?
FB: My first exhibition was a series of watercolours. But I only became interested in colour at the end; at first, I looked for form and always through scrap metal or stainless steel, and then, when I encountered car panels and car doors and started playing with that stuff, colour arrived.

I: Colour? Why colour?
FB: Because I had never used colour. Sometimes it's the colour of the car, other times I paint them. Look at that panel: that red is painted. It's fun, isn't it? Not just the form but also the colour is very important. Don't you think?

I: Have you ever been afraid of electricity?
FB: Never. Otherwise I'd be an utter masochist.
I: Do you believe in political art?

FB: Some political art. I think it's very difficult. It's the same in film. There have been one, two, or three who have managed to do it. [Sergei] Eisenstein in film. García Márquez in literature. A Spanish artist, Canogar, in the visual arts. It's very difficult to do political art without it degenerating into poster art, and that's fatal.

I: Is art critical?
FB: Inevitably. It's always been like that. If you talk about someone or something, you're giving an opinion, which is critical. It's the same with artists; capturing something you see involves giving it a critical interpretation. It doesn't matter whether the objective is political, social, or whatever.

I: Which is yours?
FB: Social and political.

I: Do you think artists should be left free to be able to produce?
FB: No. All the great masters in the history of art always worked on commission, not freely. Goya with his great portraits, Velázquez… they were all commissioned, but not directed.

I: And how do you see the situation in Colombia? Do you think the way out can be found through politicians?
FB: I think it's very difficult. Because there are no possibilities, there's no opening, you can't see a way forward. How can they give work to thousands and millions of unemployed people? How can they stop inflation? How can they provide food for everyone, education for everyone, medicine for everyone, a place to live for everyone? How?

I: Would you give up your house in Bogotá and your whole way of life and be reduced to one room if things changed?
FB: The problem is not habitable spaces. The problem is poverty. I would be much less worried living in a city like Bogotá if there were no poverty. If you knew that you can go out in the street and you're not going to get mugged, if you knew that everyone has something to eat. And if you didn't go around the corner and see three young lads dying of hunger. I think I would have much more peace of mind than I have now. It's not a question of the space you inhabit, it's a question of the environment you inhabit. I mean, in the Cuba I knew, artists had their house, their workshop, their work, their children's education was taken care of, medicine, everything was seen to, and also their work was bought and they were given a monthly wage. That's what they need to live. If you had enough to eat and a place to live you wouldn't have to charge such exorbitant prices to be able to

eat all year. Then there wouldn't be that pressure that has made artworks completely inaccessible to the economic middle class. Artists raise their prices because the art market has made this economy like that.

I: What's your favourite pastime?
FB: Sex! Ah, I've got another: cooking. I think all those who work in art are good cooks. There's something, a little bit of magic, in cooking too. What you produce, the flavours, mixing. It's a creative thing.

I: As someone who has so much respect for the public and cannot conceive artistic creation without them, how do you receive their reactions?
FB: Something wonderful occurred with the exhibition of the beds. I showed them first in Medellín and got a pair of teenage brothers to listen and note down everyone's comments. You can't imagine the things they wrote! It turned out to be an extraordinary book in which they tell us how some people shouted in front of the moving beds, some nuns cried, another person had the most unlikely opinions. It was wonderful. That's why I insist that a work is important to the extent that it arouses reactions in people. The important thing for me is what the work leaves in people who see it; the experience each person has, what they feel and think and the associations they make; what it means for everyone who looks at it; what is left behind in visitors. All this is what I really believe is important. The public decides everything; if they see it and are impressed, it's a process.

I: As happened with *Las camas*, a lot of people try to lift up the sculptures' clothing. Why do you think this happens?
FB: Because they can't really understand how they're moving. And also out of morbid curiosity and because the moving sculptures give them a feeling of hysteria. That's why I stuck the skirts on these seven sculptures. And we put a rope around the platform for protection.

I: A women's page question: for a person who moves in the world of aesthetics, how do you react to seeing yourself published – as happened recently – on the list of the ugliest women in Colombia?
FB: It was an incredible surprise. But I already have a protest document with a thousand signatures certifying that I am NOT the ugliest woman in the country.

I: What's your bedtime ghost?
FB: I have time anxiety. That's why playing seems like wasting time to me. There's so much to see, so much to read!
I: Is it true, as Gabriel García Márquez says, that you died of sadness in Paris?

FB: That's Gabo telling stories. I was sad, yes. Imagine: I'd had to leave Colombia, I'd spent 166 days away from my house and workshop, where some soldiers in plain clothes arrived at four o'clock in the morning, with machine guns under their ruanas, and dismantled even the bed, perhaps looking for my lost fucks. After the kind formalities, performed with an air of routine rather than diligence, they took away some photos I had brought back from Cuba when I was there for an exhibition and a unusable old pistol a friend had given me as a present when I lived alone. The soldiers arrested me and took me to the Brigade of Military Institutes, in "the Usaquén stables", for an interrogation. There I was sat blindfolded for eleven hours, with no food. They stuck an adhesive strip on my chest with the prisoner number: 5. That patch, with that number, is still stuck on the kitchen wall of my house in Bogotá. Before blindfolding me, the gentlemen offered me excuses for having to do so. I never found out what I was accused of and among the string of questions they asked me, one, perhaps the most intimidating, was whether I wasn't afraid of being raped. I told them that every married woman is used to being raped every night. Then they released me, but a few days later I received a summons to appear before a military judge, and we found out that on the day of the arrest the Ministry of Defence of the Turbay government itself had told Hernando Santos, editor of the newspaper *El Tiempo*, that there was a serious accusation hanging over me that he wouldn't reveal.[21] It was also said that I was a liaison between the Cuban government and the M-19 guerrilla group. I preferred to go into exile at the Mexican Embassy and then in that country I was received by Mercedes and Gabo who had to listen to the story like a broken record. I couldn't go to the United States, where my mother and my three daughters were, because they refused me a visa. Later on, we went with Pablo to Paris, where some friends got me a grant and a social security card to have my lungs treated. We went there with Mother (Alejandro Obregón), we made non-holy pilgrimages around outlying dance halls, I made Gabo his lentil soups to take away his fear of flying, and he looked after my guava plants, with carefully measured dry martinis and recent copies of *The New Yorker*. And of course in the last ten days, when Pablo arrived, I told him again and again after reading the news: "My love, the world has just come to an end!". There were just a few days left until they gave me a workshop I had rented, where I could begin again to do what I had learned here with the masters of my youth. That night we met some friends for dinner, but my heart let me down and I had a cardiac arrest. But I'm not dead. As Nene Cepeda says in his story: Dying is a drag.

The interviewer went out into the garden, and before leaving, he saw

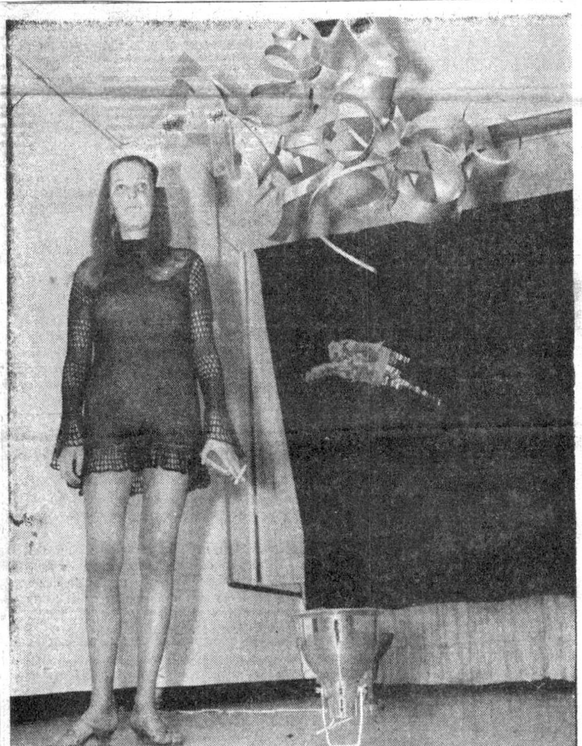

4. Article on Feliza Bursztyn's *Las histéricas* (The Hysterical Ones), published in *Diario del Caribe* (Barranquilla), 23 April 1969
Courtesy of the Archive of Pablo Leyva

something placed under the iconic images of the leaders Ernesto Che Guevara and Fidel Castro; it was a sign from the former factory of Feliza Bursztyn's father: "This company prohibits the consumption of alcoholic beverages, the carrying of knives and the use of coarse language very common in the guild of artisans on its premises. The Management" (fig. 4).

[A collage of interviews welded with pieces from texts and interviews with Feliza Bursztyn: "Entrevista telegramática con Felisa [*sic*] Bursztyn", unsigned, *El Tiempo* (Bogotá), 28 May 1972; Enrique Carrizosa, "Qué hubo… qué más", *Micro-Entrevistas*, undated; Maritza Uribe de Urdinola, "En un país de machistas, ¡hágase la loca!", *El Tiempo: Revista Carrusel* (Bogotá), 30 November 1979: 15; Beatriz Zuluaga, "Felisa

Bursztyn: La mujer de las camas", *Revista Mujer* (Bogotá), October 1975: 68–72; Lader Giraldo, "Mis Chatarras se Defienden Solas, dice Feliza", *El Espectador – Diario de la Mañana* (Bogotá), 25 July 1967; Enrique Santos Calderón, "Feliza Bursztyn y el Arte en Latas de Nescafé [La escultura de chatarra]", *El Tiempo* (Bogotá), 21 September 1964; Maritza Uribe de Urdinola, "Feliza 'baila' en Cali", *El País* (Cali), Sunday supplement, 18 November 1979: 6–7; Jorge Gaitán Durán, "La densa nube del ser", *El Espectador* (Bogotá), 12 October 1958; Walter Engel, "Poesía de la Chatarra: La Exposición de Feliza Burztyn", *El Espectador: Magazine Dominical* (Bogotá), 4 October 1964: 10-F; Gina McDaniel Tarver, "The Art of Feliza Bursztyn: Confronting Cultural Hegemony", *Artelogie*, no. 5, 2013, http://journals.openedition.org/artelogie/5561; Héctor Muñoz, "El monumento a López es un horror", *El Espectador* (Bogotá), 16 June 1967; Marta Traba, *Los que son* (Bogotá: unpublished, 1963); Alvaro Medina, "¿Feliza Krugman o Irene Bursztyn?", *La Vanguardia Liberal: Vanguardia Dominical* (Bucaramanga), 2 June 1974: 4–5; Marta Traba, "Burztyn [*sic*] por encima de toda sospecha", typed manuscript, https://icaa.mfah.org [1974]; Miguel González, "Análisis de la obra de Feliza Burstyn [*sic*]", *El País* (Cali), 25 September 1974; Gloria Valencia Diago, "Académicos vs. Artistas: el monumento a Bolivar", *El Tiempo* (Bogotá), 7 August 1980: 1-B; Camilo Leyva Espinel, "Un montón de chatarra", master's thesis in history and theory of modern and contemporary art, University of the Andes of Bogota, 2008, 11; Manuela Ochoa Ronderos, "Los escenarios inhabitados", 2013, https://premionalcritica.uniandes. edu.co/?texto=los-escenarios-inhabilitados; Nicolás Suescún *et al.*, "Un Brindis de Adiós a FELIZA", *Cromos* (Bogotá), 19 January 1982; Nicolás Suescún, "Las camas de Feliza en el Museo de Arte Moderno el 26", *El Tiempo* (Bogotá), 24 March 1974; Juan Gustavo Cobo Borda, "Entrevista trunca con Feliza Bursztyn", *Cromos* (Bogotá), 8 March 1983]

[1] Lucas Ospina, "Feliza Bursztyn: 'En un país de machistas, ¡hágase la loca!'", *070* (Bogotá), 14 January 2019, https://cerosetenta.uniandes.edu. co/feliza-bursztyn-en-un-pais-de-machistas-hagase-la-loca/

[2] Jorge Gaitán Durán (Pamplona, 1924 – Pointe-à-Pitre, 1962) was a Colombian poet and critic, founder of the magazine *Mito* and a member of the Cuadernícolas.

[3] Ossip Zadkine (Vitebsk, 1890 – Paris, 1967) was a Russian artist, mainly known as a sculptor, although he also worked as a painter.

[4] Hernando Valencia Goelkel (Bucaramanga, 1928 – Bogotá, 2004) was a Colombian critic and essayist. He was the co-founder of *Mito* together with Jorge Gaitán Durán and a member of the Editorial Board of the Cultural Bulletin of Banco de la República.

[5] Casimiro Eiger (Warsaw, 1909 – Bogota, 1987) was a Polish gallery owner, historian, and art and film critic.

[6] "Gabo" is an affectionate nickname used to refer to Gabriel García Márquez.

[7] Alejandro Obregón (Barcelona, 1920 – Cartagena, 1992) was a Colombian-Spanish painter and a mythical figure who helped build the art scene in twentieth-century Colombia.

[8] Rogelio Salmona (Paris, 1927 – Bogotá, 2007)

was a prominent Colombian-French architect who was characterized by a wide and varied work with an extensive use of brick, concrete, and water as a connecting element, through canals, water mirrors, pools, and ponds.

[9] Marta Traba (Buenos Aires, 1930 – Mejorada del Campo, 1983) was an Argentine-Colombian art critic and writer, known for her important contributions to the study of Latin American art, her combative character, and her wide influence on the perception of art in the local Colombian environment.

[10] Fernando Botero Angulo (Medellín, 1932) is a Colombian painter, sculptor, and draughtsman who has lived in Pietrasanta, Paris, Munich, and New York. His work was vital until the mid-1970s, after which he inevitably chose to copy himself.

[11] Established in 1958, the Departamento Nacional de Planeación (National Planning Department) is an administrative unit responsible for leading, coordinating, and articulating planning for the sustainable and inclusive development of Colombia.

[12] Literally "Foolish Fatherland", historical term for the initial period of Colombian independence from 1810 to 1816.

[13] Alfonso López Pumarejo (Honda, 1886 – London, 1959) was a Colombian businessman, politician, thinker, and diplomat. He was President of Colombia for two terms, first between 1934 and 1938, and then between 1942 and 1945, the year he resigned. In his first term he became known for his progressive measures, including a constitutional reform in 1936 which gave private property a social function, and in general for his government known as Revolución en Marcha (Marching Revolution).

[14] Fernando Martínez Sanabria (Madrid, 1925 – Bogotá, 1991), known as El Mono or El Chuli, was a Spanish architect considered the pioneer of organic architecture in Colombia. He arrived in Colombia in 1938 because of the Spanish Civil War and taught as a professor at the National University of Colombia. Sanabria was one of the main actors in the bohemian nights of the capital's countercultural Creole elite.

[15] The Museo de Arte Moderno de Bogotá (MAMBO) was founded in 1953 by Marta Traba and refounded by herself in 1957. It played a vital role in the programming and articulation of the local scene until the early 1980s, and then became just like any other institution with great ups and downs.

[16] *El Tiempo* is a Colombian newspaper founded on 30 January 1911 and since then has been characterized by its support of government policy with the occasional critical exercise in divergent research, often unnoticed by its own directors. Since 2012, it has been the privileged communication organ of its current owner, Luis Carlos Sarmiento Angulo, Colombia's main banker and one of the contractors most benefited by the Colombian State.

[17] Pablo Leyva (b. 1941) is a chemical engineer graduated from the Universidad Nacional de Colombia, Bogotá. He holds a PhD in Economic and Social Development from the Institute for Economic and Social Development Studies (IEDES) of the University Paris 1 Panthéon-Sorbonne. He was Director General of Colombia's Institute of Hydrology, Meteorology and Environmental Studies (IDEAM), as well as Vice Rector of Resources and Dean of the faculties of Engineering and Sciences of the National University of Colombia. He was a professor at the Universidad de los Andes and associate professor at the Instituto de Ciencias Naturales of the National University of Colombia. He was Feliza's last companion in life and, together with Camilo Leyva, took care of the good destiny of artist's work.

[18] "Little red bus" is a diminutive for TransMilenio, the rapid transit system widely extended throughout Bogotá which has privileged the bus over the construction of an integrated subway network capable of improving mobility in one of the world's worst-rated cities in terms of public transportation.

[19] "The bed must be made of stone / The headboard must be made of stone / The woman who loves me / Must love me for real." The lyrics are by Mexican singer and songwriter Cuco Sánchez (Altamira, 1921 – Mexico City, 2000).

[20] The Servicio Nacional de Aprendizaje (SENA) (National Training Service) is a Colombian public institution founded in 1957 that offers education and training services.

[21] Julio César Turbay Ayala (Bogotá, 1916–1905) was a Colombian politician and diplomat of Lebanese descent. A member of the Liberal Party, he was President of Colombia from 1978 to 1982 and became known for his misgovernment, which earned him public ridicule. He made history for the implementation of an infamous Security Statute that imposed a policy of harassment, repression, censorship, torture, and disappearances by the most fascist military wing in collusion with the political and business elite. The current President of Colombia, Iván Duque, has shown himself to be a fervent admirer of Turbay and has updated that mandate of the most inept, incompetent, cynical, and least qualified (Kakistocracy).

Author Biographies

Julia Buenaventura is a researcher. She holds a PhD in Architecture and Urbanism from the University of São Paulo, Brazil, and a Master's Degree in History, Criticism and Theory of Art and Architecture from Universidad Nacional de Colombia, Bogotá. She carried out her post-doctoral research at the School of Communication and Arts (ECA) of the University of São Paulo, where she was a postgraduate professor. She is currently a lecturer at the Universidad de Los Andes and Pontificia Universidad Javeriana, Bogotá. She is a regular contributor to various virtual and print media, including *ArtNexus* magazine (US and Latin America) and Fórum Permanente. She is the author of *En primera persona: Seis pasajes sobre Feliza Bursztyn* (Department of Culture of Bogotá, 2019) and *Polvo eres: El correr del tiempo en María Elvira Escallón* (Ministry of Culture of Colombia, 2015).

Cecilia Fajardo-Hill is an independent British-Venezuelan art historian and curator of modern and contemporary art, with a focus on Latin American and Latinx art, based in Southern California. She has a PhD in Art History and Theory from the University of Essex and an MA in 20th-Century Art History from the Courtauld Institute of Art, London. Fajardo-Hill has published and curated extensively on contemporary Latin American and international artists. She co-curated *Radical Women: Latin American Art 1960–1985* at the Hammer Museum, Los Angeles (2017), which travelled to the Brooklyn Museum, New York and to Pinacoteca de São Paulo in 2018. Presently, she is co-curating *Xican-a.o.x. Body*, a touring exhibition organized by the American Federation of Arts (2022). She is the editor of the upcoming book *Remains Tomorrow: Themes in Contemporary Latin American Abstraction* on post-1990s abstraction in Latin America, and co-editor of a publication on Guatemalan art of the 20th and 21st centuries, an initiative of Arte GT 20/21, Guatemala. In 2020 she was the recipient of the Andy Warhol Foundation Arts Writers Grant to research the photographic work by

pioneer Chicana artist Patssi Valdez. She is Visiting Scholar at the Chicano
Studies Research Center of UCLA, Los Angeles; Clark Fellow in residence
at the Clark Art Institute, Williamstown in the fall of 2021; and 2021–22
Central American Visiting Scholar at the David Rockefeller Center for Latin
American Studies (DRCLAS) at Harvard University, to develop a book
on the history of Latin American and Latinx decolonial art in the 20th and
21st centuries focusing on gender, race and ethnicity, indigeneity, African
heritage, and popular culture.

Marta Dziewańska is a curator at Kunstmuseum Bern. Between 2007 and
the end of 2018, she was curator and head of research at the Museum of
Modern Art in Warsaw and, in 2017, a curatorial advisor for documenta
14, Athens and Kassel. She has curated and co-curated several international
exhibitions, including *Things Fall Apart. Swiss Art from Boecklin to Valloton*
(Kunstmuseum Bern, 2019–20); *MIRIAM CAHN: I AS HUMAN* (Museum of Modern Art in Warsaw, 2019); *The Other Trans-Atlantic. Kinetic
and Op Art in Eastern Europe and Latin America, 1950s–1970s* (Museum of
Modern Art in Warsaw, 2017; Garage Museum of Contemporary Art, Moscow, 2018; SESC Pinheiros, São Paulo, 2018); *Alina Szapocznikow: Human
Landscapes* (The Hepworth Wakefield, Wakefield, UK, 2017–18); *Andrzej
Wróblewski: Recto/Verso* (Museum of Modern Art in Warsaw, 2015; Museo
Reina Sofía, Madrid, 2015–16), and others. She was the editor of *Tools for
Utopia: Selected Works from the Daros Latinamerica Collection* (Berlin:
Hatje Cantz Verlag, 2020), and co-editor of *Points of Convergence: Alternative Views on Performance* (Warsaw–Chicago: Museum of Modern Art
and University of Chicago Press, 2017) and *1968–1989: Political Upheaval
and Artistic Change* (Warsaw: Museum of Modern Art, 2009), among others. Her writings have appeared in numerous exhibition catalogues as well
as art magazines.

Camilo Leyva is an interdisciplinary artist and professor living and working
in Bogotá. He has conducted extensive research in the history of modern
and contemporary Colombian art. Leyva has studied the life and work of
Feliza Bursztyn for more than fourteen years. At the National Museum
of Colombia, he co-curated an anthological show as part of the National
Homage series titled *In Praise of Scrap Metal*, dedicated to Bursztyn's work.
In tandem, he published an exhibition catalogue featuring a comprehensive
commented timeline and glossary that was supported on archival material.
Leyva has co-authored a chapter on Bursztyn for the book *Pensadores colombianos del siglo XX*, vol. IV, part of a series published by Instituto Pensar
at the Pontificia Universidad Javeriana in Bogotá.

Daniel Muzyczuk is Head of the Modern Art Department at Muzeum Sztuki in Łódź. He has co-curated several international exhibitions, including *Through the Soundproof Curtain. The Polish Radio Experimental Studio* with Michał Mendyk (ZKM | Zentrum für Kunst und Medien, Karlsruhe, 2018–19); *The Museum of Rhythm* with Natasha Ginwala (Muzeum Sztuki, Łódź, 2016–17); *Notes from the Underground: Art and Alternative Music in Eastern Europe 1968–1994* with David Crowley (Muzeum Sztuki, Łódź, 2016; Akademie der Künste, Berlin, 2018); *Sounding the Body Electric: Experiments in Art and Music in Eastern Europe 1957–1984* with David Crowley (Muzeum Sztuki, Łódź, 2012; Calvert 22, London, 2013); *Gone to Croatan* with Robert Rumas (Centre of Contemporary Art, Toruń; Hartware MedienKunstVerein, Dortmund, 2009–11), among others. In 2013, he was co-curator of the Polish Pavilion at the 55th Venice Biennale with Agnieszka Pindera. He contributes regularly to several print and online art magazines and journals, including *The Exhibitionist*, *Nero*, *Mousse*, and *e-flux*. His book *Twilight of the Magicians* will be published by Spector Books in 2022. Muzyczuk is former Vice-President of the International Association of Art Critics (AICA), Poland, and a member of Grupa Budapeszt.

Lucas Ospina is a Professor at the Universidad de los Andes, Colombia. Sometimes he draws, sometimes he writes.

Sylvia Juliana Suárez Segura is an artist, art historian, curator, and teacher. Her career has focused on the modern and contemporary art history of Colombia and Latin American, the history and theory of artistic education, and the study of the links between artistic experimentation, education, and citizenship-building. In the academic sphere, she has concentrated mainly on teaching and publicizing Colombian art, the history and theory of art criticism, aesthetic theory and art theory, and supporting individual and collective creative processes. She is a member of the Critical Art History Workshop research group, co-founder of and contributor to the Social Poetics Observatory at Jorge Tadeo Lozano University, Bogotá, and a participant in the Southern Conceptualisms Network international research and creative community. She holds a PhD in Art and Architecture in the area of Art History of Colombia and Latin America from the National University of Colombia, a Master's Degree in History and Theory of Art, Architecture and the City, and a Master's Degree in Fine Arts from the same institution. She has taught at the Pontificia Universidad Javeriana (2019–20), the University of Los Andes (2008–10), the National University of Colombia (2008–10), Jorge Tadeo Lozano University (2005–06 and 2010–20), and the Licentiate

(Advanced Bachelor's) degree programme in Visual Arts at the National Pedagogical University (2007–08).

Gina McDaniel Tarver is Associate Professor of Art History at Texas State University. She received her PhD at The University of Texas, Austin, and she specializes in modern and contemporary art of Latin America with a particular interest in gender, spatial, and ecological politics in Colombian art since 1960. Her book, *The New Iconoclasts: From Art of a New Reality to Conceptual Art in Colombia, 1961–1975* (Bogotá: Ediciones Universidad de los Andes, 2016), deals extensively with the work of Feliza Bursztyn and Beatriz González, among others. Tarver co-edited *Art Museums of Latin America: Structuring Representation* (New York: Routledge, 2018) and recently contributed chapters on Colombian women artists to the volumes *Liquid Ecologies in Latin American and Caribbean Art* (New York: Routledge, 2020) and *New Geographies of Abstract Art in Postwar Latin America* (New York: Routledge, 2019).

Abigail Winograd is the MacArthur Fellows Program 40th Anniversary Exhibition Curator at the Smart Museum of Art, University of Chicago. She is the curator of *Toward Common Cause: Art, Social Change, and the MacArthur Fellows Program at 40*, a multi-site exhibition that took place across Chicago from 2021–22. Her scholarly research has focused on the emergence of aberrant abstractions in post-war South America as well as museological approaches to expanding canonical narratives. She received a PhD in Art History from the University of Texas at Austin. Prior to her appointment at the Smart Museum, she organized *The Other Trans-Atlantic. Kinetic and Op Art in Eastern Europe and Latin America, 1950s–1970s* (Museum of Modern Art in Warsaw, 2017; Garage Museum of Contemporary Art, Moscow, 2018; SESC Pinheiros, São Paulo, 2018), as well as *Abstract Experiments: Latin American art on paper after 1950* (Art Institute of Chicago, 2017). In 2016–17, Winograd was the Transhistorical Curatorial Fellow at the Frans Hals Museum in Haarlem, Netherlands, where she organized *A Global Table: Still Life, Colonialism, and Contemporary Art* (2017). In 2016 she was Research Associate for *Kerry James Marshall: Mastry* at the Museum of Contemporary Art Chicago (travelled to the Metropolitan Museum of Art, New York, 2016–17, and the Museum of Contemporary Art, Los Angeles, 2017), where she also organized *Unbound: Contemporary Art after Frida Kahlo* (2014) and *Zachary Cahill: Snow* (2014) as the Marjorie Susman Curatorial Fellow. Her writings have appeared in numerous catalogues, books, journals, and art magazines.

Lynn Zelevansky is an art historian, curator, and writer based in New York. From 2009–17, she was Henry J. Heinz II Director, Carnegie Museum of Art. There she instituted a variety of new participatory and experimental programs and co-curated *Hélio Oiticica: To organize Delirium* (2016–17) and *Paul Thek: Diver* (2010–11). Previously, she was Terri and Michael Smooke Curator and Department Head, Contemporary art, Los Àngeles County Museum of Art. Among the many exhibitions she organized or co-organized there were *Love Forever: Yayoi Kusama, 1958–68* (1998) and *Beyond Geometry: Experiments in Form, 1940s–70s* (2004). Prior to that, Zelevansky was curatorial assistant, Department of Painting and Sculpture, Museum of Modern Art, New York, where she organized *Projects* shows for artists such as Gabriel Orozco (1993) and Cildo Meireles (1990), and curated *Sense and Sensibility: Women Artists and Minimalism in the Nineties* (1994). Zelevansky has published widely on modern and contemporary art.

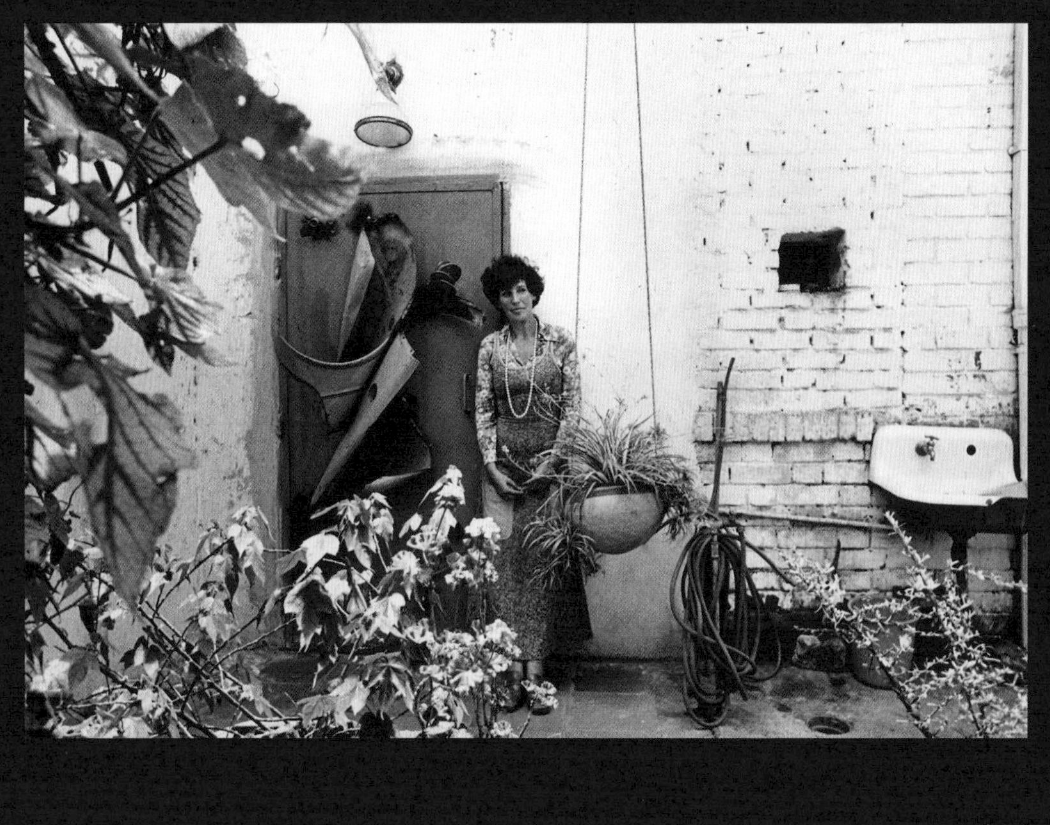

Feliza Bursztyn: Works

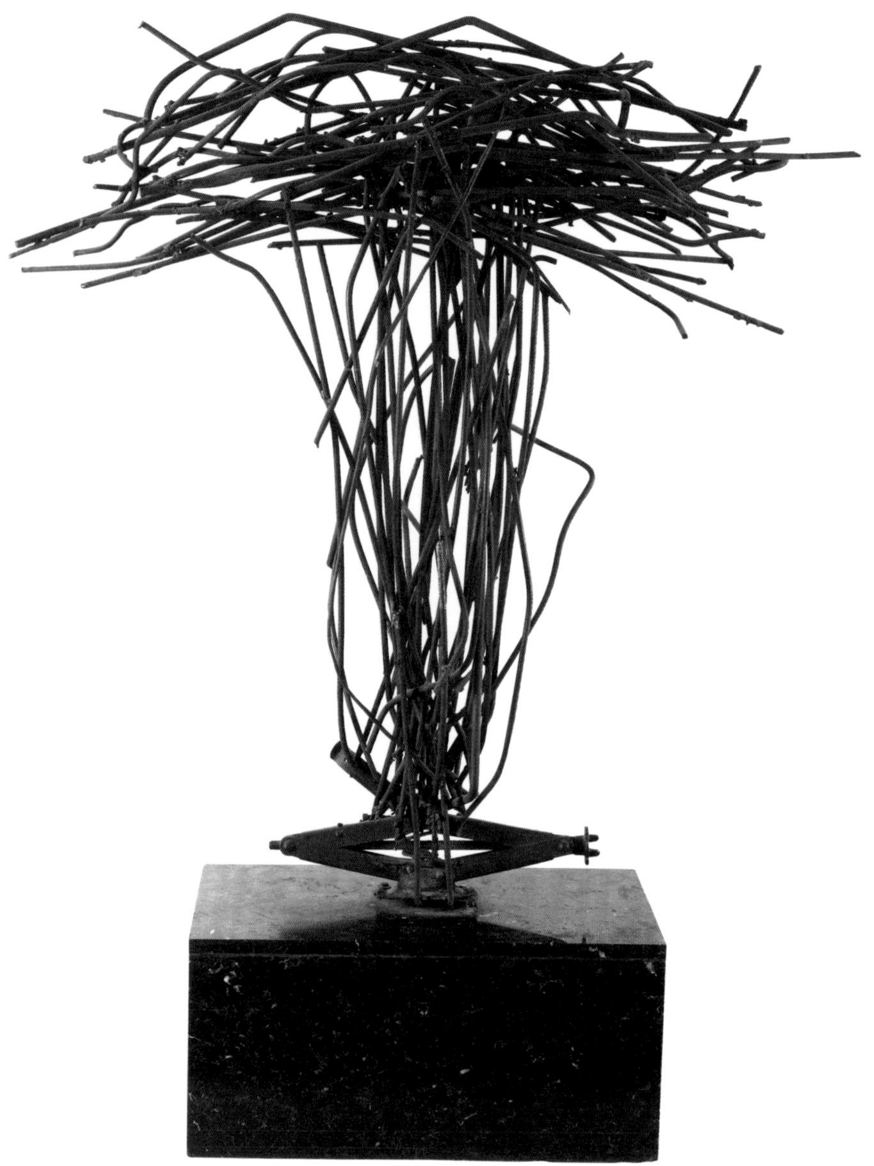

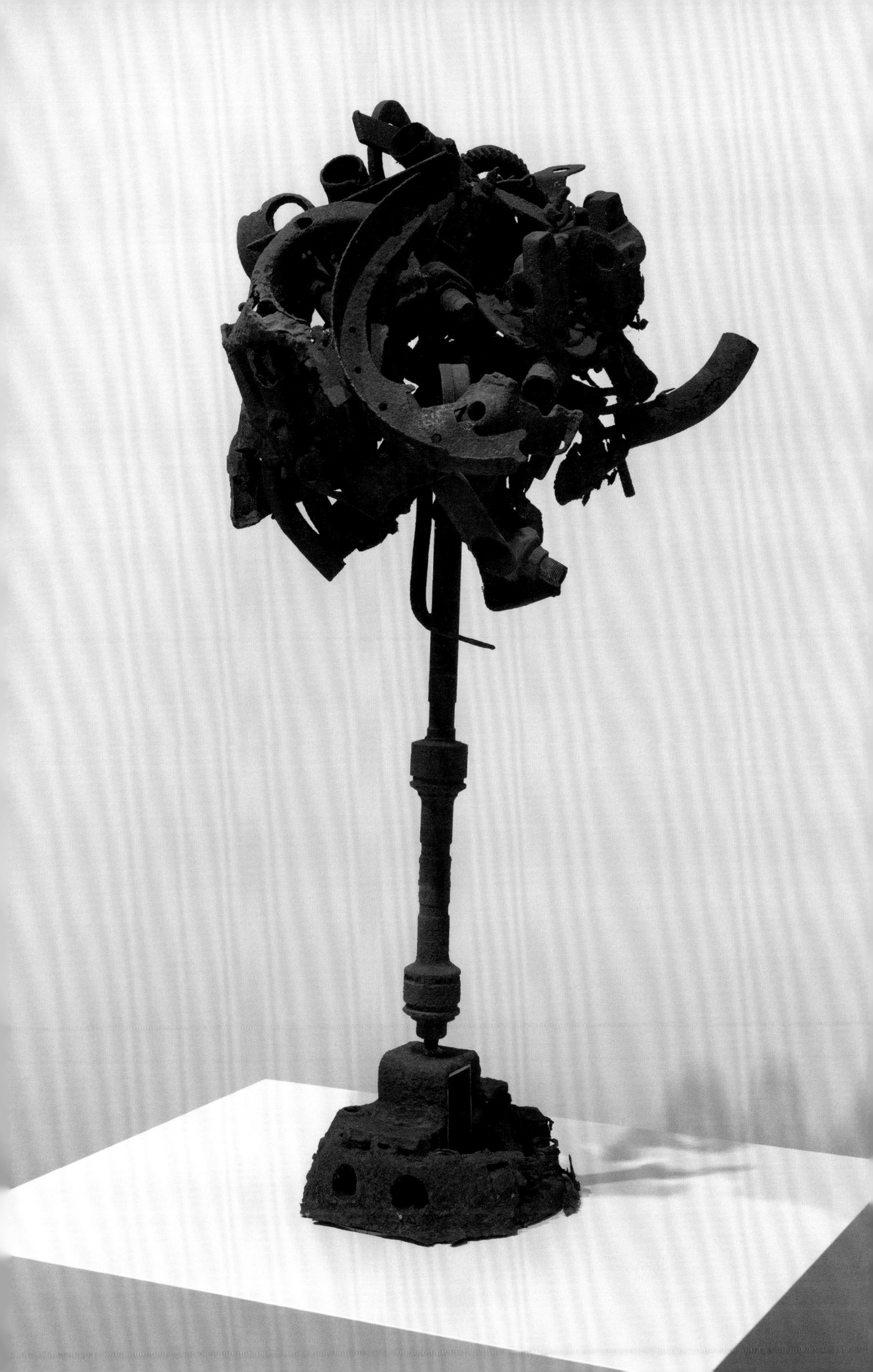

Homenaje a César
(Homage to César), c. 1971

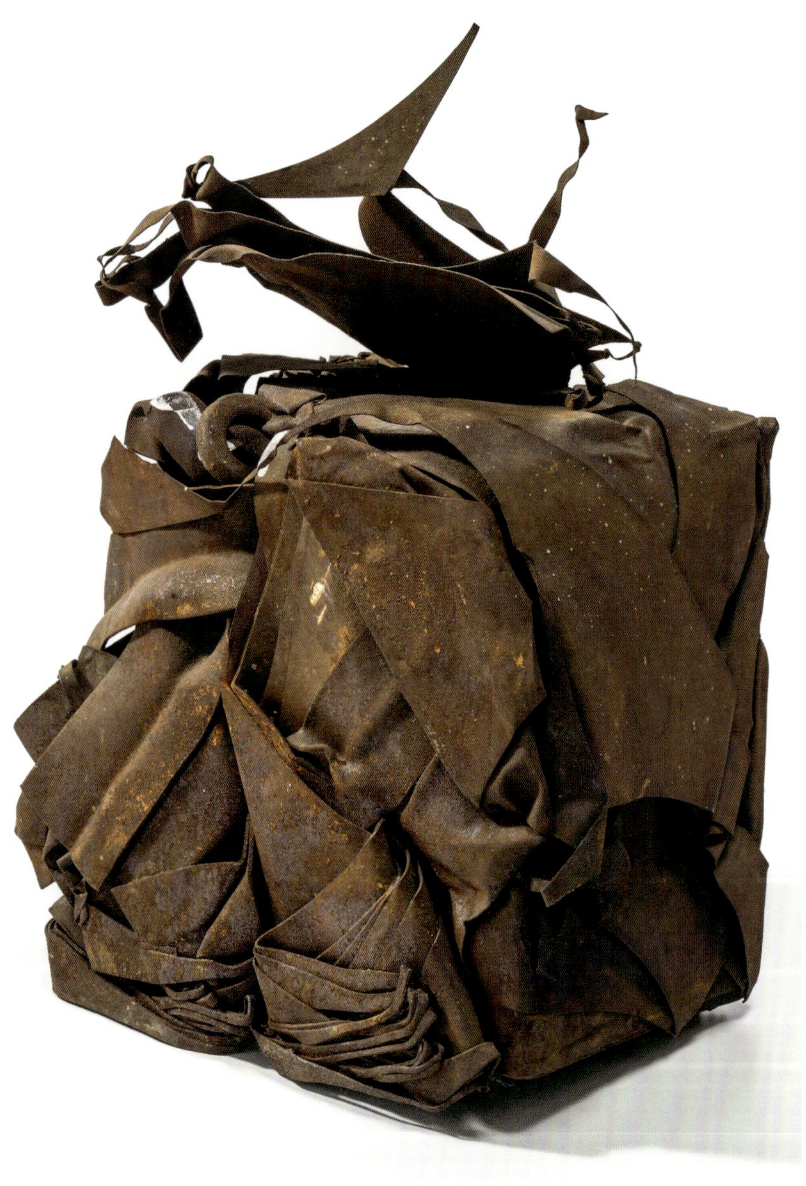

Sin título (Untitled), c. 1974

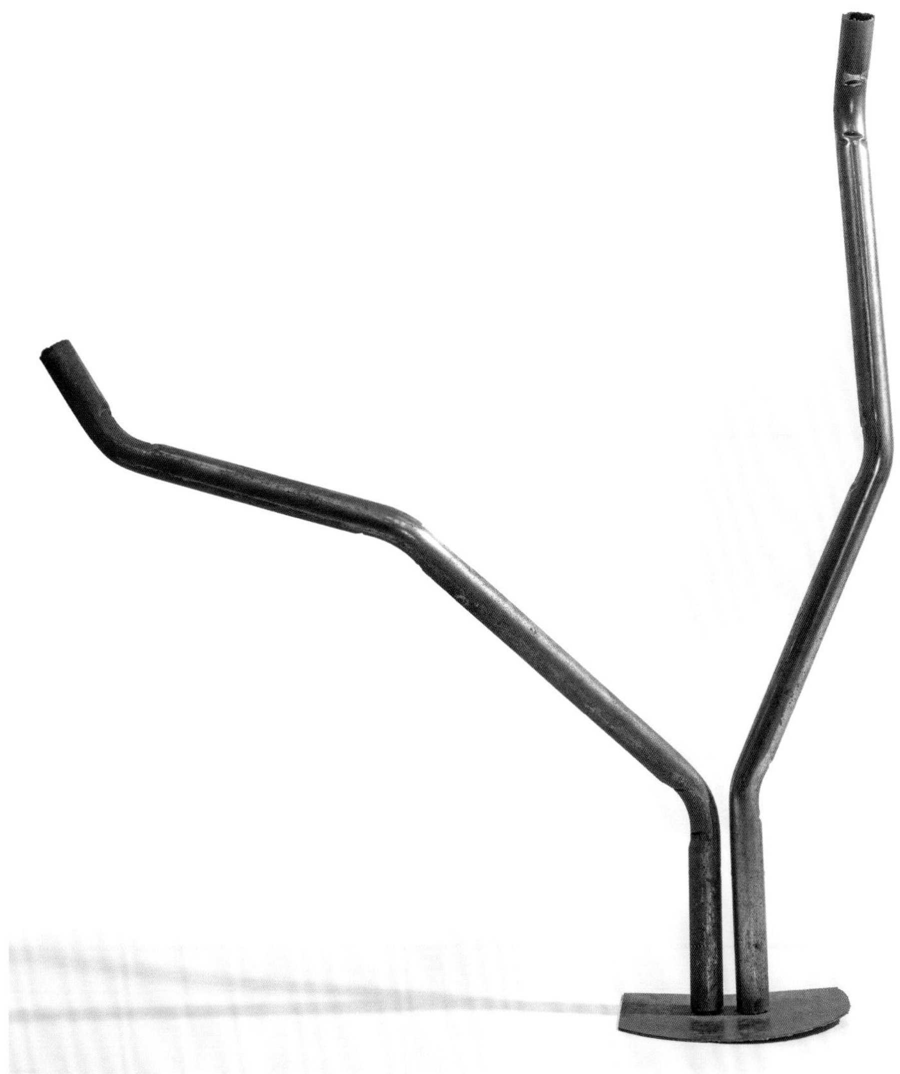

Sin título (Untitled), c. 1973

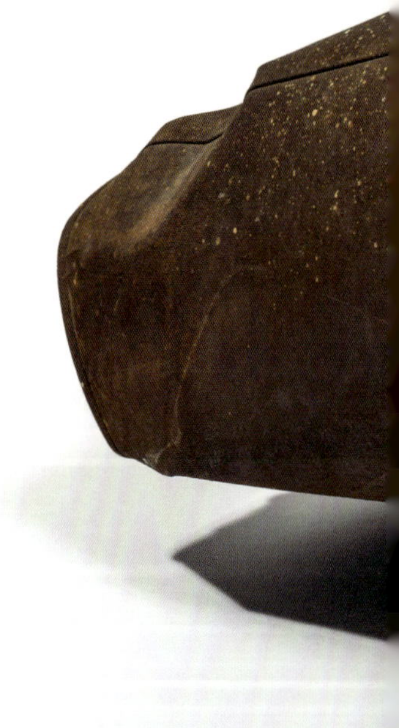

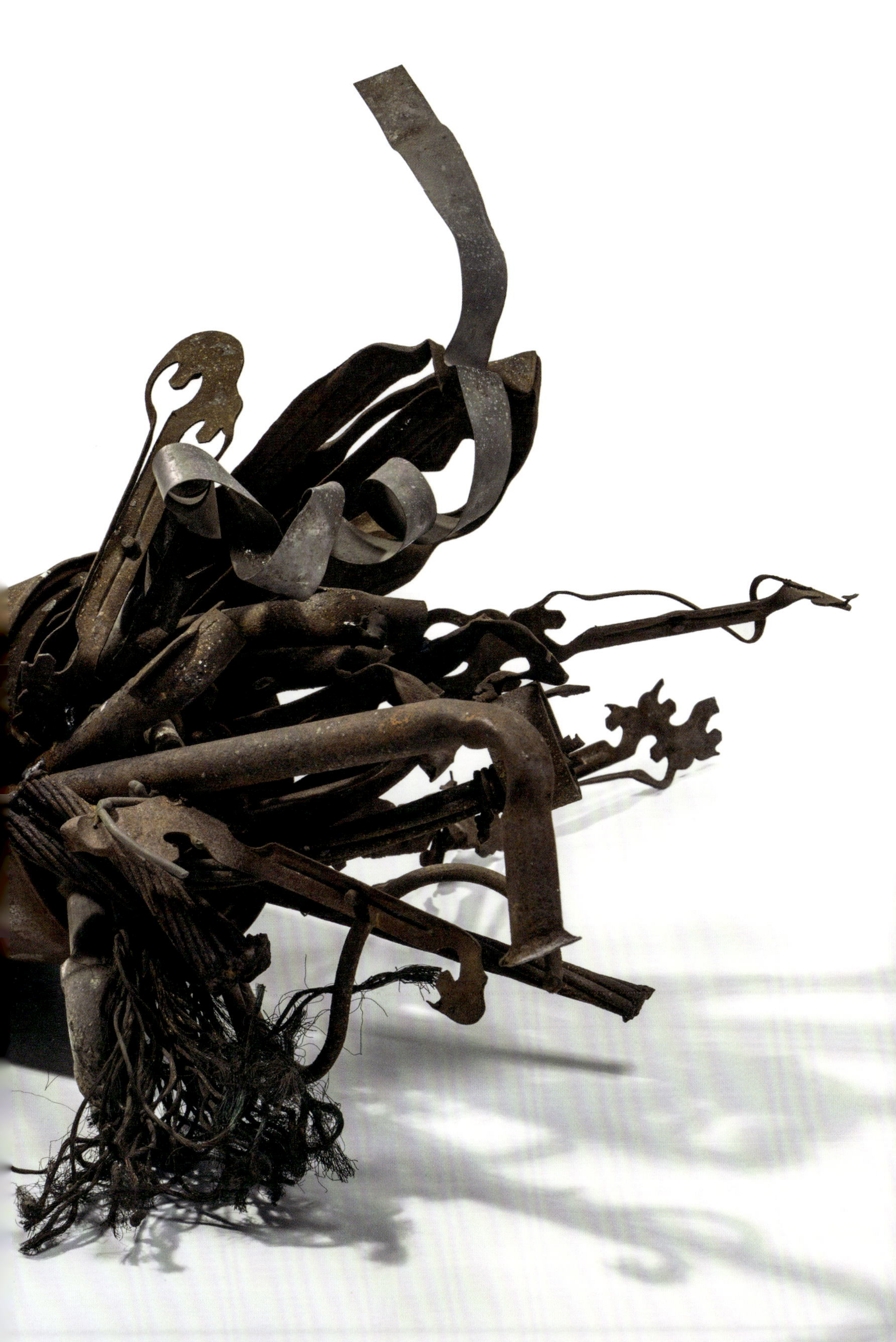

Estructura con tres arcos
(Structure with Three Arches),
1964–67

Flor (Flower), 1974

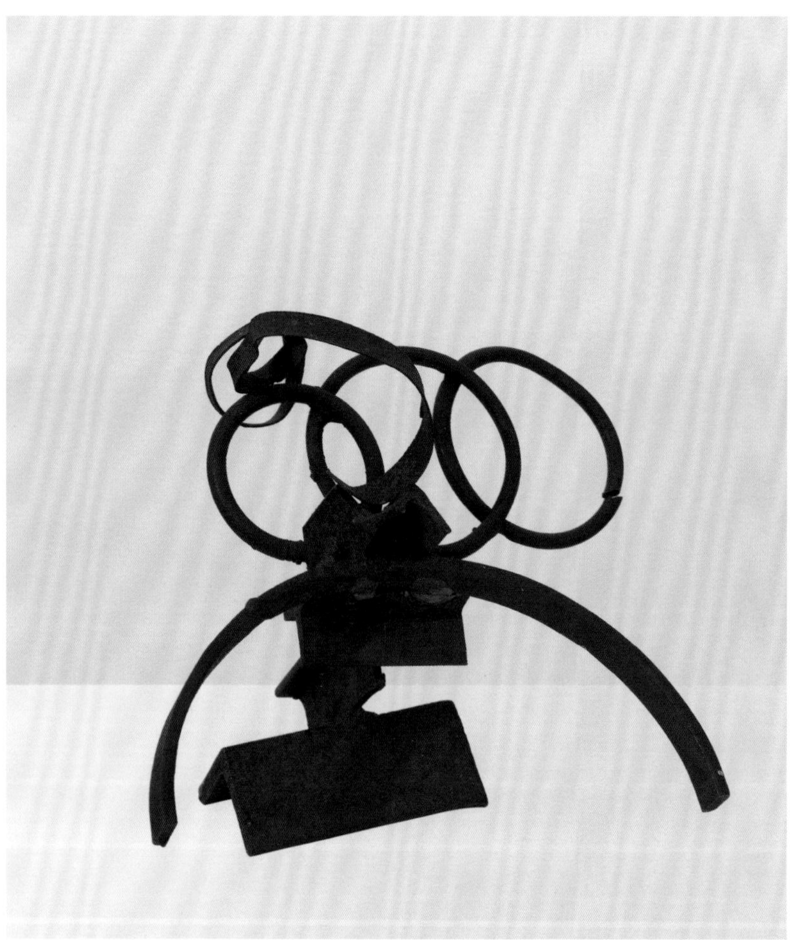

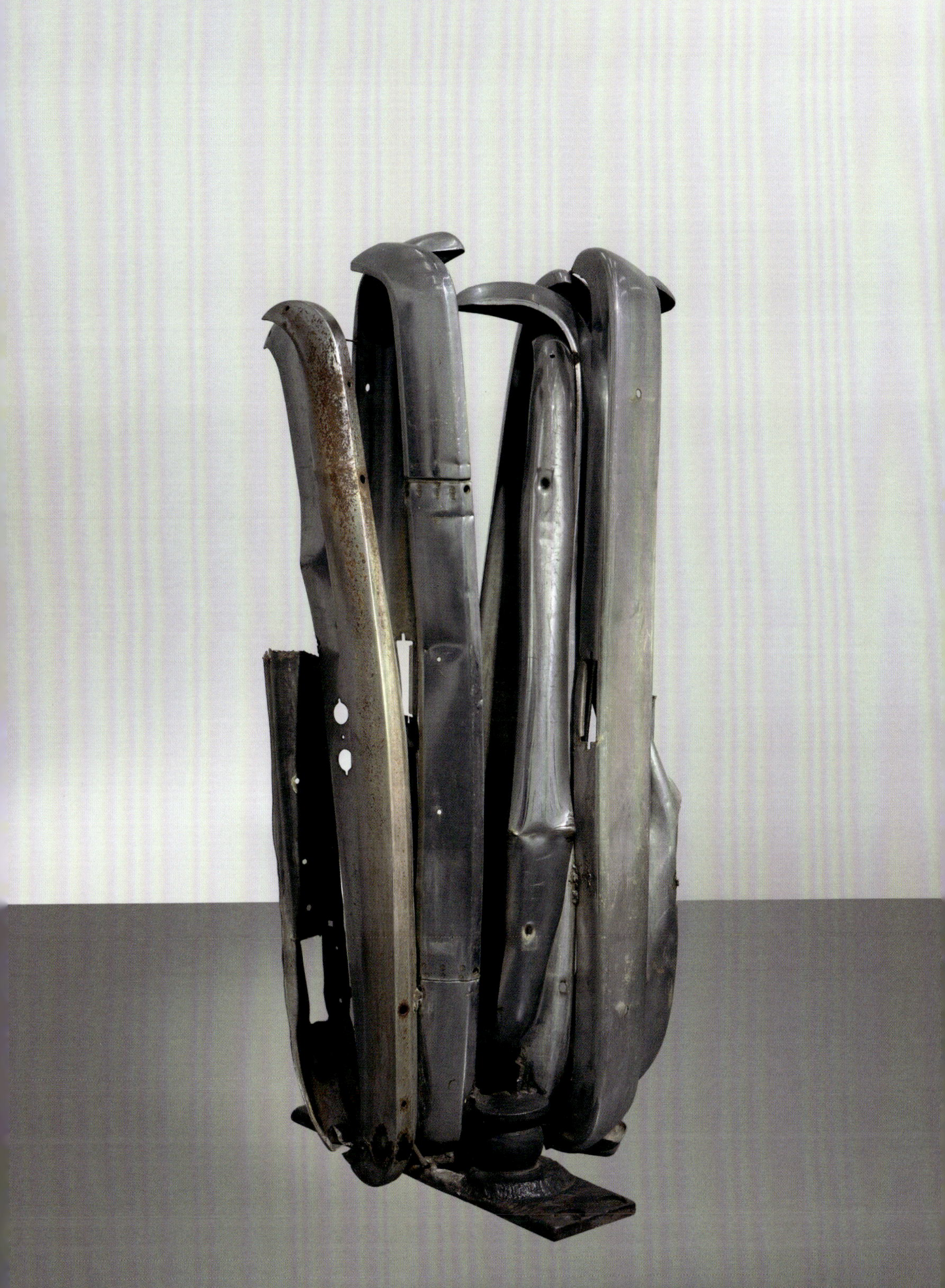

Sin título (Untitled), 1968

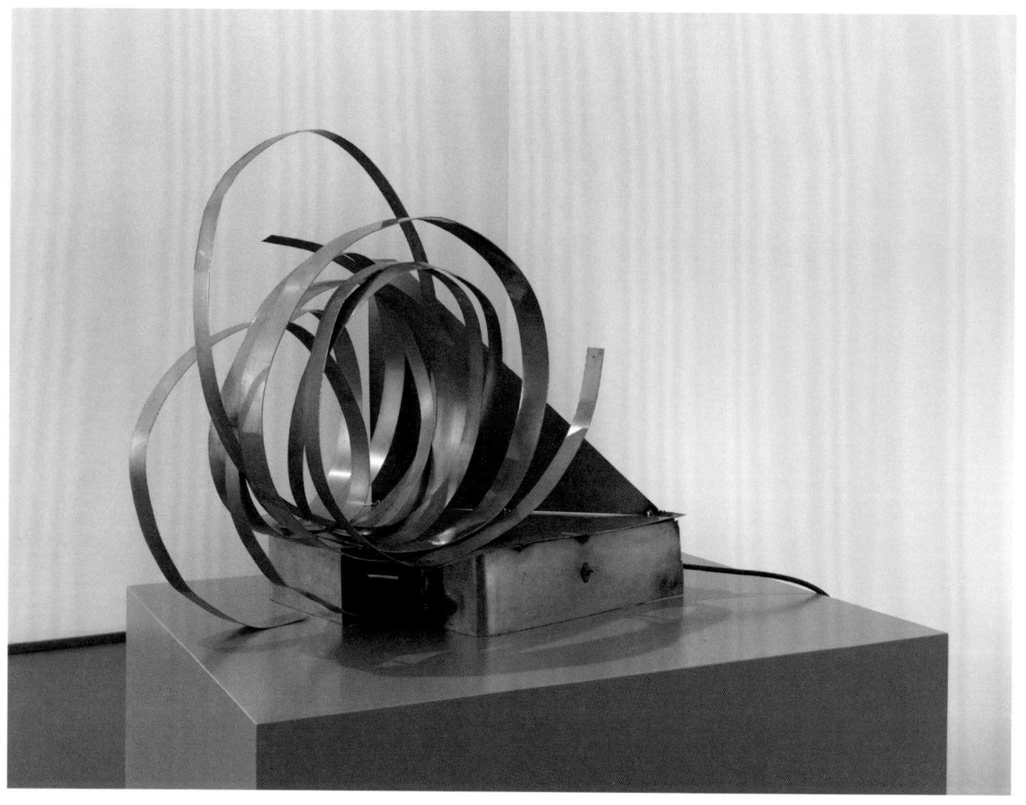

Sin título (Untitled), c. 1968

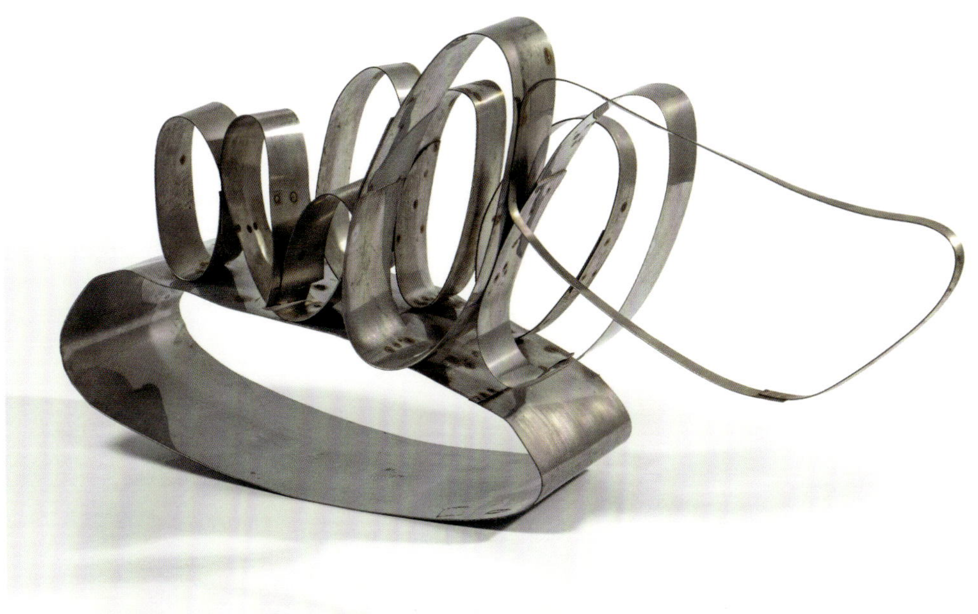

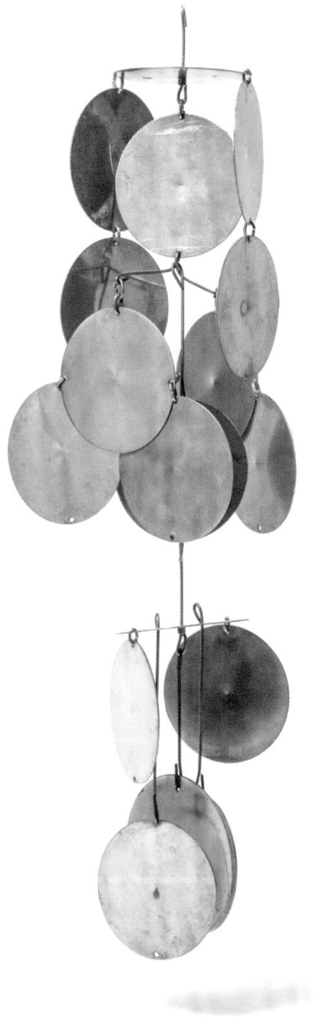

Histérica (The Hysterical One),
1968

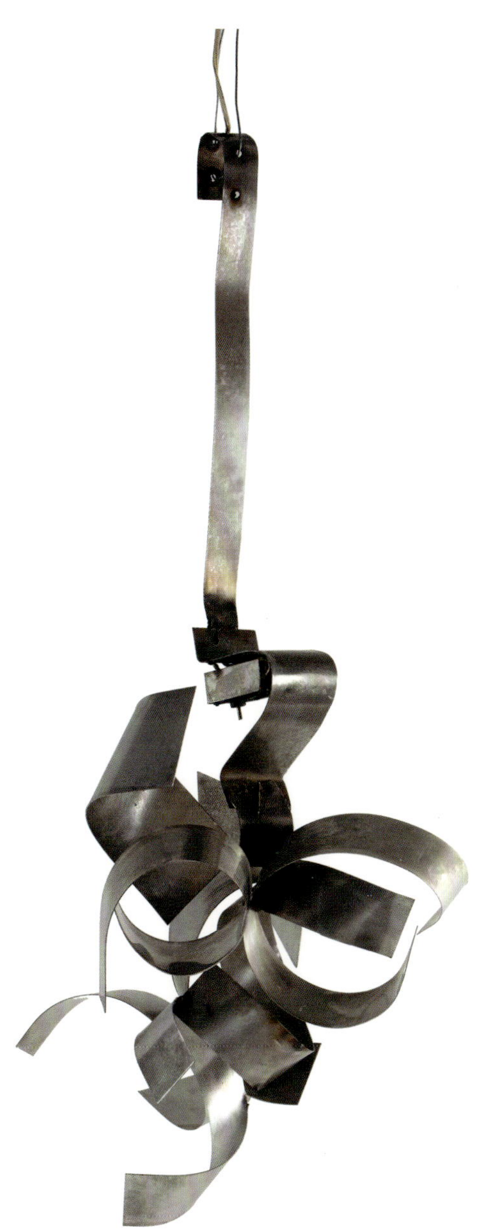

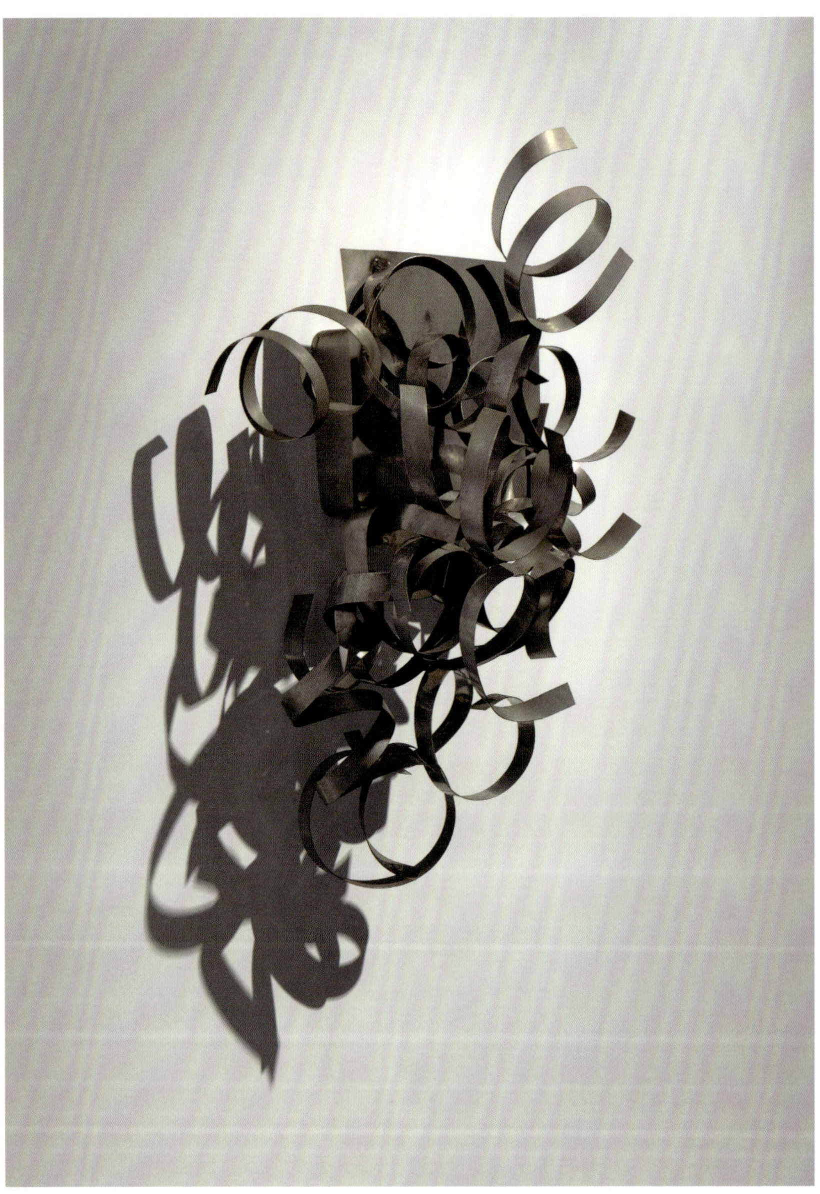

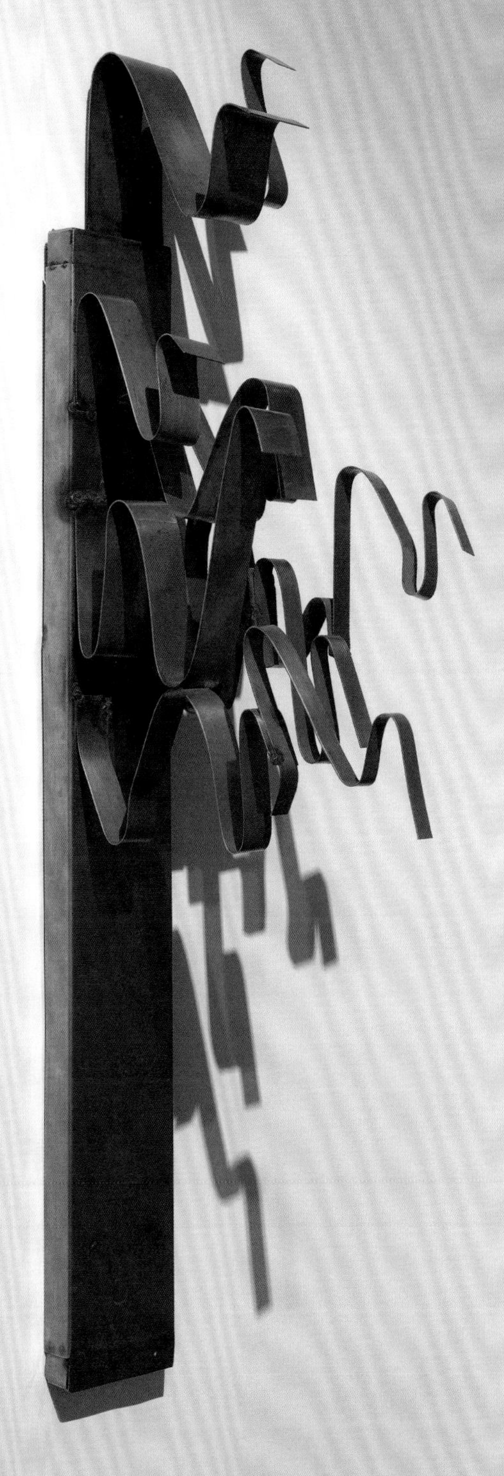

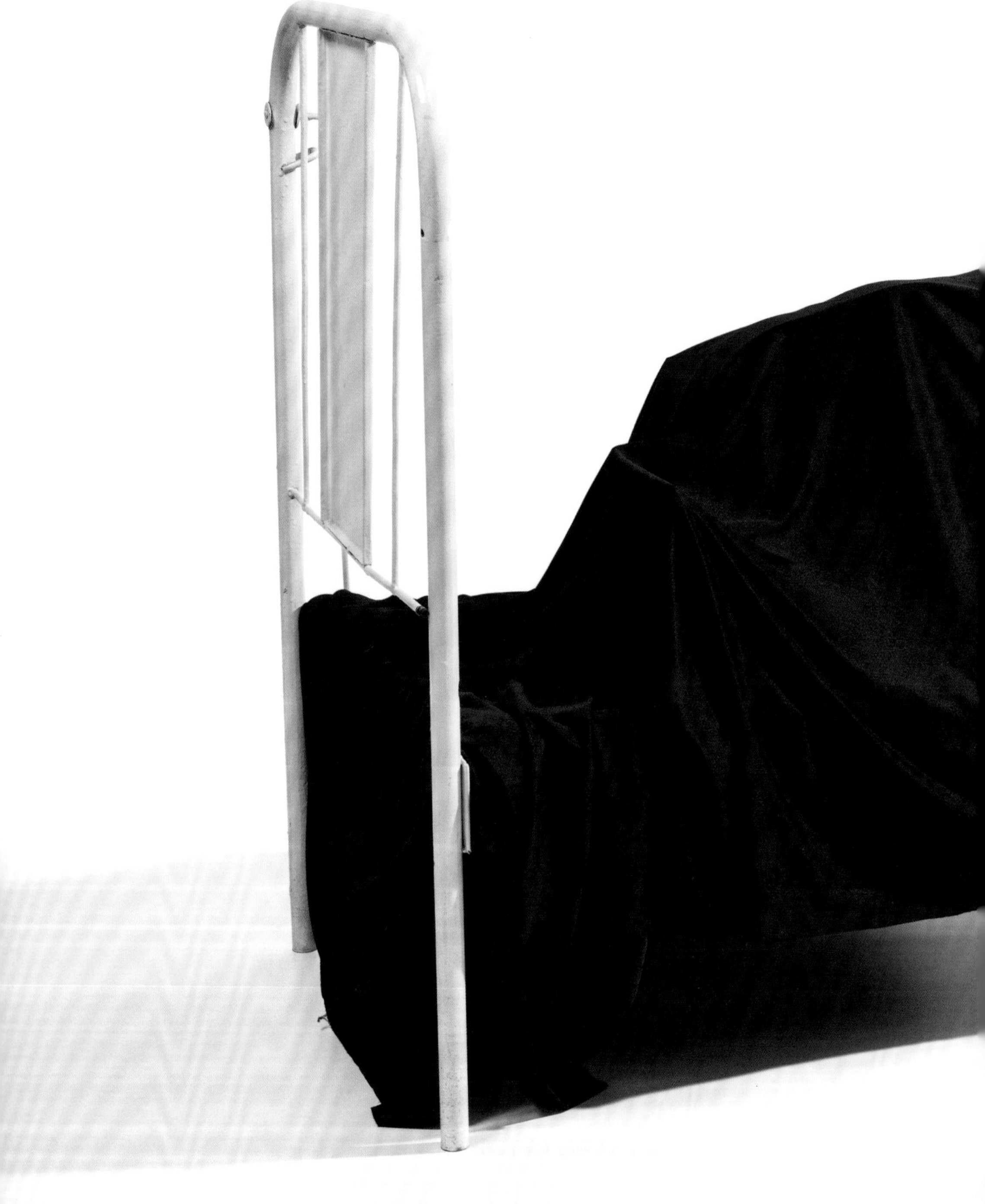

El bebé de Rosemary
(Rosemary's Baby), c. 1972

Sin título (Untitled), 1974 (2009)

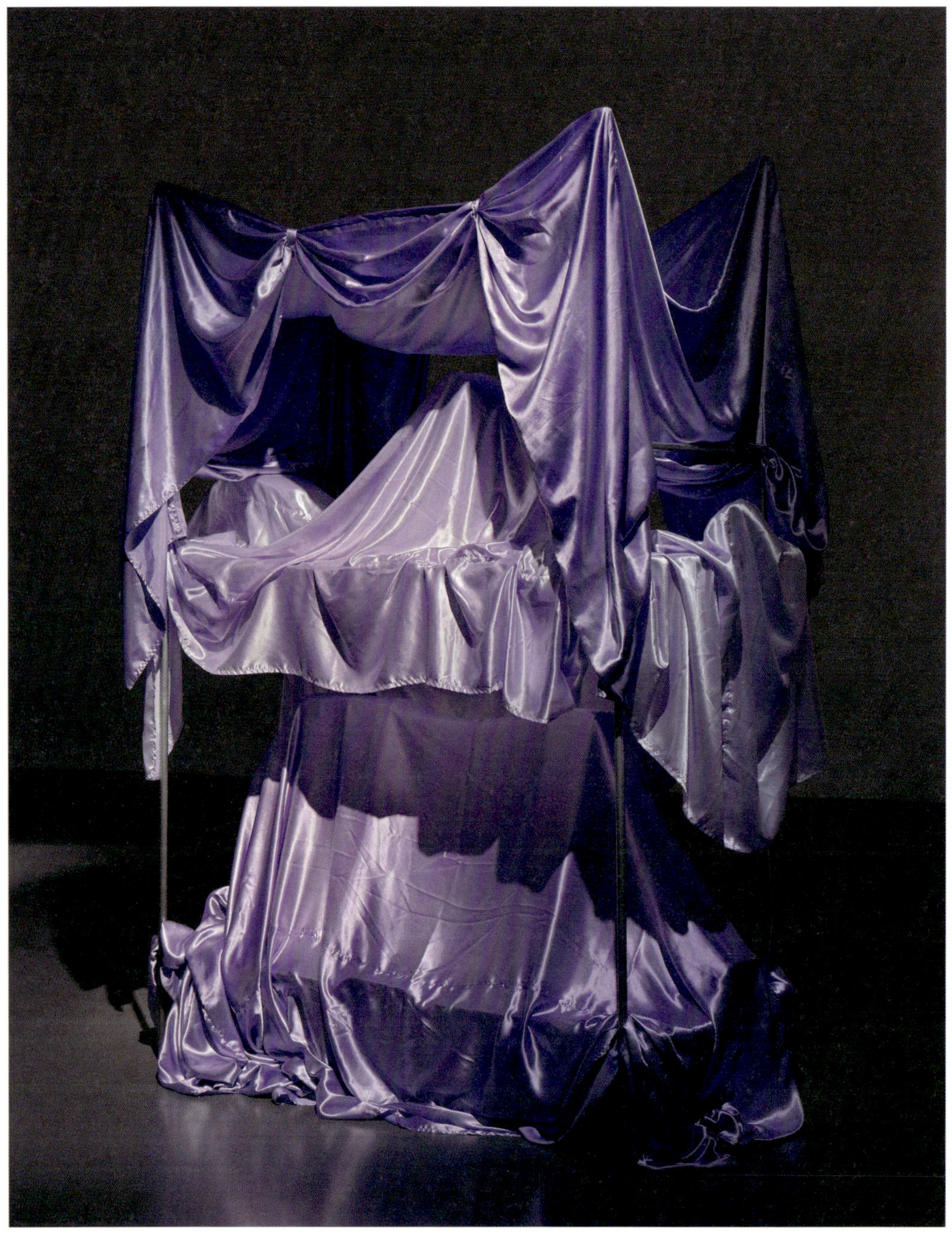

Cama (Bed), 1974 (2009)

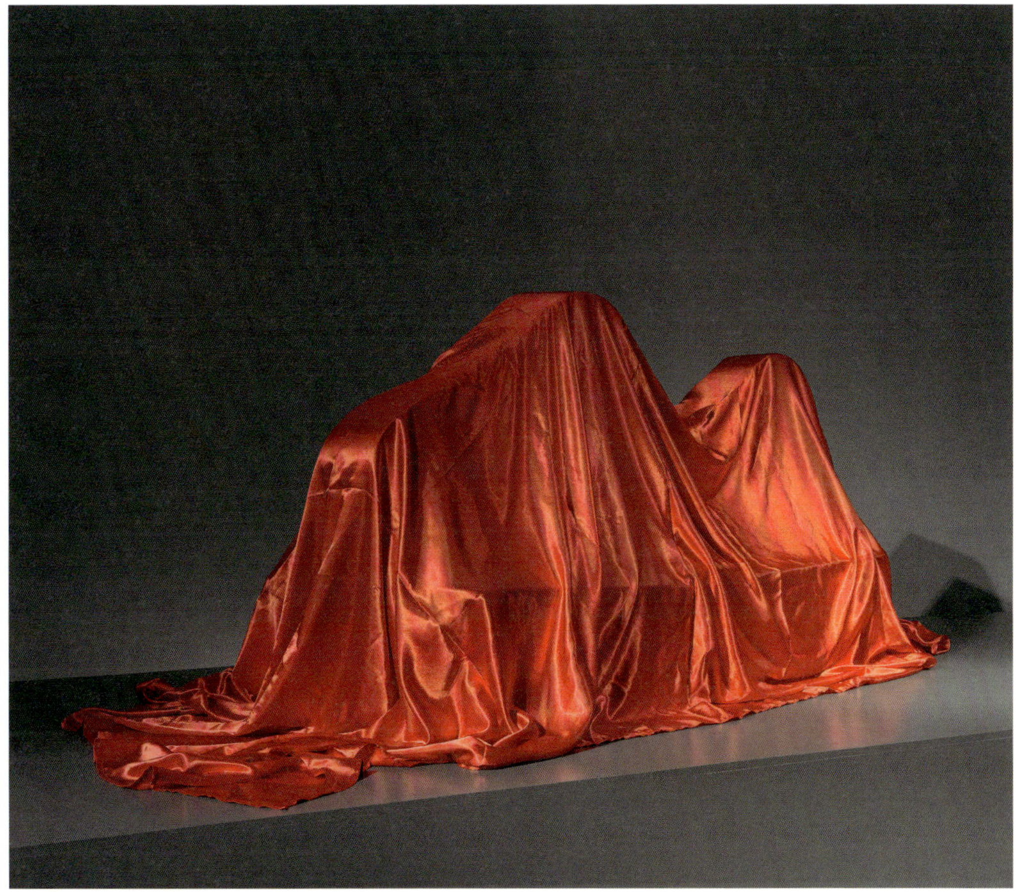

Sin título (Untitled), 1968

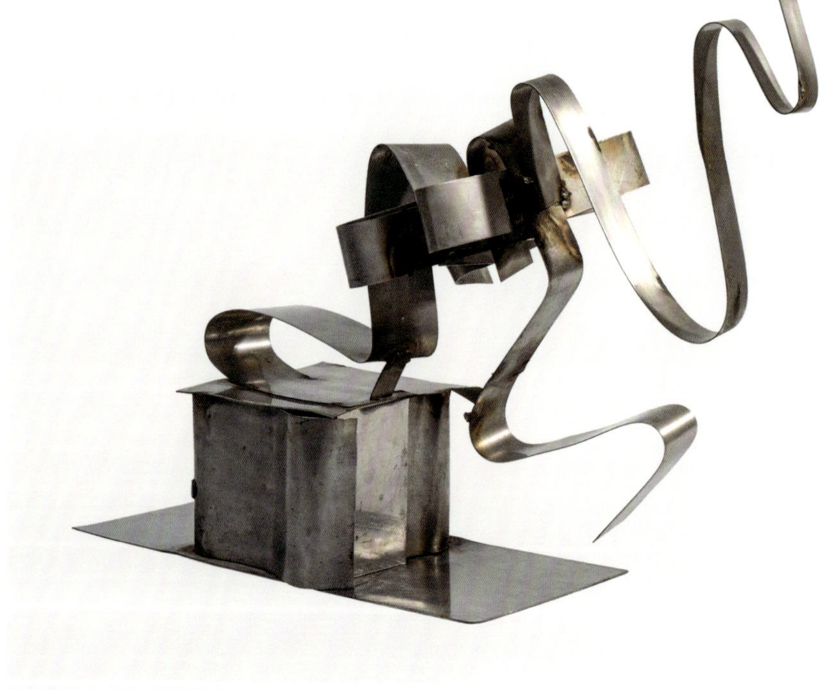

Sin título (Untitled), 1969–74

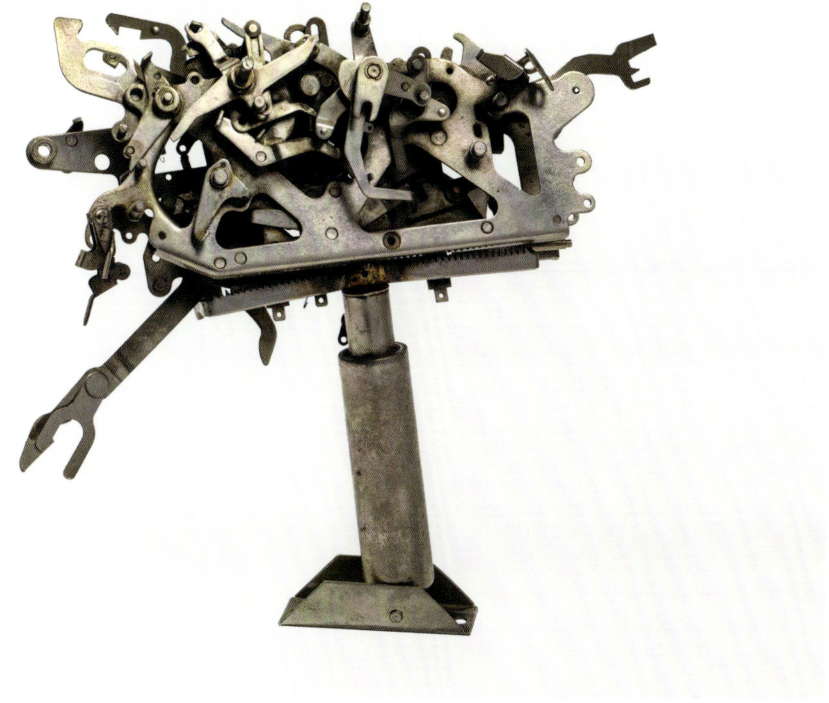

Sin título (Untitled), 1969–74

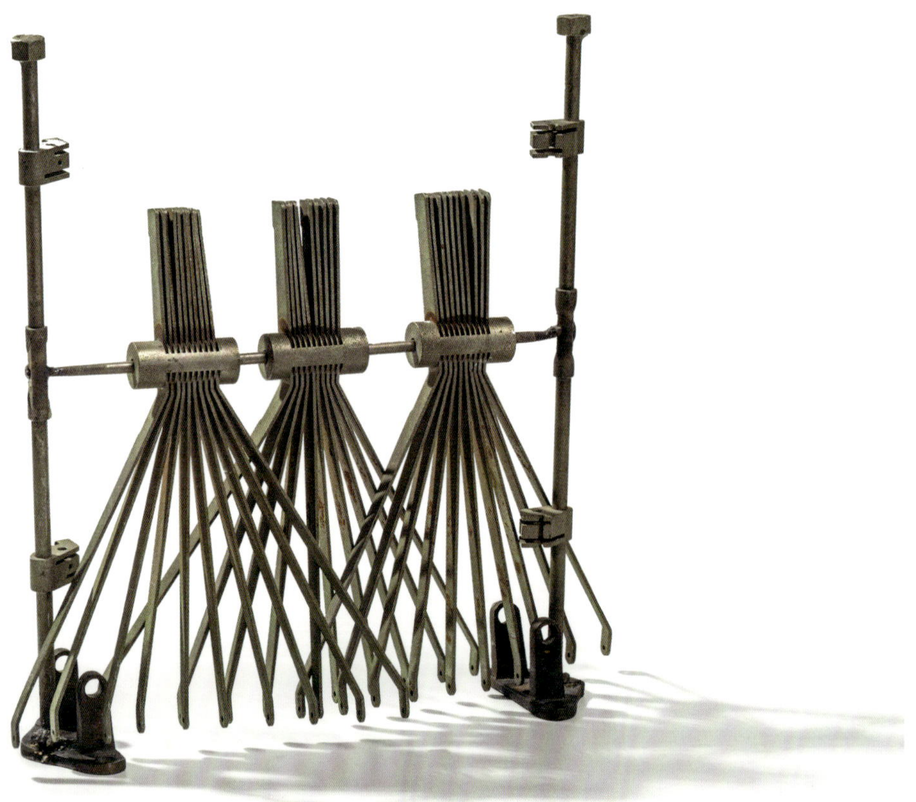

Estrella de mar (Starfish), 1974

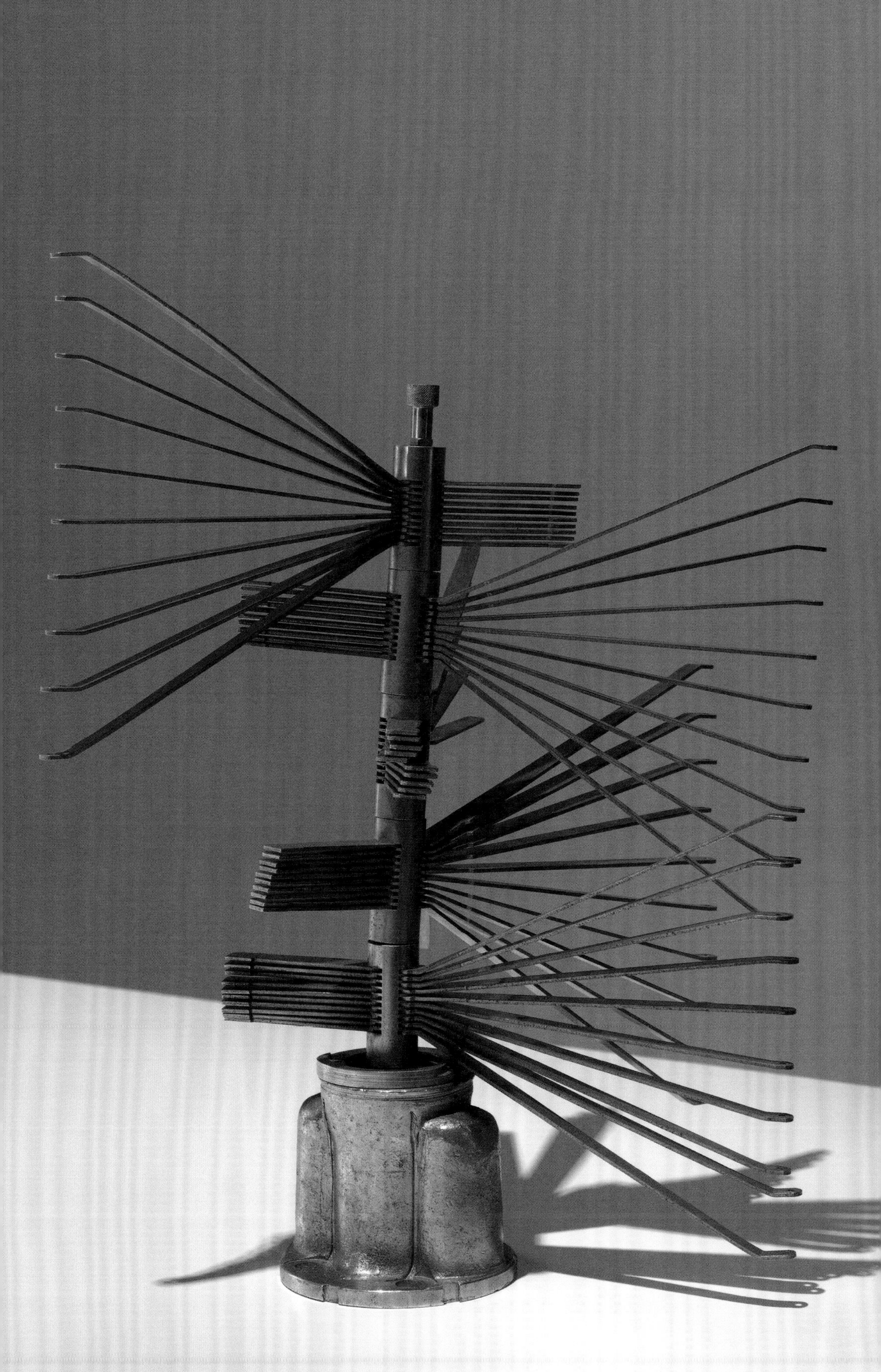

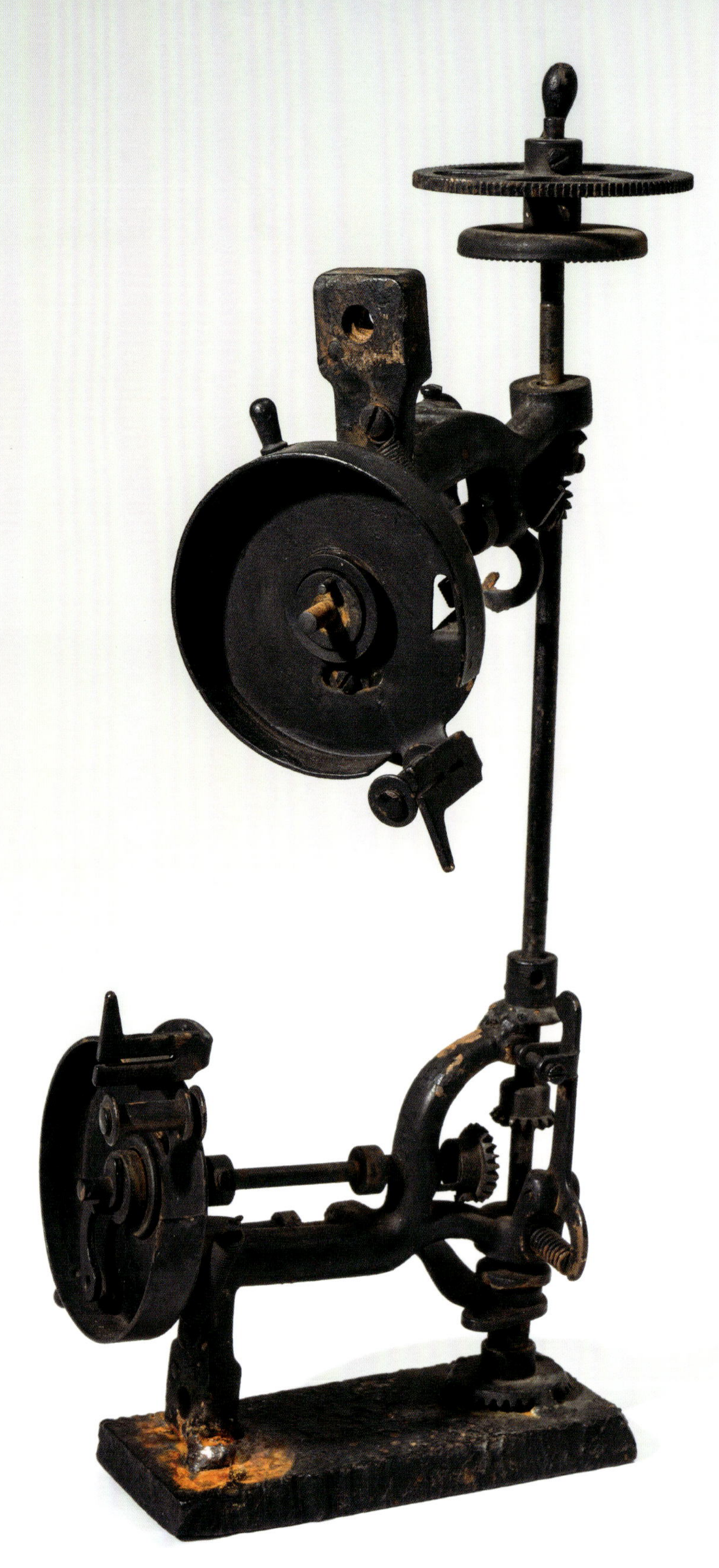

Sin título (Untitled), c. 1969   *Sin título* (Untitled), 1969–74

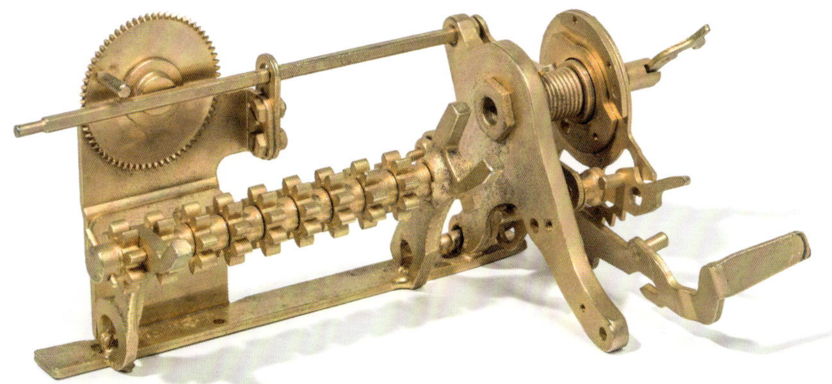

Sin título (Untitled), 1969–74

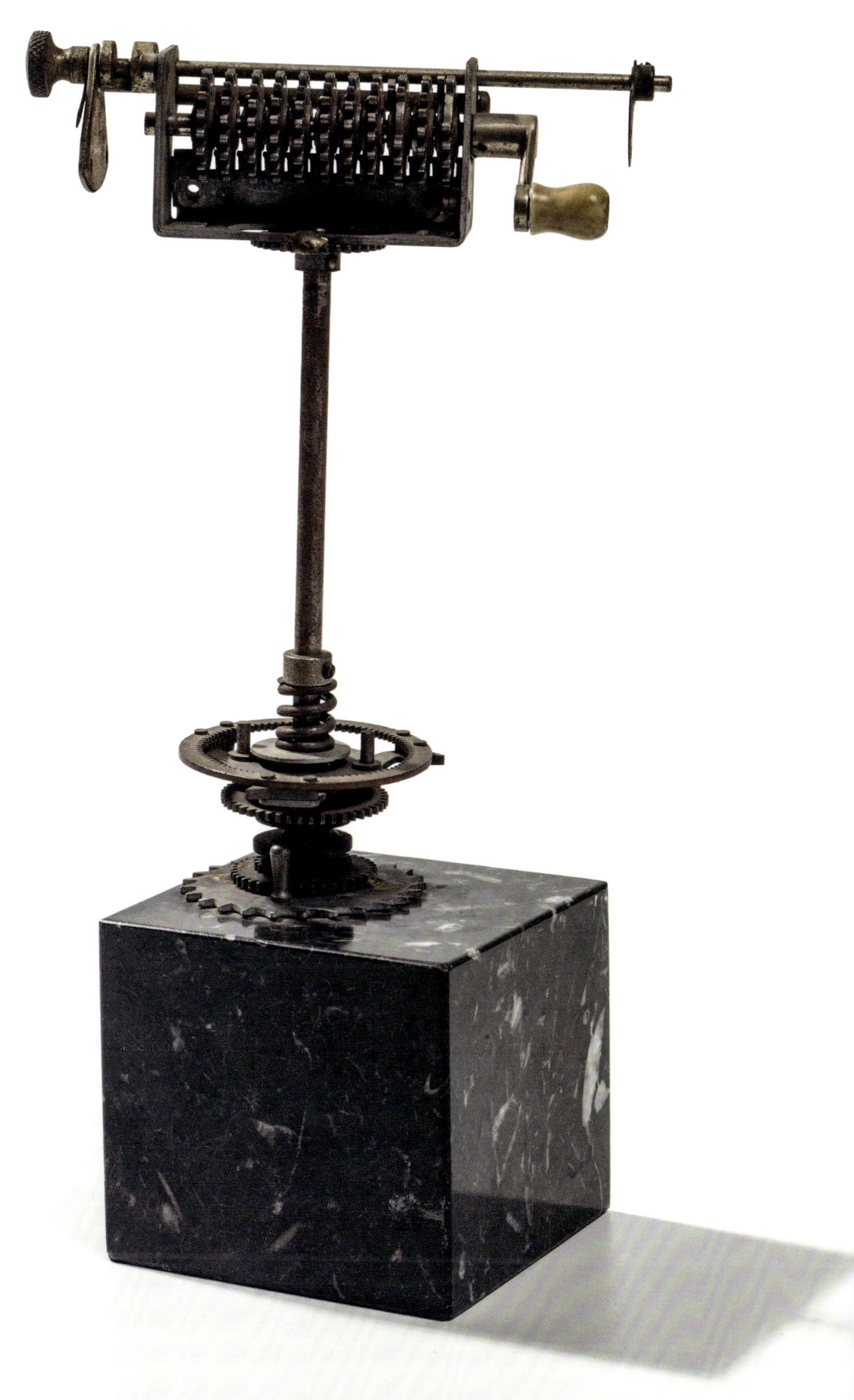

Ajedrez (Chess), c. 1972

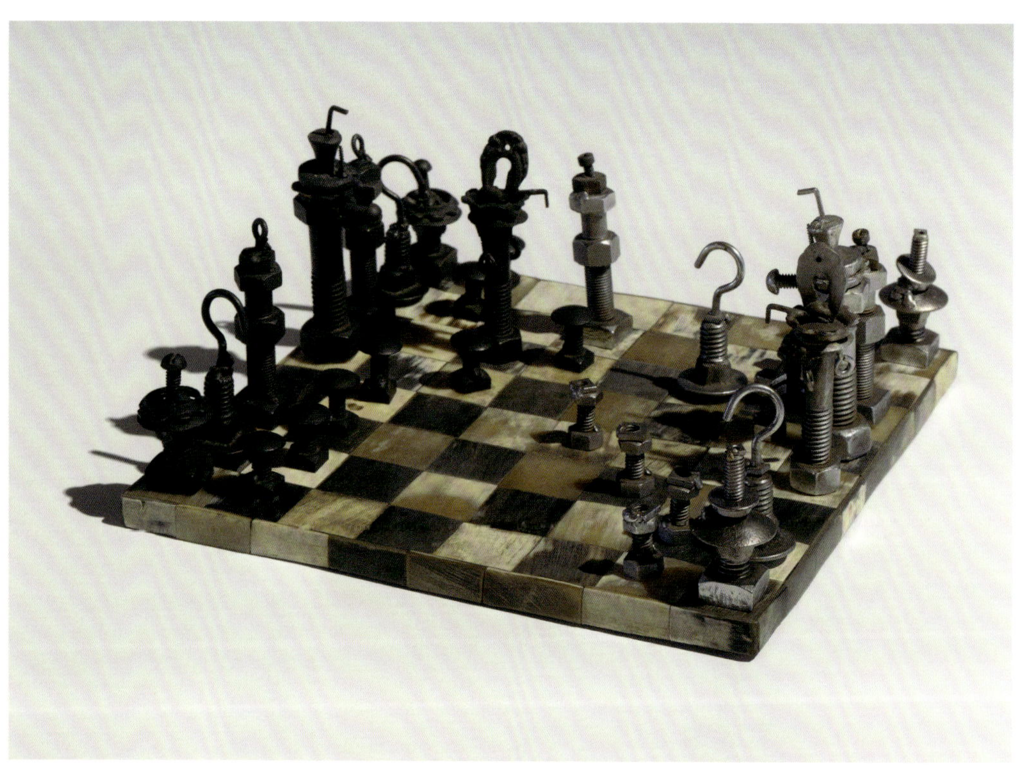

Hal, 1969–74

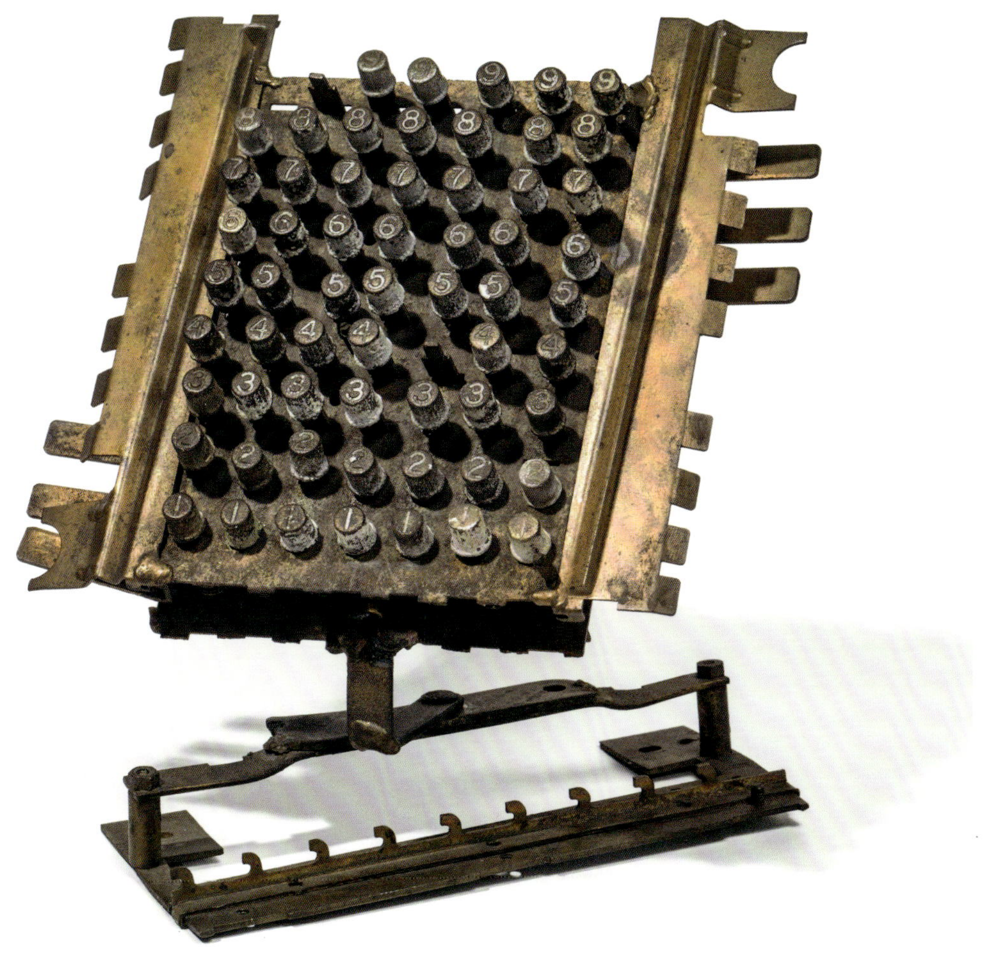

     Sin título (Untitled), 1969–74

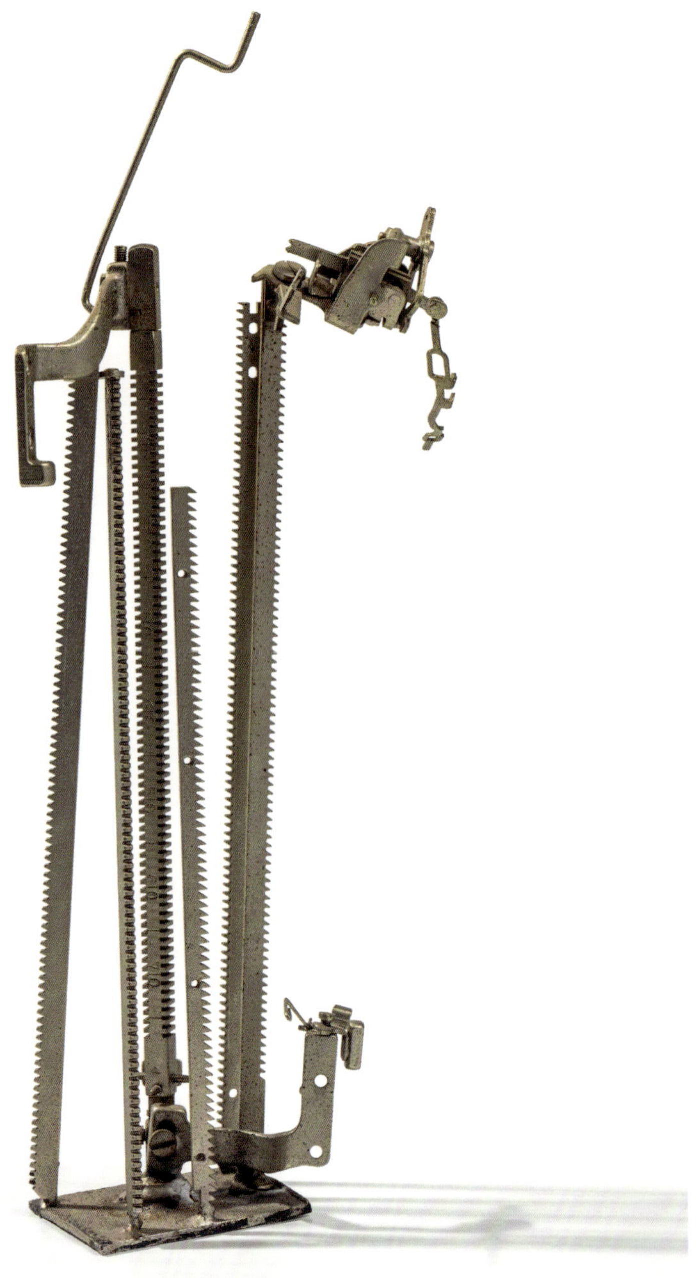

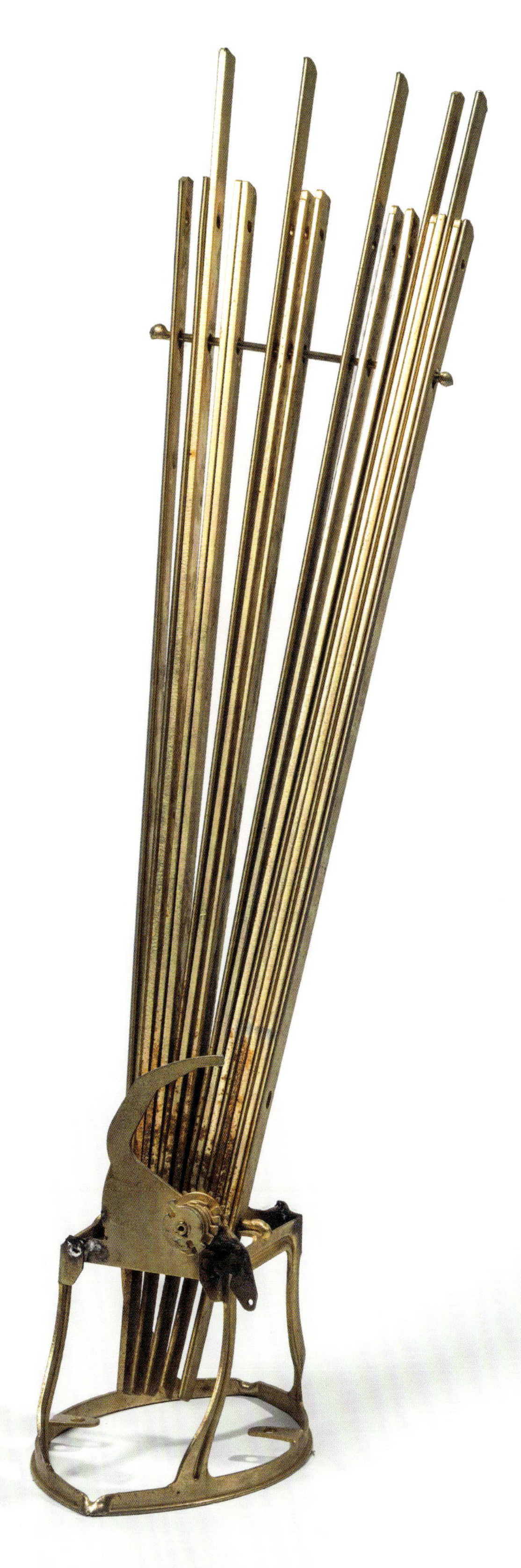

Sin título (Untitled), 1969–74   *Sin título* (Untitled), c. 1975

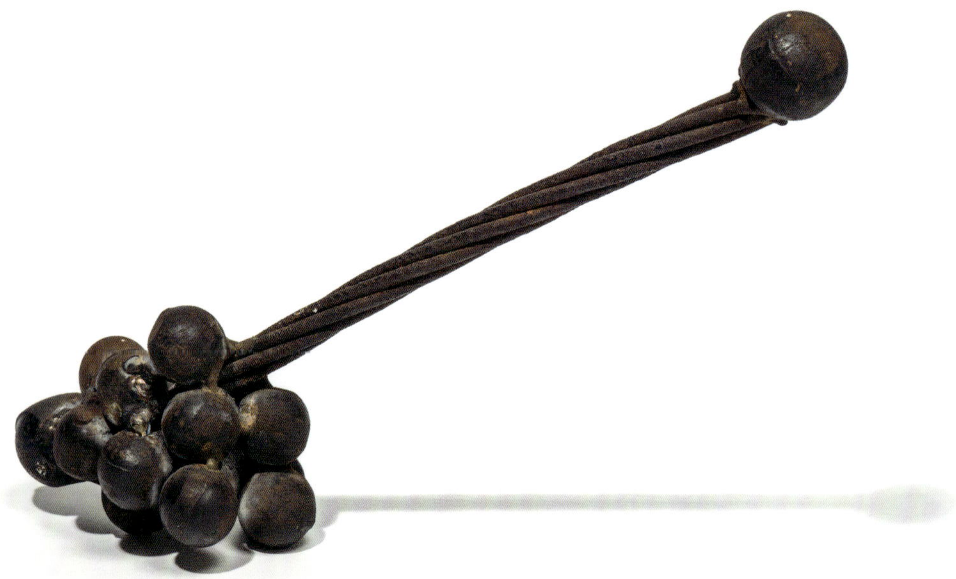

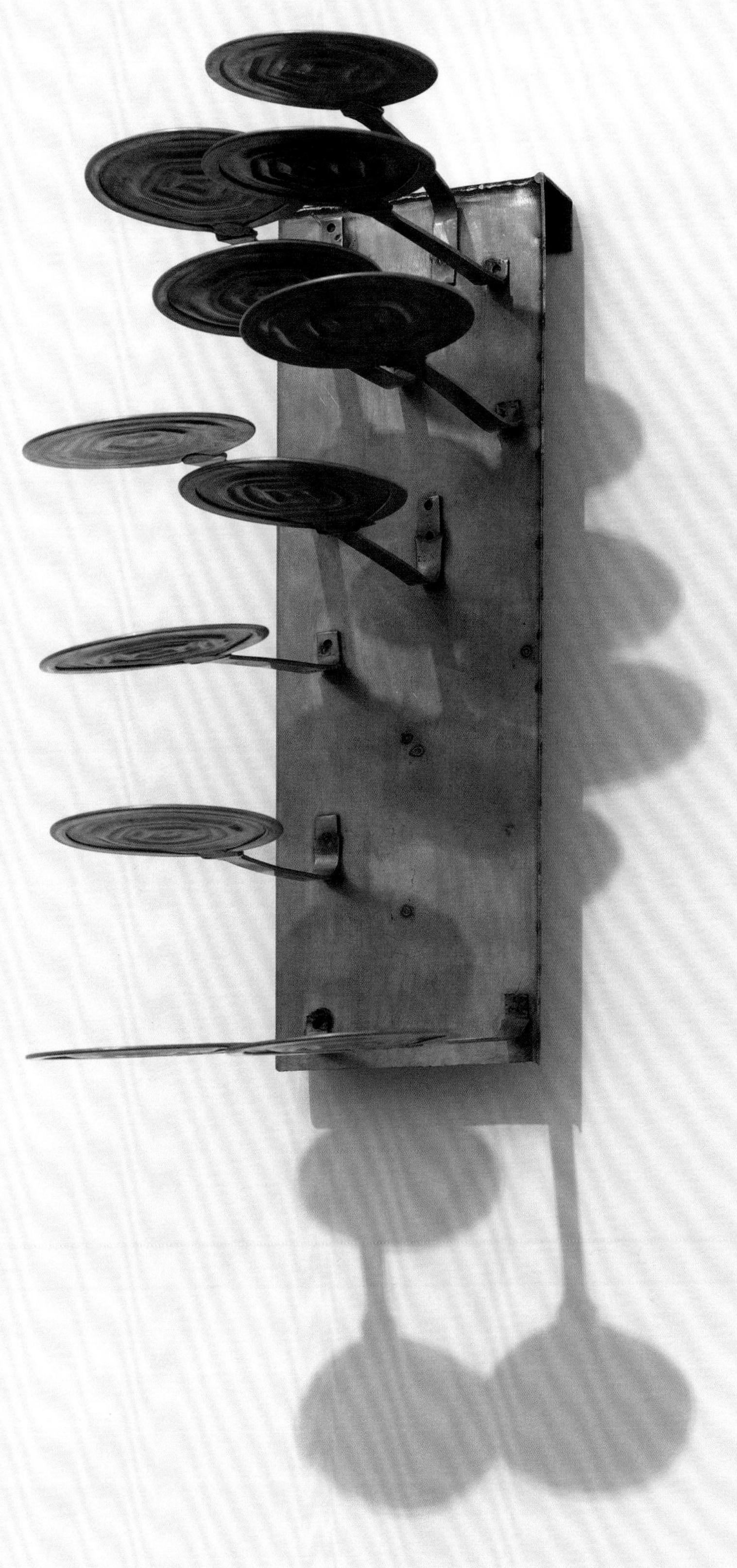

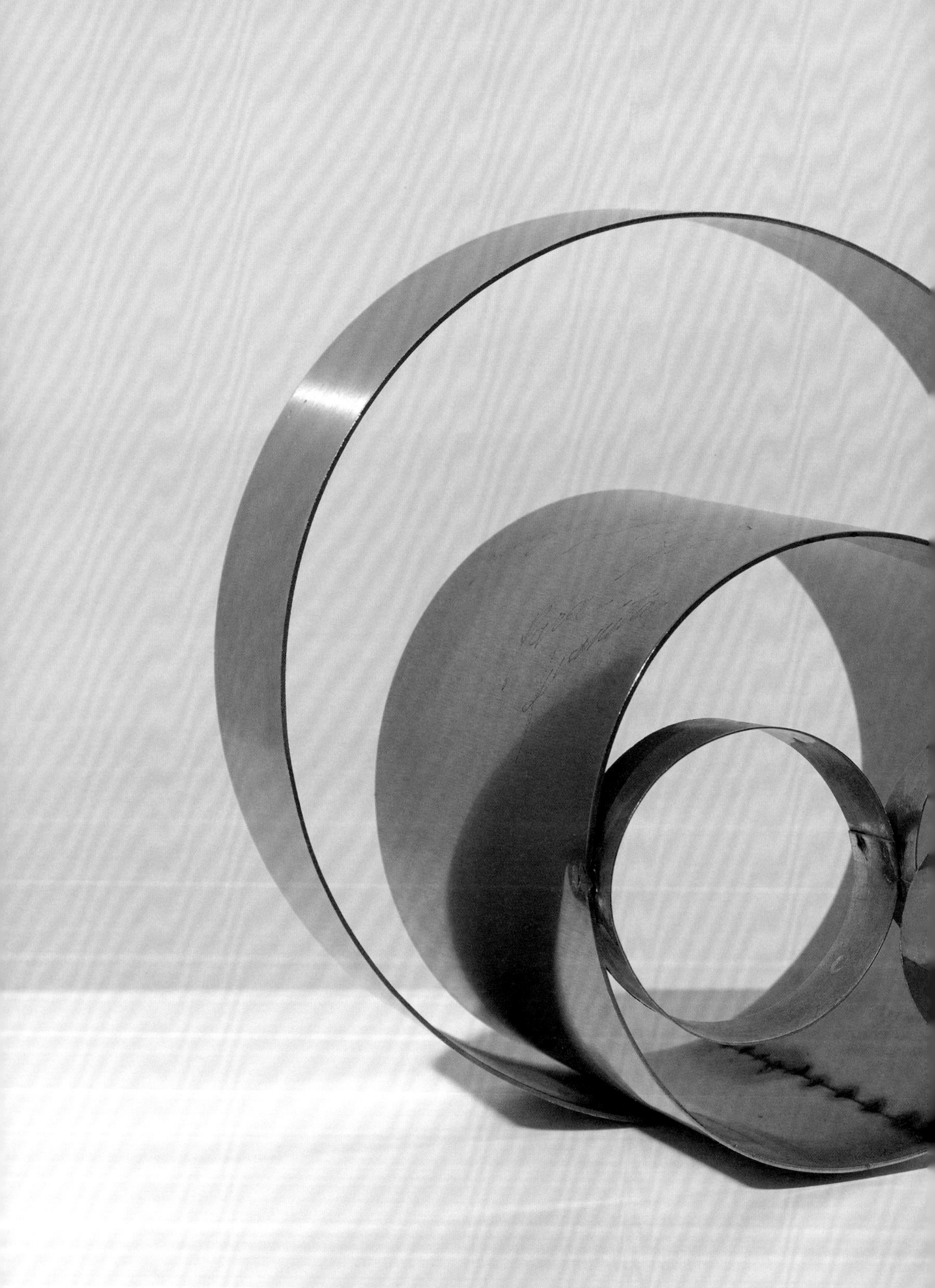

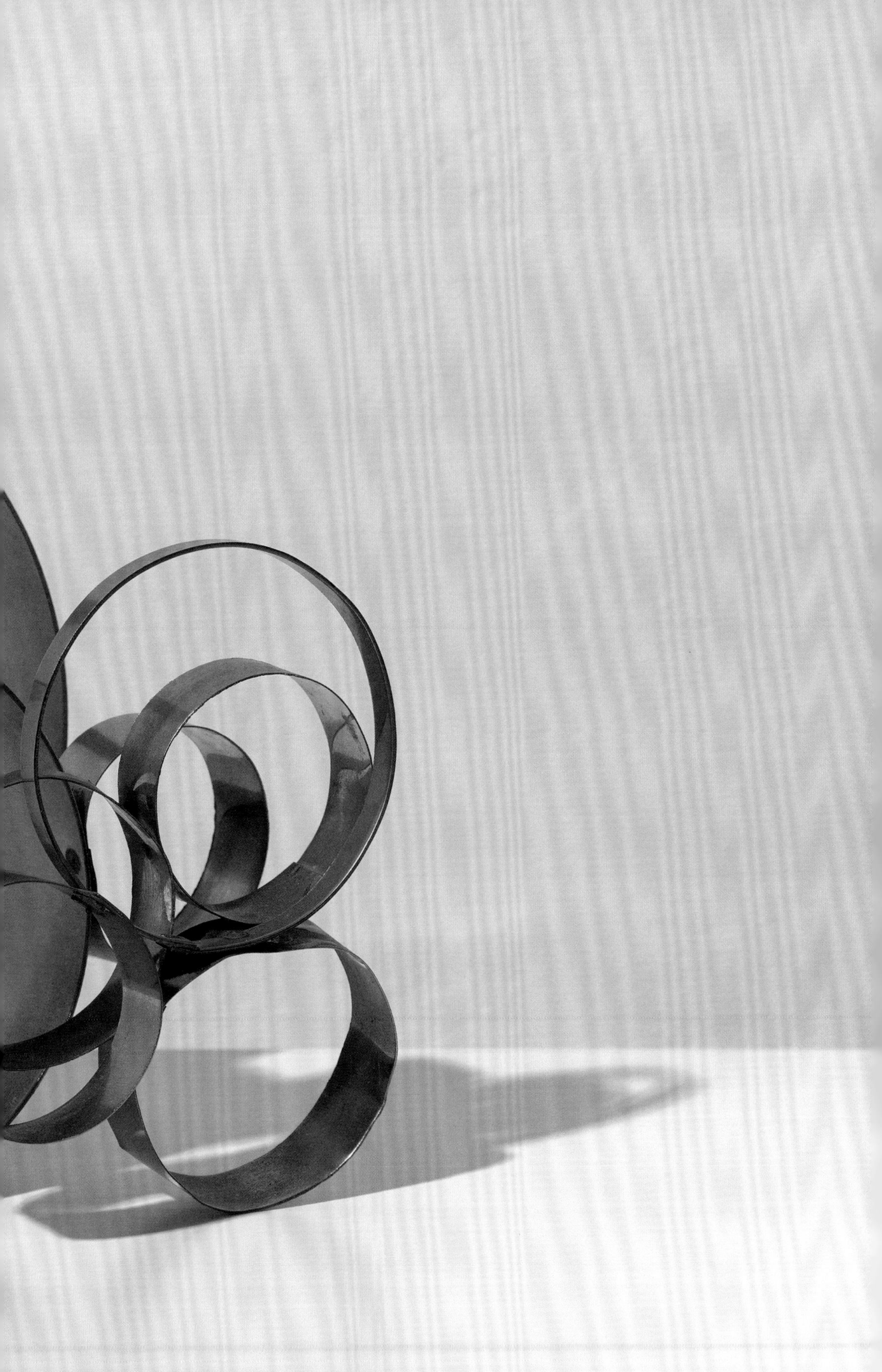

Encaje de Bruselas
(Brussels Lace), c. 1976

Sin título (Untitled), 1979

La baila mecánica (The
Mechanical Ballet), 1979

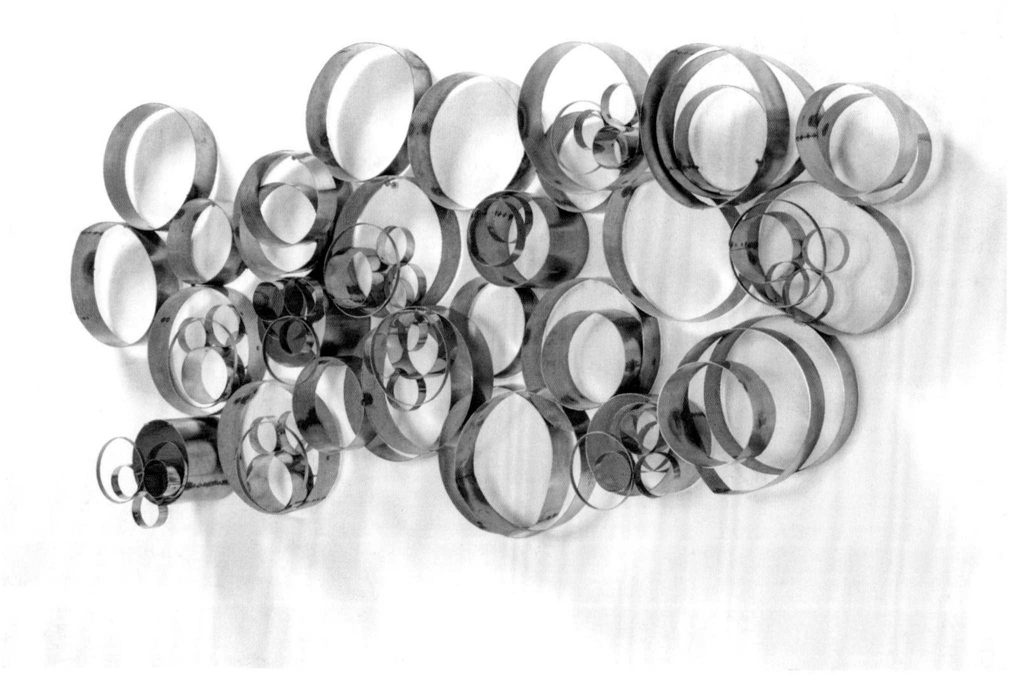

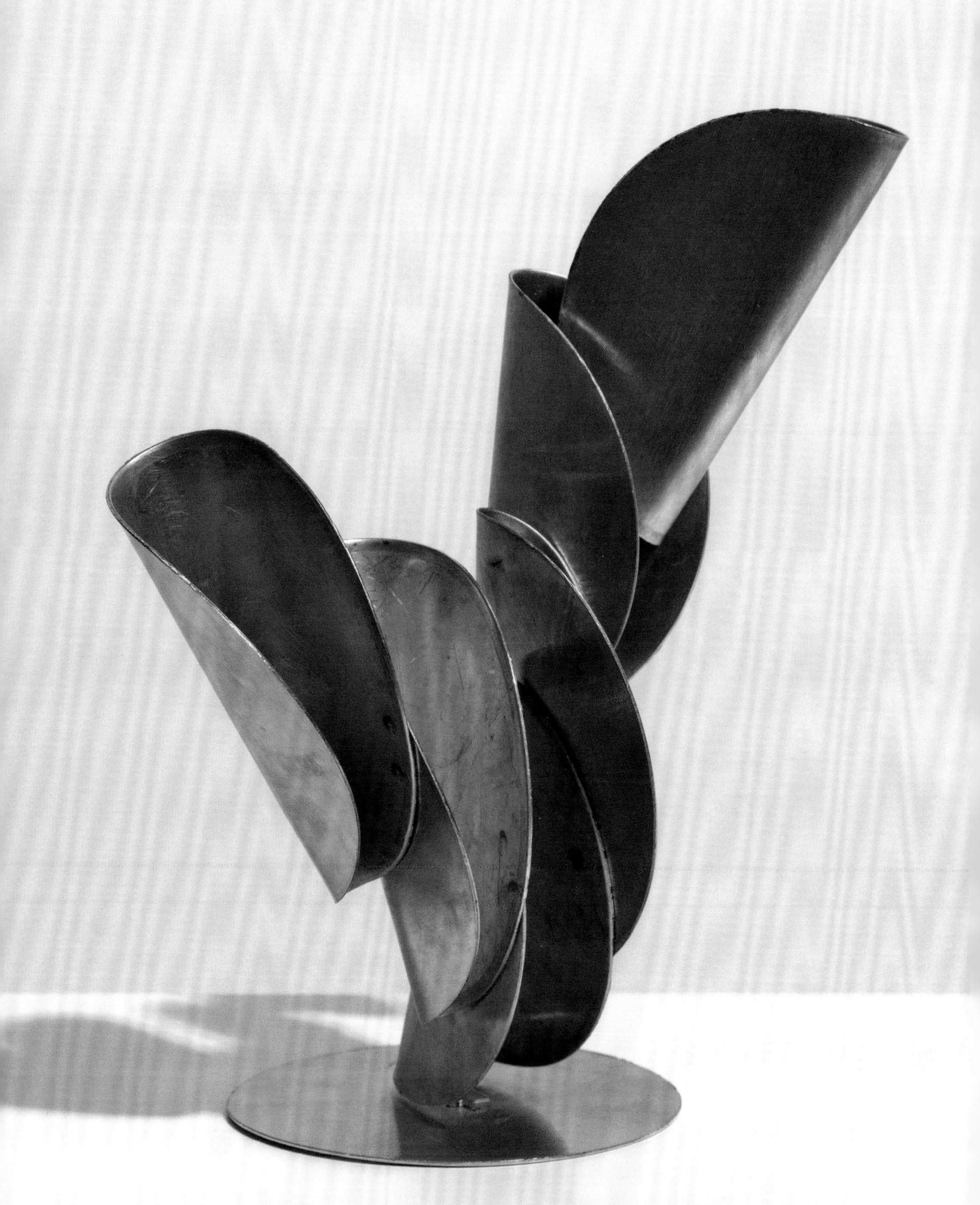

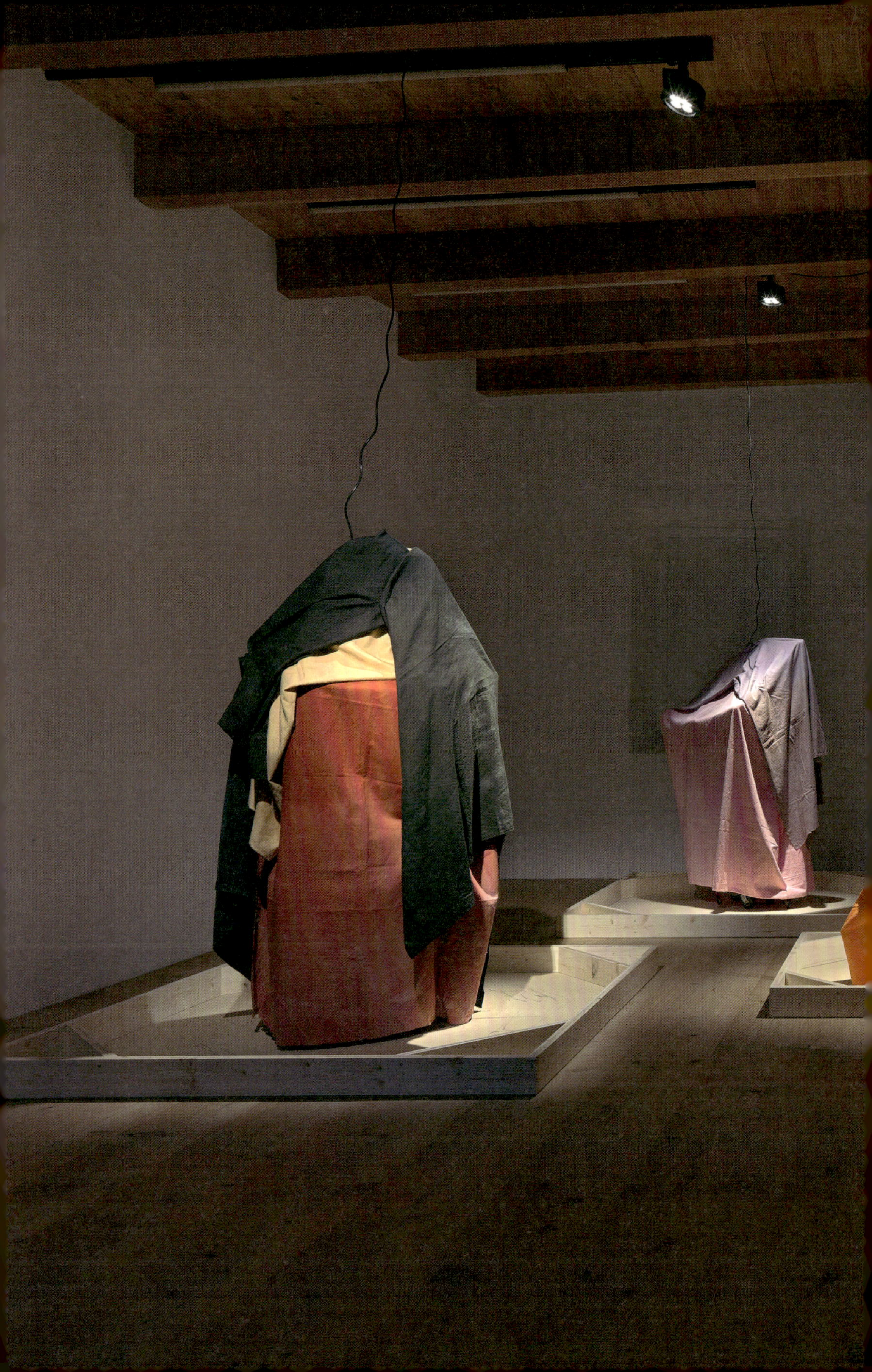

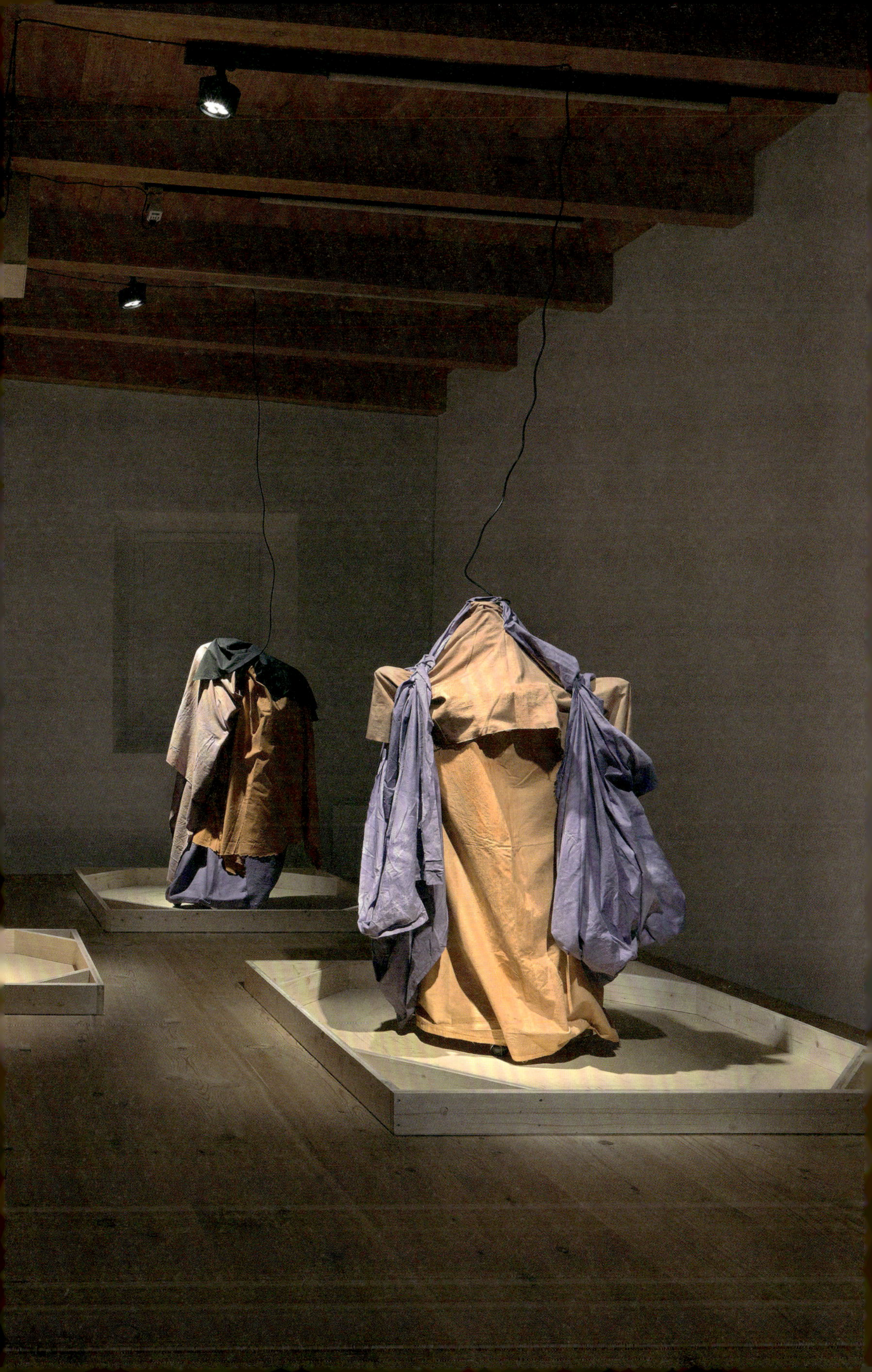

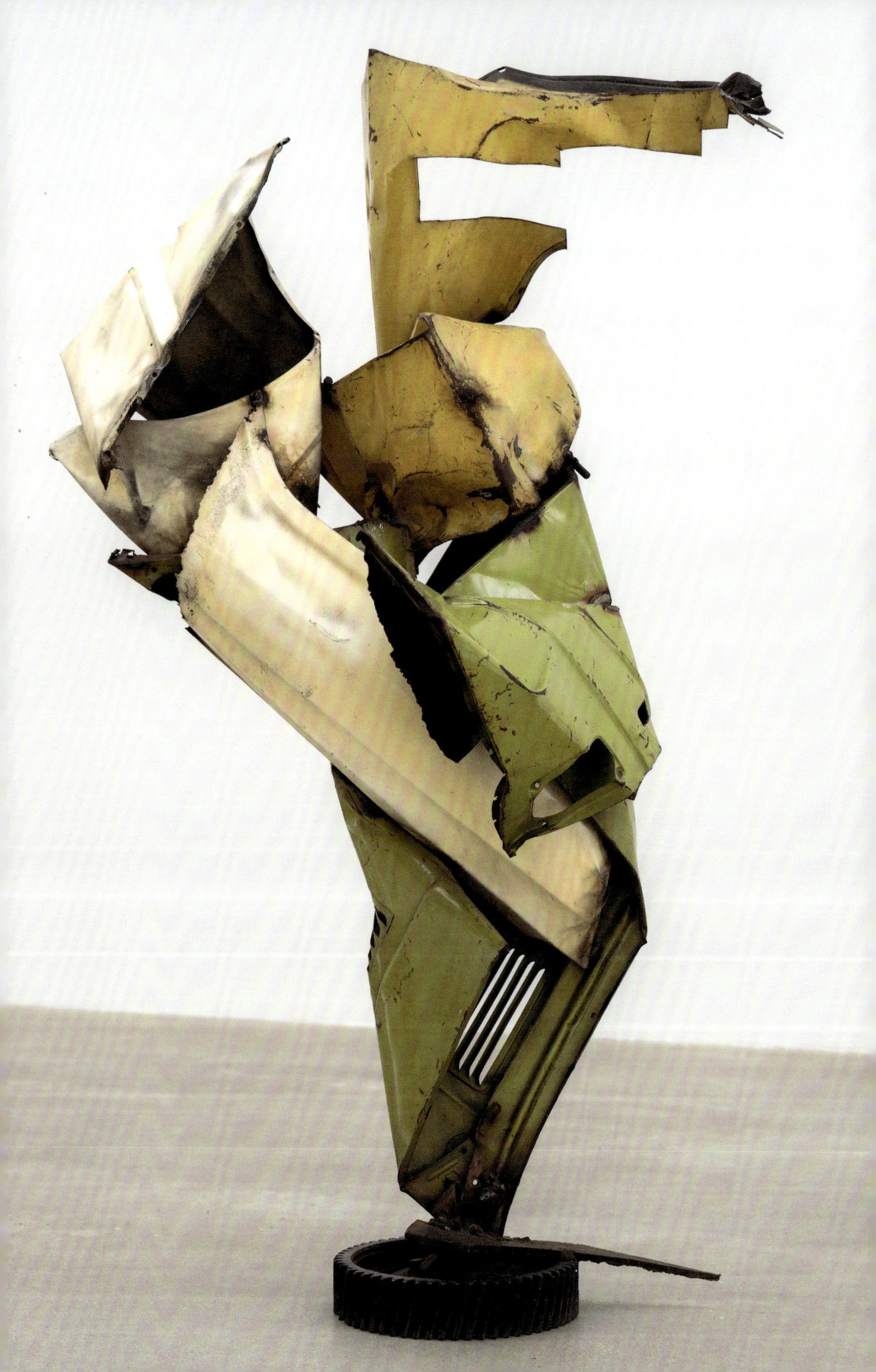

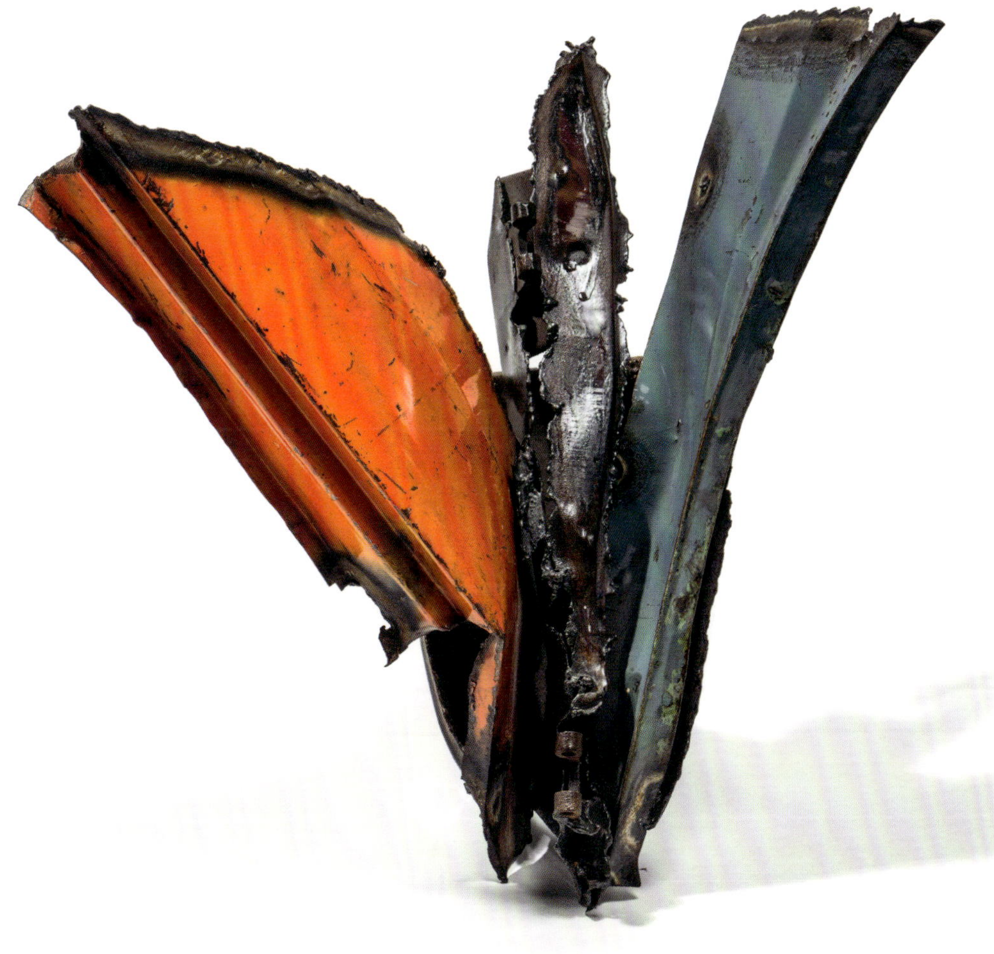

Sin título (Untitled), 1980   *Sin título* (Untitled), 1980–81

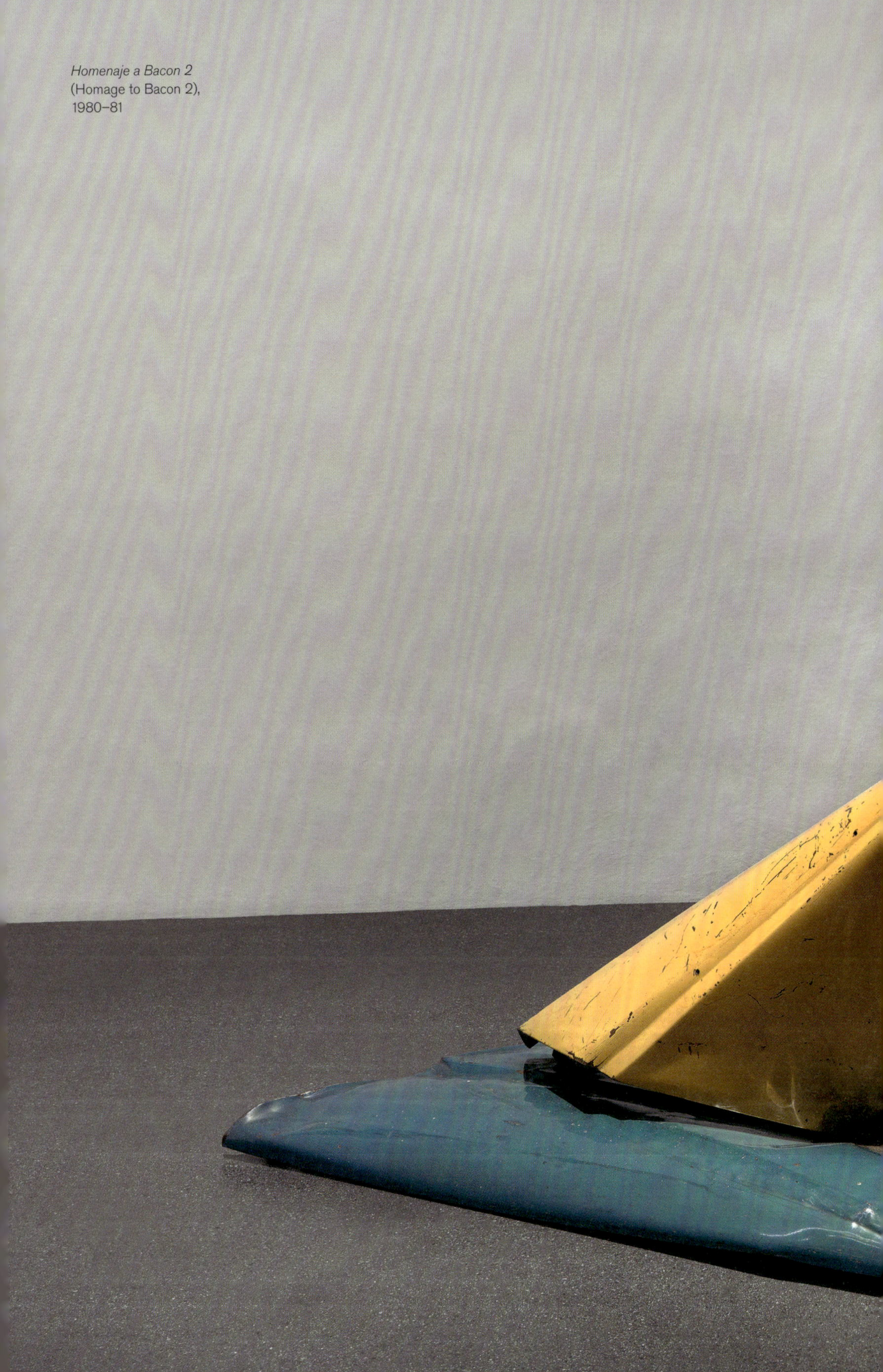

Homenaje a Bacon 2
(Homage to Bacon 2),
1980–81

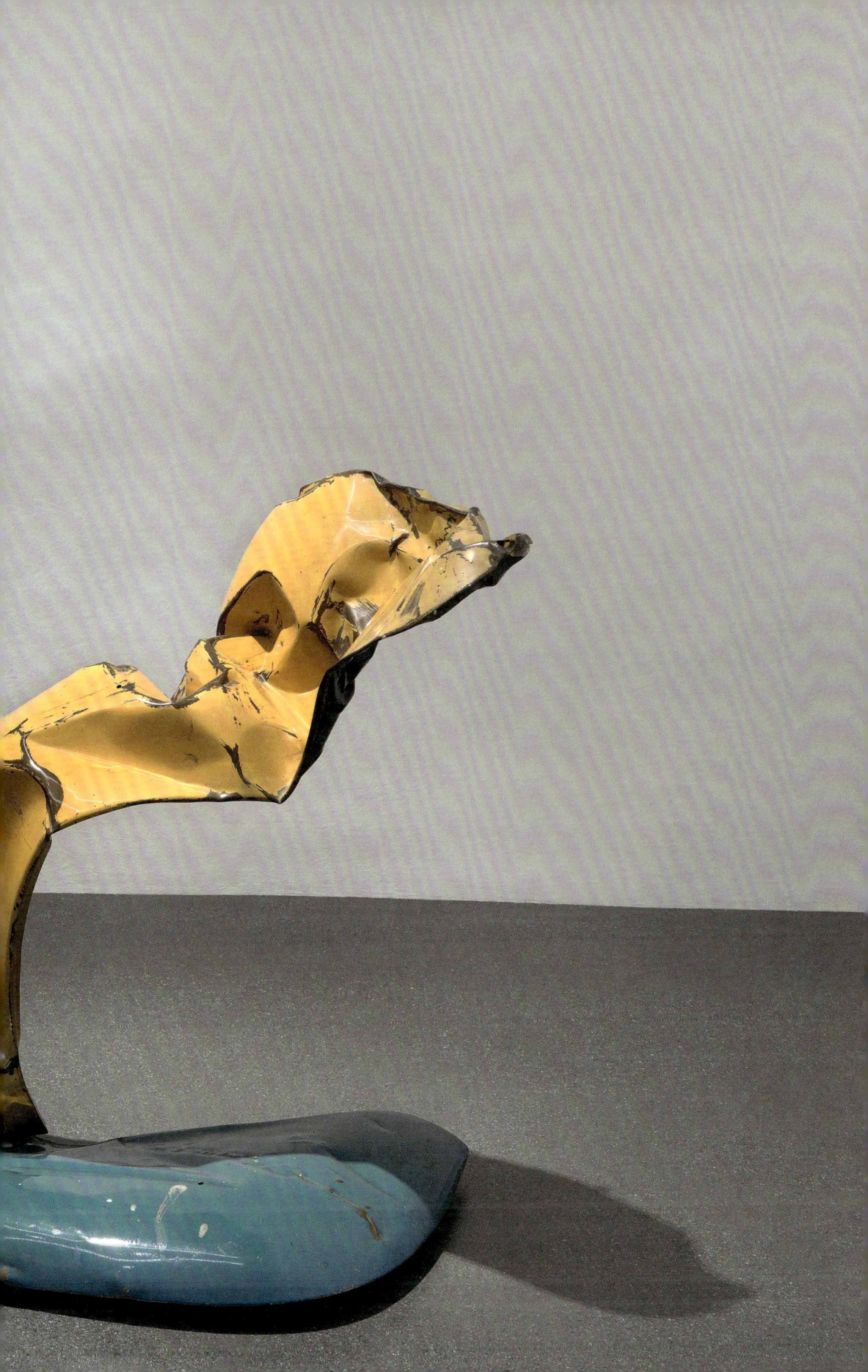

List of Exhibited Works

Escultura horizontal (Horizontal
Sculpture), 1964–67
From the series *Chatarras* (Junk
Sculptures)
Scrap metal
36 × 17.5 × 19 cm
Artwork property of the Banco de la
República Art Collection, Bogotá

Estructura con tres arcos (Structure with
Three Arches), 1964–67
From the series *Chatarras* (Junk
Sculptures)
Scrap metal
17 × 20 × 15.5 cm
Artwork property of the Banco de la
República Art Collection, Bogotá
Photo: © Muzeum Susch / Annik Wetter
(p. 200)

Flor (Flower), 1974
From the series *Chatarras* (Junk
Sculptures)
Chromed iron and recycled steel
164 × 57 × 71 cm
Museo La Tertulia, Cali
Photo: © Muzeum Susch / Annik Wetter
(p. 201)

Sin título (Untitled), c. 1974
From the series *Chatarras* (Junk
Sculptures)
Steel, chromed automobile exhaust pipes
140 × 160 × 47 cm
Private collection
Photo: Oscar Monsalve
(p. 197)

Sin título (Untitled), 1972
From the series *Botafogo*
Scrap metal parts from a car
119 × 104 × 14 cm
Artwork property of the Banco de la
República Art Collection, Bogotá

Sin título (Untitled), c. 1973
From the series *Botafogo*
Scrap metal
65 × 40 × 49 cm
Private collection, Bogotá
Photo: Ernesto Monsalve
(pp. 198–99)

Sin título (Untitled), c. 1975
From the series *Chatarras* (Junk
Sculptures)
Scrap metal
68 × 51.7 × 41 cm
Private collection, Bogotá

Homenaje a los niños (Homage to
Children), 1980
From the series *Chatarras* (Junk
Sculptures)
Scrap metal
168 × 165 × 50 cm
Collection Pablo Leyva Franco, on loan at
Museo Nacional de Colombia
Photo: © Museo Nacional de Colombia /
Ernesto Monsalve

Homenaje a Bacon 2 (Homage to Bacon
2), 1980–81
From the series *Color* (Colour Series)
Scrap metal (car parts)
69 × 101 × 61 cm
Artwork property of the Banco de la
República Art Collection, Bogotá
Photo: © Muzeum Susch / Annik Wetter
(pp. 234–35)

Sin título (Untitled), 1980
From the series *Color* (Colour Series)
Scrap metal parts from a car
125 × 198 × 67 cm
Private collection
Photo: Charles Duprat
(p. 232)

Sin título (Untitled), 1981
From the series *Color* (Colour Series)
Scrap metal parts from a car
174 × 112 × 144 cm
Private collection, Bogotá

Sin título (Untitled), 1980–81
From the series *Color* (Colour Series)
Scrap metal parts from a car
48 × 46 × 37 cm
Private collection, Bogotá
Photo: Ernesto Monsalve
(p. 233)

Muñeca (Doll), 1968
From the series *Las histéricas* (The
Hysterical Ones)
Stainless steel scrap and motor
45 × 57 × 45 cm
Private collection, Bogotá
Photo: Ernesto Monsalve
(p. 204)

Sin título (Untitled), 1968
From the series *Las histéricas* (The
Hysterical Ones)
Stainless steel scrap and motor
57 × 78 × 51 cm
Artwork property of the Banco de la
República Art Collection, Bogotá
Photo: © Muzeum Susch / Annik Wetter
(p. 202)

Sin título (Untitled), 1968
From the series *Las histéricas* (The
Hysterical Ones)
Stainless steel scrap and motor
43 × 100 × 113 cm
Private collection, Bogotá
Photo: © Muzeum Susch / Annik Wetter
(p. 207)

Histérica (The Hysterical One), 1968
From the series *Las histéricas* (The
Hysterical Ones)
Stainless steel scrap and motor
100 × 50 × 40 cm
MAMBO – Museo de Arte Moderno
de Bogotá
Photo: Ernesto and Oscar Monsalve
(p. 205)

Sin título (Untitled), 1967–69
From the series *Las histéricas* (The
Hysterical Ones)
Stainless steel scrap and motor
110 × 52 × 47 cm
Private collection, New York
Photo: © Muzeum Susch / Annik Wetter
(p. 206)

Sin título (Untitled), c. 1968
From the series *Siempre acostada*
(Always in Bed)
Stainless steel scrap
and motor
85 × 40 × 26 cm
Private Collection, Bogotá
Photo: Ernesto Monsalve
(p. 203)

Sin título (Untitled), 1968
From the series *Las histéricas*
(The Hysterical Ones)
Stainless steel scrap
and motor
66 × 36 × 32 cm
Private collection, Bogotá
Photo: Ernesto Monsalve
(pp. 212)

El bebé de Rosemary (Rosemary's Baby),
c. 1972
From the series *Las camas* (The Beds)
Stainless steel scrap, crib, black sheet
and motor
126 × 96.5 × 63 cm
Private collection, Bogotá
Photo: Ernesto Monsalve
(pp. 208–9)

Sin título (Untitled), 1969–74
From the series *Minimáquinas*
(Minimachines)
Scrap metal parts from
a typewriter
22.5 × 24 × 7.5 cm
Private collection
Photo: Ernesto Monsalve
(p. 213)

Sin título (Untitled), 1969–74
From the series *Minimáquinas*
(Minimachines)
Scrap metal parts from
a typewriter
34 × 30 × 4 cm
Private collection
Photo: Ernesto Monsalve
(p. 214)

Sin título (Untitled), 1969–74
From the series *Minimáquinas*
(Minimachines)
Scrap metal parts from
a typewriter
15 × 17 × 15 cm
Private collection

Hal, 1969–74
From the series *Minimáquinas*
(Minimachines)
Scrap metal parts from
a manual calculator
14 × 16 × 6.5 cm
Private collection
Photo: Ernesto Monsalve
(p. 221)

Sin título (Untitled), 1969–74
From the series *Minimáquinas*
(Minimachines)
Scrap metal parts from a typewriter
9.5 × 26.5 × 8.5 cm
Private collection
Photo: Ernesto Monsalve
(p. 219)

Sin título (Untitled), 1969–74
From the series *Minimáquinas*
(Minimachines)
Scrap metal
29 × 16.5 × 8 cm
Private collection
Photo: Ernesto Monsalve
(p. 224)

Sin título (Untitled), 1969–74
From the series *Minimáquinas*
(Minimachines)
Scrap metal parts from a typewriter
10 × 41 × 7.9 cm
Private collection

Sin título (Untitled), 1969–74
From the series *Minimáquinas*
(Minimachines)
Scrap metal parts from a typewriter
15.5 × 7.8 × 9.5 cm
Private collection
Photo: Ernesto Monsalve
(p. 217)

Sin título (Untitled), 1969–74
From the series *Minimáquinas*
(Minimachines)
Scrap metal parts from a typewriter
7.3 × 35 × 5.5 cm
Private collection
Photo: Ernesto Monsalve
(p. 222)

Sin título (Untitled), 1969–74
From the series *Minimáquinas*
(Minimachines)
Scrap metal parts from a typewriter
11 × 29 × 5 cm
Private collection

Sin título (Untitled), 1969–74
From the series *Minimáquinas*
(Minimachines)
Scrap metal parts from a typewriter
7.8 × 38.5 × 12.5 cm
Private collection
Photo: Ernesto Monsalve
(p. 223)

Sin título (Untitled), c. 1969
From the series *Minimáquinas*
(Minimachines)
Scrap metal parts from a typewriter
28 × 12 × 6 cm
Private collection
Courtesy Casas Riegner, Bogotá
Photo: Ernesto Monsalve
(p. 216)

Sin título (Untitled), c. 1972
From the series *Miniesculturas*
(Minisculptures)
Scrap metal
12 × 13 × 4 cm
Private collection
Courtesy Casas Riegner, Bogotá

Sin título (Untitled), c. 1974
From the series *Minimáquinas*
(Minimachines)
Scrap metal parts from a typewriter
14 × 10 × 9 cm
Private collection
Courtesy Casas Riegner, Bogotá

Ajedrez (Chess), c. 1972
From the series *Chatarras* (Junk
Sculptures)
Scrap metal and chess board
27.7 × 25.5 × 13.6 cm
Private collection
Courtesy Casas Riegner, Bogotá
Photo: © Muzeum Susch / Annik Wetter
(p. 220)

Estrella de mar (Starfish), 1974
From the series *Minimáquinas*
(Minimachines)
Recycled assembled steel
34 × 32 × 24 cm
Museo La Tertulia, Cali
Photo: © Muzeum Susch / Annik Wetter
(p. 215)

Luis Ernesto Arocha
Azilef, 1969
16mm, black and white, sound
8 min.
Instituto de Visión, Bogotá

Encaje de Bruselas (Brussels Lace),
c. 1976
From the series *Acero sobre acero*
(Steel on Steel)
Stainless steel scrap
140 × 75 × 15 cm
Private collection
(p. 228)

Sin título (Untitled), 1979
Stainless steel scrap
22.5 × 10.5 × 15.5 cm
Ed. 4/15
MAMBO – Museo de Arte, Moderno
de Bogotá
(p. 229)

Sin título (Untitled), 1970
From the series *Acero sobre acero*
(Steel on Steel)
Stainless steel scrap
59 × 65 × 18 cm
MAMBO – Museo de Arte, Moderno
de Bogotá

Sin título (Untitled), c. 1975
From the series *Acero sobre acero*
(Steel on Steel)
Stainless steel scrap
39 × 27 × 20 cm
Private collection, Bogotá
Photo: © Muzeum Susch / Annik
Wetter
(p. 225)

Siamesas, 1976
From the series *Acero sobre acero*
(Steel on Steel)
Stainless steel scrap
41.6 × 40 × 36.8 cm
Artwork property of the Banco de la
República Art Collection, Bogotá

Sin título (Untitled), c. 1975
From the series *Acero sobre acero*
(Steel on Steel)
Stainless steel scrap
45 × 51 × 48 cm
Catalina Casas, Bogotá
(p. 226–27)

Sin título (Untitled), c. 1976
From the series *Acero sobre acero*
(Steel on Steel)
Stainless steel scrap
20 × 25 × 18 cm
Courtesy Casas Riegner, Bogotá

La baila mecánica (The Mechanical
Ballet), 1979
Hand-stained cotton fabric, steel,
motors and wheels
Dimensions variable
© Tate London
(pp. 230–31)

Sin título (Untitled), 1979
Selection of 4 photolithography prints
99.8 × 70 cm
Private collection

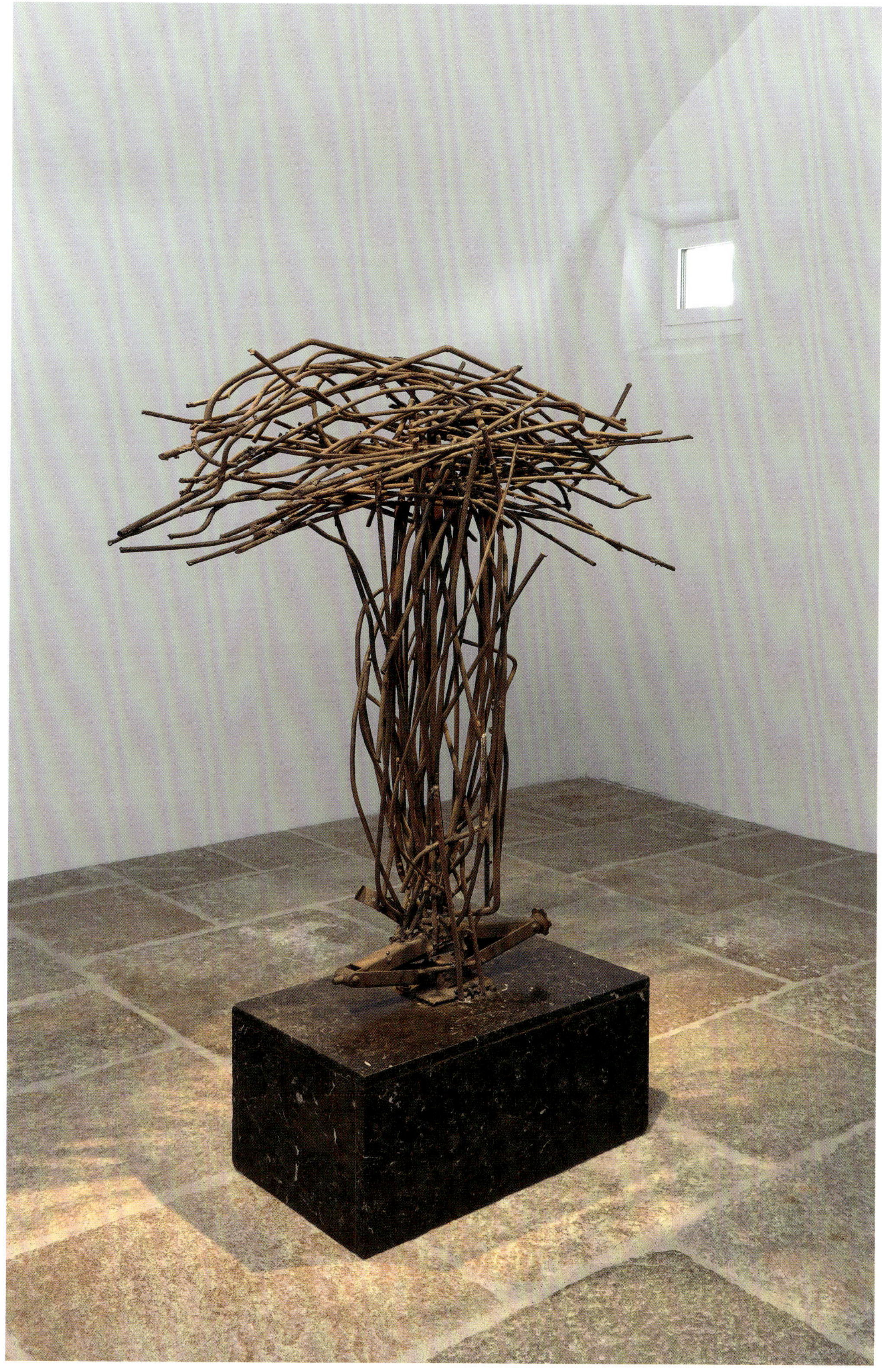

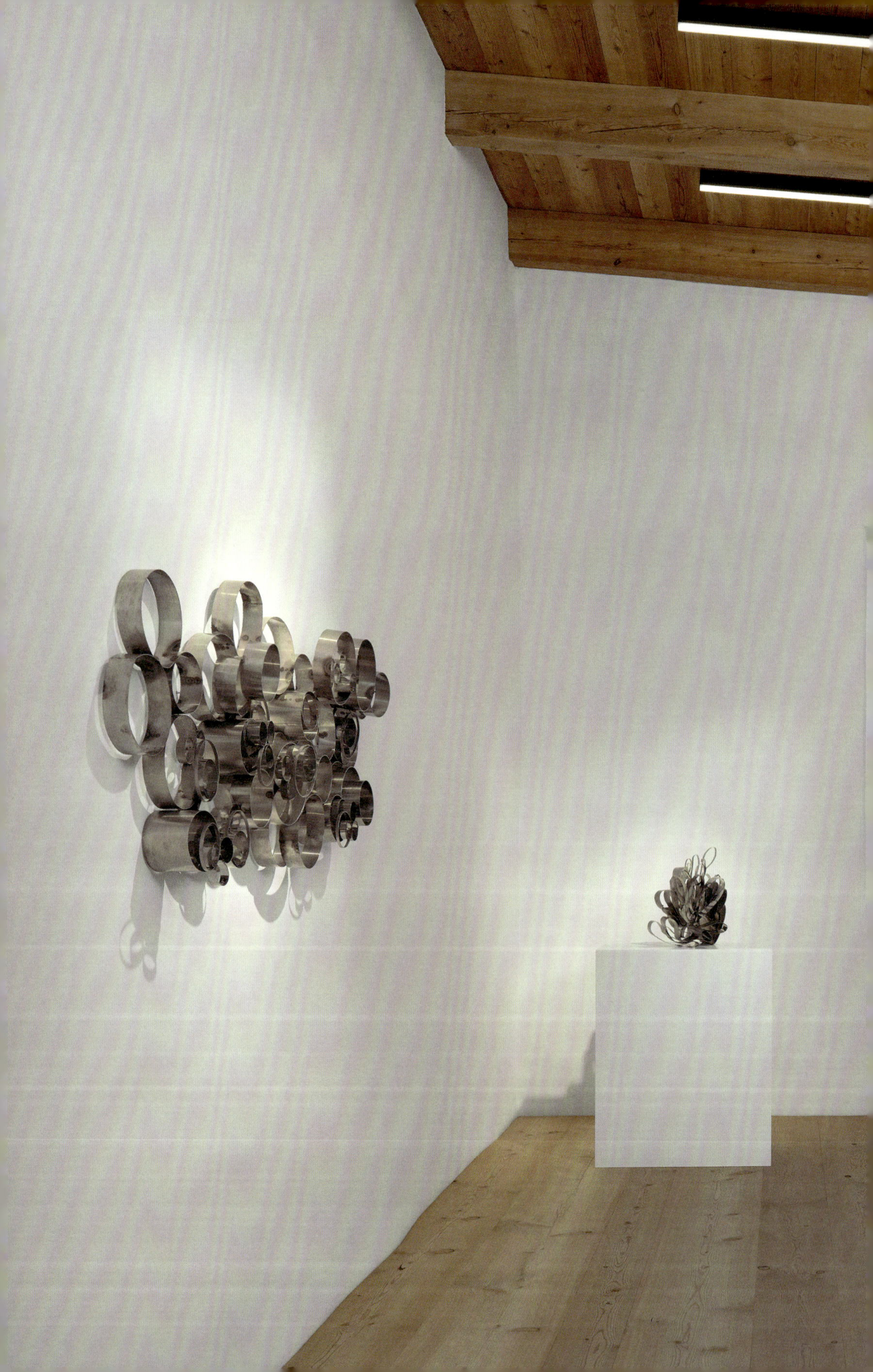

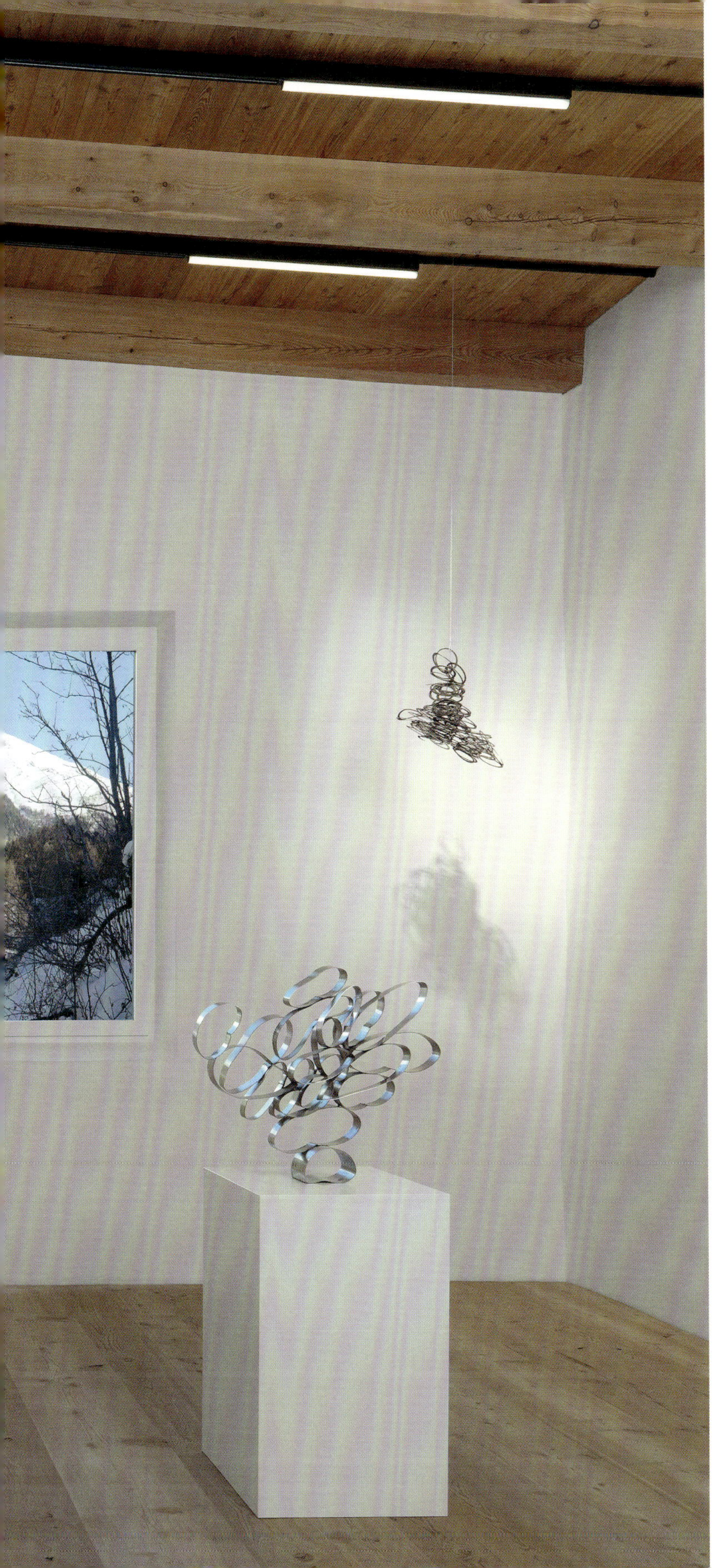

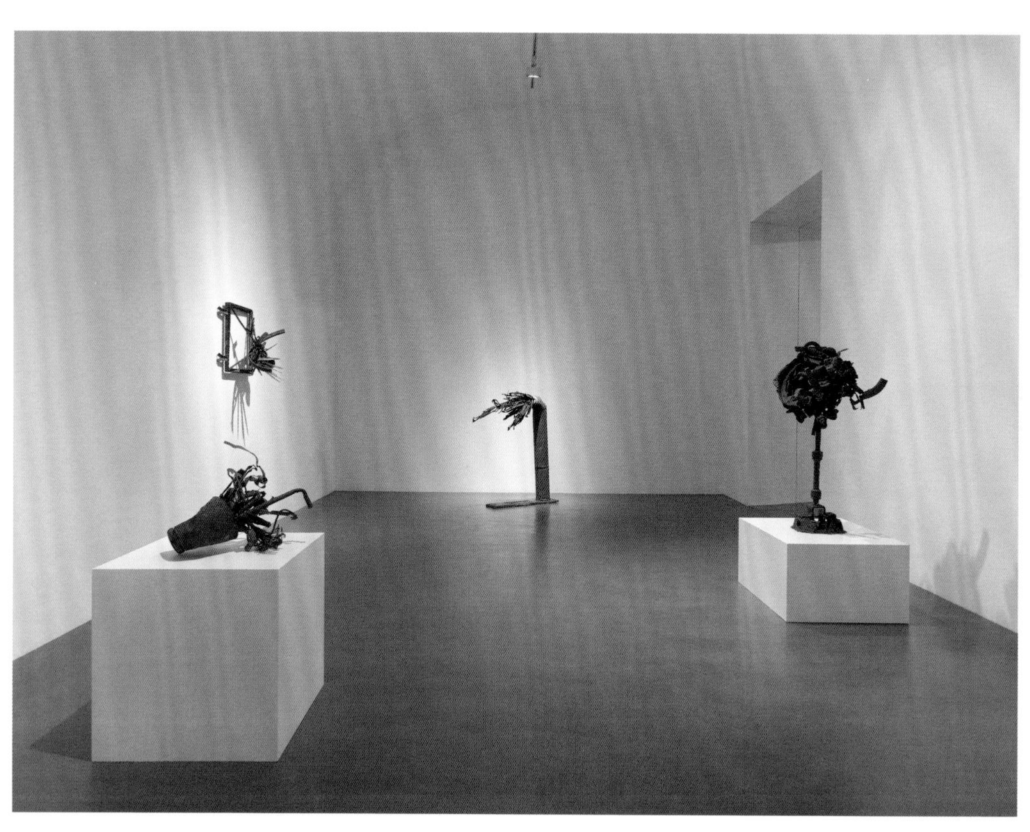

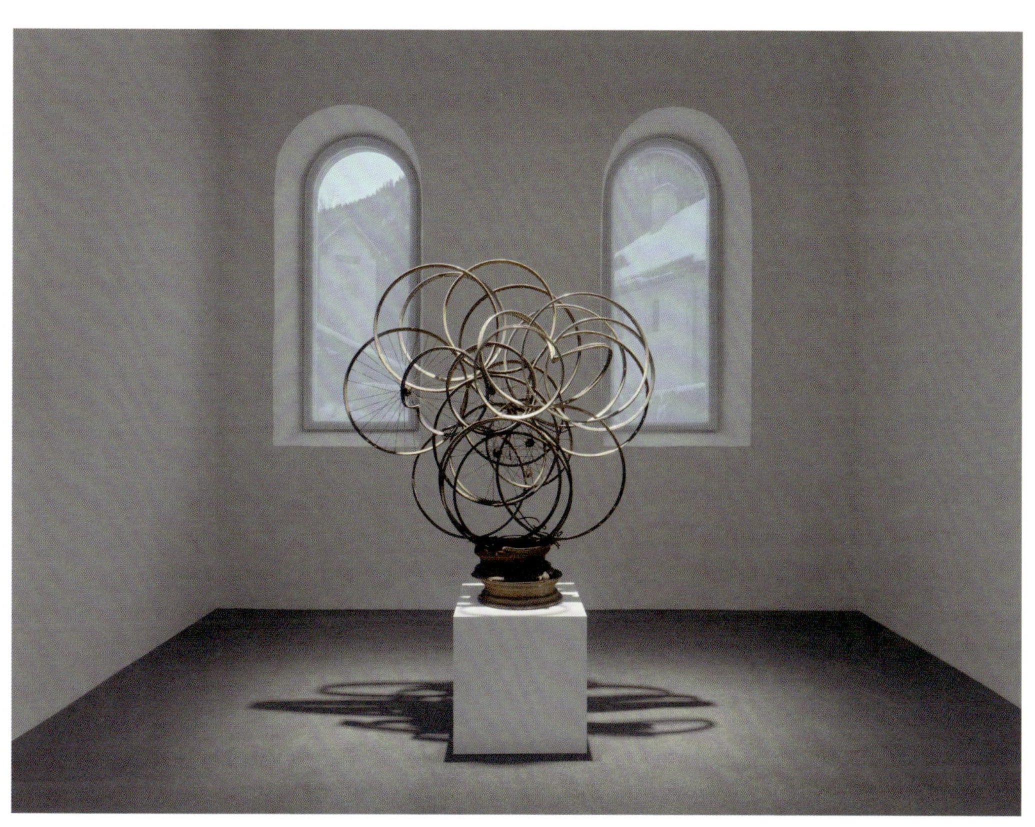

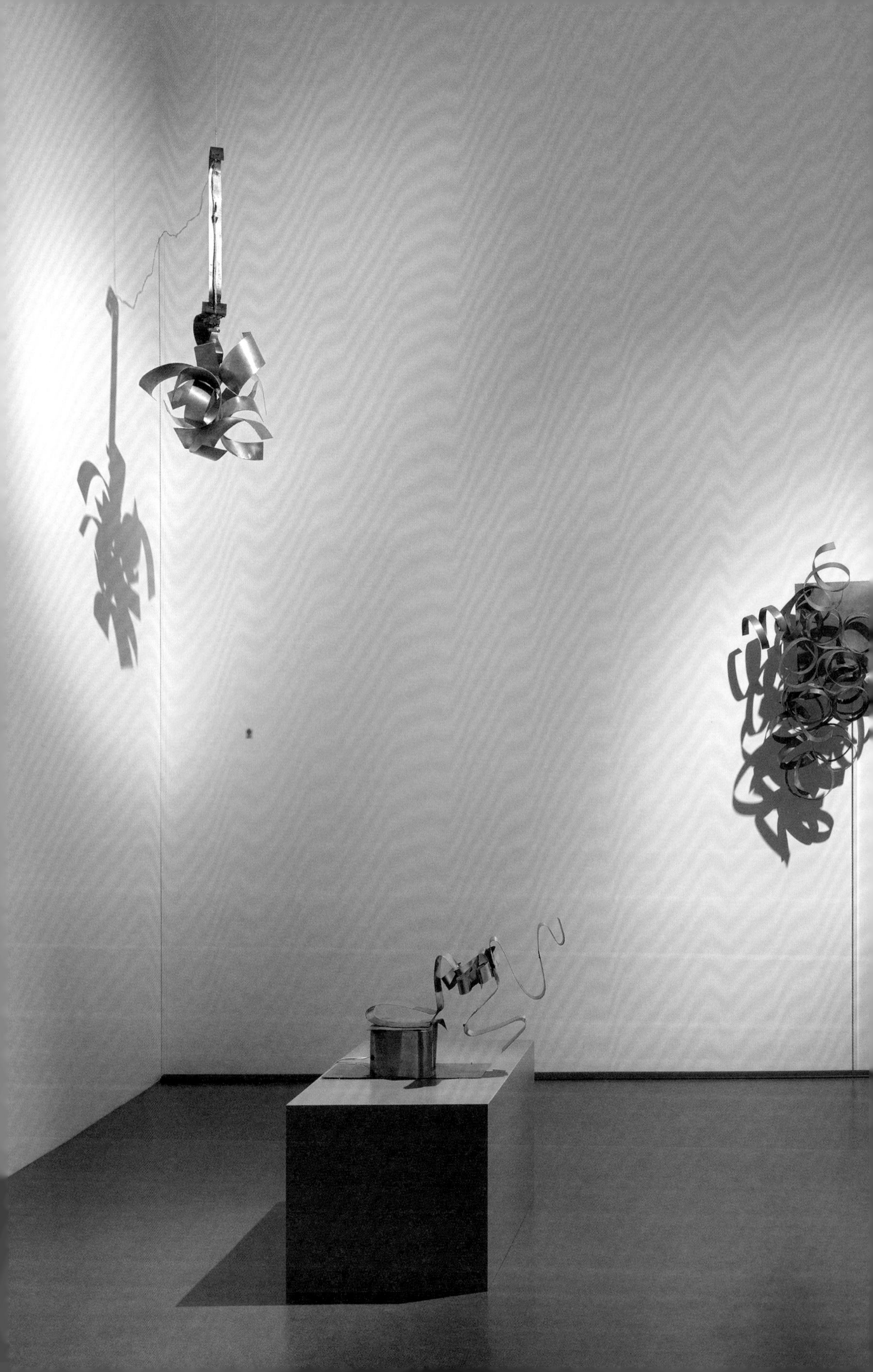

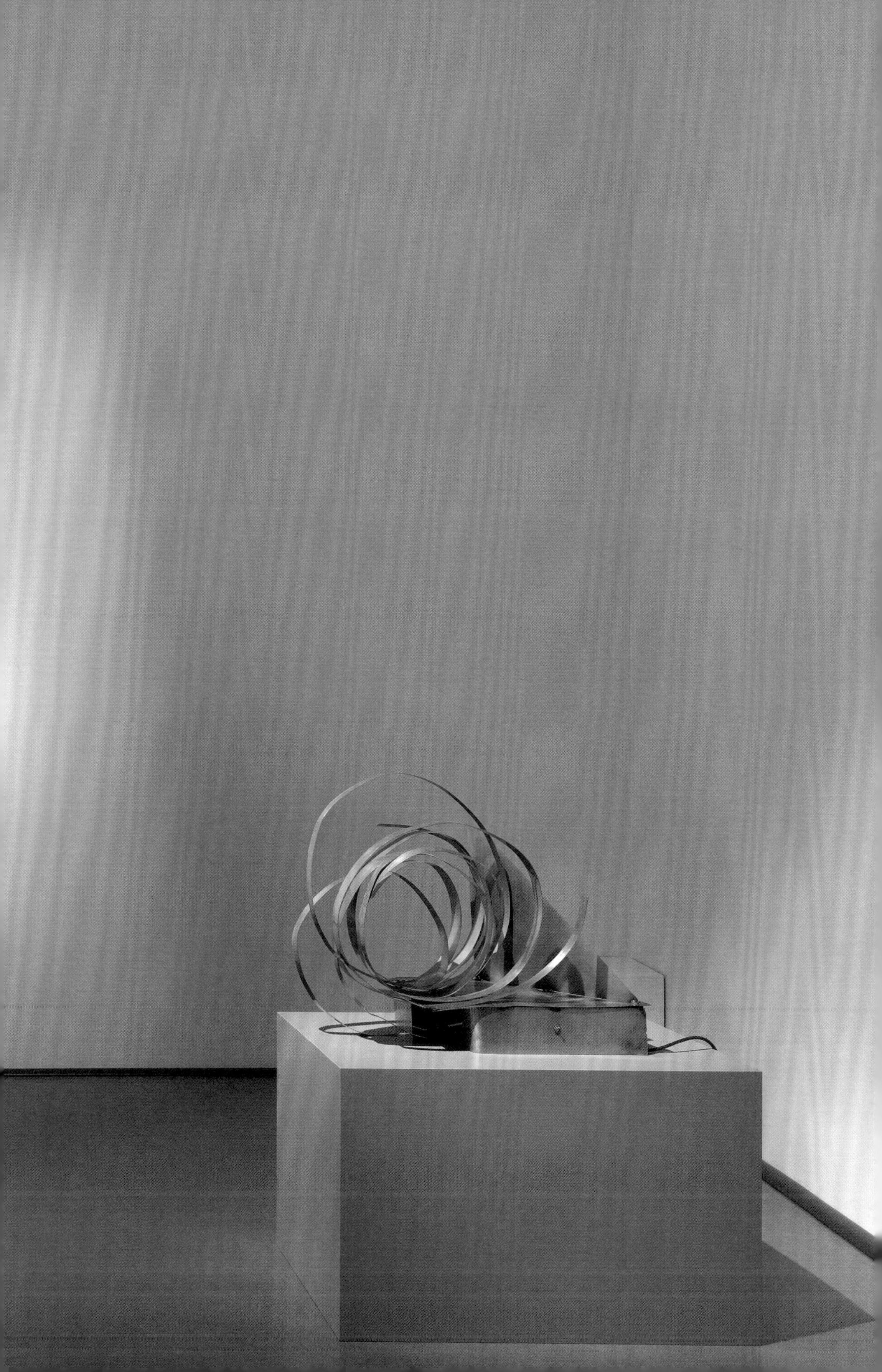